THEATRE IS NOT SAFE
Theatre Criticism 1962–1986

Gordon Rogoff

Northwestern University Press
Evanston, Illinois

Published by Northwestern University Press
Evanston, Illinois 60201
Printed in the United States of America

ISBN 0-8101-0750-3 (cloth)
    0-8101-0751-1 (paper)

FOR MORTON LICHTER
amico per la pelle

CONTENTS

Preface

I have never made my living writing about the theatre. Too busy making a life in the theatre, I was inventing survival as I went along. This collection is part of that long improvisation.

Back in 1953, when I was an acting student in London, I couldn't stop myself from joining the staff of a new magazine, *Encore,* subtitled with characteristic, humorless self-importance, "The Voice of Vital Theater." We knew—or thought we knew—where we were going. I ended up back in the U.S., moving from my one and only Broadway job as "gofer" and line-listener for Dorothy Stickney to Assistant Story Editor for General Electric Theater, where I think—oh how I should like to forget—I wrote copy for an M.C. named Reagan. I tried summer stock, Off-Broadway, and even Saks Fifth Avenue.

Then, a nourishing, painful two years with the Actors Studio, learning to sort out what I liked or needed from the Group Theatre past—denied me because I was only a kid in the Thirties, and a kid, weirdly, who wanted only to be Fred Astaire or Ray Bolger. Fresh from the Strasberg wars, I dropped into *Theatre Arts,* editing for a precious eight months—precious because I could ask writers like Eric Bentley and Richard Gilman to contribute their independent wisdom and sinewed prose. Bentley had already made himself known to me with a barrage of postcards to *Encore,* advising me where "vital theater" really was. He was always mentor, friend, and model, even when (as now) I couldn't possibly match his prodigal reach. Bentley and Gilman must be among the first to receive thanks for what follows.

If the Seventies are sparsely represented here, it is not because they were more boring than my formative Fifties or our hapless Eighties. By then, I was working more as director than critic, for half the decade outside New York. Having learned from Joseph Chaikin that theatre could make ideas and visions palpable, I tried a series of experiments with language, building theatrical events from Shakespeare's verse and prose—a dignified failure about exile and banishment called *Timon's Beach,* then a strange succession of comic productions based on the conceit that the most heavenly gift would be modern encounters where the only words available were Shakespeare's: these were called *Shakespeare Heaven, Son of Shakespeare Heaven,* and *Bride of Shakespeare Heaven.* I also made a play—or was it a Happening?—out of *Venus and Adonis,* subtitled *The Open Road,* in honor of the Beat experience I had unaccountably missed. And before the decade was over, I adapted and directed some enchanting stories from Italo Calvino's *Cosmicomics.*

I record these experiences not as memoir, rather as fragments from a theatrical life that might account for gaps in this collection. Then, too, whether you take issue with me or find a word or two compelling, you might wish to remember that I'm a New York unfrocked Jew who loves Italy and Ireland, an unmilitant liberationist who happens to be gay, and an unabashed worshiper of Schubert, Mahler, and Sviatoslav Richter. If I were to do it over again, I'd practice the piano more rigorously and hire the Vienna Philharmonic for my conducting debut. Which must mean that I'm still not sure about the theatre.

How could it be otherwise in this country? If these essays and reviews do nothing else, I hope they reveal more than my own survival techniques. One doesn't have to be Jewish to loathe American white bread. Those who write for, act, direct, and design in American theatre are among the most gallant lunatics ever invented. It's easy to be distracted from theatrical dreams while coping with peculiarly American nightmares, especially the one in which all experiment is quickly absorbed into convention, such as the Open Theater's *The Mutation Show* prefiguring the image of actors and their childhood blowups in *A Chorus Line*. The grudging Reagan years have only lifted the iceberg's tip from its moorings. Neither forum nor celebrant, theatre in America is only a hiccup away from the indignity and waste of the American farm. If anything, it has burped past the hiccup: we're not even paid for burying our crops. Like Samuel Beckett, we can't go on, we go on.

These pieces are my testimony. Representative, but not inclusive, they stand or fall now for what I wish to say, edited and trimmed for redundancies, yet published for the most part as they were, even when I might wish to hide some of my sins against plain, undecorated chat. They were written almost always under the constraints of particular journals, and often as not for sympathetic editors (none more so than Erika Munk at the *Village Voice*, the most analytical editor I've known). I hope the pieces may make a whole by tracing the pressure of one mind against the pressure of his time and place.

If one regret lingers, it is that I wasn't always writing when some particular theatrical events or astounding performances were changing the possibilities. A few of my heroes appear briefly or allusively here, some not at all: another book could be written on the performances of Edith Evans, Wilfrid Lawson, Ralph Richardson, Eduardo de Filippo, and Ekkehard Schall, all of them rule-breakers living in moment after moment shimmering with eccentric life. At their best, they communed with something holy within themselves, a transfiguration that happens only when actors are warmed by an audience. Looking back, I know that going to theatre was always a journey to the interior, great actors the lure and the guide.

Too often patronized or scorned, actors take exemplary risks unknown to the rest of us. Even Bernard Shaw had to admit that "the strongest fascination at a theatre is the fascination of the actor or actress, not of the author." Today, when playwrights may be disparaged by performance-artists, reconceived by directors, and all but ignored by literary establishments, actors nevertheless stand alone at the edge of an abyss. Indispensable, the most dangerously placed artists in the most dangerous art, they are always working within what Richardson called "a controlled dream."

Is there anything better than theatre when it shines with the actor's presence and the playwright's intelligence? Richardson was my first Prospero, not much admired at the time (1952). For me, however, he had in him the "rough magic" that Prospero would abjure, a precarious, adventurous individualism I find only in theatre, but never as often as I need or want. The dream, unfortunately, keeps running out of control. Even so, the risks are worth taking. Theatre is a fugitive form, a completely unprivate art where natural harbors, meditative sanctuaries, and safe places can't be found. So be it. In a world where Prospero's bureaucratic brother is boss, presiding over a political theatre of rant, raves, and lies, an authentic theatrical act is still the most reliably condensed means for unmasking and mastering the darkness in our lives.

Gordon Rogoff
New York
December 1986

Acknowledgments

Thanks (and apologies) to all those who didn't, like Eric Bentley, Joseph Chaikin, Richard Gilman, and Erika Munk, slip quietly into my preface: Richard Hayes, Alan Helms, Stanley Kauffmann, students and colleagues from Yale, Columbia College (Chicago), SUNY at Buffalo, the Cooper Union, and Brooklyn College of CUNY. I am grateful, too, for the fellowship given me by the Guggenheim Foundation in 1973. Rhea Gaisner and Glenn Young are among those who made encouraging noises well beyond the call on behalf of this collection. And Susan Yankowitz has been an inspiring force in my work when I was on the edge of abandoning directing forever.

Most of all, I wish to thank Robert Massa, a tireless critic of the critic, advising me what to retain and omit from the original mass. Without his unfailing guidance, I couldn't have faced my stylistic past.

The largest number of pieces here first appeared in the *Village Voice*. Other publications kind enough to invite me were the *Drama Review* (*TDR*), the *New Leader, Commonweal*, the *Nation, High Fidelity, Plays and Players*, the *Reporter*, the *New Republic*, the *Saturday Review, yale/theatre*, and *Performing Arts Journal*.

THE
SIXTIES

The Juggernaut of Production

A theatre review is not ordinarily the most appropriate forum for a discussion of trends. The strictures of space are reason enough to avoid generalities; the critic is usually sufficiently wise to leave grand design to others. I am not so wise.

There is no attempt here to claim startling originality, nor am I so foolish as to propose a rigid system of analogy. Robert Whitehead and Elia Kazan are simply in charge of the new Lincoln Center Repertory Theatre; they are not—in spite of their press releases—alter egos for John F. Kennedy and Lyndon Johnson. What I propose for myself and for readers whose enmity is not immediately aroused is a simple structure of analogy that admits only that American theatre does not happen outside of American society. This means that, as the society shows both variety and conformity, so will its institutions; that, as the society shows less of one and too much of the other, so again will its reflectors, the institutions; and finally, that, as the society today is characterized by its politics of the possible, its end of ideology, so are its institutions characterized by their lack of daring, their compromises with the heart of creative matter, their absence of ideas.

We are a severely damaged people. Under the shadow of a flag, we can be led to do or not do almost anything, no matter how outrageous. Just so do we estrange ourselves from those impulses we possess that mark our separation from dumb beasts, impulses that drive us to recognize our uniqueness, making us reach not for what is possible but for what would seem to be impossible. The process of estrangement has the appearance of an encirclement to the estranged man: he wishes to be himself, but he cannot accept himself with all his complexity unless he withdraws at least partly from himself, accepting the will of the group; but in the group he soon obliterates himself. The image is terrifying. Estrangement catches estrangement by the tail.

A man knows that he can be himself only by being himself, a unit alone, not lonely, just apart. Yet he can only *be,* that is, exist, as a unit in an organized society. He needs the group more than the group needs him. In the Middle Ages, when a man belonged to at least two groups—his family and his guild—yet made his living *from* himself (that is, whatever he produced from his own labor), the definitions of self were more clearly marked. Even the word *individual* had a different association: Raymond Williams, in *The Long*

Revolution, tells us that it meant *inseparable,* implying a direct and continuous relation with others. The word underwent a semantic change, a change meant to reflect the spirit of a time when a man was likely to make his living less from himself and more by means of working machines created and owned by other men. The machine has a life of its own; the organized industry has a life of its own; within the capitalistic structure, the industry is the pillar of society; and yet *individual* no longer means *inseparable.*

This paradox, or—if you will—dialectical tension, is the source of the modern individual's anguish. As he becomes more and more aware of his separability from the group, he becomes more and more dependent on the sovereignty of the group for his life. The fundamental group—our nation-state—involves us in its actions in the name of freedom and individualism; yet the more we get involved in and moved by its actions, the more we lose our sense of personal control. The "philosophy" by which we live is individualism; the consequence of this "philosophy," however, is a new feeling—the feeling that we are not living, that we have lost our individuality. Only by playing the politics of the possible, we say, can we put ourselves outside danger, for in this manner we accept the group as it exists, we do not try to impose on the group what *ought to be,* we exist with what is. But in so doing, we as unique beings cease to exist.

Scarred, then, by a philosophy that is not a philosophy, by a way of life that alienates us from our own way of living, by a fragmentation of self that makes us easy cannon fodder for the manufactured needs of the group, we then move into our smaller groups, our arenas of work. It is not surprising that in these groups we live a life cycle—or living-death cycle—in microcosm: we enter in order to flower as individuals; we work within the group in order to help the group work as an individual; we settle, therefore, only for what is possible; if not, we are expected to leave the group; faced with two choices each leading toward extinction, we may try to destroy the group; we are now failing ourselves as creative individuals and we are failing the group; we choose *not* to destroy the group, but to leave it; we retain, at great cost, some measure of individuality; the group continues to *be* for a time, but without the individuality that derives from individuals; it does only what is possible; it soon becomes impossible to *be* anything more than a *name.*

I have described, as you can see, a condition that is more relevant to our lives than any plays, productions, or theatres can pretend to be. But it *is* relevant to the condition of dramatic art in our country. Indeed, the cycle I have described represents in general outline the history of *group* theatres in the United States. (Not arbitrarily, I am excluding from discussion those theatres that have developed a reputation in the fifties because, with the arguable exceptions of the Living Theatre in New York and the Actor's Workshop in San Francisco, they have made no attempt to behave as group theatres, that is, as permanent ensembles. They are, more accurately, one- or two-man operations devoted to fundraising, bricks and mortar, and local reputation. They have produced plays, but they have not yet produced a theatre.) The chilling truth that emerges from our group theatre history is that we do not build ensembles, we build companies with only the outline of personal character; companies laced with good intentions, but unsupported by any substructure of good ideas. We begin forming our groups with a vague yearning toward European models, but like the heroines of Henry James, while we may love and envy Europe, we are in time suffocated by its masks and manners, which for us can have no native meaning. We are, after all, fugitives from Europe, not exiles. Our rooted wish is to forge a new world. The pull away from the old world acts like our pull away from the group: the wish may be rooted in change and isolation, but the need is linked with the past and with others. We try, unsystematically, to define our groups by fighting the psychological definition of our national character. For Francis Fergusson, the Idea of a Theatre meant the dramatic art of Shakespeare and Sophocles, developed "in theatres which focused, at the center of the life of the community, the complementary insights of the whole culture." What I am suggesting, then, is that in the United States, a group theatre, even if centered in a community, can only suggest the complementary insights of the whole culture by not behaving as a group at all.

This is a severe view, difficult to accept by anyone who cares, as I do, for what is present and potent in the real world of dramatic poetry. Yet, even as it must be accepted, it can be challenged. What is pernicious in the politics of the possible is that it neither accepts nor—by its very nature—can it challenge this view. It speaks for change, yet it works for the status quo. By playing it, whether in national or theatre politics, we succeed only in rendering impotent our drive for what is new, changing, and individual. We are not free men philosophically until we reach for ideas and ideals that make demands upon the status quo. Art, above all, as Robert Brustein reminded us in his assault on the Actors Studio, "is the politics of the impossible."

We are faced, then, with problems of so complex a nature that it is not surprising we should so often refuse to admit them. They are expressions of opposites that must be forced to live with one another: we know from European history that group theatres can serve the drama as no individual productions can, so we wish to make group theatres; opposed to this is our own special character, inherently hostile to the sovereignty of the group; we are trying, therefore, to do the impossible; yet opposed to this we persist in doing it by playing the politics of the possible. What reconciliation can be made must be attempted on the basis of reversing energies in order to bring some order *into* the chaos. Yes, we should say, art *is* the politics of the impossible, but we are simply attempting the wrong impossible for us, that is, groups modeled on European theatres. The right impossible would recognize the anarchy in our nature, and make group theatres on a new, almost literally anti-group basis.

Let me be clear about what I am not saying. I am not saying that there is nothing to be learned from Europe or the past. Far from it: for only one example, we should never forget that great theatres—from the House of Molière to the House of Brecht—have been built around great dramatists. To know Europe, however, is simply not to know—or *acknowledge*—ourselves. Yearnings are no substitute for personal confrontations. And so I *am* saying that we should know and confront our own character, our own individuality. And I am not saying that I know precisely how this can be done.

What I do know is how it can *not* be done. It cannot be done by building on Broadway or by following the model of Broadway production. In New York, we are daily witness to a war that rages so intensely on a smoky battlefield that, like Tolstoy's reeling warriors, we are not often capable of seeing what weapons are being used, who is getting murdered, or why we are fighting in the first place. The production of plays has taken the form of a huge juggernaut, inexorably bearing down upon all the embattled, confused, and angry fighters. The casualties are overwhelming. The waste is unforgivable. In bringing to bear some measure of critical reason on the plays that are produced, we are saying, in effect, that good work doesn't follow directly from the fact that we are working, that meaningless activity bears no relation to intelligent action, that movement on a treadmill is really paralysis, and that, therefore, the juggernaut must be halted, peace must be declared.

* * *

Many people suffer in the destructive wake of the juggernaut, but no one more than the playwright. He is the classic culprit, his "crimes" viewed with either cool condescension or cold fury. If the first, he is seen only as a stubborn, unrealistic, perhaps too literary man; if the latter, he is a conspirator in disguise, a wicked man bent upon upsetting the morals of the audience or the proven talents of the actors, directors, and designers. The tradition of baiting the playwright has a long and dishonorable history; in the case of Shakespeare, a tradition barely overthrown. (He is still not safe: the late critic of the *New Yorker,* Wolcott Gibbs, notably lacking in ideas or a subject he could call his own, passed himself off as a sophisticated wit by hating all the plays of Shakespeare; and only this year, a critic for one of the more reputable British newspapers complained of the "boringness" of *The Tempest,* a play he considers beyond salvation by even the most talented theatre people.) We should, of course, take the condition of Shakespeare as a useful hint. If today we are able to view a poor production of *King Lear* without declaring the play to be unactable, it is because we are willing to accept the possibility that we are not necessarily seeing Shakespeare's play, only a *version* of his play. We are, not surprisingly, more generous now toward Shakespeare than to our contemporaries. The reputation of *Hamlet* as a play survives the most outlandish whims of directors, but *Andorra*—just to take one vulnerable example from this season's carnage—will not be so lucky. We are rarely free enough to imagine new plays in other productions. We damn the playwright before we distribute the blame.

This is not to say that the playwright is untouchable, only a victim and never a clod. It is just that the juggernaut hits the *good* playwright first. For Walter Kerr, in 1956, when *Waiting for Godot* was produced, "there was something profound on the stage of the Golden Theatre . . . and that something was Bert Lahr." Beckett will survive the blush that Kerr ought to be wearing by now, but not all playwrights—particularly the young, local writers—are likely to be so hardy.

The juggernaut has a way of astonishing and then exiling those who are serious. Its main tool is compromise: somebody's vision has to be sacrificed. The onslaught may begin with what seems to be only a tiny compromise, an infinitesimal speck of matter in a universe of suns, moons, and milky ways. On the subtlest (and lowest) level, it may be the power of the playwright's agent, still believing Broadway production a signal honor, to persuade the writer that his play *deserves* Broadway. From that decision, there is likely to follow a long line of choices, of so simple or oblique a nature that they are only too easy to accept.

We are all familiar with the form: a star is hired, the star wants to be loved, or, at the least, look pretty or handsome; the director, a star in his own domain, noted earlier for his nimble choreography, or his evocative stage designs, or his days as a subleading man, then casts the other roles from a vast pool of auditioning actors who, while they are unsuitable for various mystic reasons such as height, weight, noses, and hair, nevertheless demonstrate to the director which scenes "work" and which will need surgery; then the designer sees the play in various shades of blue framing an enormous network of tin cans stapled together to form a harrowing symbol of the webs of yesteryear, leaving room for the actors to move only from downstage right to downstage left; the producer wants more laughs, egged on by the press agent who needs a gimmick; *Variety*'s out-of-town reviewer thinks it is bad B.O. for Broadway, and calls for more carefree musicals; the star stops talking to the director; the director won't talk to the playwright; the playwright is going stir-crazy in his hotel room, having forgotten what his play is about after a dream in which he saw someone else writing his play; the blue-haired ladies who sell theatre parties think the play needs more heart; the costume designer is going through her Watteau period; the *New York Times* seems to be on a "kick" for philosophical musicals concerning Chinese integration; and the *Herald Tribune*, using its inside knowledge on how *not* to write a play, says that atmosphere will never replace good, solid craftsmanship, and furthermore, there may be a touch of anti-clericalism lurking in the third act; the play closes after five performances, leaving the star to Hollywood, but not before granting interviews that express great relief to be free of that "turkey"; the director has already been called to Philadelphia to salvage a musical; the playwright goes back to basket weaving; and the producer, gazing myopically over the great literary reaches of Europe, Asia, the Middle East, Africa, Latin America, and continental United States, declares solemnly that there are no new plays anymore, and since even poor musicals can make money, he plans to produce still another, a nasty little number starring Ethel Merman and Mary Martin, based on the Bobbsey twins. We heave a sigh and drop a tear, grateful that at least one man remains a success unto himself.

My distortions are only slightly out of focus, for the juggernaut makes all things, in the theatre of the possible, quite possible indeed. There is a story making the rounds in New York this season that one playwright, awaking on the morning after the homicide, realized with a shudder that it was a matter of great urgency for him to bring himself face to face with his typewriter to begin the *physical* work of writing a new play. In pain, but saved by a still, small voice within that spoke for work instead of extinction, he sat before the machine, placed the paper, and wrote, without conscious meditation, instinctive words born from revulsion: "The curtain rises—on a bare stage."

GR(April 1963)

Brecht on Broadway

Bertolt Brecht's *Mother Courage and Her Children* comes to us only twenty-four years after it was written, which, as time travels on Broadway, is probably a quarter of a century sooner than customary practice. To do this play well, even to do it at all, is to challenge the terms of our production values at their very center.

First, there is the didactic purpose of the play, about which Brecht took pains, as was his custom, to be clear. It is not, as we would ordinarily have it, a simple statement, easily agreeable to all of us, blandly against an abstraction called war. A production should show, said Brecht, "that big business [Geschäfte] is not conducted by little people. . . . That war, which is an extension of business by other means, makes human virtues fatal, even for those who possess them. . . . That for the waging of war, no sacrifice is too great." Brecht's ironic adaptation of Carl von Clausewitz's theory that war is an extension of politics by other means is just one hint among many that he was concerned with the perversions and vocabulary of capitalism. If, like Pavlov's dog, we froth at the mouth when we hear that word, we shall then either try to erase its presence from the world of the play, or pretend in our fashion that Brecht was an artist who "transcended" the "limitations" of his views. As dogs, however, we miss the human force of his ideas.

Brecht was a Marxist. But to acknowledge this is not to say that he was ever *able* to be a Communist in what we might call the Pavlovian manner. During the middle period, in which he wrote such "didactic pieces" as *The Exception and the Rule* and *The Measures Taken,* he was surely attempting a repression of his own instincts in favor of service to a more orthodox Left view; yet even in these plays there is occasional ideological ambiguity. It isn't necessary or sound to press amateur psychology into the study of Brecht. We have only to look at the line of his development in the plays themselves. What emerges—despite his adaptation to necessity by making his theatre in East Berlin—is a strong absorption in two aspects of Marxism that tend to get lost in the distorting mirror of the cold war: the dialectical thinking process (to which I shall return later); and the classical humanism, which is a tradition far different from the Soviet managerial, conservative adaptation, with its surrender of the individual to a collective fixation.

Marx saw man in terms of his potential, not as an alienated thing; a man for whom the process of production exists, not a man who exists for the process of production. When Marx described his concept of real independence and real freedom, he might well have been describing the condition of Mother Courage in Brecht's play: "Private property has made us so stupid and partial that an object is only *ours* when we have it, when it exists for us as capital or when it is directly eaten, drunk, worn, inhabited, etc., in short, *utilized* in some way;. . .Thus *all* the physical and intellectual senses have been replaced by the simple alienation of *all* these senses; the sense of *having*." That Anna Fierling at least has the courage to *be* in spite of all the evidence against the value of being, is, perhaps, the one point that continually appears to throw the play back into the romantic, heroic theatrical tradition against which Brecht was reacting. But this is clearly in line with the tension in the play that keeps it in motion—a living, vibrant demonstration of an individual *not quite* becoming someone better during the course of history. The theatrical presentation of this Marxist view of our existence and our potential follows logically from Marx's philosophy (though we would never know it if we assign responsibility to Marx for the unresonant obtuseness of "socialist realism"). Brecht clears the stage for an action, an action that springs from our primal reasons for making plays: to show man to man. His play is a demonstration of how one person under capitalism does not learn from experience, and it is performed—or ought to be—for the purpose of entertaining us by teaching us to learn. Where Brecht failed was not in his art, which is alive, complex, comic, and deeply felt; but in any illusion he had that this play could be performed by a company of players before an audience which, like itself and Mother Courage, is conditioned by alienation from real responses *not* to learn. In short, as Brecht knew well, our theatre and our audience ask invariably that a character learn something in a play, and they ask this because they do not wish to learn anything themselves.

This philosophical challenge to our values is only the first problem for the American director of Brecht's play. The aesthetic challenge is, of course, closely related. If we are unwilling to accept a major character who does not learn, we are equally unwilling to accept the manner in which the author shows us her *lack* of development. It is at this point where a critic such as Kenneth Tynan, meaning well for Brecht and feeling something close to pity for the director and actors, tends to review the audience and daily reviewers rather than the production. It is a forgivable evasion, but no less an evasion for all that. Audience, reviewers, and players mirror one another, not as immutable beings beyond hope, but as people conditioned by the same atmosphere, the same sources of dullness. They are no different from soprano fanciers and note counters in the opera house, delighting in all that is on the surface, all that is visible to their very naked eyes, all that can be heard by untrained ears. The only crime is a note sung sharply. If it is sung loud when the composer specifies soft, if it is held long when the composer asks for the music to move on, they either do not know or do not care to know. What is fast, loud, raucous, pushy, and superficially alive is quite enough for them. What may take its time, glowing from within, at the service of the composer, is not merely unwanted, it is a genuine affront. They use the theatre as a drug, to make them high, to give them excitement. Slow movements are interludes, fast movements are fun. Pace—interminable, unmeaning pace—is our theatrical god: if the two hours' traffic upon the stage does not move fast, it moves us not at all. We come to the theatre, whether behind or before the footlights, in order to get out of it as soon as possible. What we don't see, we don't want to see. What we see, we want to see quickly. As Tynan observed of a young Chelsea girl who was "bored to death" by *Mother Courage* in the performance of the Berlin Ensemble, she should have said "bored to life."

Brecht, aware of the danger, reacting himself against the undivine afflatus of so much German art, warned the actors of the Ensemble in March 1956 to play with lightness and clarity in their London performances:

> The acting must move along quickly, lightly, and vigorously. We should act, not in order to excite, but in order to prevent lagging, not only to play at a fast tempo, but to think quickly. We must watch the tempo of the dialogue, but we must add to the dialogue our own lightness of touch. Replies should not be given in a dilatory way, as if we were offering somebody our last pair of shoes, but we must act as if we were throwing the ball quickly back and forth.

This message has the characteristic Brechtian double edge, which was undoubtedly easy for the Berlin actors to comprehend quickly: it calls for speed, but it is opposed to excitement; thus it assumes the ability to give quick thinking a steady, sensible, interior rhythm. This, like the art of true *bel canto,* is the art of propelling the melodic line forward while holding it back.

Now, this may make sense to Maria Callas, but not necessarily to most of her contemporaries, so far removed are they from the techniques and feelings of *bel canto.* Equally, it made sense to Brecht's actors, trained by him in terms of a purpose and an aesthetics upon which all, in different measure, could agree. But, as we have seen, we think and we move differently. The usual terms we read in connection with Brecht do not reach our sensibility as they must have reached his colleagues: "epic theatre," "alienation effect" do not illuminate our vision of Brechtian production; indeed, they seem to obscure it.

Again, Brecht wished to be understood, even in the West. It is not accidental or insignificant that, just before his death, he was trying to replace the term "epic" with "dialectical" in order to describe his theatre. As Peter Demetz observes in his introduction to a group of critical essays, "Brecht complained that people without a sense of humor would never be able to understand Hegel's dialectics. One might also say that these people will never be able to grasp some of the most vital implications of Brecht's art." In other words, his art is comedy that bases its drama on interior argument, the clash of opposites, the tension that exists between two seemingly irreconcilable ideas. These dialectics are at once the source of the humor, the drama, and therefore, the very *form* of the writing. We are compelled, if we are willing, to listen to every line in order to "hear" its opposite:

COOK. . . . He's completely unsound.
MOTHER COURAGE. And you're completely sound?
COOK. And I am completely sound. Your health!
MOTHER COURAGE. Sound! Only one person around here was ever sound, and I never had to slave as I did then. He sold the blankets off the children's beds in autumn. You aren't recommending yourself to me if you claim to be sound.

Suddenly—and *we* really must be quick to catch it—the virtue of "being sound" is called into question; indeed it is so completely overturned that we can no longer so easily assume it is a virtue.

In this manner, Brecht sets little dialectical time bombs underneath all our dearly held notions, theoretical and theatrical. To our actors, he seems to be saying: Withdraw yourself, do not be emotional. Yet is he really saying this, or more accurately, is he saying this alone? Is it not, in fact, a matter of *not* denying emotions, but admitting into your sphere different kinds of emotions, related perhaps, not just to the individual, but to the individual as he is connected to other people and the world around him?

In all the feelings and actions of your characters
Look for the new and for the old!

Which is to say there *are* feelings. Brecht, as Martin Esslin reminds us, was revolted by "the cramped and convulsive style of acting which is still widely prevalent in the German theatre, where actors still tend to be rated according to the violence, the frenetic intensity of the emotions they portray. The frantic *Ausbruch* (outburst) represents the highest peak of acting by the adherents of this style. The Brechtian actor is always loose-limbed and relaxed, always clearly in control of himself and his emotions." Brecht was quite simply traveling down the main stream of modern art, which has by now extended Pope's "the proper study of Mankind is Man," to mean more fully that "the proper study of Mankind is Man's relationships." Once again, Brecht tried to make himself clear: "The conventional theatre . . . derives its action from the nature of the characters," he said, whereas for him "the smallest social unit is not the single person but two people." Or as Esslin explains, "The study of human *nature* is thus replaced by that of human *relations*."

To our directors and designers, he was equally dialectical. He seems to be saying: Withdraw yourself from magic and illusion. But again, does this mean only what it seems to say? Does it deny the existence of illusion or the fact of magic? In the *Courage Model Book*, he recognizes the illusionary implication of even a bare stage:

> The completely empty stage with its circular horizon . . . undoubtedly cre-ates the illusion that the flat landscape represents heaven. *On the other hand*, it doesn't necessarily follow that because *a poetic emotional response is required* from the audience, it is fully accomplished by this *kind of illusion*. The *illusion can be created* quite easily by the mere acting of the actor. [Italics added.]

Which is to say that there *is* illusion in the theatre, and that Brecht simply wished to make it in a different way, a way purer to him, though not necessarily usable in all kinds of plays. It is, in a very precise sense, a new way of speaking to an audience: deriving theatrical "magic" not from the denial of your materials, but by admitting them, and absorbing them into the details of your performance. To the director, his instruction is plain enough:

> . . . the spectator
> Should see
> How cunningly you prepare for him
> Should see
> The tin moon come swaying down
> And the cottage roof brought in.
>
> . . . .
> Let him discover
> You are not conjuring
> But working.

To the designer, he advises specific means:

> Give us light on our stage.
> How can we disclose
> We playwrights and actors
> Images to the world in semi-darkness?
>   . . . The little bit
> Of night that's wanted now and then
> Our lamps and moons can indicate.
> And we with our acting too can keep
> The times of day apart.
>
> . . . .
> Therefore flood full on
> What we have made with work
> That the watcher may see. . . .

I have stressed dialectics because, without them as a tool of thought and work, one gets—at best—only bare Brecht without a passion. Implicit, then, in this attenuated appraisal of Brechtian purpose and practice is my view that Broadway has not only failed Brecht, but that it would have been astonishing if it had done otherwise. It is possible in this context to haggle, like Mother Courage, over details; to bargain over the chances available for making a better deal out of the production under the Broadway circumstances—a different star, perhaps, a more sensual feeling for props, light, and music. But haggling, as Courage might have learned, only plays the game according to the rules of the system, changes nothing, and sometimes leaves even greater disaster in its wake. Broadway, it is clear enough, is professionally able to cope with the details of craft, but is professionally bankrupt of ideas, and therefore, incapable *organically* of coping with Brecht.

Mother Courage on Broadway, lacking Brecht's double edge, settles for Jerome Robbins's half-world, neither all Broadway nor all Berlin, not *alienated* so much as *semi-detached,* a world in which Brecht's apparently simple means are mistaken for simplicity. It is really a sad world, wilting when it should be moving, punching hard when it should be nudging, winking when it should be insinuating. A beautiful, sweeping cyclorama is flooded with light only at rare moments. Indeed, the tricks of production are always more apparent than the work: the sources of light and music remain hidden; light is adjusted for atmosphere; and the scene changes are masked partially by the flashing of huge slides on the cyclorama showing modern scenes of war and deprivation. Yet ironically, where mechanical "magic" would seem to be mandatory—that is, through the use of a turntable—we have none. And so the play moves sideways and backwards, in and out of the wings, but never *around* the mechanistic chronicle of the war. Anne Bancroft's props are new, yet she plucks a *real* capon. Young actors gray their hair and stuff themselves with pillows, but just as they are trapped in a static world that advances yet never progresses, so do they never grow old or fat. It is all as if Robbins, following the choice of Prospero, abjured his own rough magic, but did it long before he had absorbed Brecht's potent art.

With the casting of Anne Bancroft, we have a variation on the half-world: the good actress in the wrong part. In theory, there is no one more admirable in our cautious theatre than the actor who moves away from the pattern expected by his audience, stretching his range by exploring new characters. But between the theory and the practice lies the playwright. And for him, the actor's stretch can mean his play's distortion. Several years ago, in a public performance at the Actors Studio, Bancroft showed that she could sling Eliza Doolittle over her formidable young back, and belt out "Just You Wait" as if she had been Mermanizing all her life. Belting, however, is not for Brecht. Nor is toughness without irony. Bancroft's "Curse the War!" returns us flatly to the German—and American—theatre of outburst which Brecht so carefully abhorred. She is a woman of great, good, open feeling, only inches away from inviting us into her wagon for a glass of beer. Since she can't do that, she does the next worst thing: sentimentally and tragically, in the great tradition of every theatre but Brecht's, she learns from the experience of her losses, though, of course, like her wagon on the unmoving stage, she has no place to go.

It is not that there is only one way of playing Courage. The *Model Book* makes it clear that, between Therese Giehse and Helene Weigel, Brecht was pleased with both, suggesting an idea from one, a moment from the other. Esslin quotes an observer at the Ensemble who noticed that at rehearsals "everyone is allowed to state his opinion. The actors make all sorts of suggestions to the producer." In our theatre, based as it still is on individual expression, everyone states his opinion on the telephone or in a bar. Thus, we do not see an ensemble on Broadway or a sense of collaboration. We see Jerome Robbins in a collaboration with himself where he has renounced much of himself while still clinging to a New York director's natural inclination to *save* the playwright. Unfortunately, it was not possible for the playwright to save him. Brecht, in fact, might have supplied the last warning to Robbins and the last critical word for us:

> To observe
> You must learn to compare.
> To be able to compare
> You must have observed already.
> From observation comes knowledge.
> But knowledge is needed to observe.
> He who does not know
> What to make of his observation
> Will observe badly.
>
> GR(April 1963)

The Brig: The Anarchist's Middle Ground

Parallel actions: We are so revolted by our world, by its politic solutions that corrupt what art or humanity might remain in politics, by whatever retreats we have made in the name of practical realism, by the failures in memory from one generation to the next, by the clichés of democratic culture, breaking down form and feeling into one giant platitude signifying everything and, therefore, nothing; in short, we do not wish to be ciphers, things, numbers, mechanics, engineers of souls, physicists of feelings, a faceless, limbless, collective glut of hollow statistics more alienated from ourselves than from each other; and meanwhile, in this world of clear, present, daily existential nausea, we continue in the only madness that keeps us sane, the work of making art, in itself the action that contradicts the nullifying implications of our observation. In so doing, there are some of us who are still naively surprised to find the world of art reflecting, in its corruptive behavior, the politic world at large. These actions, not new so much as intensified, are more visible to the alienated eye in the work of the American theatre than in the work of the other arts. The poets, painters, novelists, and musicians have, at least in part, acknowledged the peculiar pressures of the century. Though the *business* of their art is no less corruptive, many of them have been aware of the parallel actions, and have maintained a standard of exploration that is, by now, almost unknown in our theatre.

I say "almost unknown" because our theatre has not yet separated itself wholly from the community of art. Indeed, it is misleading today to refer so casually to "our theatre," since appearances are so illusionary.

The American theatre only *seems* to be characterized by Broadway. That, no doubt, is the way most of our reviewers, producers, agents, and audiences would have it. But the rock of Broadway ages upon which they would build our theatrical lives has long since been shattered at its base, leaving only the chips and fragments of genuine impulse behind, fossils from a time of monumental indifference. Of "ideal" theatre we have none, neither on Broadway nor in any of the legendary decentralized corners of our country. Of "modern" theatre, however, we have one—a hard, persistent, nauseated biological quirk known, with remarkable aptness in this case, as the Living Theatre.

Formed, molded, maintained, very timely ripped from the womb of Off-Broadway by Julian Beck and his wife, Judith Malina, it is a theatre which manages, against more than customary odds, to demonstrate that an idea of theatre is still possible. The Becks do not know how to play the game of parallel actions as others play it. Following the useful distinction made by Erich Fromm between the *rebel* and the *revolutionary*—the first struggling against authority in order to become authority, the second simply fighting authority with no envy—the Becks can be described without hesitation as revolutionaries. They are, in the most positive sense, revolted. The only power they seek is power over their own work, the power available to those who are free enough to make choices unmoved by the attractive suggestiveness of convention. In this respect, they begin to be unique in America. But this uniqueness, and their special kind of power, contribute, as pain follows pleasure, to their several weaknesses.

By working, in many senses, outside the system, they suffer from inevitable, continuous economic blight. Energies that might better be channeled into the making of plays and the education of a company are diverted into wars against the landlord, creditors, and the fundamental coolness of the New York audience. This beleaguered stance comes easily to them, assuming a perverse logic in relation to their theatrical stance. Economic battles represent a very real engagement in real life for them, offering always a stern reminder that art cannot live by art alone. The struggle within to make a theatre that always mirrors struggle is matched, with sad naturalness, by the struggle without to keep the theatre alive.

Adding logic to logic, the Becks maintain still another struggle. As leaders in the nonviolent fragments of our small, dispersed Peace Movement, they march, participate in sit-downs, and try not to get bashed over the head by our gentlemen police. On election day, they can be found near the polling booths in the upper west side of Manhattan, distributing a list of those few candidates for Congress who, by some generous stretch of the imagination, can be called "peace" candidates. During these moments, the theatre may well be running performances of Jack Gelber's *The Connection,* the one production in their repertory that always threatens to return its investment; but as the cause, with admirable consistency, takes first place in their passions, so must they "strike" for peace, thus closing the theatre, returning in time to an even greater economic pressure. Though they do not appear to exhaust themselves by their battles, they do exhaust the patience of their money-raisers, and, at such times, try the patience of even their most devoted actors. The necessary connections between the Becks' theatre and the Becks' cause escape none of their admirers, but a little more of the one and a little less of the other might, so their friends suggest, make a happier balance. They are, after all, too far from the world of compromise ever to feel the danger. The only temptation they suffer is the temptation to fail, carrying anarchic logic too far.

Economic weakness may well be a chronic necessity for the Becks. But it would seem to contribute little to art and even less to their work. What they *might* do some day is build a theatre that is more than the most individual idea of a theatre that we have, a kind of starveling child at war with the elements, and form at last a *continuing* theatre based more on practice than theory. As it is today, their ideas are clear and their tenacity is awesome, but the standard of their work generally raises the question of an artist's first responsibility. It has seemed as if they were choosing art by default, saying what they have to say without caring half enough in how they say it. Yet we know this can't be the case. A suggestion of a personal aesthetic impulse resides in all their productions, an impulse touched by borrowings from sources that would, on the surface, appear irreconcilable. Antonin Artaud and Bertolt Brecht, the first names that spring to mind, represent an apparently bizarre combination that can be understood only if you accept the limitless sympathies of the anarchist imagination. Nothing need be digested whole. Everything can be absorbed in fragments.

What, then, is the specific form of their default? One could point to several events as symbols, such as the fact that where once they ran some of their productions in rotating repertory (a lone defiance of American habits), they stopped doing so last year in favor of attempting a long run of their rival production of Brecht's *Mann ist Mann,* a little war they maintained against another Off-Broadway production performed in a different translation. Not surprisingly, both productions succeeded in knocking out each other, an obvious embarrassment of dubious riches. But to cite such a symbol is only to describe an effect, not a cause.

The cause, until recently, runs deeper and along lines only partially related to their exterior wars. It is rooted in a particular deficiency, a laxness in fundamental craft, a relaxation of artistic principle just at the point where most theatres live or die; namely, the area of style marked by a standard of acting.

Everything has been constructed except a company of players. True, some of their personnel show remarkable loyalty, but this is only a tribute to the Becks' potential leadership, not to the actors' useful talents. The hard fact is that the good ideas in their productions have broken down in performance under the weightlessness of most of their actors. The demands of the texts, the real life in the bleak underbrush of their subtexts, the development of character, the flashes of individuality that lift performance from the gray plains of observation into the dazzling reaches of perception—these have been largely absent at the Living Theatre. The laziness of the Becks in this respect is their most unforgivable weakness, and it forces one to wonder what conditions are finally necessary in the United States for the creation and maintenance of genuine group theatre. Other attempts have failed on the quicksands of commerce and personal compromise. The Becks, however, are belligerently uncommercial, working, as I have said, persistently outside the system. They retain their individuality, it seems, at the cost of failing as an ensemble. Where, if anywhere, is the anarchist's middle ground?

Some clues to an answer have emerged at last in their latest production. *The Brig* is the first produced play by a young man named Kenneth H. Brown; and its production, under Malina's direction, with the set designed by Beck, suddenly makes sense out of all the doubts and agonies in the past. It does so because it is a theatrical existence by itself, drawing its life not from any single participating element, but from all the elements available to performed drama. Any one factor alone would be reduced to virtual meaninglessness away from the presence of the other factors. Brown, undoubtedly, wrote his words and his directions on paper, and even without judging those words in terms of our accustomed literary standards, it is clear that they might well make striking patterns on the page, suggesting—but only suggesting—their life in the theatre. But the words surrender completely to the ritual demands of theatrical experience. They join with the lighting, setting, and acting into an occasion that is inconceivable outside of a theatre. The physical fact of theatre, regardless of shape, justifies the event. Neither film nor any other medium could contain the work: the script breathes into the theatre and the theatre breathes in the play.

We have become so inured to the corruptions of theatre—the endless adaptations from one medium into another, the active contradictions between contemplative, written prose and poetry, and the prose or poetry written to be expressed *only* on the stage—that we are none of us well equipped today for recognizing the theatrical event that is indigenous. Here, distinctions must be made. There have been, lately, various kinds of "acted" performances known as "happenings," sympathetically related to the extreme abstract painters who do "action painting." *The Brig,* inspired by similar indignation, is nevertheless a highly ordered organism. It would be misleading to think of it in terms of something that is simply allowed to *happen.* More accurately, it might be called a *becoming,* in the existential sense of truth—both theatrical and contextual—as something that emerges.

Sartre might once have been describing the subject that *The Brig* makes into a theatre metaphor:

> Nothing [he wrote]—neither wild beasts nor microbes—can be more terrible for man than a cruel, intelligent, flesh-eating species which could understand and thwart human intelligence and whose aim would be precisely the destruction of man. This species is obviously our own . . . in a milieu of scarcity.

The Brig's metaphor for this essential, *present* condition, its particular "milieu of scarcity," is the prison of a United States Marine Corps base in Japan. It is not, as some prefer to think, a simple social document about a simple national scandal. Indeed, the plea implicit in its presentation is that we recognize, for once, that the elimination of the obvious social scandal would be no more than a token action, a symbol of the thorough eliminating process that must begin if we are ever to cease our merciless reduction of one another into so many unhuman things. The Marine Corps brig represents a useful, intensified location for a general action in which we are participants and witnesses everywhere in our lives. The scandal is the mockery we make of our brief chance to seize life and make it bend to our will; for in the brig, what little will anybody has—either guard or prisoner—has been totally perverted to the uses of hiding man from himself.

The forms we know in Western theatre might have been chosen by Brown and the Becks, and if they had done so, we might have had a more acceptable, formal play; but it would then have been what several of its critics call it now—a documentary about one forgivably awful part of Marine Corps life. The story they tell—the eventless events of one day in the brig—is essentially a tale of reduced feeling, a tale in which the brutalism we use to alienate ourselves *must be felt* to be believed. The old ways—presenting a problem in the beginning that is fundamentally soluble by the end—would not be adequate to the special challenge of the theme. Nothing less would do than *physically* forcing the audience to endure, and therefore feel, exactly what the prisoners—and, indeed, the guards—feel as they enact their brutal ballet of mechanized screams and pain.

The play, therefore, though it is clearly a written work, is more a notation for an action, a symphonic scoring, a preparation for the plastic realization of an idea about our wounded indifference. Feeling is the play; the play is a feeling; the set is an actor; the actors are—horribly—walking, running, jumping, hitting, humiliated furniture on the set; and the words, sharp, denatured, constantly played in counterpoint, become a litany to what ought to be our active, involved fury. The old, more comfortable forms—and this, surprisingly, must include the innovations of Ibsen, Chekhov, Brecht, and Beckett—will not serve us today *as well* as this startling theatrical incantation. This, at least, is what the Becks and Brown seem to be saying through their work. If the solution seems either absurd or merely strange, it is, I suggest, a very temporary one; not an innovation so much as a necessary outrage, a moment in American theatrical time in which all our surrenders are suddenly called into urgent question.

Years ago, Stark Young in *The Theatre* wrote some words that accurately place the Living Theatre and *The Brig* today:

> Life, the energy, the living essence—Pirandello's "stream of life," Bergson's "vital urge"—goes on, finding itself bodies or forms to contain and express it. Behind whatever is dramatic lies the movement of the soul outward toward forms of action, the movement from perception toward patterns of desire, and the passionate struggle to and from the deed or the event in which it can manifest its nature. Behind any work of art is this living idea, this soul that moves its right body, this content that must achieve form that will be inseparable from it. A perfect example in any art arrives not through standards but when the essential or informing idea has been completely expressed in terms of this art, and comes into existence entirely through the medium of it. This is perfection, though we may speak of a perfection large or small.

The perfection here is small. But in the framework of our lives and our theatre, this small perfection assumes heroic proportions. The Becks, failing still to match some of our severe, historical standards, have shown us how momentarily obsolete those standards can be at a time when anguish and disgust cry out for new forms. They have moved their own parallel actions into one, relentlessly straight line, pointing the way to what is always possible in any theatre at any time: an aesthetic choice that does not surrender to the corrupting forces of the milieu of scarcity, a choice that clings to the perceptive life of art rather than to the deceptive trap of craft alone. In the end, their victory is greater than that of the "realists" who capitulate because, through the emergence to truth in their own stubborn way, they have also emerged into a triumph of craft, a craft which has finally revealed itself, not through talk and training, but through the logical rhythms of action.

GR(September–October 1963)

A Play by Any Other Name

"It is a strange and not undramatic fact of life," says Lionel Abel, "that something shiningly individual will continue to be seen darkly until it has been given a name." From the mouth of a babe on Madison Avenue, such a truism might be disputed on the grounds that it represents no significant discovery either about art or life; but we would let it pass as one means among many for preserving a job designed to find labels for products that few people need and more people must be made to want. From the mouth of a serious critic, it cannot be permitted to pass.

Criticism, it is true, can often be a form of promotion or a means of self-advertisement. Abel's purpose in *Metatheatre* is patently higher. Yet he does himself several disservices by relying so heavily on labels: his own considerable and potentially persuasive powers are persistently straitjacketed by the demands of words; reason is strangled at birth; and ingenuity soon becomes a substitute for thought.

Somewhere past the middle of his book, the name is finally defined: "the world is a stage, life is a dream." This is designed to bolster a form covering many plays which we had previously linked under the name of tragedy, but which now we are to accept as metatheatre. Abel asks if he can be "the first one to think of designating a form which has been in existence for so long a time, about three hundred years." The failure of the playwrights he discusses to call their plays "metatheatre," and the manner in which their work must be bent by Abel to fit his designation, offer only too painful an answer. He is the first to think of metatheatre and he will be the last.

The book is only partially unified by its title. A collection of essays and speculations written over a period of years for such magazines as *Commentary, Partisan Review,* and the *New Leader,* it makes little effort to describe and discuss metatheatre and metaplays in any systematic manner. The new word is expected to bring system and order into disparate pieces. Again, Abel does himself a disservice: the founding of a school or of a philosophy requires something written under the pressure of what amounts to a single moment of writing time. The pressure in this volume is weightless, suspending argument, propelling us nowhere in time. Lacking such heavy philosophical pressure, and depending so inordinately upon the seeming power of names, words, and labels, the book finally gives us far too much time to notice the traps, confusions, and contradictions into which Abel plunges as he laces the straitjacket more firmly around his mind.

His tendency is to discuss not the work at hand, but the word that properly or conveniently "describes" the work. What is ironic is that in the *name* of discussing form, he writes either about words or about the life and career of the playwright. This leads him into a number of romantic fallacies, the breed of criticism that was supposed to have died with those nineteenth-century actresses who were so busy justifying their own behavior on stage by making educated guesses about Viola's sighs, Rosalind's feelings before the play began, and Imogen's dreams while the shepherds speak their litany over her prostrate form.

Such romanticism domesticates the critic's world. "Shakespeare," says Abel, "might even have been pointing to the main meaning of the play, in making Macduff stress the word *all*." But the italics are Abel's, not Shakespeare's. He is obsessed by demons, by destiny, by definitions and connotations of tragedy; he is concerned with being right, with questions of true tragedy or false demons. Because Lear does not, by Abel's definition, become demonic, the play itself is not a tragedy. *Hamlet* and *Othello* are not tragedies. *Macbeth,* in fact, is Abel's—I mean Shakespeare's—"one real tragedy." Did Shakespeare call them tragedies? Well yes, but who was he? Did he leave behind a treatise on demons in tragedy? Well no, he was, after all, a careless man. Does it matter? Can we care? E. M. Forster describes how Tasso went mad trying to conform to the laws of Aristotle. Shakespeare, in his infinite carelessness, was more fortunate.

Abel is against overly psychological criticism, yet he cannot see that he himself is an amateur analyst of the playwright and the characters, often mistaking one for the others. Over and again he will refer to what Shakespeare *must have felt,* or to such personal fantasies as Racine's Athaliah bleeding a little after each chorus. In this criticism of convenience, the rule of the game is that there are no rules; or rather, that there are rules for playwrights, but none for critics. A line of Shakespeare can be used to translate a line of Racine. *King Lear* fails because the critic maintains that two remarks, spoken by two different characters in separate acts under different circumstances, contradict one another. Those who are moved by *Endgame* and *Waiting for Godot* without benefit of Abel's inside biographical view that the plays are really about Beckett's relationship with Joyce absolutely astonish him. But the critic's trickery is not clever by half: while he finds sustenance for his arguments by agreeing with himself, both his reader and his playwright prance nimbly into more relevant territory.

Strangely, while Shakespeare, Racine, Schiller, Pirandello, Brecht, Beckett, Genet, Calderón do not escape the strictures of Abel's little book of verbal rules for playwrights, Jack Gelber does. Suddenly and surprisingly, he replaces one set of critical tools with another: he responds to the play that Gelber wrote, not to the play that Abel wrote for Gelber. Momentarily he relaxes his critical guard and even asks himself what the author's view might be. No doubt he regards *The Connection* as metatheatre, but he relieves us by never bringing the word into discussion. He simply submits himself to the experience of the play, implicitly commends it for the manner in which it realizes its intentions, and moves on to several illuminating observations about the play in relation to its audience.

His perceptions here, free as they are of critical cant, are sharp and illuminating. The form of the play and the form of the audience seem to blend through Abel's eyes: the "fix" the junkies seek directly reflects the "high" experience people seek today from all kinds of odd sources because the old "high" experiences—love, friendship, heroic adventure, martyrdom, and the act of creation—are increasingly impossible for so many people today. Abel felt this. It was a play. He saw it. He wrote about it.

But in discussing other recent developments, he forgets first responses. He argues tediously against Martin Esslin's coinage of the "absurd," though Esslin has always been careful to stress the fact that the word is only a handle for a view of life, and not *in itself* a description of a circumscribed school of theatre. And when it suits Abel, he seems to forgive a playwright whom he admires when that playwright is foolish enough to use a name for his plays other than metatheatre. Thus, Abel likes Brecht, but he does not like the label "epic theatre"; no matter whatever Brecht may have intended, his work proves the viability of metatheatre. Have *we* learned anything from this verbal byplay?

It is not important to the present or future of any art that phrases be anything more than servants to ideas. They need not be definitively "good" in themselves. This is said, not because life or art should be pursued apart from theory (our nation of pragmatic realists has surely taken that "theory" too far), but because there is more to theory than the naming of it, particularly today. Forster said it well:

> In an age which is respectful to theory—as for instance the seventeenth century was respectful to Aristotle's theory of the dramatic unities—a theory may be helpful and stimulating, particularly to the sense of form . . . a theory in the modern world has little power over the fine arts, for good or evil. The construction of aesthetic theories and their comparison are desirable cultural exercises: the theories themselves are unlikely to spread far or to hinder or to help.

Abel's intention is clear: to find an alternative to tragedy. His failure is equally clear: he has not found an alternative; he has only made up a new name. The wheel by any other name would still be the first invention to set man apart from beast. But it would not have moved Abel anywhere until it had been designated muverunk, twittles, or, satisfactorily, wheel. Metatheatre by any other name would still not stand for the discovery of a new theatrical continent. What is shiningly individual to Abel remains darkly elusive to us. And not even muverunk would help. Names, as such, were important only to the Capulets and Montagues, who were rigid moralists, narrow people, and— if they were to practice the art—bad critics.

We have only a few critics who can define plays as plays. It is a loss to us that Abel, with all his suggestiveness, is not one of them. Instead, his absorption in theory, stillborn and unresonant, leads us to the most private and personal corner in a room without windows or doors, inevitably obscuring our understanding of plays, whatever they are called.   *GR(July 1963)*

Anouilh and Osborne:
Intellect without Intelligence

Jean Anouilh and John Osborne share a common absence, common, it would seem, to many dramatists. It is the absence of intellect sufficient to support the ambitious drive of their bright, active intelligence. For a playwright, perhaps, this particular gap in personal nature is not a serious one. Indeed, in most current theatrical circles, the presence of intellect is an affliction to be shunned, scorned, or denied, while its absence is meant to be a clear sign that the artist is in touch with his audience.

The theatre, runs the argument, dramatizes the emotional confrontations of men and is ill equipped to make drama out of the ideas that move them. Such an argument *might* be supportable if there were any clear, final evidence that all the men who advance it were any more adept at emotions than they are with ideas. But, while they dip their pens in emotional bloodbaths, often clumsily, their sticky fingers can scarcely resist a splash or two with the battle for men's minds. The argument, then, is founded on modesty, built on artifice, and maintained by deception. No serious dramatist really believes that the surest way to an audience's heart is through his own mindlessness. And so the only point at issue remains the quality of the playwright's mind.

In this regard, both Anouilh and Osborne are respectably endowed. Different as they are in age, range, purpose, and effectiveness—Anouilh pouring perfume on old wounds, Osborne opening them with acid—they are representative of the best kind of popular playwright who, far from scorning problems and ideas, states them all the time. The trouble is not that they lack subjects, that they have nothing to say; it is that, once stated, they rarely have anything else to say. They pose, but they do not grapple. They present, but they do not *represent*. Expert illusionists, they play entertaining war games in which ideas appear and disappear, like so many battle-weary soldiers more concerned with their own lives than with the enemy's quarrel. Certainly this is the only sensible—if unheroic—behavior for a soldier, but it is not very clever behavior for an idea.

The Anouilh of *Becket* is really only a shade of the current Anouilh, the vaguely scented aristocrat behind *The Rehearsal.* In his latest New York appearance, he is, more characteristically, a roseate, bittersweet author with few pretensions and much artfulness. Bridging centuries, he offers a pleasant charade, a wicked, precious, modest little play fashioned and played after the model of Pierre Marivaux's *The Double Inconstancy.*

In Anouilh's comedy, the contemporary Count, known by his wife, friends, and mistress as Tiger, is busy rehearsing a party performance of Marivaux's comedy, almost deliberately living out every moment of the lovely harlequinade. Tiger, we learn soon enough from the Countess, is a rake, acceptable in this role so long as he remains a man of brittle feeling. In her turn, the Countess accepts the civilized code of the libertine: both may have their lovers so long as both may have each other. Where Marivaux's play and Anouilh's little masque enter the scene is at the point where feeling and, therefore, the pain that is pleasure intervene.

Tiger actually falls in love, and is in fact rehearsing the Marivaux play in order to develop and display his love for the virginal waif who is an employee of the family. From the moment of her appearance, we can sense that we are about to witness a ceremonial performance of innocence stained by cruel reality. Wife, mistress, and friend converge on the situation with crude, desperate stratagems, and, predictably, they succeed in destroying what is good, true, promising, and impossible. Tiger, Anouilh, and the audience have had their melancholy romance and can now return to the empty, but safe, pleasures of ducal living. Moral: He who desires pleasure should possess a definition first.

If I am abrupt with the plot, it is only because I feel a gnawing impatience with the method. "Your love of paradox, Tiger, tends to lead you astray," says the mistress, a succinct, somewhat kindly appraisal of Anouilh's own substitute for thought. Duologue is almost exclusively used in place of dialogue. At all costs, two people alone must be left on stage together, removing at a stroke the dangers of genuine disputation. For the timid Anouilh, three is definitely a crowd—a mob, perhaps, that might well get out of hand, arguing concepts beyond their author's narrow grasp of dialectics.

Anouilh's words, cast as they are in the shape of sharply cut, delicate gems, cut the air with precisely considered charm, but rarely penetrate the heart of felt experience. His excuses are frankly imposed. "Like all trifles," says one of his voices, "it is extremely important." Thus, the delusion is completed by yet another paradox. Like all self-important conceits, *The Rehearsal* is extremely trifling.

Osborne's *Luther* is weightier matter. Treading softly in the beginning with sensitively observed scenes of monkish ritual, it gradually emerges from medieval darkness into the harsher light of personal drama. We remain intrigued and hopeful. Eventually, we know, Luther will have to scream his way out of the Church, and, with echoes of Jimmy Porter, George Dillon, and Archie Rice ringing in our ears, we have good reason to believe that the noise will be furious and dramatic. That these qualities arise only in Luther's sermons—accurately borrowed, I am told, from Luther himself—is a sign that the primal urges which moved Osborne in the past have begun to lose their naked, original force.

Away from the sermons, Osborne's Luther is a weirdly domesticated psychological animal who—in the manner of his playwright—can never make up his mind whether he is fighting a family or a religious battle. The costumes bespeak age, but the obligatory father-son scene might easily have been written by Arthur Miller. It is good enough of its kind, yet is its kind suitable for the titanic struggle available to this subject?

The merest suggestion of Luther's agonized responses to sin and authority creates in us a desire to see and hear more, to discover Luther engaged in trenchant, closely argued debate with himself and the princes of the Church. While the suggestions of such debates are there in several motionless scenes, they remain merely fragments, monologues masquerading as duologues, the reduction of argument to private contemplation. Ultimately, the third act is the story of evaporated drama, wispy nods toward the larger issues, finally resolving themselves in a scene of feeble nostalgia: Luther alone with his baby, almost crooning the graceless notes of hope.

Several years ago, after the visit of Bertolt Brecht's company to London, Osborne was the first young British playwright to declare, rather impetuously, that no one could write the same kind of play any more. And so, by way of Brecht's *Galileo,* we now have Osborne's *Luther.* The will once again proving greater than the deed, we ask ourselves, Why? There would seem to be few rules for epic theatre, and indeed the successful chronicles and histories of the past show that a free form can have an awesome, cumulative, tightening effect.

Brecht's Galileo is even less "historical" than Osborne's Luther, yet he relates with greater certainty to history, to the contemporary scene, and to the living tissue of theatre. One reason, perhaps, lies with the manner in which the given facts are used. Galileo, for example, suffers from ravenous gluttony. Luther, in his turn, is tormented by paralyzing constipation. But where Galileo's affliction is coolly detached by Brecht into a moral issue, related —as Eric Bentley has reminded us—to his famous line in *Threepenny Opera* *("Erst kommt das Fressen, dann kommt die Moral"*—"First comes eating, then morality"), Luther's symptoms remain psychosomatic. Osborne begins with history, and ends in the home.

Such heroes as Luther, Becket, and even Count Tiger are portraits of artists trapped by the Establishment in roles unsuited for them—poets in martyr's uniform. It is not surprising that the dramas in which they reside should be half-hearted and speculative. They are not deeply absorbed in love or religion; they are obsessed with themselves. When Luther speaks in his own voice, as author of the sermons, he is vulgar yet eloquent, personal yet apocalyptic; in short, a complex, alive dramatic figure. When he speaks in John Osborne's voice, he is, at best, only half a mind, and therefore only half a man.

Borrowings, whether from history, epic, or classic theatre, should be executed completely and confidently or not at all. Where the playwrights lead, their directors follow. Peter Coe's production of *The Rehearsal* is even more bloodless than the play, the kind of English production that mistakes good breeding for the real life of high style. Announcing their cleverness in rising sighs and broken syllables, the actors spread their arms like wings poised for flight, scarcely looking at one another and almost always forgetting that the drama is supposed to be taking place on stage. Only Alan Badel, through some quirk of eccentric suggestiveness, manages to stand human flesh on the exquisite, though very flat, surfaces of the performance: an achievement all the more admirable because it happens alone.

Tony Richardson's production of *Luther,* fluidly played against the burnished spaces of Jocelyn Herbert's handsome designs, begins as well as the play. Soon, however, it is clear that the dark lighting and the stately processions are born from notions of "poetry" in the theatre, not from engagement in the soiled life of the hero. Indeed, were Albert Finney's prodigious talents absent from the scene, the stage would look even more hollow than Osborne's rhetoric.   *GR(October 1963)*

Following Beckett

Wherever Samuel Beckett may be leading himself, he is certainly leading us back to the theatre. His timing is apposite. In the best of times—and these are the worst—defining the theatrical occasion has been more a matter of conjuring than definition. One waved a fashionably tipped wand and declared, This is a play, or This is not a play. Beginnings, middles, and ends had to be extracted from the literary texture of the object, and if it could be accurately determined that they existed and that they occurred in the appointed places, then the definers safely and sanctimoniously defined.

That a play may be *like* other works of art in certain respects, but distinctive within itself—a personal form commanding its own needs, defining its own landscapes, its own limits—never occurred to those gentlemen who have categories where their responses ought to be. Part of the trouble lies, of course, in the collaborative nature of the medium: with so many criteria to choose from—words, story, character relationships, morals, decor—it is easier to describe the occasion as the sum of one collaborative part rather than in its own embracing terms. The tree, in effect, disappears under the weight of one fragile branch.

Stark Young, the first American critic to concern himself passionately with the idea of the play as play, suggested a variety of definitions, each related to his conviction that the form of theatre can uniquely express its content. A play, he said, "is a play in so far as the idea, the content, of it is expressed in theater terms—the space relationships, the time elements, the oral values, the personal medium of the actors, and so on—as distinguished from the terms of literature." For a population of reviewers and audience educating each other about a theatre seen only as literature or theme, these words retain the sound of revolution. Telling us almost everything about the way we might submit to the peculiarly theatrical theatre experience, they confound those experts who, at all costs, would have the theatre only on its bastard, borrowing, hybrid terms.

Play, Samuel Beckett's latest excursion into the "impossible," accepts the fact of theatre, and in so doing redefines what is possible. Perhaps the first point to stress is that beyond the subterranean regions of his art, Beckett is telling the story of a rather sordidly comic and disastrous marriage triangle. While tangential to his central concerns, it remains, even after two viewings, only an outline, revealing its detail with considerable reluctance. The effect, however, is like that of those drawings by Cézanne where hands and feet are not quite drawn, possibly because Cézanne could not draw them, but more likely because their actual presence is not quite relevant. The lines leading to them, the shape of the torso, the shadings were selected to tell the story of that body in that space at that time; and the hands and feet were *unselected* for the same purpose. It should go without saying—but it never does—that both the painter and the viewer know that the hands and feet are there.

On the part of an insecure poet, selections and absences can be willful and perverse. In Beckett's work, they assume importance not only because they spring from secure deliberation, but also because they constantly reflect back on the specific reality of the work itself. Surfaces, for a start, tell much of what we need to know. Three heads—two female and one male—appear in what Beckett calls "hellish half-light" above the mouths of three huge urns. They speak first in muttering chorus, from which only an isolated word or two can be extracted. Then a cold, white spotlight turns on one of them, at which moment he or she speaks, sometimes cut off in mid-sentence as the light turns on another, bringing forth words, phrases, explanations, descriptions, exclamations, reasonings, pleas, observations—indeed, all the paraphernalia of our daily verbal relationships.

After about nine minutes of this, the hellish half-light returns, once again surrounding the choral whispers in its own ghostly, reflective silence. From the maze of words, several heard earlier spring suddenly within hearing range: the wife's "Get off me"; the husband's "We were not long together." After a moment of absolute silence, resonant with the memory of isolated phrases, the spotlight reappears, once more commanding the attention of the remembering heads.

The second half of the play, only another nine minutes, repeats the pattern. Differing from the first half more in its *im*pression than its *ex*pression, it furnishes additional information about the affair. This time, however, it is clear that the facts as we receive them could be termed accurate only by the involved person uttering them. If the light, as it continues to bear down upon these testifying heads, seems harsher now, it is because the seeds of doubt have been so carefully and selectively planted. The characters' snatches of story reveal their individual, obtuse, personally directed needs more than they reveal anything believable about the actual three-way events. Everybody tells a truth as he has seen it, but nobody is telling *the* truth, the whole truth, nothing but.

What, then, do these surfaces suggest about the interior vision of the play? For one thing, they suggest that vision is, in fact, wholly interior. The critical act, among other possibilities, is partially disarmed by such a suggestion. But like the lives remembered by the heads, it is not rendered futile. I may describe, I may even judge, and I shall certainly continue my efforts to explain. But the boundaries of my success with truth, my hope for accuracy, are circumscribed by the limited area of my head and my head alone. In this way, I present you with *a* Beckett, *my* Beckett at this instant, remembering always that each instant shifts my vision. Thus, I am a comic figure if I think I am ever presenting you with Beckett's Beckett.

The mysteries in *Play* are unerringly expressed by its formal outlines, its roughly objective exteriors. Three heads backed by hellish half-light, facing merciless spotlight: not three bodies with hands, feet, or any means of locomotion as we know it on earth, just three isolated, exposed heads. The life within these heads, the pressure clamped beneath the surface of the brain, is the real life of these people wherever they may be feeling things now.

What we see, in a strange sense mirrored by the character tricks of phrase, is an abstracted courtroom drama in which light is the judge. The tricks keep emerging, almost foolishly formal, from the denser, more directly emotional fabric of their testimony. "Judge then of my astoundment," says the mistress, or "There was no denying that he continued as assiduously as ever," and "I could not credit. . . ." But, as in most testimony from one lover to another, the embellished construction fails to hide the essential clumsiness, the justification of self that never really persuades. There are no easy explanations, no reasons clever enough, no convenient channels of escape.

Only one's head seems real, yet the evidence of its reality convinces nobody, least of all the light trained cruelly upon it.

Still, without hands or feet, having only heads, faces, voices, and words, there remains a vital hold on life and a startling kind of motion on stage. Distilling his means, choosing his theatrical language with remarkable economy, Beckett has dramatized what is perhaps the one constant available, whether in life, death, or even beyond death—the motion of the mind that has lived. In doing so, he has written yet another play belonging only to the theatre, a play severely beautiful and serenely at peace with itself.

In this production, and in the production of Harold Pinter's *The Lover* which accompanies *Play* on the program, Alan Schneider has served both writers with a fidelity to their intentions that is rare in our current theatre. He has, above all, chosen his actors well. In *Play,* Frances Sternhagen, Michael Lipton, and Marian Reardon enact roles which might well be considered ungrateful, yet they do them with a submission to the spare demands of the material that is completely admirable. Beckett offers Stark Young's space, time, and oral values, but he is less generous with the personal medium of the actor.

Pinter's play, however, suffers somewhat by its inclusion on the same bill, despite the stylish facility of Hilda Brawner and Lipton. Written originally not for the theatre but for television, it betrays its origins in a manner that would not be so readily discernible on another program. Presumably it is joined to *Play* by the fact that it, too, apparently concerns adultery. But there the resemblance ends. Pinter, neither dishonorably nor ineptly, deals here in charade, a lightweight game in which husband and wife change identities for the convenience of each other. Peppered by wit, salted by charm, and tinged with ascorbic acid, *The Lover* is only superficially related to the aesthetic world of Beckett. It appears before us as a clever idea, vaguely predictable, and so transparent that it finally disappears with ease from the memory.

Is Beckett, then, a nonexistent or ineffective influence, an artistic spasm and a theatrical dead end? I doubt it. His redefinition of theatre does not mean that he has arisen from his dark, cavernous, existential agony with a set of new formulas for playwrighting. A great dramatic poet, his influence on others is likely to touch only the shadows in their creative corners. His way, so completely his own, could never be the precisely charted way of another dramatist. But in its echoes, it suggests limitless energies yet to be released by anyone who dares as he has dared. As Joyce and Proust affected the modern novel, so Beckett's effect on the modern play: nothing, it would seem, can ever follow him, yet everything will.   *GR(January 1964)*

Blues for Mr. Baldwin

For all his eloquence, James Baldwin has muddled at least two separately vital issues in *Blues for Mr. Charlie:* the art of dramatic writing and the responsibilities of polemics. In the theatre, both have been—and can be—compatible. Shaw believed, with a measure of peculiarly personal success supporting him, that preaching was an art in which he could use "a forensic technique of recrimination, disillusion, and penetration through ideals to the truth, with a free use of all the rhetorical and lyrical arts of the orator, the preacher, the pleader, and the rhapsodist."

Taken on such terms, Baldwin's polemics might seem to meet all the central necessities of dramatic art. Indeed, given his subject and the full extent of his feelings, given so much rage undisguised, it would appear that Baldwin's promise as a dramatist exceeds Shaw's actual achievement. His concern is more directly personal. He speaks daggers to our daily headlines and exposes the heated agony beneath their cold formations. Trumpet-tongued, flinging angry grenades from the pulpit in his heart, he writes as if passion could never be spent. As Shaw would have it, he recriminates, penetrates, and makes a rhapsody of rhetoric. But for all this, for all the undoubted drama at his command, the guiding element is missing: he preaches, but he doesn't argue.

The story and theme of his play are familiar, not only from headlines and the pressures of communal and individual guilt, but from Baldwin's superb, vaulting essays. Here, shifting in and out of past and present, he tells a tale of standardized Southern murder and injustice. Whitetown is ranged against Blacktown over the combustible force of Richard Henry, the local Negro minister's son, just returned from eight years in New York where he sought and found vengeance in jazz, white women, and drugs. Back home, he has a catalytic effect on the entire community: on his father, whom he accuses of being a public man and not a private man at all; on Juanita, the tomboy left behind, now grown into a stunning, articulate woman, falling into quick and inexplicable love for him; on Lyle Britten, the poorest of oxlike whites, provoked by Richard into killing him; and Parnell, the would-be maverick editor of the local newspaper, the conciliator who fails not only both sides, but himself. Into this bursting framework, Baldwin places a patchwork of duologues, reminiscences, lamentations, soliloquies, an abstracted trial, and one brimstone-and-fire sermon. Seams crack, form never settles, choices take on arbitrary life, and people seem often to be quoting famous writers. A living newspaper, his play is more editorial than story, damaging to itself because the newsprint leaps with such startling energy from the page only to reveal its colors— blacks, whites, and emotive reds—as having been smudged and blurred along the way.

Inspired blots do not forge drama. For lack of argument, we are forced back on assertions. And these, by their documentary nature, their sense of incident untransformed, their unmediated factualness, take us toward fringe areas of truth while leaving center depths unplumbed. No play can bear the weightlessness of simple statement, regardless of its observable reality. Truths we know to be self-evident are, by definition, the last material for drama. That white oppresses black relentlessly, that the inhumanity causes psychic ruin to both, that the damage may be by now irreparable, that we are all murderous brothers under the skin, that power and lack of conscience make cowards of us all, may be demonstrated with a certain degree of assertive ease; but to make drama from the demonstration requires a submissive will, an urge to give oneself to the turbulent currents of dramatic forms, the stuff of life that can't be nailed to bulletin boards.

Further than this, Baldwin's assertions often emerge not from life, but from a tangled network of banalities, clichés, and stereotypes. "Real" life as we catch ourselves in it from day to day often consists of the most ridiculous clichés, and repetition lends the latter an equally bizarre reality. We know instinctively, however, that such automatic thoughts are not to be trusted, that our consciousness and dignity depend upon their denial. Baldwin, in almost helpless mimicry of the oppressor, uses a full battery: sexuality as a motive force, especially between whites and Negroes; love as purgative force (Juanita: "I'll have learned from Richard—how to love. I must. I can't let him die for nothing."); and first-class citizenship as a matter of manly force. Thought crumbles while effect merges clumsily into cause. The reasons for horror, the light that might be cast from history, the background clarity that must be brought to bear upon the confusion of the moment, are crushed under the load of borrowed notions.

Like the Hollywood novel, so accurate in sight, touch, and sound, yet so distant from persuasive truth, Baldwin's play is a succession of appearances without reality. His ear is good, his meaning is clear, and his essential intentions are beyond scruple. Yet his story gasps for air, never gathering its own momentum, a series of lifelike fits and starts. Alone and unregarded stands the metaphor that might have wrought transformation.

The Actors Studio Theatre production under Burgess Meredith's direction speaks fundamentally well for the play, often giving it the dramatic sensuality and thrill of discovery that are absent from the text. Much of the success derives from Abe Feder's lighting design; shafts, floods, and squares of light giving shape and point to all the scenes. Beyond the technical certainty lie at least two performances of a quality rarely seen on Broadway today. Al Freeman, Jr.'s Richard makes hatred plastic. He anatomizes impotence with sharp, stabbing thrusts at Baldwin's rhetoric, giving it a bantering liveliness not always suggested by the lines. Perhaps he unbalances events by commanding so much sympathy, but more likely, he is setting up a mirror to Baldwin's ambivalent nature. Unlike the whites in the play, Richard is seen through his humanity rather than through his color.

Juanita, more vocal essayist than character, is given enormous life by Diana Sands. She comes upon the stage as if she held in reserve an armory of vocal, physical, and emotional weapons. Nothing seems held back, yet so much more seems available. Her responses erupt with astonishing fleetness, her silences are completely filled. Given one of Baldwin's most purple passages, she builds a trembling aria, a hard, crystalline song that reaches to the outer rim of pain, the point where tears lose their meaning. Sands makes illusion where it is badly needed, pouring felt drama into naked assertion.

Even in more skillfully executed plays, we may detect a note of artful deception and evasion, a need to unmask while leaving makeup on. Of self-deception, however, the true playwright can afford only a little. He draws distinctions between questions and answers. And he knows, too, that a good answer is usually a suspended question. Baldwin, following the pattern of Richard's father, has written as a public man, not a private man at all. This may be inevitable and even necessary at such a moment in urgent history. But, within it as a choice, stands the dilemma of all socially spirited art, the cruel fact that often what is necessary serves neither cause nor art so well as what is ripped untimely from the dark regions of quarrelsome imagination.

GR(May 1964)

Hamlet without Peers

Hamlet should be measured by his ambitions. Had he not bad dreams, he tells us, he might be confined in a nutshell and still count himself "a king of infinite space." Good plays, serious, difficult, intractable, complex, transcendental, tragic plays have a way of dramatizing bad dreams. Taking them out of the shadows of experience, they make them a living, clear, present, and dangerous substance.

Hamlet, no longer under the literal scrutiny of myopic Dr. Johnsons, no longer in our minds bound by foursquare unities, domestic realities, or the simplistic rules of daily logic, is such a play. The young hero, untimely vaulted into the world of necessary action, must—unlike the court around him—make drama out of his dreams, the phantoms from his imagination possessing a starker reality for him than the directly observable facts of Danish royal life. Surrounded by a gray, politic, coldly sensual world, he is a prisoner not merely of Denmark, but of his own unique colors, his infinite variety of spirit, his warm, passionate, completely human, desperately contained heart and mind. The challenge of production lies, as it were, in the nutshell: evoking the suffocating confinement of the human condition mirrored by Hamlet's Danish prison while suggesting the infinite space over which Hamlet might be king if he could but crack the shell of his own interior mystery.

If the challenge could be met only by way of the central performance, then the new production of the play directed by John Gielgud would be a rare triumph indeed. More often than not we hear of productions in which Denmark is present and the prince is lost somewhere in the wings of the leading actor's deficient imagination. On Broadway today, the reverse situation sadly prevails. Richard Burton's Hamlet stands alone on a "rehearsal" stage almost entirely populated by a dull band of strolling players who barely manage to walk through their parts. The only excuse for such casting and the tediously neutral performances is the excuse based on a fallacy: that gray roles should be played by gray actors, somehow denatured before they begin, inert, unacting reflectors of the atmosphere they are supposed to create.

Perhaps the production was doomed to neutrality from the start. Backing away from the pit- and pratfalls of Guthrie-ized Shakespeare (the school of Wouldn't-it-be-fun-if-Hamlet-were-an-unwilling-S.S.-Officer), Gielgud backed into an idea that is notable only for its startling lack of content or useful suggestiveness. There is no set, no period, and only the players of Gonzago's murder wear formal costumes as such. This, we are asked to imagine, is the final rehearsal before a performance, with Hamlet in black sweater and Gertrude draped in Miami mink. Such a directorial choice has the negative virtue of saying little or nothing about the play, thereby sparing us all those whacky gimmicks that so often flood Shakespeare with irrelevance. But just as it keeps out of the play's forward thrust, so does it do nothing to help the propulsive force of Shakespeare's encompassing perceptions. While avoiding impositions on the dramatist, Gielgud neatly sidesteps interpretation, thus giving some muddy-mettled actors an opportunity to do their imitations of acting with impunity.

Most of them run the classic gamut from *A* to flatted *B*. Claudius clenches his hands and grits his teeth, setting down to his prayers as if he were a lieder singer launching into an assault on Schubert with little art and less voice. Polonius—always popular with an audience that loves to show its recognition of famous lines—makes more of his opportunities, but remains yet another chattering actor, no matter and poor art. And the other men—with the happy exception of George Rose's innocent, relieving comedy as the First Gravedigger—all fade into one another, a blond head here, a bland face there. Eileen Herlie's Gertrude stretches toward the horizon of character, but she too sinks into the enveloping, unfelt general mist. As for Ophelia, a critic's broken heart can barely do ungallant justice to her cracked voice and aimless hunt for motivation.

What I am saying is that in a play where events spill over one another like children at their games, nothing, absolutely nothing, happens between people. The nutshell, the space, the breaths between thoughts and feelings, the vivid, shifting motions of life, the winds of constant change, the sense of danger, are all left to the soul and devices of one man. Were he less than a great actor, the dogs would once again have had their day.

Burton strides the centuries like a colossus. Richard Burbage was said by a contemporary to be "an excellent orator, animating his words with speaking, and speech with acting," artfully varying and modulating his voice, "even to know how much breath he is to give every syllable." David Garrick's first biographer wrote a poem in which nature cried out that Garrick was the thief of her colors. And Edmund Kean, said George Henry Lewes, was remarkable for his intense, passionate expression, and more important, for a gift that Lewes called "the expression of *subsiding emotion.*" Add to these qualities, easily observable in Richard Burton, his peculiarly modern sense of psychology (about which he has the good sense to say nothing in interviews) and before you stands the most richly endowed, most musical, poetic, deeply sensitive Hamlet of our time.

In 1953, when he played the role at the Old Vic, he was closer to Hamlet's age, yet light years away from Hamlet's challenging, endlessly spacious world. His bolt was shot in the first soliloquy, and from there he had no further territory to explore. He chopped the rhythms, garbled the verse, idly playing the idol and monotonously releasing his tears, a Niobe prince of shreds and patches. Now he mines the play for surprises, none of them gratuitous, all of them illuminating. He tastes his words, savoring them for delights and terrors, their sharp reverberations. His voice cuts the air, the sound of an English horn in its lower range, the cry of a breaking trumpet above. His mind is quicksilver, darting and weaving through the underbrush of the text almost as sinuously as his body moves on stage.

Each moment represents discovery, as if he had just lighted on the words or concepts for the first time, the lines not so much written as inevitable. He shapes his scenes with the care of a sculptor. Offering no single attitude, he lets the prig in Hamlet live side by side with the saint, the tenderness of an unspent lover change suddenly to the savagery of an angry avenger; all of which would be less surprising and painfully mechanical were it not that he makes these strange companions live *within* each other rather than dealing them out in card-game succession. In short, he is intelligent, he knows how to contain and release ambivalent passions, and he has the voice, form, and mystery to sustain the agonies, to suspend decision.

That he falters toward the end, that his energies seem to drift from his pores, may best be explained by what must be an exhausting emptiness in his surroundings. An expansive, romantic, ambitious performance such as Burton's, reaching out of the darkness into Hamlet's infinite space, takes its life from abhorrence of vacuums. Meanwhile, it should be seen now as often as possible for what it is: the crown jewel of our theatre in restless search of a better setting.   *GR(May 1964)*

Joan Littlewood's Lovely War

However remarkable or desperate Harold Wilson's first hundred days prove to be, one strain in British society is likely to remain the same. The class war will continue to rage into the indolent, slippered English night, and even a foreigner must recognize that only two sides are available. Joan Littlewood, for one example—jaunty, heavily booted, defiant to the night—might appear to the outsider as the most emphatically un-English figure in British theatre. But the outsider, not for the first time, would be just as emphatically wrong. Playing the oldest theatrical game—illusion vs. reality—he is forgetting that her appearance is an invention of her own, a very real, very English, very local reflection of another side of Englishness, the attritional struggle against the Establishment. It is, finally, the war that confounds all wars because as one figure replaces another the battle must begin again. Behind Littlewood's appearance, then, lies the hard, entrenched, bitter dispute not between class and class, but rather the mortal struggle within each class to maintain itself along the lines of the revered past when Britannia ruled the imperial waves. The real canker that gnaws at almost every circumstance of British life is that the past is past.

Almost singlehandedly, Littlewood has hauled Britain's dusty theatre into the century, breaking rules and forms with as much gusto as she meant to break the content. For a start, she sought to give a working-class audience some working-class plays and productions, an *Arden of Feversham* built from muscle, a *Richard II* that had grace without a limp wrist, the Brendan Behan and Shelagh Delaney plays that always looked as if they had been born in back alleys and rooftops. Her Theatre Workshop was as far from the West End as it could be, not Stratford-upon-Avon but Stratford East. In every way it was a theatre of challenge, with Joan—as she prefers to be known—making it insistently clear that she was of the working class, by the working class, and for the working class. There was only one flaw, unmistakable even to her hopeful eye: the East End workers were staying away.

She carried on, however, British in spite of herself. Her class struggle found theatrical life even when it had to support itself on the tainted sterling and dollars of classy enthusiasts from the West End and Broadway. It was a class war with an individual tone and look all its own. The members of Joan's class are the eternal good guys. They drink good English beer in good brown English pubs. Just before 11 P.M. closing, they shoot good straight English darts. Their songs are bawdy, rousing hymns to the sturdiness of a hard-breeding race. They play soccer, not Rugby. They are tolerant, honest, brave, roughly humorous, humorously rough, dauntless, proud, gentle men. In short, they represent the ideal Britain, lean, sound, and tough as Gibraltar. In Joan's world, it is not possible to conceive that they might be the same men who defeated the new Foreign Secretary in the recent parliamentary election because—as the Tory campaign slogan went—they didn't "want a nigger for a neighbor." At their worst, as Joan sees it, they are really only victims. Yet viewed closely, their virtues have a chillingly familiar ring. By merely removing the roughness and by changing the accent and the epithets, the extolled virtues reveal the very sound, tempest, and whirlwind of British passion possessed by their opposite numbers, the bad guys of the ruling class. When those *pukka sahibs* paced the Empire, either to the stately strains of Edward Elgar or the wickedly patriotic ditties of Noël Coward, they made similar claims to pride and honor.

Joan, then, is the author of a myth, a charming, good-natured, aggressive little fiction which, several years ago, had the undoubted virtue of at least driving the old class fictions into a less respectable corner of British theatre. No more teacups at the bottom of our garden, no more stiff upper-class lips around which ideas could scarcely bend their weary way. Joan—long before Osborne, Arnold Wesker, indeed, all the members of the new ripple—had changed the face of English theatre without penetrating the heart of English society. Engaging in the war of accents, local jargon, and classless aspiration, she fell into what an outsider might consider the most obvious trap. She accepted the central terms and assumptions of the war. She couldn't lick them, so in accent proud and gesture pugnacious, she joined them. And the war plays on.

To our good fortune, Joan's war is always a miracle of theatrical vitality, sharply seen, vivaciously executed, and daringly inventive. Unjust as she may be, she is never uninteresting. *Oh What a Lovely War,* which Joan has assembled, directed, and otherwise created as her latest excursion into fancy and protest, offers vintage Littlewood, the kind of romping charade or planned improvisation to which all her previous work with other playwrights pointed: not a musical comedy, not a plotted drama, neither an abstraction nor a Happening, but something that ought to have a new name—a Gaming, perhaps, or a Playing. Before anything else, the so-called "musical entertainment" currently at the Broadhurst in New York is a theatrical occasion, not to be confused with other arts or media; which is to say that whatever her assumed disdain for words or dramatic form, whatever claims she makes for theatre in parks, streets, or fun palaces, she uses the space of theatre—its rise above and distance from the audience, its depth, its exits and entrances, lights and darks—to make a framework and a form that belong only in a theatre. This has less to do with shape than with relationships: men and women weaving in and out of each other's moments and characters, plainly acting to one another and performing for the audience. And it is from this quality of performing, this pleasure in the act, this giving to the audience, that the show derives its astonishing sense of presence and urgency. The peculiar paradox of marvelous theatre is that it must be prepared and formed without ever seeming frozen. It is possible to say of Joan's exhilarating, antic, yet intensely moving show (which I have seen twice in London and twice in New York) that it always seems to be happening for the first time: an animated, spontaneously combustible tapestry, a frieze in motion.

The method is perfectly suited to the action. A war erupted absurdly and helplessly in 1914, a senseless, infuriating war that seemed to begin with all the pomp of a ritual game, but made itself known first to the men in the firing line and gradually to history as a horrifying means to an undefined end. It is this gradual awakening that Joan dramatizes. Counterpoint is her method. Behind a simple, bemused, completely confident little Pierrot show in which the large cast sings and dances a succession of numbers created anonymously either in the trenches and hospitals at the front or in the smugly jingoistic parlors and music halls back home, she states baldly on a moving electric sign and a movie screen the brutal facts of the war, the cold statistics of money and men. The effect is at once morally and theatrically devastating. War, we are reminded while shamelessly enjoying ourselves, seems such good fun, such jolly, suggestively amusing, madly lyrical entertainment. Faced with fear, waste, and a gigantic void, the Pierrots invent "the ever-popular war games." All that remains to men is a resiliency, an incredible bounce that would seem to be a testimonial to something of value in the human spirit. Yet against the seeming good is the implicit disgust, the jolting fact that men make song—however ironic—while making or being led to slaughter. The first act ends on a note of indignant sadness. Victor Spinetti as the master of ceremonies sings "Goodbye-ee, Goodbye-ee, Wipe the tear, baby dear, from your eye-ee." Softly, with a cutting gentleness, a thrusting sweetness, he is closing not only an act but an era, saying farewell forever to a time beyond nostalgia. Hereafter, his manner suggests, you play and laugh with war at your peril.

And the class war? Hovering within perilous sight of every scene, it takes second place, for once, to the real concern and the real entertainment. It is still there, of course, partly because it is impossible to deny that some men make money from wars and others find glory. But Joan's good guys are, on occasion, seen here as easy marks and bloodthirsty dullards. It is as if her natural sentimental equation were divided by the facts of life and death, and by the logic of the theatrical art she sent into orbit. For whatever she says, she can't help making art.

Joan is an interpreter not so much of plays as of theatrical moment. And she is at her worst when she tries to make statements or uphold assertions, because the special life of her theatre lies in fluidity of thought and the unsettled nature of feeling. While it may be against her plan or will, she always crosses and crisscrosses boundaries. She wants, as she has said, a theatre that is "grand, vulgar, simple, pathetic—but not genteel, not poetical." Yet what continually surprises is that for all her vulgarity and simplicity—indeed because of the way they play against one another—she makes poetry from clowns and finds gentleness in raucous men. A fortuitous contradiction in her own person, she represents a triumph of theatrical spirit over all kinds of war.

Watch her company of Pierrots at work, especially the relaxed, contentedly alive Spinetti, whose mercurial wit, cartoon clarity, and startling inventiveness make viciously funny sense out of Cockney and French gibberish. What you will see—through him, through the collective sensitivity of the others, and by way of Joan's controlled abandon—is a theatre that honors a vast part of an original art, a theatre that celebrates an odd wisdom and a haunting elegance. Class war notwithstanding, Littlewood is a proud inheritor of an ancient tradition—of all things, an aristocrat with a smudge on her face.

GR(November 1964)

Lee Strasberg: Burning Ice

To dispose at once of some necessary self-consciousness: Lee Strasberg and I have been associates. At one time, indeed, we shared intimations of friendship. While it should not have to be said, it *has* to be said that this association, far from disqualifying me for a critical appraisal of the man, the teacher, and the director, does, in fact, qualify me more than nonacquaintance might serve another critic. Fashion, of course, dictates otherwise, which is why this ancient argument must be labored again.

"It is the capacity," said Shaw, "for making good or bad art a personal matter that makes a man a critic." The true critic is not an arbitrator between artist and public. Neither is he a labor mediator between management and artist. Whatever social role may be his pretense, his real concern rests between himself and the artist, treating the public, in fact, as a welcome eavesdropper on a deeply personal dialogue.

In short, the critic knows and cares. Three years away from the Studio have brought me detachment, but I remain, if anything, more involved. My role having changed from participator to critic, I am now no less concerned with what I know and what I see than I was before, when critical awareness was almost too much to bear.

My time as Administrative Director of the Actors Studio—a shade less than two years in 1959 and 1960—was not a relationship of critic to a theatre. The performance, for me at least, never took place. When Elia Kazan hired me to "push us to do what we want to do, even in spite of ourselves," he was suggesting that the Studio could continue to have meaning only if it were to become a theatre. Considerations of joining Lincoln Center, though at the time an issue between Kazan and the Lincoln Center Board, and also between Kazan and Strasberg, were not really the point. What was at stake, in effect, was the life of one man: Lee Strasberg. Was he willing, first, to breathe the air beneath open skies, to turn preparation into performance? And second, once willing, whether charging forward on his own momentum or being dragged into battle, what would he reveal? The first question concerned me then. The second can at last be answered now.

*   *   *

If the symbol was a hard nut for Stanislavsky to crack, so is Lee Strasberg, symbolically and literally, a hard nut for anyone, friend or foe, to crack. He is one of those figures who, like a supreme politician as opposed to an expert statesman, invites no middle ground, no neutral view. He suggests, as much by his nodding silences as by his little attentions, a classically formed love-hate relationship. But when the nut is cracked, it comes out melting love or towering hate, rarely both together.

Tony Richardson once wrote, "It has been claimed, and on the record not unjustly, that he has done more for the American theatre than any other man in history." A minister, disturbed by Strasberg at work in the Studio, borrowed a phrase from Luther to describe what he saw: *incurvatus in se*—turned within itself. A New York University psychologist wrote to me in 1960, "My first reaction to the question, 'Is Strasberg practicing psychiatry without a license?' is to pose a counter question, 'Are psychiatrists practicing Strasberg without the requisite experience?'" An English actor, Richard Johnson, said in an interview, "I went to hear the high priest of the Method, Lee Strasberg, the other night. He spoke for an hour and a half about Brecht and the Brecht theatre in East Berlin. It seems extraordinary that he should have discovered Brecht twenty years late." Kim Stanley says, "Strasberg is not interested in exploiting talent but in maturing it and making it go." Robert Brustein, calling him the Keynes of Times Square, wrote, "The fact is that Strasberg's reforms have all been too limited, too timid, too superficial—like those of a prose stylist who raises the quality of advertising copy. Unlike Stanislavsky, who invented a new acting technique in order to mount dramatic masterworks, thereby transforming the Russian theatre, Strasberg has been the interior decorator of a crumbling structure whose foundations he has done nothing to change." Members of the Studio, with the latter-day exception of a hard core of unemployed actors (unemployed, at least, by the Actors Studio Theatre), go to Strasberg as some people travel to Sunday morning Mass, the news from Nietzsche that "God is dead" having not yet reached their prickly ears.

Strasberg himself does nothing to discourage awe either way. A visibly quiet man, outwardly contained much of the time, withholding words, keeping to himself, dressed almost always in what looks like the same black shirt, the same dark tie and sports jacket, he seems to be locked in constant thought. His appearances and habits at the Studio always take the same form: roughly five minutes before a session's scheduled beginning, he arrives downstairs, stands expectantly in front of the secretary's desk, says nothing until he is addressed, then answers wordlessly with a nod if the question or statement is routine, or embarks upon an elaborate discourse; at least one time a week he sits beside the desk signing checks placed before him; then, just as suddenly as he appeared, he moves upstairs to where the sessions take place, his entrance signal enough for settling down; as he sits on a director's low-slung deck chair (the only one of its kind in the room), the stage manager next to him cues for lights; a card is handed to Strasberg, who reads aloud the title of the scene, usually omitting the names of the actors or the author; then the scene or exercise is presented, after which the lights come on, and the customarily exhausted actors sit in the center of the playing area in order to describe the intentions of their work; when they are finished, there is a pause, Strasberg holds his position, his back still to the viewers, and says in a low voice, "What would you say?" to which there is usually an extended pause broken finally by the stage manager calling upon one of the members for comment; after several people have had their say, Strasberg shifts his weight in his chair ever so slightly, the stage manager clicks the switch of the tape recorder sitting in front of Strasberg, and the extended assessment (not criticism, as Strasberg takes many occasions to stress) begins; when this is finished, a second scene is usually performed, with actors' intentions, "What would you say," members' comments, tape recorder, and long assessment following in direct, predictable order. If, as it sometimes happens, only one scene is scheduled, or by a stroke of ill luck, no scene is ready, the two-hour session takes the shape of a disquisition by Strasberg, his subject usually a variation on one of two themes: either his distress that time at the Studio is not better used, or his interest and concern over misunderstandings about the Studio's work. Finally, Strasberg rises and the session is over.

Ordinary actions of men never appear to be his. After each Studio session he would join the members in a nearby café and automatically receive and eat the same sandwich and tea; then he would allow a member to hail a cab for him, in which he returned to his apartment on Central Park West. These Tuesday and Friday rituals, like the unchanging form of Studio sessions, were signs that Strasberg *ordered* daily life as he might wish to order theatre. They looked like real behavior, but the unyielding repetition of even these spare, minor actions contributed to an unmistakable, perhaps wishful, aura of immortality. No wonder, then, that a timorous Studio member, upon discovering Strasberg before a urinal after one session, rushed out immediately to convey the alarming and surprising news to his fellow members.

One does not visit Lee Strasberg, nor does one chat. One simply pays court. In paying homage to an Eastern potentate, there is an orderly sense of ceremony, a bending of the knees at this moment, a bow here, a gentle scrape there. To any child of the thirties the image remains indelible: a vast and mysterious kingdom lies somewhere beyond the Himalayas, a place which is in some odd, inverted way associated with Ponce de León and fountains of youth that might have been seen by Marco Polo; the horizon is lost, of course, and inside, seated rigidly and sternly on a golden throne, is an ancient man, apparently carved out of some withered prune tree, his eyelids permanently drawn down upon his eyes, a living statue dedicated to staying alive and infinitely wise for a minimum of two thousand years. Buddha, Mohammed, or High Lama not yet ready to pass his power to Ronald Colman: whichever he may be on the silver screen of his imagination, Strasberg invites not honor, not homage, not mere appreciation, and never understanding; rather does he ask—implicitly in his silences, explicitly when praising himself—for worship.

He approaches the road to worship, however, by making a detour into the land of the querulous and humble. "The next few years," he said in one interview, "will have to be dedicated to a search for what should be the Studio's future direction." This is what might be called Strasberg's rhetorical-earnest mood, after which he eased himself into the rhetorical-depressed: "I began to question our reason for existence. Perhaps we had contributed as much as we had to contribute. Or maybe we hadn't been as valuable as we thought we had been. Was there something new we could go on to do? Or was there, possibly, no need for a Studio?" With nobody there to supply him with an answer, he then moved on, unsurprisingly, to offer his own, at last in the spirit and language of the rhetorical-triumphant: "I realized how important an institution like the Studio is by its very existence, by sending a constant stream of young people bursting with enthusiasm into the theatre . . ."

If God sounds at moments like a huckster, it may be that no other language is available to him. For Strasberg is Lord over a small temple, a Greek revival building on 44th Street that once looked down upon the Hudson, now crushed on all sides by the ratholes of Hell's Kitchen. Such surroundings have their own importance and urgency, placing the problems of theatre in a perspective that most actors, directors, teachers, and producers scarcely think about between jobs. To be heard not merely in the world, but first amongst colleagues, one must shout. And in the theatre, the press agent's handout is the equivalent of anyone else's scream. Thus, when Strasberg said at the first rehearsal of *The Three Sisters*, just before playing a recording in Russian of the Moscow Art Theatre's version of 1940, that "this is a historic occasion"; or when at one of his recent classes he called himself "the most important person in American theatre," it is possible that he was exaggerating—as he often says when assessing an actor's problem—to make the point. Such exaggeration may be necessary: it is one matter to have disciples, quite another to win an audience. And Strasberg has been battling for an audience all his life.

In Group Theatre days, he came in time to a double horror: he lost his standing with the actors, and he never captured the imagination of a large audience. Was he ever a good director? It is not easy to say now, so tactfully has the subject gone undiscussed by the disciples, almost as if they dared not breathe their doubts in open rooms; and from Strasberg, even in the long period between directing jobs (1952–64), his direction was referred to in persistent present tense ("When I do this," etc.), and his past loomed always as a time of lost glory when what was less than splendid could be laid at the door of commercial theatre and what was marvelous was a moment we can never know.

The record after the Group and before the Studio is dim where it is not plainly inauspicious. Stark Young, reviewing Strasberg's 1942 production of J. M. Barrie's *A Kiss for Cinderella,* starring Luise Rainer, was not impressed:

> It might seem to Mr. Strasberg that there is something intellectual in thus muffing the moon and happy sugar in Barrie's writing. We have had plenty of these examples of intellectualism, where the director or the producer or both knew only too well the follies of his author and how to set all that straight. . . . It is really a subtle form of the obtuse. Nothing is less functional—to use the highbrow cliché—than the right brain in the wrong skull. There are times when we are well sick of these people in the offing who know better what the author meant than the author himself knew. The sum of all which is to say that it is hard for second-rate people to let anything alone.

What can be surmised about Strasberg in the forties is that times were fundamentally hard and possibly more cruel to him than to any of his former friends in the Group. In 1947, Cheryl Crawford was producing *Brigadoon* successfully on Broadway, directed by still another Group colleague, Robert Lewis. The Strasberg family had just returned to New York in distressed financial shape. There were no offers from producers, there were no huge private acting classes, and the Actors Studio was only an idea in the minds of Lewis, Crawford, and Kazan, the latter saying—according to Kevin McCarthy, a founding member—that the one man they must keep out of the Studio at all costs was Lee Strasberg. Crawford, whose bleak exterior—lips drawn tightly, nose set in sniffing readiness for the unacceptable odors accompanying bad news, her entire frame poised, as it were, for that Medea moment when she can dust the blackboard—hides a heart of soft, crumbling granite, felt moved enough to put Strasberg on the *Brigadoon* payroll as an acting coach, though, as she puts it, he wasn't really needed.

It can be said obliquely in his favor that he suffered exile quietly, that he may well have been exercising an uncompromising conscience all those dark years, and that—whatever may be said of him as a man, a teacher, a leader, or self-styled prophet—he was certainly more serious and thoughtful than most of the directors who thrived then and now on Broadway. One might argue, in fact, that had he been consigned not to temporary oblivion, but to continual work as a director, he might by now have clarified his life, his role, his mission. As it is, he has been a teacher and a gradually influential aesthetic force, but he has never wholly surrendered to a teacher's life. The consequence is that, where American theatre was failing, he became at once physician and patient, prescribing a remedy while just as busily nursing his own wounds. He whose religion is certainty could never make up his mind.

In the *sanctum sanctorum* of the Studio, however, he could be certain, at the least, of his command. Upon his late arrival, war was declared, and since then, it has been carried to many fronts. What must be distinguished are the tanks he sent personally and precisely into battle, and those that got away from him through attrition.

Of the first, there can be no ambivalence: Strasberg has tried quite genuinely to develop a specifically American adaptation of Stanislavsky's System, a way of making Stanislavsky work for what he took to be a uniquely American character. Behind this lies an abstract, scarcely defined notion of nationalism in acting, coupled with a conviction that this barely tapped source of acting power might be channeled to serve plays of the classical, international repertory. Others in America have taught what they called "Stanislavsky," but no one else has ever built so systematically on the dogma of inherent American superiority. Students of Strasberg, particularly those admitted to the Studio, are continually reminded that they are the best actors in the world. Inspired by a sort of rage for recognition, he will exhort them, assure them, cajole them, sometimes tease them into accepting the evidence of his confidence against the evidence of their eyes, their sporadic, narrow achievements, their empty pockets, or their experience of good acting from other countries. In short, outnumbered, besieged, not always popular with the masses they are fighting for, these soldiers go into battle not merely determined to win, but persuaded by their commander that they will never lose.

Here, however, is where attrition enters the scene. As Napoleon's army failed to reckon with Russia's bitter winter, Strasberg's beleaguered, out-of-practice legions more often than not neglect the conditions of American theatre and those aspects of the general's personality and ideology that are less than conducive to fruitful struggle. The two elements—the worst in American theatre and the worst in Strasberg—form a common design, the one wedded to the other as if nothing was more natural than an alliance between idealism and corruption. Setting his sights on one central target—the extension and codification of the art of acting by stressing the special aliveness in each actor, "to bring the actor *alive* on stage," as he put it in his 1958 Harvard lectures—

Strasberg allows his thoughts to stray to other targets, some outside his range of perception, some which contradict by definition his claims for his ideal theatre, and finally, some which simply reveal his abject surrender to commodity. What he gives the actor in concern, precise awareness of personal problems, and sensitive, informed analysis, he too often takes away by presenting vulgarized personal goals, his own ignorance of and bad taste in plays and playwriting, and his intransigence in the face of whatever is aesthetically new in world theatre. As friend to his actors, he offers running evidence that he responds to people and ideas as potential enemies. If he is a genius at anything, it is in the fine art of inspiring insecurity.

The central enemy, of course, is bad theatre; or at least what can be commonly agreed upon as bad theatre: very roughly, almost all that is seen on Broadway. In general terms, Strasberg shares with his severest critics a distaste, even a hatred, for many of the same impurities. Where they part company is in the scope of concern. Strasberg, like the surgeon who wants only to operate, is a specialist compounding solutions almost exclusively from one element—in his case, acting. Often, the surgeon pronounces the operation a success even though the patient is dead. Strasberg's critics, while seeing the same desiccated spirits on stages, view acting as only one of many problems.

His arrival at the Studio in the early fifties was really a new beginning for both. Several life members suffered sudden death. There were denunciations—particularly of Daniel Mann's brief regime—banishments, and promises. Strasberg was announcing in his private, authoritarian way that the revolution was on. Seriousness was in, dilettantes were out. Talent was to be cultivated under hothouse conditions, the chosen few to consider themselves delicate plants finally receiving constant care and attention. To be overturned was everything in American theatre that contributed to the destructive usage and abusage of the American actor. No more polite acting, no more physical crutches, no more vocal tricks. Nothing, indeed, alien to the actor himself was to be developed, and everything human, alive—therefore, personal—was to be encouraged. Beauty in theatre was to be found not so much in the artifice and design of art, least of all in the artificial frippery of so much boulevard, West End, and Broadway theatre, but rather in the work of art that is man himself. The key philosophical figuration was a type of humanism, proposed first as a technique and a modest antidote, but developed in time into something with wider pretensions: an all-purpose, dramatic, theatrical *aesthetic*.

Joseph Ernest Renan, brooding over what he considered to be the "deplorable reputation" of Mme. de Sévigné, wagged his head, says the de Goncourt journal, and, repeating silently, let fall from his lips, "She is not a thinker. . . . She is not a thinker." Conditions have changed only a little and reputations continue to be built from mountains of muddled heads. In Strasberg, the obvious presence of thought does little to hide the absence of thinking. His wiring, it might be said, is faulty and shows signs of constant crossing, blunting short circuits, a network of spindly strands that only rarely connect. In carrying an impulse or observation into an idea, he travels in detours, almost as if he were afraid that the snapping of the switch might actually lead to the turning on of the light.

Where he is most at home—directly coping with an actor's immediate problems demonstrated moments before in a scene or exercise—he is still unable to match his passion to a clear expression of it. His sentences wind their way in jerky, fumbling patterns through cluttered underbrush, most of them masterpieces of how not to use the language. Studded with qualifiers, parenthetical clauses, and jumbled syntax, the only miracle is not that his message is widely misunderstood, as he so often complains, but that it is understood at all.

A written transcription of Strasberg's extemporaneous spoken words can be only partially evocative of the sound he makes; indeed, to transcribe him to paper is to transform what is essentially an astounding run-on sentence into a series of reasonably intelligible single sentences with commas, semicolons, and full stops. Here, however, is one typical, necessarily abbreviated, extract, taken from the tape recorder that regularly commits his extended apostrophes to documentary immortality. Directing his remarks to an actor who was trying to master a scene from *Henry V*, Strasberg said:

> But for instance, when you spoke I got only a general thing. I didn't see you were somebody there, and somebody there, and so on. The gesture was always rather general, within a general area with almost one person that you were sort of speaking to. But I don't know why you need to fluctuate between the extreme of one or the other. I think that if you find something, hold onto that thing, also then use another thing, you see, finding new things; otherwise you are now almost too concerned with finding the right thing, and the right thing is not something to be found, it will happen. You find little things here for yourself, easy things, some people here have already mentioned, and to be willing to go a little bit more easily with that. And even with the voice thing, or so on, if we say we don't hear, fine then, the next time, a little bit more, but not suddenly very full as it was here where the tone was very definite and very vivid, but where the tone unfortunately and unconsciously reminded me of an actor who was trying to do the words well, of an actor, you see, who was acting, so to say, with the words.

By itself, internal contradictions notwithstanding, the general point made in the criticism is accessible even to the dimmest wit. So fraught is it, however, with vague references—the reliance continually upon the word *thing*—with *so to say*'s, *you see*'s, and in other examples, with *so on and so forth*'s, that it is difficult for a listener to dislodge himself from the oppressive sensation that either everything or nothing is being said. In the land of Strasberg, the persistent *et cetera* has never found a more congenial or spacious home. Again, a subliminal triumph for insecurity: the mask of certainty itself masked by obscurity, by speech in the form of spasm.

The use of language, however unregarded, reveals important clues, and often clear warnings, about the state of a mind. While in a teacher it need never be poetic nor even relentlessly grammatical, it should always serve to illuminate its subject. It must, in fact, show that the mind has done its work at home, and that in public it is prepared to make that work not only well meaning, dogmatic, or emotionally charged, but clear, shaped, and intellectually felt.

Surely, too, a hardened *aesthetic* would be better served by a more articulate spokesman. What use can it be even to him for years to pass in a state of acknowledged public confusion about his beliefs and his work? An aesthetic philosophy requires at least two forms of explanation: the publication in carefully developed, systematic chapters, of its several meanings; and—in the case of a performing art—a long, grueling, experimental succession of public demonstrations. Miles upon miles of recorded tape, even when someday they might be edited, may give—as they do in the Studio—a sense of presence and imminent discovery. But like the exercises, which do not necessarily lead to art, they cannot be expected to drift automatically into philosophy. Similarly, the practice of so contentious and remotely comprehended a philosophy should have been tested repeatedly in a continuing, permanent theatre long before Strasberg and the membership created their producing unit out of envy and anger at Kazan's commitment to Lincoln Center. Even then, the late and laborious emergence of Strasberg as a practitioner indicates further that understanding—far from being sought—was feared; that there may have been fewer *things* in this philosophy than were dreamt of in heaven and earth.

Within so much willed mystery, there still must lurk some meaning. What, after all, is Strasberg's message? By asking this, I do not mean to imply that all his convictions should be easily reducible to one or two naked statements. Nor am I referring to those unarguable aspects of his teaching (and those of other Stanislavsky descendants) which can be listed under the heading of intentions: that the actor has available to him actual *techniques,* psychological and imaginative, for helping him to come alive on stage; that the actor first of all has only himself to work on, that this self is his instrument, and he can practice on it as a musician would on his; or, to shift the metaphor, that he works out in his classes as an athlete works out in the gym, or as a dancer uses the bar. What I am suggesting is that Strasberg *does* convey at least one surprisingly simple message to his actors in spite of his upside-down, roundabout, prolix method of conveying it. And this message, I suggest further, may be not only the first source of confusion among critics and audience, but, more disastrously, it may be a powerful interior source of confusion within the actors who place so much faith in him.

Threaded into the tangled webbing of his talks to the actors, he will almost invariably say what he said to that same actor after the *Henry V* scene:

> The kind of technique that we have, as separated from the work that we do, is directed towards . . . building the actor's faith in himself. Since *an actor cannot have faith in himself,* that's too general, we build faith in things, in objects. . . . [Italics added.]

The actor, in brief, *must* build faith in himself, yet he *cannot* expect to find it or have it.

Now, sometimes even in the highest reaches of art the artist cannot be permitted to luxuriate in ambivalence. Had he wished, Rembrandt might have declared for our enlightenment that paint was his medium, but having said that, he could not then pour potash, lime, or scent of tartar on his empty canvases. In like fashion, only those actors mature and developed enough to ignore or withstand this invitation to confusion and frustration can be expected to separate what is useful for them in Strasberg's classes from what might well be pernicious or frankly obstructive in the theatre. As it stands, most of the faithful are young and essentially unformed, and even the older, more accomplished and experienced actors still require *direction* when performing not in exercises, but in plays. Meanwhile, with objects and things standing in for self, it should not be surprising that where psychology and imagination are called for, most of Strasberg's students offer helpless, undirected, undisciplined, frequently disconnected exhibitions of behavior.

No dirtier words exist in the Strasberg actor's book of dos and don'ts than *external, indication,* and *results.* While no one could seriously quarrel with the principle that an actor must first of all be at home on stage, quite literally living in ease, naturalness, and comfort with the objects around him, still more is it true that this relaxed acceptance of objects does not imply or require *dependence* upon them. To gain faith by reaching out for the support of an object is, by inescapable definition, to gain faith by being external, indicating to the audience that one is alive, while hoping somewhat aimlessly for consequent results in dramatic truth. Behavior, in fact—what we do—is not psychology, it is only the indication that, as in all men, a psychology exists. Moreover, in life, behavioral actions often tell lies about the truth within, frequently without planning to do so. These are the lies that the System was initially designed to intercept. And indeed, since no drama, be it verse, epic, absurd, *or* naturalistic, was ever intended by any dramatist, living or dead, to be unselectively lifelike, it follows that what may be called the Strasberg flaw puts serious obstacles not only in the paths of learning actors, but interferes, in fact, with the vaulting intentions of good dramatists and their plays. Furthermore, to supply the actor with dependable objects is to demand a heavily furnished stage. And, quite plainly, this won't do for many—perhaps most—plays from Aeschylus to Beckett.

One part of the mystery, then, is not half so mysterious as it might like to be. The teacher is less misunderstood by others than he is misunderstood by himself. When even an older actor frequently complains—as one of the male leads in *The Three Sisters* regularly did—that he is unable to bring any of his work in the Studio into his work on stage, then it is clearly because what is alive in exercises, whether Private Moments, improvisations, or scenes, is not necessarily transferable to the sustaining demands of fully developed, incessantly moving, drama. Alive in the actor at the Studio are some gratifying moments, some beautifully felt and observed instants in time, none of them by themselves inherently useful or relevant for those long arcs of dramatic confrontation that must have constant, selected life on stage.

Among the obscurities that continue to pass undiscovered by the Studio advertising is the element of responsibility. The question can be asked in several parts: Which thriving careers, which continuing displays of excellence, can be laid to the hand of Strasberg? Granting the loyalty of most of the actors, youthful and mature, conceding the conviction of so many that Strasberg has—as they say—freed them, helped them, or inspired them, which actors, then, languishing with personal, unsolved difficulties, unable to keep the art in themselves in motion, are also to be laid to the same hand? If he is given credit for the genuine achievements of actors such as Kim Stanley, Geraldine Page, Maureen Stapleton, Eli Wallach, Anne Bancroft, and many others who are not stars, should he be credited also with their less distinguished performances, the signs in their work of only modest growth and development; and further than that, is he responsible for the increasing number of careers, undistinguished or halted, that form a vast part of the large Studio membership?

It is not uncommon, and certainly not unjust, for a teacher to receive full and proper credit for the excellence of his pupils. When Van Cliburn emerged in triumph from Moscow, suddenly the public was made aware of Mme. Rosina Lhevinne as an honored teacher at Juilliard. But never was it suggested that Mme. Lhevinne was the real winner of the Tchaikovsky competition. Traditionally, the best teachers carry with their knowledge and perceptions a sensible, balanced share of humility and proportion. They know, ideally, that they can be the first liberators of talent, that they can even point the best ways of using and developing that talent, but that they can never hope to liberate everybody, talented or not. They know, too, that by their actions they are as influential as by their words; that what might be called their spiritual underground message is just as important—sometimes more so—as the message they think and hope they are saying.

Strasberg's underground message, as I've been suggesting, is a smoothly meshing network composed of studied omissions, marketplace values, darkly inspired insecurities, and downright spiritual paralysis. I have stressed the insecurities in some detail because they are the elements in Strasberg's pedagogy least understood by his actors. The other elements, surprisingly, are understood and conceded by the faithful. What is not surprising—and what makes the membership no less culpable in its individual and collective fate—is that these corruptions are also forgiven, indeed, often shoved under the public rug.

Most of them, however, are widely familiar in one form or another. The omissions, for example, range from the basic to the strangely personal: the Studio is run deliberately along casual lines, with no one compelled to do anything but watch and listen; concurrently, lip service is occasionally paid to the need for an actor to develop his body, his voice, and his mind, but with the exception of one session a week with a speech (not voice) teacher (also not compulsory and sparsely attended), and two brief, abortive periods with mime and movement people, the many strings of the actor's instrument are left to the gods of spontaneous development.

On the personal side there is the omission of other theorists of acting, most seriously, Brecht. As it took five years for Strasberg to develop one exercise, so did it take him five years to admit publicly that he saw—and was impressed by—the Berlin Ensemble production of *The Caucasian Chalk Circle*. And then he did so without making it clear that the five years had passed.

In 1961, the Studio hired the Morosco Theatre to present a talk by Strasberg on his trip that summer to Italy, Germany, and France. One of the lecture's features was an account of his welcome by Helene Weigel to the Schiffbauerdamm in East Berlin. Strasberg then went on to discuss the qualities in Brecht's productions of *Galileo* and *The Caucasian Chalk Circle* that caught his attention. He presented his glowing remarks as if in response to productions seen only that summer; indeed, as if he had never before seen the work of Brecht's company, as if the news of the Ensemble's excellence had reached him in the past only by way of the theatrical gossip route. What the majority of his listeners didn't know, and could scarcely be aware of, was that the *Chalk Circle* was *not* in the Ensemble's repertory that summer because the only actress available for Grusha was no longer with the company. Strasberg had, in fact, seen the production (along with *Mother Courage*) on the Ensemble's visit to London in 1956. What had happened, most probably, in the intervening, silent five years was that Brecht had by then been safely stowed away in his less threatening grave. But whether Strasberg is merely slow, or simply an innocent, or, in more complex terms, a deeply disturbed, defensive man, the point remains that it took him almost indecently long to give his seal of approval, his imprimatur, to a move in the theatre that should long ago have reached New York's actors, directors, and playwrights. And then, like the other forms of omission, it was a seal made only from the lips.

Strasberg's marketplace values are even more notorious, compressible as they are into one magic word—Hollywood. His attraction to manufactured fame, to engineered personalities, to empty stellar vessels born, it would seem, to be filled by him, is one of those bumbling corruptions that is often referred to as funny were it not so sad. Young, talented actors stand in the Studio wings while Strasberg defers kindly to big names built under the Hollywood sun. When *The Three Sisters* was first offered to him as a Studio production in 1959, he declared that he would do it only "in the rhythm of art," and that in any case, "Jennifer [Hollywood's own Miss Jones and *not* a Studio member] is not ready yet."

Less well known than the Hollywood frenzy are the cautionary commercial impulses that are remarkable only in that they are almost always wrong. Two examples should suffice: *Who's Afraid of Virginia Woolf?,* said Strasberg at a time when it seemed as if it would be the Studio Theatre's first production, is the kind of play the Studio should do even though it would never be commercial; when the Studio was looking for a new secretary, he suggested that Carmine de Sapio's completely unqualified daughter should be hired because she might lead the Studio to people with money—this at a time when her father's political star was clearly falling, and against the obvious fact that fantasies about the Studio operating in the orbit of political parties should best go unspoken.

These flights of fancy, comic only as they hit the ground, are perhaps less serious as indications of confused or corrupted values than they are of an assumed omniscience designed to increase the faith of the faithful. But the accumulation of Strasberg's lapses do little to discourage true believers, possibly because all of them hope that this comedian of errors has not done it yet again when he declares after Studio auditions—as he did in 1960—that "we never make mistakes."

Finally, as he tends to visit his corruptions upon the atmosphere of learning, so would he visit his working paralysis on all who work around him. Linked closely with the lures to insecurity is the fact—long acknowledged by his friends—that Strasberg is barely able to move into any overt, committed action. When he does—with his concession that the Studio might die if the actors weren't given permission to create a producing unit, or with his eventual production of *The Three Sisters*—it is because he has run out of bluffs and alternatives. I am referring here not to cause—which can be surmised only on the basis of direct, analytical evidence—but of what is socially, at least, more important: the effect of the interior life that he reveals. A man alone who cannot move is, beyond question, a figure of sympathy and compassion. A man *in power* who cannot move—though still sympathetic on a personal level—is a figure of grave concern.

Meanwhile, how has he kept such power? Why are the actors unable to make distinctions, unable to keep him where he might serve their personal needs as they see them while deflecting him from those areas where even they admit he does irreparable harm? Why, as Kenneth Tynan once asked of Kazan, can't Strasberg be turned to peaceful uses? The answer, I suggest, rests with one of those unspoken agreements between leader and followers that mark any autocratic society: what Max Weber, borrowing from the New Testament, developed as a sociological theory—*charisma.* Weber described charisma as the kind of social authority acquired by a leader not on the basis of law or tradition, but more subtly, on the basis of his or her unusual impact. What is particularly relevant in the case of Strasberg and the Studio is what Weber called the "routinized" nature of the charismatic movement as it entrenches itself. The almost inevitable decline and fall of revolutionary fervor leads the leader into a gradual acceptance of society's less radical standards. The dreamer is replaced by the executive, the prophet on the mount by the trial lawyer. In time, the new order absorbs the "practical" characteristics of the old, gradually making itself indistinguishable, except in its claims. Most ominously, charisma has a short life and seldom survives beyond a single generation. The new order changeth, ringing in the old.

Still, charisma only defines Strasberg's position, not the peculiar qualities and undoubted forces within him that make charisma possible. Like it or not, Strasberg's impact on actors drawn into his circle is a real one. The conditions allowing for charisma are first of all marked by a tightly interlocking relationship between the leader and the led: charisma is, by definition, a description of shared needs. Both sides, in effect, are filling yawning gaps in their emotional and, to some extent, intellectual experience. Classically, somewhat simplistically, charismatic relationship is the extension of byplay between parent and child, neither side willing or able to break the cord.

One point in this regard is all too easily overlooked: to choose an actor's life in this society is still to choose against accepted standards. In spite of Henry Irving's knighthood, acting continues to be a vagabond profession, not entirely suitable for respectable men and women. Only the most unusual, calm, liberated, and generous parent—with one cool eye directed to the instances of spectacular financial reward—will launch his child unhysterically into training for the stage. When, therefore, the average hopeful actor arrives at Strasberg's feet, he has usually bounced there after a violent wrench from his family. With revolution in his heart and only a protracted education in his head, he comes in search for more than an ordinary profession, he comes in search for a home. Stronger men than Strasberg have not been able to resist the plea of a perpetual child for care, confirmation, and—veering toward the sinister—severity, reprimands, and the hovering threat of being cut out of the will.

Shared needs represent signs that he, like them, is vulnerable; that he, like them, needs help and understanding; that he, like them, feels an outcast from society. The equilibrium of the relationship, however, is maintained by other means, no less emotional in origin, though flying under the flags of age-difference and intellect. Protecting Strasberg's authority now, as it couldn't have done with the Group Theatre, is the simple accumulation of years. White hairs may not a grown man make, but they certainly help the illusion. And in the theatre, sometimes to its cost, illusion often has higher standing than reality.

Beyond his age, however, Strasberg answers yet another need: that of the deprived, the earnest, the half-read but still curious, for a figure of letters, a scholar above all familiar with the books, history, music, and painting denied for one reason or another to them. In this respect, at least, Strasberg offers more apparent reality than real illusion. By his metaphors, references, and library, he reveals a grounding, a preparation for either art or bibliography, that few teachers of acting could ever hope to match.

An inveterate collector, he is quite literally the man who has everything in the way of books, recordings, and *objets du théâtre*. Had he not cast himself in the image of an American Stanislavsky-Vakhtangov, he might easily have made his living by being the Baron Duveen of the theatre. His mantelpiece is crowded with fragments and pieces left over, in some cases miraculously, from theatres and actors long since absent from the scene. A lock of Eleonora Duse's hair, sealed hermetically from the air that would finish it forever, lies there in helpless anonymity.

In like manner, the devout collect themselves around Strasberg almost as if they hoped one day to be worthy of his permanent collection, to be added to his trophies and mementos, living monographs sitting in dusty eminence on his bookcase. The connective tissue between master and man tightens its grip, the services to be performed, one for the other, a hopelessly undefined blur. One life blends into the other, never to be alone again, never to be apart, seductive dancers in a dream they call theatre.

Ivan Turgenev, writing of Mikhail Bakunin long after the latter's spell had worn off, said, "People did not tumble to the fact Bakunin was such an amazing fool because he was such an involved and subtle fool—and we always suspect depth in a case like that: a man mumbles because his tongue is too large and we think: oh, he has so many ideas that he can't express them all." Moving on to a discussion of Mephistopheles's character, Turgenev later added to the portrait an observation about the men who follow the involved and subtle fool. They are

> lonely people given to abstract reflections, people who are deeply worried by some trifling contradictions in their own lives, but who will go past an artisan's family dying of hunger with complete indifference. . . . Such a man [the leader] is alarming not by himself, but by the influence he exerts on a number of youths who, thanks to him or, to put it more plainly, thanks to their own timid and egoistic minds, never leave the narrow confines of their own charming selves.

What Turgenev described novelistically, Erich Fromm has discussed in the terms of the social psychologist. Holding a view with passion, says Fromm, does not necessarily mean one is a fanatic:

> [The] fanatic can be described as a highly narcissistic person who is disengaged from the world outside. He does not feel anything, since authentic feeling is always the result of the interrelation between oneself *and* the world. . . . He has found a way out of acute depression . . . built for himself an idol. . . . He then acts, thinks, and feels in the name of his idol, or rather, he has the illusion of "feeling," of inner excitement. . . . He is passionate in his idolatric submission and in his grandiosity; yet cold in his inability for genuine relatedness and feeling. His attitude may be described symbolically as "burning ice."

Whatever the evidence may be, Strasberg's bubble reputation should be no surprise. The public eye, separated as it is from the private fire, can be scarcely expected to distinguish between the warm flame and the cold. The

smokescreens, up to now, have done their work with remarkable effectiveness. Though Strasberg uses many words, he is not a conversationalist; indeed, within the carefully guarded walls of the Studio, he is known not for dialogue, but for monologue, a seemingly endless discussion with himself. And
this verbose silence, this studied disconnection from potential challenge,
should never have been mistaken—as it has been—for eloquence. The best
men—at random, Freud, Stanislavsky, Chekhov—share even their most private searches with the world. They do not shroud them in mystery.

For more than ten years, then, Strasberg preached only to the converted.
Somehow, the "rhythm of art" never fell into step; the production of *The
Three Sisters* was confined conveniently to the theatre of his mind, more real
to him than life, more real to him indeed than real theatre. When it finally
emerged, it came within the rhythm of the foreshortened rehearsal period
common to all Broadway plays. This cannot have been agreeable to Strasberg. Yet, as he had finally to commit the play to production, so was he compelled to do it outside the rhythm of art. In the event, Jennifer was not only
unready, she wasn't even in it. By now, the Studio's leading ladies had eased
themselves into the power suggested by their names, one of them—Geraldine
Page—having become, in fact, a Studio director. Clearly, the days of delay had
to come to an end.

I should be deceiving no one if I pretended at this moment to give the rest
of my words an atmosphere of suspense. The ice that burns in class is not
likely to be transformed into authentic fire just because it has at last moved
into a theatre. On that same "historic" occasion when Strasberg played the
Moscow Art's performance of the play to his cast, he also announced that he
wouldn't block the play because, with such a company, it wouldn't be necessary. To the extent that he could depend upon many of his actors to place
themselves with ease and some intelligence into the most telling relationships, or that he could be certain of the way they could work on their instruments, he was quite correct. Characteristically, what this evasive tactic
threatened was not several good actors, and not the director, but the pressures, the design, the special life and meaning of Chekhov's play.

This, of course, is far from a new event. Strasberg, in choosing a play by
Chekhov for his Studio Theatre debut, was placing himself in the hands of international theatre's most publicly safe and foolproof inheritance. Without rehearsing the documented history, it is enough to recall that it all began with
Stanislavsky and the Moscow Art, treating their frequently reluctant and outraged playwright as if he were some sort of a spoiled, unconscious genius
who couldn't expect to come to theatrical life without their often misguided
and irrelevant interventions. Strasberg's production, following the precedent,
has acquired some of its most respectable reviews from those, like Brooks Atkinson, who feel that Chekhov was a lovable man who "wrote it so well that it
does not seem to have been written at all," existing "as life exists, without
conscious purpose or design." In other words, the production succeeds first

with those who are still a little embarrassed by the presence of planning, thought, imagination, shape, indeed art itself.

For all the authentic art and feeling in Kim Stanley, Albert Paulsen, and Geraldine Page; for all the bird calls, the heavily authentic Biedermeier furniture, the exquisite lighting of Abe Feder, and the delicate magic of the stage manager's wind machine, there is still not enough art on the stage to go around. Casting is quixotic, ranging, of course, from the galvanic emotional force of Stanley to the neuter presences of others and the lowest mugging of one. On the barest naturalistic level, it is impossible to tell from the physical or psychological life on stage that four years pass from beginning to end. Chekhov's drama of indirect action is taken, so it appears, as an invitation to let the play get by undirected, a formless, uninflected evening by the samovar.

It is not difficult to guess at what Strasberg might have wished from his disparate, unevenly talented actors. In his lectures at Harvard, he drew a distinction between Stanislavsky in 1920 and in 1936, the old man writing toward the end about the kind of work never actually or fully tried at the Moscow Art. This work would have realized the "deep and heartfelt notes of superconscious feeling." Strasberg's *Three Sisters,* it can be assumed, was his attempt to pick up where Stanislavsky left off, with Strasberg hoping against hope that the truest deep notes would prove to be his by usurpation if not by natural inheritance.

Ironically, what he would call the "quietism" of Kim Stanley developed into a deep note that at once harmonized and clashed with the themes and variations of the play. Lacking an interpretation from her director, giving off waves of power as other actors simply give off words, Stanley inadvertently redirected the play into a story of one woman, a woman who lives brilliantly, eccentrically, exotically on one stratospheric plane of what may well be superconscious feeling. Never reproducing daily, momentary, domestic reality, always presenting images selectively in the shape of pared, economized realities, Stanley in one extraordinary gesture saves the theatrical life of the occasion—and therefore, Lee Strasberg—while tipping the hand to what isn't there. For a few blessed, intensely human and moving moments, she rescues the fire from the ice.

But where will the fire be next time? How long can a myth perpetuate itself in the teeth of the evidence? And how much, in the end, does it really matter? Theatres built upon internecine warfare, upon nostalgia and the petty squabbles of rival leaders, would be sufficiently sabotaged even without the flaws within. As it stands now, the choices posed seem as artificial and irrelevant as the war.

It was the late Molly Kazan who, when asked to comment to the Actors Studio membership about their plans to form a committee and build a producing unit, looked around the room at the aging ingenues, the graying young leading men, the forty- to fifty-year-old students, and implored them to come to their senses about who they were. They were still referring to themselves

as "kids," she said, and after fourteen years at the Studio, it was time to realize that they should have grown up. Kids they weren't then and kids they
aren't now. They can be forgiven for hanging back with their dreams, for falling into the trap of certainty, for giving their lives to the only man who *seemed*
to be there—through force of his own tenacity, his capacity for staying firmly
rooted in the same earth for over thirty years. But it is possible now that the
arguments for and against this settled issue, this diversionary tactic—the
Method, which has done its service to the state and knows it—that these arguments, and the great battle for an American theatre, will have to be taken
elsewhere, leaving some of them behind, using what has been learned, dis-
carding what has clotted the brain and paralyzed action, movement, and
growth, building theatres where the eternal child will find no comfort, where
dramatists are respected, directors are encouraged, and where actors no
longer sing in chorus that their hearts belong to Daddy. Indeed, if theatres are
ever to come alive at last in these peculiar States, it will be necessary first for
them to hang signs over their entrances making their position unmistakable,
signs that declare in the plainest language available that Daddy doesn't live
here any more.   *GR(December 1964)*

A Streetcar Named Kazan

"A thought—directing finally consists of turning Psychology into Behavior."
Thus Elia Kazan seventeen years ago in his notebook for *A Streetcar Named
Desire.* Earlier, somewhat before his major triumphs on Broadway, during rehearsals for S. N. Behrman's *Jacobowsky and the Colonel,* he put it another
way: "I will say nothing to an actor that cannot be translated into action."
These twin remarks would seem to constitute a reasonable definition of
directing, suggesting a firm combination of the ideal and the practical. But
dramatic art must be more than the sum of behavioral parts, more than psychology alone. The actions of men and women are one matter, the actions of
art quite another. And this is true even of theatre, the singular art that uses as
one part of its medium the very sounds, souls, and bodies of men and women.

To be fair, Kazan was not trying to define for the ages; perhaps he was
not trying to define at all. In 1947, it was only "a thought," a rare reflective
moment, a pause in the business of simply getting on with the job. He was

never one for dark philosophies. Reliable legend has it that he was a good actor in his Group Theatre days. Quick on the draw, he had the pugnacity of a kid slouching outside the corner drugstore coupled with the aw-shucks lazy charm of a ranch hand at a square dance. It was not a performance of infinite variety, but of personality there was never any doubt. This held, surely, in his productions. For once, the American theatre had a serious director who didn't fade into the scenery, palely mimicking the postures and rhetoric of European contemporaries. Kazan made it clear in the late 1940s that he was our first wholly native director, an individual in touch with the nerve centers of the nation. He didn't have to define; his productions did it for him.

The best of them, *Streetcar* and *Death of a Salesman,* revealed less psychology than stance, a certain kind of physical conduct. The human form, forced to float in a sea of dimly lit illusions, was trying against all doubts to be more than a piece of driftwood. Bodies aching from inarticulated pain moved hypnotically from scene to scene, accompanied by a wistful flute or a trumpet riff, so many anguished objects in search of character and meaning. The key to survival was suggested by a succession of turned backs: Willy Loman weighted by his suitcases or hunched on the ground shouting, "I gave you an order"; Stanley Kowalski bellowing for Stella, embracing her hungrily at the foot of the spiral staircase, the rounded muscles of his powerful back moving in sobbing rhythms outside his artfully torn shirt. Beer bottles weren't merely opened, they were shaken into gushing fountains, life seen as constant climax, active symbols for what a man takes when there isn't anything better. There was never very much time for thinking. Drifters may drift, but the pace around them had to be frantic. If the spirit wouldn't work, there was always the body, something to plunder, something to kill. Suddenly, the musicians under the stage uttered the whining blast that heralded an announcement, the perhaps ultimate turning of the back: Willy off to his suicide, Stanley at his rape. On Kazan's stage, life came to a halt only after the body had been throttled into submission.

It was, as the phrase goes, good theatre, stamped with a life of its own, and therefore in its own way unique on Broadway. If, when appraising it, one still tends to blur the lines between Kazan and his playwrights, it is because the blur was intentional, and from all accounts agreeable to Miller and Williams. For a time at least, they had found their man, a kind of co-author to a theatrical event, the expert reader between the lines, the man who literally put flesh on their dreams. In Kazan, they possessed—or were possessed by—a Svengali that O'Neill never had. However they might be judged later, whatever would be said finally about the quality of their writing, they had an ever-present, physically urgent *now* in the theatre. It was as if their plays had been written on stage, their words acting as understudies to the real star.

If the director as dramatist, magical as he was in one startling area, seemed a strange usurper, what then was he ever intended to be? Always being compared to an orchestral conductor, he would thus seem to be at once an interpreter, a complete commander, and even a performer. The comparison, however, neat as it looks, is flawed by one central difference in their roles: the conductor is present, indeed necessary, at the performance, while the director is just another helpless member of the audience. Or to put it another way, the conductor rules over people who play instruments clearly defined in sound, capacity, and temperament, whereas the director can never quite rule over a disparate band of actors who *are* their instruments. The director, in fact, has done his job well when his absence is least felt. Yet it is no wonder that the analogy with conducting is not only drawn but actively sought. The art is a relatively new one, and, to make its place in a collaborative world, it has been compelled to cast a net wide enough for catching the few passing precedents.

In the absence of a chartable history, the precedents had to be taken pragmatically, from people more than ideas. In the beginning were the *author-directors,* Shakespeare perhaps, Molière certainly, and in this century most notably Bertolt Brecht. Later there were *teacher-directors* such as Stanislavsky, followed in our time by Michel St. Denis and Lee Strasberg, men who changed the face of acting, leaving almost untouched the look of the stage or the shape of the play. Stage imagery was the sweeping infatuation of the *scenic directors,* men like André Antoine, Adolphe Appia, David Belasco, Max Reinhardt, and lately Franco Zeffirelli, covering every kind of play with the same kind of sensual splendor. Alone, with a corresponding lack of immediate practical effect, were the leaping *visionaries*—Jacques Copeau, Gordon Craig, Vsevolod Meyerhold, and Antonin Artaud—touched by the kind of sane madness that rips change from a stone, but fifty years later. More articulate than their ancestors, but still left over from a faded tradition, are the *actor-directors*—Jean-Louis Barrault, Laurence Olivier, John Gielgud—Hamlets giving advice, and perhaps a few paralyzing demonstrations, to the players. Lately, the *choreographers* and *improvisers* have dashed into the theatre, such masters of mercurial movement as Joan Littlewood, Tyrone Guthrie, and Jerome Robbins. And finally, the visionaries are having a part of their way at last in the work of the *idea-directors,* pragmatic idealists and embryo philosophers such as Jean Vilar, Roger Planchon, Peter Brook, and—not to be too easily placed—Brecht again. From all this, a pattern emerges that hints at definition even if it doesn't specifically provide one: direction, we might say, is the art of persuading a doubt to look like a certainty, a bias turned into a craft, the most evanescent phase of the most evanescent art.

Kazan refuses to be one type. He commanded image, mesmerized actors, tore drama from the inert, raised theatrical movement into a style, and—before anything else—mastered the tricks of authentic illusion. In his productions, what happened had to happen; no other way seemed possible. The knack of fooling, seriously inclined, was his. Yet for all his ingenuity, he couldn't temper tremors of doubt: his work, unlike that of his predecessors and contemporaries, was devoted exclusively to new plays, the settled art of the dead being all outside his reference; moreover, he rarely worked with the same actor twice, hardly a good omen for repertory. His best productions, galvanizing as they were to an arid scene, seemed to have spent their passion in preparation. What we saw was the end of the line, and at the end was exhaustion.

"The acting must be styled, not in the obvious sense," he wrote in the *Streetcar* notebook. "Say nothing about it to the producer and actors." Here, at last, was a definition: the director as cunning diplomat. Secretive yet seductive, he would say nothing in order to say—what? Perhaps nothing. Everything was pat, ordered, fluid. Even so, whole worlds were missing—other plays, other styles, other tempi, other nuances, other shapes, other lives. For the sake of an image, he shifted from stage to screen and back again, he hesitated between the Actors Studio and Lincoln Center, he wrote a screenplay and published it as a novel, and he stayed entirely away from the stage for nearly five years. He was hitting, running, seducing—and abandoning. This was our best director doing his best acting, a cycle in relentless motion—his best and most alarming performance.

What has been more alarming this last year, however, is that, where he should be home free, safe and relaxed in the soft, unpressuring arms of the Repertory Theatre of Lincoln Center, he has looked like a fugitive still madly on the run. Given time, a permanent company, and an open stage, he has looked restless and uncomfortable, at peace neither with the theatre nor with himself. Even as co-author, he no longer had a presence, no longer made a mark. *After the Fall* took center stage and never left it, rarely probing the sides and corners of a splendidly flexible playing space. A three-hour indulgence, weirdly uninflected, it moved as in a bad dream from symbols to realities. Most of the actors strained and growled and tore at rubber faces. Props were suddenly real, and just as suddenly imaginary. The play wasn't happening any more, it was being pushed on. In even more desultory fashion, Behrman's *But for Whom Charlie* came over as a comedy of manners without comedy or manners. True, it was an unlikely choice for him, but even within that melancholy context, it kept giving off signs that he was in retreat, that he was not only tired of running but tired of the will to stop.

In this manner and mood, he came to his first play from the dead, his first battle with absent writers, Thomas Middleton and William Rowley's bleak, hard, and violent study of thwarted innocence and unstoppable corruption, *The Changeling.* If direction for him is still turning psychology into action, then the choice would seem to have been apt: the play has uncanny links to our psychology and responses. All that remains is to make the action alive and relevant. For Kazan, the bouncing, shifting, vibrantly alive stage was never any problem, and relevance always seemed to be his personal obsession. The possibility that Beatrice might become a Jacobean Maggie the Cat with slippery de Flores her very own Kowalski seemed inviting, even though it would have been a vaguely perverse and obvious way of serving relevance. But at this point in the Lincoln Repertory's life, the combination of a good play and an energetic production, however eccentric, was not one to be scorned easily after the company's first joyless season.

But nothing was changed between seasons. If anything, the company looked and sounded wearier than before, their hollow monotones crashing senselessly against the shoals of simple verse. Where was the old Kazan, the director who gave bodies a stage reason, who could draw blood from a zombie or squeeze an hour into an instant? But had he ever been wholly there? Is not *The Changeling* too much to ask of him or his young, casual, unformed company? With the best will in the world, for example, Benny Goodman never *came to* Mozart as well as he had *lived with* Swing. Can we be classic before we know how modern we are?

Kazan stands, finally, for several confusions: the play as screenplay, the screen as stage, both supported by running sound tracks designed to underscore emotions, point moments, or bridge scenes. His vision and his range of concern were always limited. But once, years ago, there was something more than a glimmer, something vital in everything he did, some sharp thrust of feeling, some roaring climax, a moment of daring terror here or grinding tension there. Yet for all that, for all the gritting teeth, the clenched fist ready to punch down every door in the universe, the hard center of his work was always too brittle to bear the load of lost convictions and aimless fury.

GR(December 1964)

Longing for Moscow

Chekhov is traditionally loved for what he considered the wrong reasons. What was comic or satirical to him is tragic or melancholy to others; what was characterization is real life; and what was precisely ordered is taken for happy accident. Of Stanislavsky's original production of *The Cherry Orchard* for the Moscow Art Theatre, Chekhov complained: "With the exception of two or three parts, nothing in it is mine. I am describing life, ordinary life, and not blank despondency. They either make me into a crybaby or a bore."

It is an odd tradition, one that has been widely and persistently accepted by the English-speaking world ever since the plays were popularly successful in Stanislavsky's productions. Disparate acting approaches have made little difference: Eva Le Gallienne's grand manner has the same effect ultimately as

Lee Strasberg's behavioral psychology. Drift and melancholy prevail. Most American and English productions make the plays and the characters sound alike, as if Chekhov had only one story to tell, unvaried in tone, focus, or tempo. The price of being an innovator was that his name could be so easily transformed into an adjective.

Similarly, Stanislavsky has become—in America at least—a figure frozen in a pose, the father of "truth" and "reality" in acting. Nothing was inherently wrong with the religion built around his name. Indeed, his effect on the art of acting was profoundly liberating. All that went wrong was that his American disciples, arguing among themselves, seemed to stop where Stanislavsky said he was just beginning. Inner truth became an excuse for ignoring the compelling outer realities of dramatic art. Stanislavsky was interpreted just as Chekhov felt he had misinterpreted him: as a means to a monotonous end.

Against this background, the recent visit of the Moscow Art Theatre to New York seemed to promise few surprises. It seemed reasonable to anticipate only a peek behind a moldy curtain, a glimpse into a complacent past. In the event, there was both mold and surprise.

The first clues came with the adaptation of Nikolai Gogol's picaresque novel, *Dead Souls*. All the signs of museum deadness were there: the staging was said to be preserved-Stanislavsky, presented essentially as he himself had charted it toward the end of his life, in the 1930s; also, the dramatization used only lines by Gogol, with nothing new added and nothing old left out. Yet for all the willed mustiness, the stage shivered with life. Gogol's fascination with grotesque humors and Hogarthian conceits became the occasion for an extraordinary actors' festival. As his sly, wickedly lubricious anti-hero, Chichikov, traveled from one confidence trick to another, uncovering characters even greedier and more unconscionable than himself, it became clear that this actors' theatre was using the flimsy dramatic line more as a theatrical offering than as a play.

Never has there been such a concentrated display of virtuoso acting to so little sustained purpose. Chichikov's journey into swindle-land—buying up lists of deceased serfs in order to turn them into some form of peculiar profit—can only repeat itself, drawing what little variety it can from the quirks and tics of the idiots he is fleecing. Boundless energy and invention were poured into every motion, small or large. No wheeze was left unturned. Actors sighed, giggled, roared, simpered, puffed, and belched. It was like a celebration of all the gestures and noises available to the staged event. The actors were enjoying themselves in character, not the character in themselves. This was the initial surprise: the gaiety, the delight in caricature, the obvious pleasure in acting as, first of all, a *performing* art.

Late in the Moscow Art's New York season, one of its "modern" plays was introduced into the schedule, *Kremlin Chimes,* or as it might have been more aptly titled, *Nick Lenin in Illinois*. To an even greater extent than *Dead Souls,* this was less than a workable play, so crowded was it with pompous incident, poster characters, and slogan thoughts. Yet for all its stolidity, its stumbling idolatry of an energetically lifeless hero (Lenin), its sudsy socialist realism (Girl meets Sailor, Sailor serves Lenin, Lenin meets Girl's reactionary Father, Father meets Progress, and so on), it was still used as an excuse to present actors as live, throbbing, responsive instruments tuned to the art of being selectively human on stage. Boris Petker's Watchmaker, for only one example, had an encounter with Lenin that might easily have become as dull and automatic as the writing, but he covered it with a kind of centered acting that would make even a zombie look personable: he was speaking of his humble craft while attracting attention not to his words but to the strange, almost feline wanderings of his hand on the table. These quietly anxious motions were more emblematic of his need for work than all the hollow phrases placed on his tongue.

Thus, the second surprise of the Moscow Art today is its aggressive awareness of everything physical. Actions are spacious yet contained, recognizably lifelike yet artfully planned, visible yet suggestive. An aging Boris Livanov, for instance, plays the stormy, lustily alcoholic, youthful Nosdrev in *Dead Souls* for all the world as if he were a bellowing, imaginative Douglas Fairbanks. A somewhat younger Angelina Stepanova plays the isolated, wishful, aging governess in *The Cherry Orchard,* Charlotta Ivanovna, with a drooping bounciness that constantly betrays how prim and finished she really is. The outward show is used always to stress an inner tale.

Behind these gestures lies yet another tale to add to the Stanislavsky legacy. According to Mikhail Kedrov and Iosef Raevsky, both students of Stanislavsky and now director-actors with the company, his later years were devoted primarily to two somewhat obsessive lessons: that his work was never meant to remain the same, and that the most difficult and essential part of rehearsal (after discussing the characters for several days) is the quest for physical behavior in relation to the given circumstances of the scene set by the author. The current mode of the Moscow Art Theatre places unexpected stress on the dramatist. While its repertory, sets, and lighting reflect the tatty, tremulous, unsearching methods of the orthodox, its acting hints today at a minor revolution. If the company is a kind of museum, the present directors made it clear that they think of their job as experimenting with the new as well as preserving the old.

The greatest pleasure of the Soviet company's visit was the discovery—and I hope this is taken as neither frivolous nor obvious—that *The Three Sisters* and *The Cherry Orchard* are two very different plays. When Chekhov referred to the first as a drama and the second as "a comedy, almost bordering on farce," he knew what he meant, even if Stanislavsky couldn't accept the distinction at the time. True, the dramatic surfaces are similar: comings and goings, reflections and musings, hopes, longings, and all the configurations of nostalgia. But, as Raevsky put it—and it was he who redirected *The Three Sisters* in 1958—this nostalgia was an *active* emotion—a mood, yes, but one propelling the characters into a reiterated wish to *do* something about their lives.

Not that many of them ever really turn wish into decision; it is only that, in expressing the world of the plays, the actors need not behave like depleted, motionless figures in a dream. In the drama, *The Three Sisters,* the central characters are almost always aware of their ineffectualness. Hence they derive their forward motion from a gathering sense of resignation. In *The Cherry Orchard,* however, speckled as it is by scene after scene of gentle farce, they are almost completely unaware. (Lopakhin is the single exception, and therefore, to Chekhov, he is the hero of the play—not, as it is usually performed, Madame Ranevsky.) The result is motion based upon the events that needlessly and ridiculously turn against the characters. They don't linger over disaster or memories, they move swiftly and almost carelessly from one to the other. When they do hang back for a moment—such as in Gaev's extravagant apostrophe to an antique dressing cabinet—they are meant to look and sound preposterous. In short, to play Chekhov sensibly, the actors must press on with the play, skimming lightly and fluidly over surfaces so as to leave that many more reverberations behind. Lingerings and sadnesses are the audience's privilege, not the actors'.

"When a man," said Chekhov, "spends the least possible number of movements on some definite action, then that is gracefulness." It is this essential grace and economy that mark the work of most of the Moscow Art Theatre's players. Moments are carefully measured and stresses are delicate. Never unnatural, always believable, they manage to let us know precisely where our eyes should turn. As actors, they are rarely *in* tears; they follow Chekhov's repeated assertions in the stage directions that they are talking *through* tears. They present character and represent life. They do not pretend that what they are a part of is something different from—and therefore something less than—art. They act rather than behave.

It is regrettable that the actors are supported by such laggard notions of stage design and lighting, since theatrical perfection, for once, almost seemed possible. Surely, too, Alla Tarassova should now retire from the role of Madame Ranevsky: she is not without grace, but she tends to bring an unyielding lumpishness, a star-turn quality, that is too heavy even for this unromantic view of the character. A great soloist, however, such as Alexei Gribov—the oaken Firs in *The Cherry Orchard,* the crumbling nihilist doctor in *The Three Sisters,* and the almost immobile great bear of a schemer, Sobakevich, in *Dead Souls*—thrives within the ensemble.

Whatever the misunderstandings between Chekhov and Stanislavsky more than sixty years ago, there is clarity and aptness today. The playwright, in fact, has been rescued from the dust that was threatening to overwhelm his plays in England and America. One's abiding memory of the superb Moscow Art Theatre will always be of coolness released, of rhythms shaped, forms contained, of art honored by life.   *GR(March 1965)*

Shakespeare with Tears

We enter the theatre. There is no curtain. A raked stage extends well beyond the formal proscenium arch, reaching in almost desperate appeal to the audience. We see an enormous, high-beamed gallery, a candle chandelier hanging over a floor of heavy oak boards, supporting the barest furnishings, surrounded on three sides by towering, dark redbrick walls; a delicately curtained archway breaks the upstage center wall. This is the only suggestion of mobility in the entire set. All else is weighted, durable, lived-in, lending the atmosphere a peculiar, autumnally colored sense of permanence. This room, we feel, is definitely in a theatre, but just as surely it has known life, an existence away from us, somewhere remote, in a past that we had comfortably connected only with the pleasing unreality of history. It seems to be weathered, like most English rooms, by a stern assumption that winter belongs inside as much as out. Here is a world where a man is forced upon himself; not, as in France, on his spirit: here it is his body that must survive before his soul can even begin to discover warmth.

The place, then, is England, a precise, physical, richly caparisoned Tudor England. It is the background and considered atmosphere for Peter Hall's production of *A Midsummer Night's Dream* at the Royal Shakespeare Theatre. Were this the setting for almost any other Shakespeare play, we should not, perhaps, feel such skeptical surprise. The custom for *Dream* productions is to reach for the properties of dreams, the lands of nod and never-never where nothing is more urgent than the resolution of happy, fathomable mystery. No other play by Shakespeare attracts so many flights of supposed poetical fancy. No other play invites such untroubled delight. And no other play can be viewed, under ordinary production circumstances, with such painless detachment. Serious actors shear their tragic locks for a chance to play Bottom; clowns assume his ass's head for an easy, larkish, intellectual spree; and dancers—lithe, bony, endowed with thin, piping, mincing voices—will surrender a hundred Swan Lakes for those moments that find them flitting from wing to wing as Titania or Oberon. Indeed, the play, following that mysterious, traditional English habit of absorbing its rare gold into its common dross, has been produced generally as the harmless old grandfather of Christmas pantomime. Farce and fantasy are used by *Dream* directors to induce in the audience a comfortable sense of lethargy. Forgetfulness, they seem to be saying, can be a way of life.

They are, of course, forgetting the play and the poet. What is remarkable about Peter Hall's production is that it reaches for so much remembrance. In the *Dream,* Shakespeare drops a clue that no director should gloss too casually. Like Hamlet's soliloquies, the Fool's seeming nonsense in *King Lear,* and perhaps most relevantly, Ulysses's speech about degree in *Troilus and Cressida,* Shakespeare gives Theseus a speculative and reflective set piece which—coming as it does after four acts of gaming byplay—pulls the comedy back to philosophical and dramatic reality:

> The lunatic, the lover, and the poet
> Are of imagination all compact:—
> One sees more devils than vast hell can hold,—
> That is, the madman: the lover, all as frantic,
> Sees Helen's beauty in a brow of Egypt:
> The poet's eye, in a fine frenzy rolling,
> Doth glance from heaven to earth, from earth to heaven;
> And, as imagination bodies forth
> The forms of things unknown, the poet's pen
> Turns them to shapes, and gives to airy nothing
> A local habitation and a name.

> (V.1)

Hall's production, undaunted by the mystery in Shakespeare, makes all compact, bringing the lunatic, the lover, and the poet into working harmony, the one within the others, the others all one. The three personal worlds in the play—mortal lovers, rustic workers, and fairies—unite within themselves the qualities of lunatic, lover, and poet: they suffer or enjoy momentary madness; they love; and, wittingly and unwittingly, they make verbal, visual, and metaphysical poetry. The unnerving and often puzzling task of the director, the actors, and the designer is to join with the poet in giving "airy nothing a local habitation and a name."

Creative challenge has rarely been expressed more succinctly: if we wish to be general we must lodge ourselves firmly in the particular. Peter Hall's way, assisted by Lila de Nobili's solidly conceived design, is to be real before he is fanciful. The lovers, particularly Ann Bell as Hermia, are not excessively romantic in either appearance or manner. They are somewhat hard little creatures, clumsy, troubled, silly, a set of awkward young does taking their first baby steps into a gently painful world where love's facts are always arguing with love's illusions. Similarly, the fairies are spiky, tough spirits, jagged at the edges, though no less charming because of their links to familiar emotions. Bottom, miraculously, is not a star turn: he is completely integrated into the earthy community of the other rude mechanicals, sweetly comic would-be gentlemen, touching, though hilarious, in their anxious will to please. Against the sharply hewn background of the Tudor gallery, a very substantial and basic world is presented, a world in which man's hope lies in his capacity to be lunatic, lover, and poet in one. Failing such capacity, freezing himself out of any available feeling, he faces implicitly the physical fact of unfelt life: around him only the dank, imprisoning walls of a world indifferent to his loneliness and his look.

The first shock we encounter upon entering the theatre, then, is the sudden awareness that we are not to be lifted on a highly magical carpet to ancient Greece, but that we are to be rooted carefully within the geographical limits of Shakespeare's charted world. Hall, in short, is making what is now a bold, eccentric suggestion: that we can begin by returning to the poet.

                        *   *   *

If this is only a beginning, it is easily the most rational, contemporary, *and* poetic effort of the current Shakespeare industry. Is there any artistic phenomenon more dangerous than a poet unscorned? The prevailing misery of art in this century is that it is so cultured, a viral specimen, to be seen only through a microscope darkly. Shakespeare, helplessly in thrall to the critical biologists who break him down, cell by cell, into protoplasm, signifying nothing, has become the darling of this separated culture. Once he was a dramatist. Now he is a Summer Festival.

A working paradox persists in most of the reverential activity. Faithful to the idea of producing limitless cycles of the thirty-six plays, few of the faithful really like their playwright. Or, to give them the benefit of grudging doubt, they may well like, but they do not trust him. The familiar gamesmanship of our mushrooming Shakespeare festivals—as in most production ruled by commodity—is to see how the plays can be "improved" in production. The directors and designers, to borrow from Stanislavsky, love themselves in Shakespeare more than they love the Shakespeare in themselves. Their reputations, founded upon a succession of external tricks, lead them away from the text and back to their last emblematic mannerism.

Unpolitically, I am giving myself away early because it is futile to pretend that my pilgrimages to the Shakespeare festivals in Connecticut and Canada were made with a mind as open as the new stages. I have been to hell before, and—despite a sometimes absurd personal optimism—I did not approach the journey again in a mood of mindless delight. Long ago, Margaret Webster's painless dentistry set the average American standard, simplistically dressing productions in gowns, codpieces, and gimmicks that were designed to bring us Shakespeare without tears. It was always a patronizing standard, both to the poet and to the audience, clothing itself in the mantle of forgetfulness while teaching the great unwashed groundlings that learning can be fun. Webster's *Richard III,* fearful that the message would be missed, opened with a projected montage of swastika, *fasces,* and hammer and sickle, thus betraying within thirty seconds an ignorance of political sublety that could only add insult to the subsequent injury of the play. (In that single flashing moment, we knew already that José Ferrer could scarcely make matters worse. He did, of course, but we had been suitably forewarned by Webster's slick inanity.)

Webster's standard easily suited the undubbed knights and dames of the American stage: Katharine Cornell on the Nile, Helen Hayes in all her sugared piety, Louis Calhern mistaking Lear's heath for a suburb of Hollywood, Raymond Massey mistaking Prospero as an early study for Abe Lincoln, Maurice Evans mistaking everything—these followed tediously in Webster's tearless wake. When the Theatre Guild decided to finish its long betrayed revolution with ye olde compleat imitation of Stratford-upon-Avon, following closely on the heels of Tyrone Guthrie's hit-and-run appearance in a similarly arbitrary Canadian town, then we knew that we were destined for a long series of neo-Websterian productions. Beatrice and Benedick out West probably represented the zenith of our American nadir. Only the costumes and period change. The witless, condescending, empty-headed standard remains relentlessly the same.

Even so, there is method to festival-hopping in 1963. For one reason, there is always an abstracted hope that miracles can happen. England has had its festival and its murders in the old vicarage for more than half a century; and in that time, where the productions were capricious, there was always the possibility of some sudden illumination, some splendid illusion of richness if only through the force of an ingenious star performance. The line from David Garrick and Edmund Kean to John Gielgud, Laurence Olivier, Michael Redgrave, Paul Scofield, Albert Finney, and Peter O'Toole is, even modestly, a strong and logical one, providing reason enough for repeated production. That we have a right to expect more, that we wish for more reason than stars alone can give, that we ask, candidly, for modern relevance—such expectations do not deter us from welcoming moments and scenes touched by the glory of great acting. Equal precedents in America are, within memory, few, but their absence has little to do with the irrational mechanisms behind hope.

Another reason, more central to my motives, is that the voice of a new Shakespearean turtle is being heard in the world. Or at least it is being heard and acted upon across the Atlantic. It has made reflected noises in Charles Marowitz's *Lear Log* and John Russell Brown's *Shakespeare's Subtext*. It is a voice born from a curious network of cross breeding: for example, the Polish scholar Jan Kott has written a book called *Shakespeare Our Contemporary;* in it, he gives considerable space to an appreciation of Peter Brook's 1955 Stratford production of *Titus Andronicus;* Brook, in turn, is said to have been strongly influenced by Kott's existential study when he moved into production of *King Lear;* meanwhile—and I shall return to this strain—the names of Beckett, Brecht, and, most strikingly, Artaud are beginning to be named by continental directors, particularly the young leaders of the Royal Shakespeare Theatre, in connection with all their new work on Shakespeare. Americans, so long missing a native reason for producing Shakespearean cycles, have borrowed in the past from the native reasons of another country. One travels, then, to see if we are borrowing from the past or the present.

Indeed, both Canada and Connecticut have produced *The Comedy of Errors,* basing their "style" on principles of *commedia dell'arte,* and, therefore, one year behind a similarly conceived production in Stratford-upon-Avon.

The *Comedy* is a play about which it would be difficult to maintain sacred thoughts. Antiquarian curiosity is the strongest reason for keeping it alive. Yet the coincidence of three productions springing from *commedia* lends it further interest at this time, suggesting as it does that directorial choices are either severely limited by the nature of limiting material or that there is a universal poverty of imagination in most contemporary Shakespearean theatres. Such a play, less "Shakespearean" than the others, offers through its limitations at once a greater and a lesser challenge: greater because it is so difficult to make its ancient humors amusing in our theatre, lesser because it simply stands as itself, a naked farce with few intimations of immortality, no hints of allegory, metaphor, or myth. As a directorial exercise, it asks only for a jubilant return to what might be called basic theatre, what Gilbert Norwood describes in *Greek Comedy* as primitive mummeries, lampoons, and Dionysiac celebrations, the original and persistent comedies of mistaken identity. Indeed, the exercise would seem to be sensible for a director, if only to help him draw energy from the play itself, rather than searching for energetic means outside. There may be little inherently wrong in choosing *commedia* for production background, but it is, at the least, less right than the available choice of earlier models, the Roman perhaps more than the Greek. The influence of Seneca's plays on Elizabethan tragedy is always taken for granted; even if there is less scholarly evidence for an equal Plautine influence on Elizabethan comedy, it would seem to be a more logical source than *commedia*, which in fact is its descendant. If transplantations are to be made, why leave the roots behind?

The Canadians and Americans made different effects through sight-and-sound gags that were, of course, independently conceived. But the productions were, nevertheless, more notable for the similarity of their solutions than for their differences. In Stratford, Connecticut, Douglas Seale mounted a play behind the play on an upstage platform, performed by *commedia* figures miming and dancing as mirror images of the play proper. These silent figures were masked. In Stratford, Ontario, where the quantity of Jean Gascon's cleverness was certainly greater than Seale's, the quality was still a matter of indifferent taste. He too had his crowd of Punchinellos sitting in the foreground pit, participating not as mirror images, but rather as Mack Sennett cops, pushing pratfalls, making noise, and generally acting as tormentors of the two Dromios. Here, *all* the characters were masked, players and Punchinellos, with the odd exception of the two leading ladies, Adriana and Luciana, a comment—if it is one—which remained thankfully obscure. The Canadian clowns, looking like those incisive Callot lithographs, had a merciful directness to their actions, representing something of an improvement on their shadowy American counterparts. But it was impossible to escape the feeling that Shakespeare's little play remained, in both theatres, a fundamentally closed question.

Were we faced with a desert island choice of productions, the Canadian would have to be preferred. Connecticut, in settling for the mirror image of *commedia,* was settling for a half-hearted half-world that, at best, can only be half an experience. This was plumbcake Shakespeare, illustrated like a Sunday comic strip with a panel for every line, each spoken as if contained in a puffy "cloud" above. It is as if Seale were afraid we might think for a split moment that he enjoyed the play. Given half the archness of his droningly physical production, however, we should know that he was filling what he considered a vacuum with even more vacuous material. The disservice to the young Shakespeare takes on strange, geometric reverberations: if what appears to be a hole is covered by another hole, which hole, observably, is the real hole?

Gascon, in Canada, answered the question, not by ignoring it, but by ignoring the play. Faced with a modest, elusive comedy by Shakespeare, he produced, with mercurial swiftness, a running-jumping-dancing production of a play by Goldoni. Thus, the hole is filled by an alien solid, which is, at least, a fuller, more confident way of evading the central issue. Meanwhile, both productions stand eloquently as arguments against production for production's sake. Why the *Comedy* if it must be couched in *commedia?* Why *commedia* when truer antecedents exist? A conductor restudying the score of Bach's *St. Matthew Passion* ought to know his plain chant, but it is doubtful that any musician would recommend that the chant should usurp the Passion. Our Shakespeare theatres, conversely, are usually posing one final question: Why Shakespeare?

Already, they are responding to their own futile question by producing Bernard Shaw (in Connecticut) and Edmond Rostand (in Canada). A sad impotence lies behind their surrenders. Committed to the *fact* of Shakespeare, they cannot find an engaged reason for doing Shakespeare. They can see him blandly as a man of the theatre, but of what theatre they cannot say. Verse drama is presented as its own reward. The contrast between the Canadians who sail boldly and dashingly into Rostand's empty, florid seas and the same company sinking wanly into the seas incarnadine of Shakespeare could scarcely be more apparent. How can it be, one wonders, that these same actors are so much happier and freer in *Cyrano* than in *Troilus and Cressida?* And then the answer rises from the ashes of burnt Shakespeare: for them, there is no marked difference; Rostand *is* Shakespeare, albeit a more fluent, delightful, romantic, touching poet. They pay homage to Shakespeare because they are compelled. They make love to Rostand because he never threatens them.

*   *   *

The stance of the English has been slow in revealing itself, and has only lately become a matter of official commitment. London's *Observer* reports that Peter Brook and Peter Hall have plans that "are pervaded by the heady influence of Antonin Artaud, the French propagandist for the 'theatre of cruelty'—a concept based on ritual, instinct and violence, a return to myth and magic. . . . Peter Hall sees the Artaud theatre-stream as stemming from

Shakespeare's poetry and violence, and now—appropriately—inspiring Stratford's new work."

Is this yet another imposition on Shakespeare drawn from an alien land?
Artaud himself, without question, would have been outraged at the suggested
marriage of his theatre with Shakespeare's. Middle-class theatre was, for
him, a maddening mixture of illusion and falsehood, with Shakespeare, un-
forgivingly, the leading villain. If we think of the theatre as an inferior art, he
said,

> it is because we have been accustomed for four hundred years, that is since the
> Renaissance, to a purely descriptive and narrative theater—storytelling psy-
> chology; it is because every possible ingenuity has been exerted in bringing to
> life on the stage plausible but detached beings, with the spectacle on one side,
> the public on the other—and because the public is no longer shown anything but
> the mirror of itself.
>
> Shakespeare himself is responsible for this aberration and decline, this dis-
> interested idea of the theater which wishes a theatrical performance to leave the
> public intact, without setting off one image that will shake the organism to its
> foundations and leave an ineffaceable scar. . . .
>
> If Shakespeare and his imitators have gradually insinuated the idea of art
> for art's sake, with art on one side and life on the other, we can rest on this fee-
> ble and lazy idea only as long as the life outside endures. But there are too many
> signs that everything that used to sustain our lives no longer does so, that we
> are all mad, desperate, and sick. And I call for *us* to react.

Which, of course, is precisely what the British Shakespeareans are doing,
within a framework, however, that absorbs Artaud into Shakespeare. It is a
daring move, surprisingly free of dogma. Peter Hall, in a talk to his company
called "Avoiding a Method," leaves the door open for further absorptions. He
is concerned lest they be engaged only in what he calls "an archaic exercise,
an act of historical interest for those who are culture-conscious." Shakespeare, he says, liberates them because he is "domestic as well as tragic, lyrical *and* dirty; as tricky as a circus and as bawdy as a music hall . . . realistic
and surrealistic." Toward the end of making dramatic sense out of multiple
images, of synthesizing Shakespeare's freedoms—"of expression, of place, of
time, of stage"—Hall confronts the poetry. Not through the poetic voice, the
lyrical, romantic obfuscation of meaning, but through a wider, more far-
ranging response to all the elements in stage-verse: the structure of lines, alliteration, rhythm and counter-rhythm, imagery, and rhyme—these made to
modulate effortlessly between several worlds, seemingly real, always theatrical. Peter Brook, releasing Shakespeare from the stifling compartments that
separate story from characters and verse from philosophy, adds in his essay
that "we are beginning to see that Shakespeare forged a style in advance of
any style anywhere, before *or since,* that enabled him, in a very compact
space of time, by a superb and conscious use of varied means, to create a realistic image of life." The actor's problem, he suggests, is that if he copes with
verse only emotionally, he is likely to conclude in bombast; if he is intellectual

alone, he may lose the line of humane feeling; or if he settles for what is literal, he will simply be common, a world away from Shakespeare's extensive meaning.

As essayists, neither Hall nor Brook is particularly helpful to those who require specific solutions. Theirs is a reaction *against* boredom with the past, and a move—however tentative—*for* something related to the present. "We must move the productions and the settings," says Brook, "away from all that played so vital a part in the post-war Stratford renaissance—away from romance, away from fantasy, away from decoration. . . . Now we must look beyond an outer liveliness to an inner one. Outer splendor can be exciting, but has little relation with modern life: on the inside lie themes and issues, rituals and conflicts which are as valid as ever. Any time the Shakespearean meaning is caught, it is 'real' and so contemporary."

If Hall and Brook are correct in their approach, if, indeed, there is any theatrical gain to be had from all their suggested mergers, marriages, and reconciliations, then it is clear that Artaud's quarrel with Shakespeare was based less on what he read than on what he saw. It could have happened to anyone. The experiences in North American Shakespeare theatres today, despite the illusion of freedom presented by Guthrie and Tanya Moiseiwitsch's open stage in Ontario, would leave Artaud no less angry. True, he could never be reconciled with a theatre that communicated first and incessantly on a verbal level—and in this respect, he would still be baffled or furious with Hall and Brook—but our dress parades would undoubtedly remind him of the fatted Shakespeare so beloved by gentlemen's theatre. The effect of mounting a mannequin instead of a man is, in fact, the reverse of what might be expected: a type of man emerges, a psychological man who contradicts psychology, a reduced quotient, all boundary with no horizon, no frontiers.

Hall and Brook's case for Shakespeare, however, is based on the assumption of clashing, yet coexistent, strains, romance seen unromantically, myth seen naturally, ritual seen realistically. Their words, of course, would mean little were they not supported by their work. It may be that I have not yet seen the central linchpin on their Shakespearean wheel: Brook's *King Lear* with Paul Scofield is said to incorporate most of the dialectical tensions between past and present, Beckett and Brecht, ceremony and humanity. But Hall's production of the *Dream,* as I have said, and more recently, his work with John Barton in making a workable, full, yet compressed experience out of the *Henry VI* plays and *Richard III* under the comprehensive title *The Wars of the Roses,* indicate some guidelines. What began, perhaps, as a series of inspired gropings is now emerging as a considered practice grounded in flexible theory. The "new" trilogy is, in one sense, less of a test than *Lear* or several of the plays likely to be taken more seriously. It was patchwork Shakespeare even before Barton adapted, cut, and added to it. So this is a case where "improvements" of the text are not a betrayal. The patches of Barton blend seamlessly into the fabric of Shakespeare. By combining several dukes into one more readily recognizable duke, by adding bridge passages, above all by presenting an opportunity to watch the same actor develop and change in one role, the unstoppable ritual movement of history informs, attacks, and hurts directly.

We enter the theatre. Again, there is no curtain. At the foot of the raked stage an open coffin faces us. It contains the corpse of Henry V. We are in a huge feudal hall, austere, gray, seemingly constructed from steel and copper mesh. It is grand, cumbersome, cold, completely awesome. The lights are still on in the theatre. A voice is heard. It is the dead king, commanding his family "to love and join together into one league and one unfeigned amity" (taken from the Tudor chronicler, Edward Hall). The theatre lights dim slowly, focusing attention on the flickering candles round the coffin. The boots of men make a harsh, hissing noise on the metal-plated floor. This too is a room that has known life, and for nine hours (with intervals, of course) we shall be lured into it. There is nothing comfortable or comforting about this open, heavy space. To live in it is only to endure. To survive within is probably impossible. Existence here is always in question, leading men into labyrinths, the winding corridors of bad, but very real, dreams. Beyond, the theatre is never absent. It is the beautiful but horrible castle ground for a rite. Life happens here, but only in the measured pace of ancient ceremony.

And so, again, we are in a physical, ancestral England. Princes and kings appear and vanish. Conspirators caught in the web of their own conspiracy are replaced by younger men who haven't learned. Ambition is stern, forbidding, and finally, absurd. Battles, pervaded by weird, slithering electronic sounds, and looking like slow-motion, almost frozen sarabands, repeat themselves, monumental swords glinting in the thickening air, swinging clumsily against the resounding floor. Everything is hard, substantial; every move reverberates, sound compounding sound. Heads literally roll. Blood spits from bodies. Shock deadens shock. It is the numbing brutality of history come to frightening and personal life. No one—least of all the audience—can be spared.

The actors, too, are unspared and unsparing. With few exceptions, they join in an extraordinary company performance. Artaud proposed "a theatre in which violent physical images crush and hypnotize the sensibility of the spectator seized by the theatre as by a whirlwind of forces." Against John Bury's ingenious design, these actors play the whirlwind, flashing image after image on the screen of our imagination. They play—most of them—as if possessed, driven by furies hacked out of bleeding stone. In control of the martial rhetoric, they are at once distant and involved, savage and human, sculptured and fluid. Stalking one another through history, they are always—as actors—responding to another's action, to the situation of the moment. The halls, cells, and battlefields stay fixed. Only the people change, growing into old, embittered, plastic images of decay, men and women weighted by their own souls, stubbornly insisting on their own destruction.

This is basically the work and expression of a young ensemble of players. Yet links to what was best in the past have not been forgotten by Hall. Peggy Ashcroft's Margaret of Anjou, the only character seen in all three plays, stands firmly at the center of this terrifying occasion. If Rachel, as George Henry Lewes said, was the panther of the stage, Dame Peggy is surely the tigress. She has suffered criticism in the past for her Kensington manners, her air of graces untouched by human dust. She would, in fact, often preside over the stage like a hostess at a tea party who would never fling a cup at an offending guest. In *The Wars of the Roses,* however, she flings roses, swords, and animal curses at the whole tribe. By means of what might have been an obtrusive trick in a lesser actress—the assumption of a rolling French "R" in her accent—she remains the intriguing outcast of the cycle, an alien spirit in an alienating world. Her range is startling: from girlish flirtation to haggard old age, she twists and darts through the political and personal lives around her as if people were only trees in what ought to be her private jungle. Gliding effortlessly through lines that are frequently craggy, poetic obstacle courses, her voice—now trumpet, now flute—supports her shifting, melting, piercing, flaming, tender, exhausted emotional responses. She exists on stage as a constant, passionate, and angry metaphor of human waste, the animal always breaking from the woman. It is a formal, yet human, performance, a life cycle seen through an hourglass, never more moving than when it is suggesting the beauty within the ugliest and most violent encounters. One moment was a summation: Margaret throwing a paper crown on the captured Duke of York, smearing his face in the blood of his son, murdered by her, hurling curses at the head she will lop off, but stopped momentarily by York's prolonged curse at her. Dame Peggy chose a network of surprise: at her own viciousness in attack, never certain herself if she is laughing or crying in her raillery; and then, surprise at the horrible truth behind York's last words. Past redemption, she listens, not reluctantly, but unwillingly enthralled by his fury. Her arms descend wearily to her side, her head turns slowly away. She is moved, anger spent, listening always, and sinking into age before our eyes, a tear withheld turning to rock.

Images of violence, propelled by poetry, can stand only for a part of Shakespeare. Yet that part is large enough to stand as a portent for the whole. The paths, from period to period, are difficult to map: so much is missed by gentility, so much is gained by reaching into the underground, the hidden recesses of men's minds. Lear's words should be ignored. If we begin, irreverently, from nothing, then something—an event, an occasion, a personal experience—will occur. Shakespeare has become too daunting a figure, the Jesus of the poetic world humbling all before him. As Shaw might have said, he is too true to be good.

The contemporary experience, though received in many senses by the Shakespearean experience, is new nonetheless, as he would have been the first to chronicle. He is *completely* modern only to those who would contradict his own perception. The first great English poet of exploration, he was the first to expose himself to the probability that there is always something new, even under the severely proscribed Elizabethan sun. He would know today when he is relevant, and he would acknowledge those modern instances when he is thoroughly, if charmingly, irrelevant.

Peter Hall's approach to a comedy and to one set of histories is, in fact, not so much a test as an implication. What has been given up for dead in Shakespeare, what we have lost by the power of our own indifference, what we once hoped to gain by fanciful snippings away from the text, can be found again by making several concurrent return journeys: to the origins of theatre, to the dense yet translucent atmosphere of Elizabethan England, and to the dramatic poetry of the relevant material itself. Shakespeare's imagination, shaded by light, and colored by darkness, had a terrible splendor. And it is being honored today by England's young Shakespeareans.

Meanwhile, our theatres whimper where they should roar, tiptoe where they should stride, and withdraw where they should lead. They ignore the journeys, the imagination, the terror, and the splendor. Separating art from life, they fragment what was meant to be compact.   *GR(Spring 1964)*

Sean O'Casey's Exile

Sean O'Casey would understand when I say that the news of his death last month came almost as a relief. He would understand, but he wouldn't cover me with garlands for saying so. Life was more precious to him than any knowledge he might have had that, like so many a venerable figure before him, it was no longer sitting well upon his brow. He made the shortest possible shrift out of wasteland prophets, those monarchs of gloom he saw hiding under almost every contemporary literary bush. "They are not for those in the Spring of life," he wrote recently, "not for the young who are seeing visions of great things in the future, as I do, even though I be old and grey." Yet—and with O'Casey there was usually a splendidly testy *yet* and a peculiarly confounding *but*—Samuel Beckett, for one, "wears his rue with a difference— he is a poet."

It was always like this: arguments, fights, riots in the theatre ("You have disgraced yourselves again," said W. B. Yeats to the audience that was breaking up *The Plough and the Stars*), disputations with the named and the nameless, thundering rages against hypocritical politicians, ascetic clerics, savage militarists, and those stuffy theatre types he once dubbed "Dramama-mannakeens" and "Criticonians." But when the dust of battle settled, a responsive, gentle, lyric artist was revealed, a man in love even with those he was committed to despise.

Hanging heavily over him in later years, however, were the sad ironies born from his firm persuasions. He was in self-appointed exile from his country and his theatre, an exile that had been chosen decades ago after considerable provocation from both. (Sending writers into exile has always been one of Ireland's most popular tribal customs.) But neither theatre nor country cared as much about the absent lover as he cared for them underneath his growls and grumps. Oddly, it was his mentor Yeats who, as leader of the Abbey Theatre, provided the final push by arguing with him over *The Silver Tassie*'s innovations. Yet his exile came at a time when he was transforming not so much his style as the theatrical context in which his rebellious dramatic comedies would be played: on the broadest level, he was done with the urban naturalism that framed *Juno and the Paycock* and *The Plough and the Stars*, replacing it with choruses and fantasies, the material of dreams inherited from Aristophanes, Shakespeare, Strindberg, and Yeats himself.

It was a bad time to quit land and theatre, though it is always easier to argue from the distance of time. In moving from Ireland to Britain, he was trading a place where he felt unwelcome for a place that had neither the resources nor the feeling to take him in as he deserved. To write plays is to need a theatre. But England's theatre, trapped then in its own stiff upper accents and its four-walled drawing room, was hardly the spiritual or actual home for a rough Irishman treating every kind of wall as a personal enemy. So O'Casey did the next best thing: he wrote plays that went largely unproduced, and to keep the endless dramas in his mind alive, he wrote a great book about himself.

Meanwhile, the ironies continued to unfold. His young spirit scarcely touched a young audience. In England, especially, he seemed never to be talking to the people around him. His great champions were American, reviewers such as George Jean Nathan, Brooks Atkinson, and Richard Watts, names he only recently invoked to challenge Kenneth Tynan. As always, it was a proud invocation: "Is Sir Kenneth Tynan right about the play, 'Purple Dust'? Does he see clear, does he hear well, does he understand it at all? . . . I call friendly drama knights to my aid, who come cantering up, and let out a bellowing cry of 'No, Ken, No!' "

Behind the shrillness and reversed snobbery of the defense (Tynan has not been knighted *yet,* and should he ever be, it will not be a disgrace or a triumph for the ruling classes), there is the charm of the exile, the man protected from the currents and trends of daily intellectual life, unaware that, out of time, he has called clumsily upon champions who, with good will and limited sensibility, have done as much as any to make Broadway inhospitable to art. Or to put it another way, Tynan's idea of theatre—even when it excludes some of O'Casey's best plays—would at least furnish a better climate for O'Casey's ideals than the accommodating notions of theatre represented by Nathan, Atkinson, and Watts. The most devastating fact of O'Casey's exile from Ireland is that he so often seemed to be exiled from the world.

In time, it will be easier to know who was most at fault—O'Casey or the world. At present it looks as if they neutralized each other, wall against wall; O'Casey stubborn and unyielding in his opinions, the world equally resistant to his titanic will for change. It isn't surprising. He made the tactical error of following the logic of his life: from slums and the Irish Citizen Army where he tried to square the wonder he felt with the horror around him, to the discovery of books and theatre where equally bloody ritual wars were waged, he withdrew finally to a Devonshire outpost where wounds could be nursed and new battle plans hatched in the relative privacy of creeping age.

Clinging to the images of change—in science, social order, and the theatre—he held fast to early innocence. Against the odds, he persisted. Great nay-sayer that he was, he tried to say yes at every turn. A visionary, he suffered continually from a childhood blight on his eyes. A devoted father, he lost a dear son only eight years ago, wishing for once, that the death had been his. Still, he said yes. The world, so it seemed, would have to be marvelous even if he had to knock it senseless first. From a quiet corner in England, he followed his beloved Whitman by sounding barbaric yawps over sleeping rooftops. From darkness, he insisted on light.

If these are contradictions, then so much the worse for us. The point of a life like O'Casey's is surely that, faced with pointlessness, it goes on. Most of us speak—as I have—from naked embarrassment with life, a little unsettled by O'Casey's presence, put out by his tattered dignity, his indifference to the rules. Like Yeats before us, we would have him as he was, the crude young poet of pubs who was supposed to father a thousand Joxers and Junos. Instead, we took to the less complicated epic liberties of Dylan and Brendan, forgetting that Sean—stretching life as far as it would take him—had written the tunes to which they danced toward early graves.

What Yeats damaged and we've missed can't be comfortably assessed. One thing is certain. The theatre without the playwright lost more than the playwright without the theatre. Literally from the day after the Abbey's rejection, it ceased to be a lively, imaginative, and productive home for drama. But O'Casey's later plays—however unwelcome they were to critics and friends—were bubbling with spirit, busily extending for others, if not always for himself, the frontiers of theatre. It can be argued, in any case, that they were never given a chance. Published and frozen before ever reaching the stage, the most intriguing of them—*Red Roses for Me, Purple Dust, Time to Go,* and most of all, *Cock-a-Doodle-Dandy*—never found *their* director. At best, they suggest the need for a company of exiled Irishmen, mercurial actors aware that conventions change, that character is more than behavior just as acting is more than a brogue. What may well be missing is some gloriously dotty Irish Berlin

Ensemble led by an equally improbable Bertolt Littlewood. Before agreeing with Yeats, we should have given the plays a hope.

Certainly there is a terrible lesson in O'Casey's history for theatres everywhere. Whatever the tempers of the moment, whatever may be said for the rising stars of actors and directors in this century, the dramatist—particularly when he and the theatre have shared an interweaving success—must be given his head. The mistakes he may make are as nothing compared to the irreparable error of holding him back or rejecting him outright. The saddest, silliest, most wasteful part of the O'Casey story is that, for all his pride and eloquent bluster, he was not as strong as he wanted himself and us to believe. The hurt cut deeply, not only to his heart, but to his vaulting but vulnerable theatrical talent. Despite his gallant stand in the wings, he wanted and deserved a welcome on stage.

The final irony is the theatrical presence—the star quality—of his autobiography: scenes connected by passion, comedies of terror, death agonies, love play, farceurs who kill, melodramatists who laugh, a stunning rhetoric that aches to be heard, crowned finally by moments like the ending where hushed reverberations are meant to fill the silent theatre's air: "Even here, even now, when the sun had set and the evening star was chastely touching the bosom of the night, there were things to say, things to do. A drink first! What would he drink to—the past, the present, the future? To all of them! He would drink to the life that embraced the three of them! Here, with whitened hair, desires failing, strength ebbing out of him, with the sun gone down, and with only the serenity and the calm warning of the evening star left to him, he drank to Life, to all it had been, to what it was, to what it would be. Hurrah!"

For such a man, grief lacks eloquence and mourning is an indulgence. To honor him, we must live a little higher, we must dare again. I am relieved because the test comes now. If he is set aside in death as he was cast aside in life, we shall have disgraced ourselves again.   *GR(October 1964)*

The Companies They Keep

Historians, speaking of origins, refer to the *immediate* causes of war and the *real* causes. One could say, then, that the appearance of John Osborne's *Look Back in Anger* on May 8, 1956, at the Royal Court Theatre, London, was to the new move in British theatre as the assassination of Archduke Ferdinand was to the initiation of World War I: it triggered the action, but in itself it was more effect than cause. When India finally severed itself from Britain's imperial grasp, the appearance of the first "angry" play was only a matter of incidental time. The sceptered isle, the precious realm, that earth, so long a powerful world unto itself, was at last compelled to join the world. The beginning of painful, yet splendidly alive, discovery, it was also the beginning of fresh perceptions, a new awareness, an unavoidable sense that the fragmented world outside was a useful mirror in which to view the new, emerging, terrifyingly real Britain. By the time of *Look Back in Anger,* long before the Profumo scandal, the breakdown was complete. This is not to say that men didn't move mountainous obstructions into their minds in order to ignore it. But they did so only at the cost of increased isolation. Their masquerades, built on the scrapheap of past glory, had nothing to do with the present. "We are *Great* Britain again," said one of the headlines during the Suez crisis in 1956. In the event, the triumph was an illusion. The old, mannered, parasitic greatness was disappearing against a litany of nostalgic whimpers. That may be serviceable behavior for a dying social order, but it is hopelessly corruptive to art. Indeed, a theatre that whimpers has lost the name of theatre. Thus Osborne's resounding bang, while limited as art, was the first necessary cry in the battle to save an art.

But actors fought the war. Only once in its history could the English theatre be described accurately as a playwright's theatre; and in Shakespeare's case, with that kind of social logic that history is heir to, the playwright was himself an actor, indeed, an actor in a repertory company with a "permanent" home on the banks of the Thames. One can babble—as critics, including myself, invariably do—of this trend or that strain, or some other tendency, without quite catching the strangest strain of all: namely, that actors mark the difference between library and stage. For the most part, playwrights represent recordable theatre history while actors, forlornly in the wings to the end, stand for unrecordable history. And precisely in those wings stands the real history and dependable vigor of England's theatre.

I am not speaking here of what is right or wrong, desirable or deplorable, only of what *is*. At any time, in any country, a Shakespeare would be a more elusive blossom than a Burbage, Garrick, or Kean. But, in England, the playwrights after Shakespeare were nipped harshly and early when, in 1642, the Puritans closed London's theatres, giving their war against the Crown as an excuse. The wounds are still being felt. Images of respectability, for what little they are worth, were effectively removed; to this day, the vagabond art has a bubble reputation. People like it more than they respect it. More to the point, the dramatist continues to be a second-class literary citizen. In universities, Shakespeare is admired primarily as a poet who happened to write plays, rather than—as he was—a playwright who happened to be a poet.

The actor, by tradition, cuts a handsomer figure than the dramatist. Scattered to the winds, chances, fate, what-you-will by that same puritanical repression, he proved less vulnerable finally than the playwright. Perhaps it was because he neither expected nor claimed respectability. Once theatres were reopened, all he had to do was to act whatever was given him, and it is only a small exaggeration to say that what was given him was Shakespeare; or rather, whatever else he might be doing, he would always return to Shakespeare. This has been the testing ground, the summit. For Garrick, Betterton, Kemble, Kean, Macready, Gielgud, Olivier, and Scofield, there has never been anywhere to go from *Lear, Macbeth,* or *Othello*—nowhere to go but down. In short, England's theatre in its worst days—days when poets such as Byron and Shelley were running aground on theatrical shores—survived as an actor's theatre. It follows, then, that in better days—and the last decade following Osborne's explosion surely qualifies—it would stay the same.

And, indeed, the past decade, while adding refinements of its own in the form of vital, social, mysterious, and unquestionably talented playwrights, as well as equally imaginative, probing, and technically brilliant directors, has probably made more of the actor than any of the golden periods before. It was bound to happen. When Henry Irving was knighted by Queen Victoria, it was only a matter of time when every tailor's or collier's son and every publican's daughter would set his or her dewy eyes on the actor's life. (In America, at the turn of the century, a similar move in a similar field was being promoted by immigrant mothers discovering that Mischa Elman made $1000 per concert; suddenly every good Jewish boy was taking violin lessons.)

To be sure, the first wave of Knights and Dames came from the gentry, fathers and mothers who were stalwart pillars of Church, Commerce, State, or Education. Until the mid-fifties, the crown could always feel comfortable in the choices selected by the Prime Minister for gentle shoulder-dubbings: whatever else may be said of them, Sir Cedric, Sir Ralph, Dame Sybil, Sir Lewis, Sir John, Dame Edith, Sir Michael, Sir Donald, Dame Peggy, and Sir Laurence have certainly made reliable, well-dressed, and thoroughly proper dinner partners. Which isn't to say that Kenneth Haigh, away from the howls and furies of Jimmy Porter, would be any the less a gentleman; only that his accent and stance represented very different bloodlines.

Ironically, then, what the Royal Court Theatre released with its production of *Look Back in Anger* was far more than a great new wave of playwrights. What it unleashed was a pride of lion-like young actors and actresses into a world of roles formerly denied to them. If you came from the bleak wastes of the North or from the Rhondda Valley in Wales you were automatically limited to comic charladies or wizened postmen; and if you were really distinguished and suitably overweight from all those fish and chips you'd been eating during all your ragged, lower-class life, you could be a gravedigger in *Hamlet* or the porter in *Macbeth*. So far as the good, brave causes lamented by Jimmy Porter were concerned, there was none more swiftly won than the victory implicit in Jimmy's presence on stage. One knew, instinctively, that the next generation of Hamlets, Shylocks, and even Restoration wags and fops would never quite look or sound like the heroes known and often loved before.

The Royal Court had, of course, different plans. As founded and run by George Devine for ten years until just before his death this winter, it was meant to be a theatre that would uncover new playwrights, particularly by encouraging novelists and poets to move their energies into the theatre. It was a scheme, like so many others of its type, that gave way almost immediately to the strange laws that have nothing to do with men's best-laid intentions. These laws, I suspect, have something to do with the fact that most novelists and poets, while craving to be transformed like Dr. Jekylls of the written word into Mr. Hydes of the acting word, never quite find the strength to sustain the adventure, thus clearing the field for writers who need no magic to feel at home on stage.

Once Angus Wilson, Ronald Duncan, and Nigel Dennis had their flings with plays, helping Devine set the machinery for a writer's theatre in motion, it was necessary only for them to fade away, leaving the Royal Court ready and able to produce the plays of Osborne, John Arden, Ann Jellicoe, N. F. Simpson, Arnold Wesker, and Alun Owen. For all the undoubted evidence of these names and their numbers, however, the Court was still far more than a writer's theatre.

Theatre is so much a game of illusion versus reality that the trick of looking like a writer's theatre, while behaving like an actor's and director's theatre, is simply a natural part of the game. Two reasons, more than others, account for the success of the masquerade. First, English theatre was clearly in search of a Movement; or, if not the theatre, certainly journalists, hungry for copy, were only too quick to pick up the Court's claims and the Osborne play and turn them into a convenient label; a label, too, that could be applied easily to actors. Thus, it scarcely mattered that Osborne, Jellicoe, and Arden were not really Angry, Young, or all Men, it only mattered that everybody should have a sense of motion, that it should be clear to the public—if, thankfully, unclear to the writers—that Something was at last happening in the English Theatre.

The second reason for the illusion's staying power was ordinary theatre-audience economics. The fact is that, apart from John Osborne's plays, the new dramas made—to borrow the title of N. F. Simpson's comedy—only *A Resounding Tinkle* in the Court's cash register. Quite early in the game, it became clear to all but the most relentlessly journalistic minds that the new plays, fewer than one might imagine, were quite literally being paid for by way of successful star vehicles drawn from the past and present literature of world theatre. Peggy Ashcroft in Brecht's *The Good Woman of Setzuan* and later in Ibsen's *Rosmersholm,* Vivien Leigh in *Look after Lulu,* Laurence Olivier in Osborne's *The Entertainer* and Eugene Ionesco's *Rhinoceros,* Rex Harrison in Chekhov's *Platonov,* and finally the Court's very own home-grown star, Joan Plowright in *The Country Wife* (also starring Laurence Harvey) and in Arnold Wesker's *Roots*—these were the attractions that kept the Court alive. It is difficult to think of any theatre with a history quite like the Court's, one whose reputation and fame rest almost entirely on a body of new plays seen, understood, and admired by only the tiniest fraction of its regular audience. Never have so few carried so little so far.

Shortly before his death, George Devine called the National and the Royal Shakespeare the "great battleships" of the British theatre. He might well have drawn a finer distinction; for example, the Royal Shakespeare as the battleship or destroyer, the National as the aircraft carrier, scattering its weapons in all directions—to the old, the new, the tragic, comic, melodramatic, farcical, and sentimental. The National, by design and in nearly three years of phenomenal success, is what might be called a performing *museum,* with none of the mustiness that word implies; a breed of theatre attempted, but really unknown, in America; one whose primary purpose it is to present the best and most representative plays from every major period in the national literature, while by no means ignoring the Greeks, French, Russians, Spanish, Americans, and Scandinavians. Within ten days during February of this year, for example, it was possible to attend the National almost every day—sometimes twice a day—and see a different play every time: John Arden's *Armstrong's Last Goodnight,* *Othello,* Georges Feydeau's farce *A Flea in Her Ear,* Arthur Miller's *The Crucible,* William Congreve's *Love for Love,* Peter Shaffer's *The Royal Hunt of the Sun,* and, on a double bill, August Strindberg's *Miss Julie* and Shaffer's farce *Black Comedy.* Obviously, if this list seems eclectic, it is, and was never meant to be otherwise. In effect, the National has been playing the same kind of repertory that used to be common at the Royal Court (which is hardly surprising, since Dexter was one of the Court's leading directors, and Tynan, as a critic, was the noisiest drummer for the Court's ideals); but with this difference—that the National, cushioned by the largest subsidy ever granted by the government to a theatre in England, and by the undisputed eminence of Olivier, has been able to insinuate itself into the nation's consciousness without making heavy social assertions. It isn't a theatre with a mission because, for its purposes, the mission has been accomplished.

The National's character derives fundamentally from an actor's imagination; fortunately, in this case, from a great actor, one whose every gesture and audacious choice set incredible challenges for the others. In practice, this means not that everybody acts *like* Olivier—an inconceivable suggestion—but that almost everybody acts with a comparable sheen, precision, and largeness. The National's actors take the stage like so many thoroughbreds, proud, relaxed, and almost haughty; off not to the races, but to the hounds. Above all, they are versatile. Albert Finney ranges from Arden's dour and earthy Scot to a double role in the Feydeau, and in the Strindberg-Shaffer evening from stern sensuality to outrageous effeminacy. Robert Stephens offers a performance as Atahualpa in Shaffer's *Royal Hunt* that would look natural in the Kabuki theatre, while in the Arden play he presents a suave, self-possessed man-about-town. Colin Blakely's Pizarro in *Royal Hunt* matches Stephens note for note in intensity and spirit, while his Ben in the Congreve play is the very definition of a sea-swept bumpkin. Maggie Smith and Geraldine McEwan are just as protean: Smith as Olivier's soft but formidable Desdemona, as Strindberg's repressed and hysterical Miss Julie, and in a total shift of styles, as Shaffer's witty, playacting, thoroughly modern girl; McEwan as an insanely funny French intriguer in Feydeau's farce, as a rueful Restoration lady in the Congreve, and finally as a free, uncomplicated Scottish courtesan in the Arden play. In their separate ways, they all declare the "message" of the National—that so much of living is the playing of roles, and that this game, like any other, can be the source of more pleasure than pain. In short, going to the National is invariably an engaging experience, even though one never emerges with a committed social or philosophical idea. And this is the most English quality it possesses.

GR(Winter 1966)

Tennessee Descending

That Tennessee Williams is currently in crisis probably goes without saying. There are reasons, however, why it should be said yet again; not the least of which is the need to name the crisis, place it, forget about it, and move on to more helpful abstractions. To name it, at least as it comes to us from the theatre page of the *New York Times* or the gossip columns of the *New York Journal-American,* all we have to ponder are those twin obsessions, money and sex.

The popular image of Williams is that of the Successful Playwright, man about many towns, suavely wearing a pencil moustache that seems to have been bought as an elegant accessory to his debonair tropical suit. He looks to the public eye like a smooth man, a bit reserved, perhaps, a trifle nervous, but for all that, calm, civilized, and much less troubled than his plays suggest. Above all, he is a success. A new play by him seems to be an annual event; so far as most of us can tell, an event that need only be announced to bring long lines to the box office.

Meanwhile, his private life, though something of a mystery, yet known to be a heavily psychoanalyzed one, doesn't really look so unpleasant, considering that half the theatre world is doing its work between analytic sessions anyway. If Williams has been doing the same, for whatever problems he may be suffering from in love and work, he is not so unique.

Thus—the popular image, supported as usual by half-truths. The harder facts are these: Williams's name, unlike the names of Richard Rodgers and Mary Martin, has never been a guarantee for box-office success on Broadway; and even off Broadway, where the pressures were once lighter, his *Garden District* lost money. Two of the four plays directed by Elia Kazan—*Camino Real* and *Sweet Bird of Youth*—had relatively brief runs on Broadway, and *Camino* was never even saved by a film sale. Indeed, each year the battle for "smash" success has been more brutal and discouraging. The middle-class intelligentsia has always considered Arthur Miller a more important playwright, even during his seven-year silence. The literary monthlies have given Williams the kind of lofty disdain reserved once for John P. Marquand and lately for John O'Hara. And, in the case of the two Broadway productions of his last play, *The Milk Train Doesn't Stop Here Anymore,* nobody came, even Howard Taubman demurred, and those few remaining shook heads sadly or laughed. So extensive is the kiss of death associated with his name now that last season the producers of his latest work, *Slapstick Tragedy,* had to cancel production plans because investors couldn't be found. This year, cash was found for it more because of Margaret Leighton's presence as star than Williams's collateral as dramatist.

As for his private life, it is even less encouraging. He supports his eighty-one-year-old mother and his beloved sister Rose, the latter living for many years in a private institution. Two years ago, his best friend and secretary-companion died of cancer. He seems to enjoy giving the impression, at places like Sybil Burton Christopher's discotheque Arthur and Andy Warhol's studio, that only regular doses of vodka and drugs keep him alive. In short, he appears to be less wealthy than he might be, and less wealthy in more ways than money—a lonely, often clownish figure, well past his better days.

To call all this a writer's crisis, however, may be too easy. In the case of a writer, knowledge of his crisis, whatever its character, is no guarantee for knowing his work. True, the lives of the poets are more popular than their poetry. This says more about readers, however, than it does about poets.

The most interesting feature of an artist is his imagination, not his life. T. S. Eliot was a publisher, Charles Ives sold insurance, and Dylan Thomas flooded his liver with booze, but these were only the outward shows, the necessary signs of living and—for Thomas—dying. As facts of life, they have only the remotest connection to the central fact of art, namely that it is the pressure of the mind on experience, not the reverse, that marks the source and substance of art.

Williams's private crisis is of concern, then, only insofar as it touches his public work, and then only as a peripheral concern. Somebody once said that the only writer worth worrying about is the one who has stopped writing. In such a case, obviously, the private and public crises are one. We are all involved. Otherwise, interest in a writer's life, prurient or sympathetic, carries with it the heavy luggage of continual frustration and, at best, partial relevance. Whatever may be said today of Tennessee Williams, playwright, it can never be said that he has stopped writing plays. And in his case, at least, the evidence is clear enough by now that the quantity of his work is *some* guarantee of frequent quality.

There is evidence, anyway, that when journalists and the public refer to private crisis, they are usually speaking for their private wish that an artist should repeat himself. When Williams alternately pleased and shocked the public with *The Glass Menagerie* and *A Streetcar Named Desire* in the mid-forties—in both cases successfully—he was virtually sealing one part of his critical fate. Thereafter, all his work was pressed into comparison, as often as not unfavorably, with his first successes. It didn't matter which strain was, for the moment, the preferred one. The nostalgia in *Menagerie* or the sexiness in *Streetcar* quickly became critical touchstones. Henceforth, he was expected to be our official Southern playwright, spiritually languid, emotionally torrid, technically predictable. Ever and again, he was to be a chronicler of other people's nightmares, never our own, a colorful exotic guide to a never-never underland. Beyond that, he was to be used as one of his favorite writers, D. H. Lawrence, had been used before, as a kind of voyeur-in-residence.

Indeed, it is this latter role which accounts for the repeated cry of crisis. Writers such as Lawrence and Williams invariably inspire an ambivalent response from serious critics and public alike. For one thing, they are approachable. They come at us not so much with grandiose theories of life as they do with galvanizing concepts of aliveness. They speak in the language of forces, unions, eruptions, fusions, pressures, tensions, monstrosities, and an endless succession of mysterious presences. Flames and the phoenix are their comfort and weapons. By turns brutalized and lyrical, they are not read or viewed for the quality of their minds. Part of the ambivalence they inspire derives, in fact, from a general feeling that what genius they possess has little or nothing to do with powers of thought. On the contrary, they are admired precisely because, like occult cats in mythology, they seem to be our familiars, hosts to our darkest longings, our blackest fears.

Put another way, even the most severely learned critic holds Thomas Mann, James Joyce, or Marcel Proust at various levels of awe. He knows that

he himself can never compare with at least one major part of their achievement, Mann's philosophical grandeur, for instance, or Joyce's linguistic invention, or Proust's sustained transformation of memory into art. With them,
he is just another member of the audience. With Williams and Lawrence, on
the other hand, the audience can—and does—easily fancy itself the critic, severity, learning, and all.

Here, then, is a peculiarly convenient, while ambivalent, relationship between writer and public. As a "familiar," the writer gains popularity. But with
that popularity comes a certain legacy of guilt, and therefore, suspicion of his
talents. He has shown raw nerve in simply "acting out," at least in his plays
or novels, some of those fantasies that may well be all too real in most of us,
but equally he can be respected only for his nerve, not for his actions or the
closeness of his fantasies. He is, in short—and this has been true of Tennessee
Williams for two decades—both liked and disliked for the wrong reasons.

Somewhat remarkably, America's best drama critic, the late Stark Young,
then writing in the *New Republic,* predicted the confusion when *The Glass
Menagerie* first overwhelmed the Broadway scene in 1945.

> The author is not awed by the usual sterilities of our playwriting patterns. On
> the other hand he is too imaginative, genuine, or has too much good taste, to be
> coy about the free devices on which his play is built, a true, rich talent, unpre-
> dictable like all true talents, an astute stage sense, an intense, quivering clarity,
> all light and feeling once the intelligence of it is well anchored—a talent, too, I
> should say, that New York will buy tickets for in later plays, especially if enough
> of the sexy is added to things, but will never quite understand.

The addition of the sexy was at once inevitable and—so far as understanding was concerned—fatal. Understanding and sex ought to be the best of
bedfellows, but they rarely are; more so where art is in question. In life, secret
or otherwise, the violent puritan can always make peace with his impulses.
But when responding to art, he feels free to take a public stand. A good work
of art is meant to fill the gaps in his own nature, telling others, if not himself,
what is really good, true, or beautiful. What he desires from art is the restraint, control, and decorum that he can barely maintain in his own life. Art,
for him, is his altering and flattering ego.

At what, after all, was Stark Young hinting? Knowing only *The Glass
Menagerie,* what precisely was he sensing—and so accurately—about Williams's future? For a start, of course, he was acknowledging something in
Williams that is all too easily overlooked by moral arbiters of public taste: his
"true, rich talent, unpredictable . . ." Further than that, he could see plainly
that the play represented a necessary beginning, the story derived directly
from self, that " first novel" usually in every writer, the calm that helps release the storm. Williams, it is true, had been writing plays for years, long
since a fugitive from mother's savage solicitude. *Battle of Angels,* the play
that was later reshaped into *Orpheus Descending,* had already suffered the
fate four years before that Boston traditionally reserves for imperfect young

strangers. *The Glass Menagerie* was his answer, slow in coming, as it had to
be; but for all that, a fresh start, the young man's summation before crossing
the shadowed line into maturity. Above all, Stark Young was hinting that only
maturity lay in waiting, the play having described ever so delicately the absolute, titanic absence of sex in both Tom and Laura's lives. Young foresaw not
really the addition of sex, but rather its discovery.

Had Williams merely "added" sex to his work, there would be neither serious dramatist nor reputation at issue. In their place would be talk of surrender, compromise, or corruption, all the words we call upon whenever mourning a lost talent. Against him we should level the charge of cynicism.
Literature was meant to be his art, we might say, and instead he chose a
tremulous pornography as his trade. Williams's earliest detractors—those
who pretend, at least, to speak for a scandalized public—held modified versions of such a view. But again, this was always the easy way to mislead the
public about both the nature of crisis and the wellsprings of art.

It can be described, not too roughly, as the conspiracy view of art—the
notion that serious artists often *plan* to diddle their audience, quite literally
preying upon gullible passions, campaigning like generals to put one over on
the enemy. The difficulty is, of course, that books have always been published
and plays have always been produced by ravenously cynical men. The first
baby step in any critical act is to draw lines between the man who shows his
anguish and the man who uses ours. What happens, for example, in Faulk-
ner's Yoknopatawpha County may conform to the "Southernness" and violence of our expectations, but it happens on an indisputably loftier and more
complex level than the blowzy events in Caldwell's little acre. One is real
imagination, the other feigned reality.

And so it is that Williams, in discovering sex, plunged into that delicate
area where life invariably insists on confusing art. Or rather, confusion sets in
if the artist himself begins to share the vulgar confusions of his audience. Williams's plays after *Menagerie,* then, became subjects of inquiry, not so much
for what the plays revealed in themselves but for what they exposed of Williams. A crude chart of the sexual territory covered by the plays would be
headed by Blanche DuBois's nymphomania and Stanley Kowalski's urge to
rape both it and her sanity out of existence, followed by several subheadings
borrowed from Krafft-Ebbing.

This is how the inquiry works: Blanche is a nymphomaniac; she is a brilliantly realized character; yet how can a man *know* so much about such a
woman?; it is not really possible; besides, the author shows so much understanding and sympathy for her even though he brings her to a rather messy
end; then, perhaps, as a character, she is only a disguise for the author himself; it is clear, anyway, that he doesn't really like women (look at that mother
in *Menagerie*), so the only conclusion available is that he is more or less expressing his own experience *directly* through the medium of Blanche; in
short, it is a dishonest characterization, and therefore, a sensationalist play;
Blanche is not a woman at all, she is a man in drag.

The inquiry is, of course, even more sensationalist and twice as misleading as anything in the play. But that doesn't stop it from going on, until by now it has become accepted form even in serious criticism; used most effectively on the work of dramatists known to be, at the least, more homo- than heterosexual in what is intriguingly called real life. Philip Roth, in the *New York Review of Books,* lacerates Edward Albee's *Tiny Alice* not on the basis of its very vulnerable dramaturgy, but on his certainty that Julian, like Blanche, is really a sexual hoax. Similarly, George and Martha in *Who's Afraid of Virginia Woolf?* (and one hopes that this isn't devastating news to Taylor and Burton—or their admirers) are not a married couple at all, but a pair of sex-crossed male lovers, doing a breed of psychic mayhem to one another that simply has nothing to do with *any* heterosexual experience. (Tell that to the divorce courts!) The list of masked ladies and gentlemen goes on: Adriana del Lago in *Sweet Bird of Youth;* Flora Goforth in *The Milk Train Doesn't Stop Here Anymore;* the Reverend T. Lawrence Shannon in *The Night of the Iguana;* and so on forever, giving the inquiry the benefit of having it all ways at once. Whatever the nature of the play, whatever the *stated* conflict of the characters, the playwright is supposed to be suffering from one central, debilitating crisis—the suppression of his real experience. His plays, therefore, cannot be valid because—placed against real life, particularly the playwright's alleged real life—they cannot be true.

This style of criticism, carried to its logical ends, yields a howling multitude of fallacies. No writer, be he major-minor-homo-or-hetero, could truthfully escape censure. Shakespeare, who (arguably) revealed something of a homosexual attachment in his sonnets, must perforce have given much of his energy to masking his homosexuality in his plays, helped psychologically, it is true, by having his women played by boys in drag anyway. Thus, the intractability of Hamlet's character might be explained by the terrible unspoken truth in his life; or the girls pretending to be boys (Viola and Rosalind) were really, in Shakespeare's mind, boys revealing more boy-psychology than girl-, a convenient mask-on-mask technique designed to fool most of the people all of the time. Similarly, the young Christopher Marlowe, a known homosexual, had the courage to put one real homosexual relationship on stage in *Edward II,* thereby making psychological nonsense out of his other work; unless, of course, one really imagines that Tamburlaine, Faustus, and the Jew of Malta are all queers or ladies in complex disguise. And what this reasoning does to such aggressively heterosexual writers as Lord Byron, Ernest Hemingway, or Arthur Miller one shudders to surmise.

The fact is, the writer whose sexual practice has been deeply, neurotically, and even pleasurably homosexual is expected today to reveal more graphically and directly the nature of his experience than the writer whose sexual practice is common to the majority. This expectation is derived from one part curiosity, one part resentment, and two parts utter confusion. Moreover, as the literary market has become more free, the expectation has been met, in fact, literally dozens of times; and, not surprisingly, the real homosexual between covers or on stage is found to be no more an assurance of artistic cohesion or indigenous honesty than the so-called disguised homosexual before him. Blanche, in short, still looks like a rich, full character study, very much and every inch a woman.

The crisis of veiled homosexuality is, then, one of those decoys invented by a critical fraternity which is itself in crisis. The plays, singly and together, are nothing if not revealing. What is revealed has something, perhaps a good deal, to *do* with homosexuality, but it has nothing to *show* of the deed itself, which is hardly surprising. Drama is not yet documentary, despite all the ill-conceived efforts of newspaper naturalists with their well-made plays. On the contrary, drama selects from experience and transforms it into something else, something with a substance, order, and life all its own.

The life of Williams's plays, like the life of Shakespeare's, Strindberg's, or even Beckett's plays, is meant, of course, to look like life as we think we know it. But this is no more than to say that plays are not paintings, buildings, or symphonies; that the element in them corresponding most directly to the paint in a painting, the mortar in a building, or the instruments in an orchestra, is something that looks alive, acts as if it is alive, and is, in fact, very much alive: the actor taking the *role* of a human being. The illusion, such as it is, depends finally upon the persuasive union of the actor and the character *invented* by the author. Which means quite plainly that nothing in the end is ever really real on stage. The illusion is real enough, but the medium used—a person—is no more real aesthetically (which is to say animate and alive) than an oboe, a pigment, or a stone. Whatever he may say, if a dramatist had no ambition beyond the literal presentation of reality, he would not then be writing plays. He would be making personal appearances.

Williams reveals, for better and sometimes worse, areas of thought, feeling, and imagination that extend above, below, and frequently beyond the literal details of any man's daily life. He is not always strictly modern in his technique, though with *Camino Real* he tried to build—not always successfully— a romantic abstraction into a sustained drama; and in his latest work, *Slapstick Tragedy* (two short plays), he aims for what he calls "vaudeville, burlesque and slapstick, with a dash of pop art thrown in." But whether he is "current" with any given play, whether he succeeds or fails with technical experiment, he is surely modern in temperament, though never making a sound quite like anyone else's.

On occasion, he has a character say something so direct, so reflective, and so final as to be unmistakably representative of himself. "We are prisoners inside our own skins" (*Orpheus Descending*) is surely a formative, motivating conviction, one that speaks immediately for the currents and tensions in all his plays. What is fascinating about the conviction is what it means for drama: from it springs unique, dramatic life, the urge in any character to free himself from the prison, to reach insistently—as men do—for what the mind insists is unattainable. No thought could be at once more revealing and more nourishing to dramatic life than that.

Now, it would be possible to minimize the effect of such a thought by interpreting it not as a source of personal drama but as a source only of personal anguish. One clinical interpretation could, with some justice, lean again toward homosexuality. To view life from a homosexual bedroom, cluttered as it is with the memories of scattered partners, angry justifications, and broken dreams, might be to view life as a prison. One might wish to be plural, but one is continually and often agonizingly single. That is generally a simple, not easily changeable, fact of homosexual life. The mind thinks it is calling for one thing while its sexual surrender is moving it toward another.

But even the clinical is not so conclusive. The plural urge has never been exclusive homosexual property, even though the homosexual himself is freer, by marital definition, to turn the theory into more frequent practice. No. To be clinical alone about Williams's prisoner theme is to be simultaneously half-truthful about life and almost entirely unenlightening about drama, particularly Williams's drama.

Deep within the theme is something modern, dramatic, and expansive; something that might be called a demi-existentialism, a half-formed, incomplete, fundamentally unphilosophical view of man's condition; a sense of futility playing against a sense of struggle; a feeling that much of survival depends upon the discovery not of the imprisoned self alone (that, after all, is already known once it is stated), but of the many selves coexisting or battling within the prison. It is almost like adapting Whitman's nineteenth-century, romantic humanism—"I am large, I contain multitudes"—into twentieth-century terms: tensile, anxious, extravagantly austere. For the dramatist, it is anything but clinical or limiting. It is one way, particularly useful to Williams, of filling the stage with *different* characters. The inner territory being so richly populated with shadows of dreams and dreams of shadows, it is an endless source of character, a natural source of conflict, and a rich source of dialogue and monologue. The plays of Tennessee Williams are, therefore, something like variations on his own skin game. Breaking loose is the motive, some kind of drama the inevitable reward.

What kind of drama? Drama, first of all, that succeeds in part *even when it fails in sum* because it is always rooted psychologically in the central urge peculiar to drama as a form; drama, in a word, that is founded on motion. In one sense, there is nothing unique about this quality. Indeed, it is something of a technical necessity for almost all drama. The curtain rises, the lights begin to cast bright transparencies or gray intensities on corners of the stage, someone on stage stands, sits, or moves to another corner, or someone else enters from the right just after still another person has exited at left, and the drama begins. Events occur on stage because, in effect, people are moving from one position to another. And this is meant to be a parable of life; as Jaques says in *As You Like It,* "All the world's a stage, the men and women in it merely players. They have their exits and their entrances . . ."

Williams, however, is not only making use of entrances and exits, he is really writing about them. Look first at those who appear to be his opposites,

who use the *absence* of physical motion to describe their dramatic world:
Samuel Beckett, placing characters in ashcans, mounds, or urns in order to
center the "action" on the movement of the mind; Richard Wagner, who, as
interpreted by his grandsons at Bayreuth today, has characters stand like
rocks on rocks hour after hour, thus centering the "action" on the movement
of the music. Motionless bodies, in these cases, stand for an attitude as well
as a technique. Beckett for philosophical endurance, Wagner for fatalistic acceptance.

Williams, on the other hand, moves his characters almost ceaselessly because he has to. Perpetual motion, in his case, is also an attitude. Women, for
example, are usually his pivotal characters for a reason. Their very presence
challenges the truth of appearances. They look fragile, but as often as not,
they prove strong. One runs to them for help, yet runs from them for relief.
Some, like Amanda in *Menagerie,* are autocrats of the dinner table, psychological vampires, helplessly enthralled by the sound of their own needs, and,
therefore, suffocating to the child unable to leave them. Others, like Laura in
the same play, are natural victims, delicate and helpless in the larger world,
but quite adept in the narrow, circumscribed privacy of their own creation,
people who need protection, but only at the expense of one's own more natural life. A man's life cycle in a Williams play is to reach out to a woman (either
the strong or the weak, it doesn't matter), and just at the point of contact,
run. In a recurring phrase, used first for an early play, later as the title for the
movie version of *Orpheus,* a man is almost always "the fugitive kind." *Camino Real,* the play least concerned with naturalistic torments, was said by
both Williams and his director, Elia Kazan, to be quite literally about various
states and stages of "flight." Men may come and men may go, but in a Williams play, they are likely to be coming and going forever.

Everybody is a traveler. They told Blanche to take a streetcar named Desire, transferring for Elysian Fields. Ten scenes later she is leaving for a mental home, having found and lost Mitch (who ran like hell back to his mother),
and having lost her balance in a tug of sex with Stanley (whose way of life is
to crawl back to Stella). The absent father in *Menagerie* "fell in love with long
distance"; and his son dons sailor cap, tells us the family story, and leaves
home. Val Xavier in *Orpheus,* guitar over his shoulder, *is* the fugitive kind, descending into yet another disappearing act. Sebastian, the central but recently
dead figure in *Suddenly Last Summer,* was a poet of blank pages wandering
first from mother, then from wife, into oblivion on a Spanish beach, an end he
came to after walking his eventual killers for miles. Similarly, the actress in
Sweet Bird of Youth is running anxiously *from* Hollywood just as her male
stud hopes he is running from his hustler's beat by way of her bed *to* Hollywood. The Milk Train, we learn, doesn't stop at Flora Goforth's Italian villa
anymore; and so her wandering poet, Chris, clearly has no place to go. As for
Mrs. Goforth, she is no longer a way station for anybody because she, like Big
Daddy in *Cat on a Hot Tin Roof,* is sounding a losing battle cry against the inevitable—and very last—exit.

These arrivals and departures, then, are the special stuff of Williams's drama, the force that informs all his work. Once again, it is possible to observe both homosexual and biographical connections: wandering comes with homosexual territory; while Williams is the most peripatetic of playwrights, making homes in Key West, New Orleans, Rome, and New York; up until recently, at least, always in motion, the act of writing seemingly the only constant in a sea of travels. But what is known outside the plays tells only a little, as always, about the plays themselves. What, besides weaving its way into both the form and content of his drama, does motion do to their relative success or failure?

The word failure, of course, shifts attention back again to where we began—to crisis. But this time, at last, the concept of crisis has some direct relevance. To be sure, Williams is in no way a failure when measured against most American playwrights now writing; and in the relatively brief history of serious American drama, his work has already taken a significant place, richer perhaps, more allusive, fluid, personal, and suggestive than the plays of any other American dramatist, Eugene O'Neill's included. Yet, however unfounded and unjust some of the charges against him may be, there is still a persistent, nagging doubt about how successful he has been when measured against himself—a very different matter.

In part, this is a critical stance taken frequently on dramatists. Sean O'Casey, for one, became heartily sick of the praise heaped on *Juno and the Paycock* and *The Plough and the Stars,* usually at the expense of his later, more experimental plays. And the same is undoubtedly true of Williams when he hears *The Glass Menagerie* and *A Streetcar Named Desire* discussed in reverent tones. Still, the ambitious nature of later work is never a way of insuring a success equal to the more modest claims of the early plays. The fact remains, even the best of the later plays—and here I place *Cat on a Hot Tin Roof, Suddenly Last Summer,* and *The Night of the Iguana*—miss the cohesion, force, and above all, the formal inevitability of *Menagerie* and *Streetcar.* And one cause of this is that his later work is paying a price for the stress on imprisonment and motion.

The price is one that ought to have been guessed from the beginning. In *Menagerie,* scenes followed one another, fading in and out behind the filmy scrim, almost before there was a chance to feel their presence. Similarly, the eleven scenes of *Streetcar,* though never arbitrary in their endings, seemed almost more compact and complete individually than the entire play itself. Williams, in short, was never so much an expert *play*wright as he was a superlative *scene*wright. He was always disappearing moments after he had arrived.

It is a strange problem for a dramatist. On one side, he seems to be writing in quicksilver—easy, direct, and emotional. On the other, he is cluttered and disjointed, cutting into the line of drama with sudden fits and fresh starts. It would take a genius at mental welding to link the first act of *Sweet Bird of Youth,* for example, with the second, and the second with the third. At best, it seems like one promising one-act duologue inexplicably tied to one distinctly unpromising bellowing contest. Williams is never less at home than when he is trying to be large, grand, and cohesive. For him, the great arching curve of epic or romantic drama is an alien line, whereas a tight succession of full stops represents a natural language for dramatic action.

The problem is, of course, more than a formal one. By itself, a drama of sharply punctuated successive scenes is not necessarily the opposite of good playwriting. If such were the case, Shakespeare and Molière would be more culpable than Williams, and we should not be turning to them for dramaturgical knowledge today. For Williams, the short play and the attenuated scene may be expressive of his pervasive themes, but they are also indications that, for all the motion, he is never really going anywhere; or to be more accurate, he is rarely moving artistically as far as his native powers have promised. Every writer has lapses, but plays as abortive as *Sweet Bird* represent something more serious, particularly in view of subsequent history.

Even as early as *Cat,* there was evidence that he was uncertain of more than technique. His sureness of touch seemed to be abandoning him. The subject of a play, as presented in the first act, faded into unsolved mystery in the second, like one of those favored fugitive characters of his, making a mark on life only to leave no trace behind. It is almost as if he hasn't wanted to change, or grow, or make an impression. He starts with Maggie the Cat, abandons her for Big Daddy, leaves Brick on his crutches far behind, and ends with two warring versions of the third act. *The Night of the Iguana* is all coming and going, hordes of fringe characters shouting or mumbling in German or Spanish, saved finally by one extended, trembling scene between Shannon and Hannah. Grandfather then finishes his poem—one symbol—and Shannon cuts loose the iguana—the other. The scene is like a resting place for the jumbled events, characters, and symbols of the play; a place, as the Carolers sing in *Slapstick Tragedy,* "that quiets the outraged heart." If it fails to convince, it is because there has been so much withdrawal, by which I mean writer's withdrawal, before it. There is another verse sung by the Carolers which tells more, perhaps, than Williams meant to say: in order to love, the lost will need to know

> How to walk upon fresh snow,
> And leave no footprint where they go . . .
> A miracle, a miracle!
> No footprint on new-fallen snow.

A miracle indeed, but not one by which a writer can move from one scene to another. There is no Virgin Birth in writing. The self intervenes between the pen and the thought. There is no other way.

Perhaps *Slapstick Tragedy* will mark the end of a desperate line. Two versions of *Milk Train* made heavy footprints on the gray Broadway snows. Something profoundly personal was hanging in its atmosphere, but it was hanging like Chris's mobile, a spinning, aimless, undefined abstraction in search of an idea. There was pain in the play, but no shape for it, no interior logic, no place to go.

The two plays that form *Slapstick Tragedy*—two plays otherwise unrelated by characters, narrative, or setting; two separate plays, nevertheless, trying to live under the umbrella of one title!—are different from *Milk Train*, not so much because they are more coherent, but because they are not pretending. As Williams put it: "a dash of pop art thrown in." The style is unsure, the symbols are shaky, the stories more remembered than dramatized, but at least the uncertainties have been frankly announced from the start. And curiously, in both of them, the portents of change may lie within their plotless tales: these are plays that describe human dislocation, but of a different order from before, a fragmentation lived in *one* place. Celeste and Trinket in *The Mutilated*, and Molly and the title character in *Gnädiges Fräulein*, are where they are to stay. It isn't necessary for them to move anywhere in order to feel the force of dislocation. Life, in these plays, sits at a jerking standstill, busy only with the memories of past motion.

About Williams, then, one can only hope. Nothing has really changed since Stark Young welcomed him so eloquently twenty years ago. He has proved his "astute stage sense" time and again. He has been always the charmed possessor of a vivid talent, "an intense, quivering clarity, all light and feeling." He has the gift of humor, a stinging laughter never very far from even his darkest visions. And unlike some of his contemporaries, he does not try to make a statement serve for a play. But his traveling heart has betrayed him, perhaps once too often. If, as Stark Young hoped, his intelligence could be "well anchored," held firmly but still floating, he might yet reach that golden moment finally touched by O'Neill in his last plays, that time when one's past is recollected in tranquillity, abandoned to memory, exchanged for present dangers, future doubts. Then, only then, might we know what we have missed, and what we have been waiting for. Only then will we know that the restless days were worth the failures and the loss.   *GR(September 1965)*

The Impossible Herbert Blau

I see too many plays, too many mealy productions, too many actors trained neither to play nor to dis*play,* only to indulge, too many mixed styles, too many misappropriated actions, too many actions turned into stasis, too much of the dull, lifeless, shallow, droning, thoughtless, earthly, timid stuff that most men are made of when faced with other men. Truth marches on. The art of theatre draws almost to a standstill. Enthralled by fanciful notions of reality, the American theatre has lost its sense of fancy.

Until now, the mind turned within itself has seemed to be the only mind in our theatre; or if not the only mind, surely the moving force. Whether reacting to McCarthyism or to the pleasurable discoveries that followed from acknowledgment of Freud, our theatre has certainly turned its back on the world; and in doing so, it has lagged dangerously behind the art practiced, the rage felt, and even the humors developed elsewhere. Meanwhile, it has been building new houses in communities where the business of art and the possibilities of theatre are as alien as toilets and jets are to Australian aborigines. Which is an outrageous way of stressing that nobody—neither audience nor players—has been prepared long enough and well enough for the staggering demands on imagination that are so much a part of collaborative art.

Into this atmosphere came Herbert Blau. For most of us, knowledge of his work with San Francisco's Actor's Workshop depended upon secondhand reports. Wherever these reports differed, they all shared one central view: that Blau was dedicated, complex, and possessed of a hard, ranging intelligence. Moreover, the repertory of plays chosen by him and his partner, Jules Irving, revealed a taste so far advanced as to suggest that all other resident companies were hanging back with the brutes. Over the years, one read open letters from Blau to his actors, letters written, it would seem, in the spilled blood of dead theatres and dandified artistes. They were outbursts, they were aware, they were political, they were visionary, concerned, anxious, ironic, and even dreamy. Indeed, if nothing else was clear, there could be no doubt that he saw his theatre as a microcosm, a wondrous rehearsal for the greatest production of them all: making the world outside a better one.

Nothing else, unfortunately, was half as clear. The letters, like the book that followed, could only be felt to be believed, for in the making of them Blau seemed to have neglected technique. They were, in short, unreadable.

*   *   *

During the run of Blau's opening production of Büchner's *Danton's Death* at the new Vivian Beaumont Theatre in Lincoln Center, a joke began to make the inevitable New York rounds:

FIRST MAN: You must see *Danton's Death,* especially the second act.
SECOND MAN: Why the second act?
FIRST MAN: Because it has become a collector's item. No one has seen it.

I saw it. Somewhere in the middle of the act, I scrawled a note to myself: "I don't want to have subtle parallels rammed into me anymore; I want to see an urgent event told for the sake of its own narrative strength."

*   *   *

Faced with unreadable prose, I cease to read. Faced with undramatized theatre, I see only as in an anguished dream and I hear the sound only of my own detachment. When less is occurring on stage than might happen in the privacy of study, the stage as such is pointless. No *idea* of a theatre can afford the luxury of boredom.

*   *   *

Within two pages in *The Impossible Theatre* Blau makes references to Khrushchev, Nietzsche, a San Francisco columnist, Mann's Aschenbach, Hannah Arendt, Janet Lewis, Othello, Desdemona, and Emilia, the Kafka-esque, King David, Jehovah, Luigi Pirandello, Artaud, Hamlet and Gertrude, Freud, the arms of Venus, Maya, Madison Avenue, the president's cabinet, the CIO and AEC, Organization Men, Levittown, the Lonely Crowd, Francis Gary Powers, the Senate Foreign Relations Committee, the CIA, Realpolitik, *Angst,* the Theatre of Cruelty, and the Void. Also—God.

"Amidst the glut of energy," he writes on these same pages, "and prodigal motion, the atomic-powered windlasses and assays of bias, the task of all the arts is to protect the residual will against the tyranny of multiplicity." If one's glutted, prodigal mind seemed to be shattered out of its residual will (wherever that resides) by so many proper nouns so improperly placed; if one, indeed, cannot really decide what any of this means, at least there is a clue in the last phrase quoted: Blau is stunning us into senselessness by way of his own nemesis—the tyranny of multiplicity.

It is not—putting it gently—a tyranny that works well in the theatre. Theatrical art knows little or nothing of philosophical bias. The artist turned outside of himself may be, by definition, a better man. He is not necessarily, by any stretch of multiple wills, a better artist. Blau's predecessor at Lincoln Center, Elia Kazan, was in thrall to the tyranny in his production last year of *The Changeling.* Where his work was actively hysterical, Blau's in *Danton* was hysterically passive. The distinctions, finally, erase themselves. Both productions were funny without seeming detailed, rhetorical without pas-

sion, activities without a central action. From opposing directions, the two directors arrived on the same threshold. The theatre, as always, is a ruthless
autocrat. It cares not a jot for good intentions.

Danton, in Blau's new version, says at one point, "For God's sake, you
want to hear me shout?" The answer, of course, is No. But in the inert person
of Alan Bergmann, he kept on shouting. And he wasn't alone. Everybody
shouted. The mob shouted. Robespierre shouted. St. Just shouted. If they
didn't shout—as in the cell scene—they crooned, the other side of the same
oratorical coin. "I demand that Legendre's motion be rejected," someone
shouts. But what *was* his motion? The lines kept passing one another like
proverbial ships in the night. They blew their whistles incessantly, but after a
time, only a passing bat could hear them. (Bats in the ocean? Why not? The
mixed metaphor has become, at Lincoln Center, a theatrical way of life.)
Shouting is, of course, only the surrogate villain. The evil genius behind it is
the absence of selection.

*   *   *

How odd it is that Blau, the enemy of what he calls "prodigal motion"
and "atomic-powered windlasses," should be so much in the power of machinery. True, it is his inheritance and, therefore, only to be borne. This is the
house that jackasses built, plushy blue on red lulling one to sleep even before
the production has a chance to do the same. Too large as an auditorium for a
varied repertory, too distantly deep for the sight lines of those sitting on the
side of the amphitheatre curve, too niminy-piminy in its apron thrust, it must
be the all-purpose theatre that absolutely defines lack of purpose. Added to
this, however, is a stage that moves relentlessly even in the teeth of a production that stolidly refuses to move at all. The twin revolves, as used by Blau
and also by his associate, Robert Symonds, in the second production, *The
Country Wife,* create a ghostly effect. Tribunals are whisked forward and
whisked back, covered with actors representing the mob, lawyers, and other
rhetoricians. The scene over, it is mysteriously pushed back, the unseen
agent of this action more interesting—and more terrifying—than anything
happening in the play. Perhaps the machinery is no more villainous, in itself,
than the shouting. Here, it seems to overwhelm a company already overwhelmed by the complex demands of its material. Powerless in their art,
Blau's actors become shifting pawns of backstage power. The spectacle is appalling: mechanical actors denied even their own entrances and exits, the
helpless led by heartlessness.

*   *   *

Sparkish, in *The Country Wife,* is described by Lucy as "a great bubble."
As acted by Robert Symonds, the play's director, he is neither bubble nor bau-
ble, only an actor in costume; not clothes—costume. A bubble, presumably,

takes some kind of airy, abandoned flight. Like the mistress in Shakespeare's Sonnet 130, when Symonds walks, he treads on the ground; and just as surely, when he speaks, music hath a far more pleasing sound. His voice emerges, both in this production and as Robespierre in *Danton,* as from a great distance, as if a bee were buzzing into a microphone from the bottom of a well.

He came from San Francisco to New York as the company's leading actor.

*   *   *

I have no memory of Pinchwife ever touching Margery in Symonds's production. Perhaps, indeed, he did brush a casual hand over her dress on occasion, particularly when urging her into her offstage chamber; but of lasciviousness, of the roughened, coarse, slavering sensuality that marks this filthy old man, there was not a tittle. One lingering impression left by both productions is that few, if any, in this company feel comfortable about *handling* other actors. Short of initiating a course in company orgies, there must be a way in which an extended ensemble can learn to *feel* one another's physical presence. It is a symptom, of course, more than an effect. What it describes is the neglect of presence in the company, the total absence of the here and now.

*   *   *

Elizabeth Huddle, in the role of Margery Pinchwife, is the first person to appear in a leading role in this theatre with the slightest suggestion of resources held—or not yet tapped— in reserve. Not surprisingly, she comes most alive when alone on stage. Spreading her legs under the table, making a wiggling character out of her feathered quill pen, letting it tickle her bosom at precisely the moment when she is almost completely abandoned to the delicious idea of an affair with Mr. Horner, she makes of the difficult letter scene the only sustained comedy of the evening. Surrounded by others, she almost fades into the decor. Alone, she is bright, cherubic, and relaxed, a sweet butterball bouncing for the fun of it. She may not be funny enough, but anything more extravagant within this casual, humorless atmosphere might easily have looked foolish and misplaced.

*   *   *

My notes, finally, are designed to be inconclusive. Long ago, Coleridge set an impossible task for the critic: to consider rather than to judge, to reflect rather than to decide. It may indeed be true that I see too many plays, that in traveling extensively to resident theatres in the past two years I have merely hardened my responsive arteries. But, as you might expect, I don't think so. Instead, I feel myself emerging with suggestive impressions: namely, that American directors may be, for the most part, weaker than their actors; that everybody needs more intensive technical training; that there is probably very little reason to believe that Americans are natural inheritors of European tradition; and that the best kind of theatre we are now performing is native, contemporary comedy.

Herbert Blau, known in New York now from his book and from the emblem he has undoubtedly set on two productions, may well be an eccentric exception to all the warnings and all the fears. For me, however, he seems currently to be a misplaced person, Saul Bellow's autodidact, Bummidge, gone completely haywire, a mind absorbing like a sponge and squeezing out dry. I do not disagree with his suggestion (at *Tulane Drama Review*'s Theatre Conference last November) that the theatre is a political institution, merely the sense he conveys in both word and action that he places the political first. Worse, I cannot imagine how he can make any artistic choice clear for actors when he cannot make any philosophical or political choices clear to me.

In his book, he speaks of "his acquired apocalyptic vision." He confesses next that he refrained from introducing it "wholesale" to the company "for fear I would be incoherent if not irrelevant." Multiplicity, I fear, must be a crushing burden. Somehow, it seems relevant to say that apocalyptic visions are best left to popes, angels, and other assorted troublemakers. In art, coherence and relevance can be left as afterthoughts only at the artist's grave personal risk.   *GR(Spring 1966)*

The Myth of Director's Theatre

At least three times during the maniacally hilarious events in Murray Shisgal's *Luv*, it is impossible to look at anything on stage except Alan Arkin's hands. The first time he is caressing Anne Jackson's head. The second he is waving and shaking his right hand, imploring her not to jump from the suspension bridge that is the setting for the play. The third moment, no less ordinary in outline than the others, comes as punctuation to an apparently casual and innocently intended suggestion: "We should get to know one another," he says, pausing for a trembling instant, "and then . . ." His hand sweeps out, as it were, from under those two last words, suspending both himself and the thought in mid-air. There it rests for a matter of seconds—a mobile question mark, a talking exclamation point, an animated comma capable of launching a thousand quips, attracting attention not by its beauty or unusual expressiveness but rather by its placement in time and space. Gesture, in these instances, becomes the actor.

In Molière's *Tartuffe* (the last production of what is already the old regime at the Lincoln Repertory Theatre), Joyce Ebert, playing Orgon's mightily abused young daughter, takes at least four occasions to hold her hands before her, gesturing always in the same way for attention, the hands fluttering loosely like paper tassels in a strong breeze. Provoking a respectful giggle the first time, this action thrice repeated leads only to diminishing returns, surely the primal threat to comic spirit, at all costs to be avoided by comedy directors. By the fourth time, one can only center upon the bony, sinuous delicacy of Ebert's hands, the moment and the play no longer half as interesting or relevant. In these instances, gesture masks the actress and submerges the play.

Not that Ebert is a fool and Arkin an instinctive genius. On the contrary. Ebert has in the past, and even in the opening statements of the girl in *Tartuffe*, shown boldness, sensibility, and inventiveness that need never give way to Arkin. Both stand, in their different fashions, for what is best in our best young actors: a certainty of attack, blessedly unneurotic, that is never afraid to yield individual psychology to the demands and suggestions of dramatic situation. On the evidence, there is no reason to believe that Ebert could not think of anything else to do with her hands. It is that she has not been helped by William Ball, her director, to do anything else. Where Mike Nichols seems to have led Arkin, Jackson, and Eli Wallach into bubbling passacaglias, funny fugues, and endless variations on Shisgal's theme of obsessive uncommittedness, Ball has led his actors into a cleverly arranged series of repetitions not so much on Molière's theme as on an alien's idea, three hundred years removed, of Molière's theatre.

"To present the necessary in the form of the accidental," said Hebbel, "that is the whole secret of dramatic style." He was speaking of dramatic writing, yet the same can be said of theatrical moment and direction, perhaps the comic event and directorial demand more than any other. Comedy presents several paradoxes: at once the most difficult form to write, act, or direct, it is nevertheless the form most easily scorned or disdained; frivolous, light, and antic as it must always appear, it can succeed at none of these unless its essential seriousness is both observed in action and deeply felt in spirit; mad on the surface, it is purposively sane beneath. While tragedy (or, more accurately, high seriousness) seems to rest comfortably in higher public estate, looking down its haughty nose at the allegedly lower form, comedy maintains itself by suggesting continual unsolved mysteries. Scorned or not, it survives even at a time in literary history, such as our own, when the "higher" form is constantly sent to an early grave. Men think they know tragedy, thus feeling free to respect it and bury it at will. Yet luckily they know they can't know comedy, and so its challenges persist.

Hebbel's perception casts refracted light on the special challenges of comedy. Any theatrical event, portentous or lilting, must give the appearance of happening that moment for the first time. The heavy load of tragedy, however, can afford to relax imperceptibly, if only because great weight suggests predictability anyway. Comedy, on the other hand, can never relax. The action that can be anticipated ceases, by definition, to be a comic one. Comedy is so difficult because it must always astound while still preparing the characters—*and* the audience—for another astonishment. Necessity is the mother of its invention, accident the constant midwife. It isn't only a matter of funny lines or tricky business, though these, when organically conceived and executed, fit neatly and helpfully into the comic texture. What is required for its fullest success is an interior freedom, a sense that whatever seems amusing now might be catastrophic later, a confident feeling that even certainty and finality have no endings. Obstacles, says comedy, are not so much broken as endured. Life, in its infinitely capacious way, goes on, precarious, amoral, ridiculous, indifferent, and—most astonishing of all—enjoyable.

This appreciation of accident for its own sake is what is missing from Ball's encounter with Molière and what is so extravagantly present in Nichols's surrender to an embellishment of Shisgal. The use of hands is only one way of centering on their differences. It is a viable clue in spite of its narrowness; a close, picky concern that mirrors critically the narrow momentary concerns that must occupy the director as he builds his house of comedy. More to the point, perhaps, are the performances of the leading actors and the uses to which they are put.

If the quality of comedy could be measured by the quantity of laughs, then Ball's Tartuffe, Michael O'Sullivan, might be counted every bit as successful in his style as the Wallachs and Arkin are in theirs. Pragmatic as theatrical art must necessarily be much of the time, it must still withstand the crass appeal, the amusing, though irrelevant, vulgarity. This, O'Sullivan's Tartuffe never does. In a voice that gurgles and growls when it isn't raucously shouting, with arms flailing like spinning windmills, and with spindly legs that seem always on the verge of collapsing under the weight of his own obviousness, O'Sullivan executes his choices well while insistently *ending* the play. Molière's subtitle is *The Impostor,* but it is beyond the most generous suspension of disbelief to imagine anyone being gulled by O'Sullivan.

Fundamental to drama is the fact that the characters on stage don't really know who or what they are. Evil, indeed, thinks itself good, and the clownish figure sees himself a god. When Olivier's unctuous Richard Crookback wooed and *won* Lady Anne, he was convincing to the audience because he so clearly might have convinced anyone on stage, so sensually and irresistably attractive was he through all his blazing nastiness. When O'Sullivan's Tartuffe woos Orgon's wife, Elmire, it is clear from the start that he could never win. Grotesque, thick-tongued, noisome, and uncannily reminiscent of Edna May Oliver hooting her way into Jane Austen's porcelained society, he is predictably the same in all his encounters. In consequence, while the laughs might conceivably go on forever, the play has no place to go at all.

No doubt O'Sullivan enjoys his own misplaced virtuosity. It isn't every day that a serious and talented actor can make a vaudeville exercise out of a seriously intended character. Given the terms of the production, however, the performance tells more about his director than it does about himself. Ball shares with too many of his colleagues a distrust of his material. He doesn't interpret what is there so much as he compensates for what he thinks is missing. At times this is not a hazard: for example, the charm he derives from moving the swaying Orgon family around the stage as if the people formed one body; or the brittle, delicate undertone he supplies by way of an occasional use of harpsichord accompaniment; or, finally, the startling humor he discovers in an inanimate object such as a broom that looks for an instant as if it could sweep on its own. Such simplicities, unfortunately, are not his common style. More typical is a taste for what can only be called the playing within plays, those bravura fantasies that engaged him so much more strongly than the harsh realities in his production two seasons ago of Pirandello's *Six Characters in Search of an Author,* and the bumbling playacting nonsense of the Pyramus and Thisbe scene in Benjamin Britten's *A Midsummer Night's Dream,* which he directed that year for the New York City Opera.

Tartuffe, of course, has no such set piece, a tactless omission on Molière's part redressed by Ball in an ingenious fashion flattering both to him and O'Sullivan, but crippling to the play. Where Molière prepares patiently for our first view of Tartuffe by keeping him off stage for the first two of his five acts, Ball brings him on at the very beginning, continuing to insert him regularly between scenes in a succession of dumb shows. In short, even before he opens his mouth to Molière's lines, O'Sullivan has several chances to trigger his infinite monotonies, thus ending the drama even earlier than it might have done had Ball permitted Tartuffe to enter at the moment planned by Molière. This is a *Tartuffe,* then, without dark harmonies. It is as if Bach were to be represented only by his ornaments, comedy seen here only as an entertaining collection of imposed grace notes.

The acting trio in *Luv,* by contrast, seems to be moving and decorating the text all the time, yet without push or imposition. Resisting easy bids for sympathy, each plays for the larger stakes available: savageries, unconscious humors, hysterias beneath the skin. Laughs spring from a miraculous combination of preparation and surprise. Shisgal's cool geometry, marked by a barely hidden cold loathing of domestic sentimentalities, is matched by the actors' manipulation of moments and physical details. The stamping of a foot, the crossing of a leg, the baring of teeth—all suggest more than what they are, and all are good for a laugh and, remarkably, a thought. Meanwhile, sight gags flood the sparsely decorated stage, but derived as they so clearly are from personalities and situation, they never sink the play. Indeed, for all its ingenuities, Nichols's direction of *Luv* succeeds so well because it still suggests things withheld. The wonder is that so little strain shows on something so well ordered.

On one side, then, effort; on the other, seeming ease. Ball impresses himself upon the play, Nichols impresses the play upon his actors. Ball invents too much, Nichols races past his innumerable inventions pretending there is more. One director of comedy constantly makes statements, the other suspends questions. It is a pity, finally, that Ball could not, at this time, heed his own words. "Bright-idea productions," he wrote over three years ago in reference to the superfluous rites regularly enacted over the battered body of Shakespeare, "indicate that the director admits that (1) he considers the play, as written, dull or incomprehensible, and that it desperately needs his help, or (2) he assumes his audience to be so dull in the wits that they require graphic illustrations, a directorial browbeating in order to understand and enjoy the work, or (3) he is personally bored with the basic theme of the work and probably considers his boredom universal."

*   *   *

Directing in our theatre remains the most fugitive art; this despite all the earnest tracts, notebooks, and suggested codifications that have tried to urge solidity into what is persistent evanescence. There are schools for acting, so many indeed that the laws of supply and demand in an overcrowded profession are mocked by their number. Similarly, classes and special units for playwrights seem to emerge wherever communities or universities pretend to care for theatre. But for directors there is almost nothing, no pretense, no huckstering teachers, no therapists, no laws, no Systems; which may, under the circumstances, be just as well. A disjointed, fragmented, necessarily impure art such as the theatre needs the reminder in one area that fragmentation—despite the appearances of schools and lessons—is the reality. The young director in our theatre learns from the start that where he may be needed he is certainly not wanted.

Yet for all his indignity and isolation, a suitable, though paradoxical, reward has awaited the patient and tenacious novice: in time he often became a leader in what is known popularly today as a *director's theatre,* the man in the end to whom everybody turns. His is not, of course, an orderly art, by which I mean that, once accepted, he is likely to be cast to type as often as he does the same to actors. Mike Nichols is now *the* light comedy director, the man who makes miracles out of miniatures, the natural inheritor of George Abbott's weightless mantle. Before him, Elia Kazan was the master of one side of Americana: what might be called *exotica neurotica,* the subhysterical, tense, limited view of life seen from a couch darkly. Positions are frozen at relatively early ages. One man is known for his ability to move actors with lightness and speed around the stage; another for his sense of lush, scrim-covered romance; still another for the grotesque; or archness; or domestic gentility; Shakespeare-black; Anouilh-rose; and on and on into narrower concerns. Renaissance prodigies—directors equipped for dramas, farces, two or three periods, working well with actors, commissioning organic, expressive design—are not merely few and far between, they simply are not. This may be both natural and desirable. In music, for example, the nineteenth-century romanticist is rarely adept at the baroque or the atonal. People are specialists usually for a reason: what they do well they know they can do better.

Even so, the estate of directing, so firmly entrenched, so much the maker of manners, is in a sorry condition that squares uneasily with the power it has assumed over dramatic art. The arguments for or against a director's theatre, an actor's theatre, or a playwright's theatre are, of course, futile, absurd, and away from the point. Forgotten in them is the central need: the drama's theatre, that place where all gestures and actions converge into a singular occurrence recognizable as an act belonging only to that space. The source, we know, is the dramatist, the medium is the actor and the properties around him, the interpreter and organizer is the director. Between the dramatist's impulse for theatre art and the actual realization of that impulse lie countless mediators, pressing vitally individual impurities into an event that must finally appear whole, inevitable, and commandingly pure. While the director represents, in a sense, the master mediator, he is also something more: a receding presence, the artist who is felt most when his hand is seen least. And it is on this point that the director's theatre, particularly in the United States, has diverged.

Having taken almost full command, it produces only the impurities, calling attention primarily to itself, stressing not the occasional genius of the playwright but the ingenuity of the director, manipulating rather than drawing upon the actor, placing sets rather than designs upon the stage. This is not only a matter of warring egos or arguable differences, it is a matter of attitude. The director's theatre, by definition, misplaces the desired end by redefining the meaning of drama and theatre. Its first error, not easily hidden by cleverness, is that it barely approaches the playwright. At its best it makes scattered moments of feeling, light, sound, and sense merge into something ineffably beautiful, precisely right, where statement and shape are one. At its worst—by now what is common and expected—it seems to be caught in frenzy, busily striking out in all directions for an effect and an impression not necessarily related to the play. Missing more often than not is a feeling for all the elements not immediately *visible* on stage: the spaces between words, the polyphonic lines of almost any considered text, echoes acting as reminders and prophets, the relationships in theatrical performance between thought, words, objects, persons, light, shape, and time. For the lucky break of a flashing moment, the director's theatre will sacrifice the resonant world of a play.

Its history has been rehearsed often enough. A few representative names, flourishing at their highest in the fifties, tell all: Elia Kazan, Joshua Logan, Tyrone Guthrie, Peter Glenville. Not that they should be cited for malice or inordinate ambition. Conditions summoned them just as surely as they served conditions. They were simply the right men—talented, aggressive, adaptable—at an unfortunate time; a time when everybody else was abdicating, a time when playwrights were disappearing into movie sales and actors were retiring to school. It was impossible to think of certain shows going on without certain directors: Williams needed Kazan for his universal sex appeal and the reconstruction of his third act; Miller renounced Kazan politically and lost some identity theatrically; Logan gave Mary Martin and William Inge a lift into sensual glory, his kingdom for a belly dance; Guthrie played hit-and-run driver with everybody from Marlowe to Paddy Chayefsky, dropping theatres and frivolities like so many pebbles in the wilderness; and Glenville moved from elegant stage to chichi screen as if *Rashomon* and *Becket* couldn't possibly have happened on separate tables. Every director stamped a manner on stage, often at the expense of an apt and relevant style. Directors were the new theatrical royalty. The king might have been a little bit dead, but long live the king.

Thus, the mid-sixties arrived, a moment of retrenchment, an instant of educated doubt. In the middle of it, one can see the portents of change, the emblems of refinement. Nobody trusts the doctor-director anymore, nobody wants a wizard. Williams can't live with him, and, like any errant spouse, he can't live without him. Miller can rule him, but he can substitute only pose and posture, the fine points of detachment and sensibility proving elusive. Logan can repeat his sexy tricks, but not his commercial success. Guthrie can continue—but only just—to play parlor games with masters. Kazan, finally, can play martyr to a board of directors, a Reinhardt manqué betrayed by absence of taste, scope, and penetration.

The death knell of the director's theatre was sounded this season by Kazan's incredibly awful production of Middleton and Rowley's *The Changeling,* his grotesquely comic exit line from the management of the Lincoln Repertory Theatre, his first murder of dead dramatists, and thus his first crime against the unprotected. As in his weirdly boring production of *After the Fall,* the stage design looked as if it was in agonized, cluttered search for a proscenium, the first two scenes, in fact, being played—locked would be a better word—on the forestage and semicircle down front and center. The play is supposed to chronicle the somnambulistic collapse of Beatrice's virginal innocence, yet when she was first seen, she hit a blind beggar with her beads, in one stroke making clarity and development impossible, no more virginal than Ava Gardner in a Hemingway jungle. Failing psychology, voice, or a sense of period, could nobody have taken a moment to give her line readings? "To such," runs one line, "gold tastes like angel food," clearly referring to the way in which certain people take to gold. But not to Kazan's Beatrice: to her, a breath after "such" would keep her too far away from the end of a gruesome evening; and so, what tasted like angel food was "such gold," leaving the people in the reference to fend for their very absent selves. All that could be worse—a hollow mirror turning up later as a real one, helpless hands always illustrating lines, the players in Rowley's comic subplot casting knowing winks to the audience, the Bedlam scenes danced as if amateur Apaches had just been hired for a low-budget Western romp around the totem pole, actors followed by spotlights in the dark scenes—all these and more were hideously and embarrassingly present.

It was as ignominious and cruel a death scene as anyone could have imagined, matched only by Joseph Anthony's massacre of Saul Bellow's first produced play on Broadway, *The Last Analysis*. Here again the play was simply a peg on which to hang a string of directorial whims: the casting of melancholics for clowns, New Englanders for Brooklynites, heavies for heroes. Astonishingly, nothing worked. Only through closed eyes could Bellow's play be "seen": listening to his blowzy rhetoric (something I feel like calling Elizabethan-Yiddish), peopling the imagined stage by way of one's own imagination, guessing blindly at what Bellow must have envisioned. A frenetic, funny, passionately serious play concerning the ridiculous, yet noble, wishful thinkings surrounding American dreams, it was played by a strutting and screaming cast as if subtlety had gone out of fashion. The set looked like a junkyard, the light fantastic wit was moved around the stage as if it were heavy furniture, and reflective moments were passed with lightning speed almost in the hope that they wouldn't be noticed.

So ran the elders. The younger directors—Ball even in his evasions and self-betrayals, Nichols in his exquisitely detailed comic etchings, and Jonathan Miller in his somewhat shy, ceremonious confrontation with the stately line of Robert Lowell's *The Old Glory*—showed, at the least, a sense of proportion, a gift for placing themselves, a talent for humility. Miller, it is true, received more homage than he yet merits, possibly because the old pros had been directing so poorly by contrast, or perhaps for his alliance with a superb poet's introduction to our theatre. But, given the recent past fraught with so much directorial chaos, so much frantic irrelevance, it is not surprising that this should happen. Lowell's adaptations of Hawthorne and Melville stories, written in spare, measured verse, needed more pointing, more rhythm, and a sharper sense of character. If the entire vision was to be realized, a tougher theatrical technician might have served better, someone with a firmer grasp on the economies available to theatrical development. Lowell wrote three plays designed to be played together, each supporting and amplifying the others, casting different shades of light on the central theme of America's stained, faded innocence. It was meant, presumably, to be three separate acts finally forming a whole. As it happened, Miller could manage only two of the plays within a reasonable playing span; then too he saved everything for a last-minute explosion, content before that with an imposed political cartoon for the first play (*My Kinsman, Major Molineux*)—madly rushed, coy, and inappropriate—and a languid, heavy, uninflected air for most of the second (*Benito Cereno*). Still, he did not press hard nor did he decorate the stage with substitutes for thought or imagination. Making a virtue out of inexperience, he did not try for more than he could currently manage. Reticence was the watchword, modesty the key.

It's a useful key, one that appears already to be opening some doors in our somewhat closed-shop theatre. Optimism, I admit, sits uncomfortably upon my brow. One season in New York, after all, differs little from another. Yet the signs are there. Events that look purely social, political, or economic—such as the ticket scandals on Broadway, the prevalence of low comedies and dull musicals, and the Kazan-Whitehead disaster at Lincoln Center—have at their base a genuine unrest in the community of artists. Theatre, even of the ruthlessly pragmatic American breed, can lag behind the other arts only so long. When the artist's private despair becomes society's public scandal, it is usually society that adapts. Commerce, if it does nothing else that's positive, bears clumsiness, open vulgarity, egomania, and all the cumulative signs of failure even less patiently than art.   *GR(February 1965)*

Auschwitz and the Illusion of Docudrama

According to the transcripts of the Trial of Mulka and Others, the occasion on which Germans examined the crimes of Auschwitz for the first time within German legal structure, one of the judges asked the accused "to reflect most earnestly whether you do not wish to break, at this last minute, the ice of silence." No one wished. No one broke. The essential silence was maintained, filtered through an automatic language of detachment. Where blood had once been their argument, now it was ice. Germany's frozen warriors, these were twenty-two men unwilling to be guilty alone. Implicit in their silence was the wish to turn on their accusers a phrase that has become familiar to everyone: "We are all guilty." Implicit in the court's sentence was the equally familiar, lofty response, at once unanswerable and paralyzing: "Perhaps, but some are more guilty than others."

Breaking the ice of silence is, if not the only business of the dramatist, surely one of his imperatives. It is a silence, however, that can be broken only from within. Edging his way into this observation, more than two years before his presentation of the Mulka and Others trial as *The Investigation,* Peter Weiss said that "it is most important that a production [of any play] should express a play's dualism." Earlier, he had referred to a novel of his which, though finished, he could view only as a fragment. "It is an interior monologue," he said, "and an interior monologue goes on as long as one lives." There is, of course, no dualism in these remarks. Weiss was saying over two years ago what he would never permit himself to say today. The experience of a play, he was suggesting, may be directed toward the arguments of other people, but dramatic pressure is derived from the arguments sealed into the mind of someone alone.

As a man alone, Weiss first chose painting. Of all the oddities beginning to converge upon his public stance, the strangest, perhaps, is that he presents himself so firmly—and now famously—as a dramatist. Behind the image, surely, lies something like a submerged experiment. Weiss, after all, though not a young man (he is in his middle fifties), is very much a young playwright. His first teacher, indeed his first model, was Breughel, followed quickly by an assortment of fantasists, men whose work and lives could be described in common jargon as theatrical or dramatic, but who worked with materials different from or even alien to the actual language of theatre. In his teens, there was Hermann Hesse. Later, he felt himself influenced by people such as Max Ernst, Salvador Dali, Franz Kafka, and in yet another reversal of taste and inclination, Henry Miller. His career reads like a map of Europe and a survey of the verbal and visual arts: once a Czech citizen, he writes in German and lives in Sweden; once a painter, he wrote novels, directed his own "underground" films, and now makes a show of writing plays. It would probably not be out of character for him to move now from Stockholm to Moscow, and from plays to symphonic dramas. A man with a thousand talented faces, Weiss seems to be skimming the surfaces of art while casting a watchful eye over its shifting fashions. That he is a serious explorer of what might be called the deeper surfaces goes without saying. In his travels he has at least admitted the fixed, unremitting fact of the interior monologue. Clearly, however, he is committed to wandering, a style of living that leaves only the narrowest of echo chambers for the voices inside.

There is little way of knowing what might have been. Weiss's paintings, if they are known at all, are certainly not as available as his two plays, *Marat-Sade* and *The Investigation*. His novels, too, are a relatively German secret, though his *Abschied von den Eltern* was published here in 1963 as *Leavetaking*. Those of his films seen here last winter proved to be little more than fragmented games, as if Ingmar Bergman had been trapped feverishly in Dr. Caligari's cabinet. It was possible to link them with the imagination behind *Marat-Sade* only in terms of the concern with madness in one of them. Tics within the soul, the gesture broken only by afterthought, the relentlessly open eye staring only at itself: these were Weiss's characteristic images, notations not of loneliness, but of a brain detaching itself from alien intrusions.

Marat-Sade, even apart from Peter Brook's chilling inventions, those startling actions quite often deliberately not suited to the words, had already provided similar clues. Here, as Brook liked to put it, was density of experience. Like a three- or even four-part fugue, the separated dramas had to impress themselves into one event: the play about Corday's murder of Marat, the play about the asylum of Charenton, and the play about social revolution all surrounding the play about Marat's philosophical quarrel with Sade (as written by Sade!). This last is, by transparent deduction, the play about Weiss's mind. The quality of mind mattered less than the fact that it was willing to use itself, to *play* itself out—a good literal reason for its successful life in the theatre, *any* theatre in *any* production. The interior monologue was, in short, being honored, not denied.

With *The Investigation,* however, the denial is astonishingly absolute. The central event is a place remembered: Auschwitz. The central action is the process of remembering: affirmations and denials. The eye behind the action is meant to be, in effect, the hand of a reporter, presenting the trial itself, truth unadorned. He cuts, selects, and edits the voices of other people; and he does so, presumably, less from respect for his idea of documentary than from awe before the horrors of the event. There is no other way, he seems to be saying. Anything more selective—which is to say, anything more from himself, any more art—would defeat the purpose and vulgarize the event.

As presented under Ulu Grosbard's direction, the most telling defeat is dealt to the reporter. For a start, unadorned truth is a lie. The living newspaper—that is, the one outside of the theatre—pays daily witness to the improbability that the naked sentence will ever tell the same fact to different people; just as even the most warmly motivated relationship will be shaken for a moment by the discovery that the objectively seen event was seen differently by the other. If Weiss, therefore, was trying to pretend that, once in a theatre, he needn't be trapped in theatricality, he was miserably mistaken. Art can contain objective reality even less comfortably than life. The smallest choice, no matter how it would like to be seen, remains a choice. Choose to enter the theatre, whether director or audience, and you are in the insistent presence of art. That it may be good or bad art isn't the first issue. That it isn't life, is.

More confusing is Weiss's misreading of documentary as a legitimate, expressive form. At its best, when the camera rather than the writer is the eye, it is still only a secondary, highly mediated, manner of seeing. A documentary film about war, for example, shows real soldiers at war. The stage, obviously, can do nothing of the kind; and this is, of course, the origin of its separation from the realities of both film and life. Thus, when Weiss and Grosbard collaborate in the fiction that documentary reality is possible on stage, they are bringing us to neither tears nor thoughts, rather they are reducing us to a numbing sense of disbelief.

Inevitably, theatre intervenes between the recitation of facts and the way they can be received. The tiniest gesture, the briefest pause, the most casual gaze beyond the proscenium have a way of inflating themselves into portraits, moments, even statements, none of them necessarily in line with the thrust away from decoration, comment, or interpretation. Worse, the ponderous laboring of behavioral truth on the part of all the actors in Grosbard's production succeeds only in blurring available reality. An American actor's sense memory exercise put to the service of a memory beyond the power of our ordinary senses is finally just a conceit, designed—if not calculated—to place the emphasis where it cannot belong in such a presentation: namely, on the relative skills of the actor. The better actor might conceivably offer the more persuasive document. Yet I doubt it. Good or bad—and here the acting is almost uniformly bad, bad in the sense that it is sententious, self-conscious, heavily illustrative—it would still be acting. Under the lights, there must still be make-up. As a produced play, there must still be a designed environment; in this case, a courtroom almost ravishing in appearance, a grouping of cells for each actor in the shape of a honeycomb, all of it in sleek, paneled surroundings of gorgeous blond wood. Finally, there must still be intermissions between the acts, a convention left as unmoved as the spectator by the added conceit of calling them ten-minute recesses.

Nothing is more dismaying now than playing the rating game with such material. Critical custom suggests a conclusion at this point, a yes, no, or maybe. Faced with the unspeakable event of Auschwitz, one is finally driven to speaking of art. I am left not merely bored by the "play"; I feel pole-axed by frustration, defeated even before having had a chance to begin any effort I might make simply to *know* Auschwitz. I have been given an immobilized list of facts, a droning succession of words. But it is a communal cheat. The theatre has been trying to be everything but itself, and in so doing, it has left the most agonized moment in human history without an image. Drama, finally, is not recorded. It is an act of the imagination, the willingness of a mind to break the icy silence.   *GR(November 1966)*

Olivier's Vaulting Art

Laurence Olivier's Othello is clearly an actor's creation, a triumph for the special quality of theatrical occasion. This was true when I saw it last year in London, and remarkably, it is no less true on RCA's new recording. There is a paradox here: a recording, a moment for the ear, suddenly seems like theatre, a moment for all the senses. It is a reminder that the ear can open worlds. It is, indeed, a way of *knowing*.

Although recorded in a studio, this *Othello* has none of the defects suggested by packaged and homogenized studio recordings. A wise compromise has been drawn between "live" and hermetically sealed performance. Olivier and his National Theatre company, acting before hidden microphones, freely used their original stage blocking, even to the point of bringing props and costumes with them, reproducing as closely as possible the pressures and momentum of actual production. The absence of formal audience is scarcely felt; nothing is cool, nothing is detached; never is the performance far away from the urgency usually given to it by direct, human response. Whatever may have been lost away from an audience is recovered by the latitude and flexibility offered by the studio: no accidents, no lapses, indeed a firmness of outline, a driving confidence that literally seduce one into the heated extravagance of Shakespeare's Cyprus. Where stereo has so often been a trap, ruling the shape and sound of performance, here it is the servant of a life already formed, a superbly managed eavesdropper of a human event. The listener stages the play in his mind's eye; the actors prowl unobserved, as it were, through the corridors of Shakespeare's awesome imagination.

Othello has an odd history in the theatre. Of the four major tragedies, it is meant to be the easiest to produce, the one most available to comfortable interpretation, the one least likely to fail because of an inadequate actor, a dull design, or an uninventive director. *Hamlet,* we are told, is a study in ambiguities, *Lear* an encounter with the heavens, and *Macbeth* a tragedy without a hero—a hard, unyielding play which, in its definitions, alienates the most fundamental sympathies. *Othello,* in contrast, is said to be a simple melodrama that hangs upon a handkerchief, a domestic tragedy of the human heart, an immediately gripping tale of an exotic but always recognizable jealousy. Yet for all the deceptive simplicity of its plot, for all the transparent ease with which Iago's poison invades Othello's reason, the play has had less success—at least in this century—than several *Hamlets*, *Lears*, and even *Macbeths*. It has, in fact, confounded the British in performance since Kean proved to be more adept with Iago than Othello. The most notable Moor, strangely, was Tommaso Salvini, touring in the part during the late nineteenth century, and playing it, of course, in his native Italian. No wonder, then, that Verdi's *Otello* has often seemed a better *drama.*

Olivier's achievement can be marked in a phrase: he has rescued the drama from Iago. At the heart of the play's erratic theatre history lies the fact that Iago's villainy in action can easily be more subtly persuasive, more attractive even, than Othello's seeming nonresistance to it. "O fool, fool, fool," cries Othello when truth is upon him, and it is difficult—in most performances—not to concur. Here, however, balance is restored.

One of the sources for this necessary reversal is the clear stress Olivier and his colleagues place on the play's military background. This is the story of a *general,* an enormously gifted leader born to command. But as leadership is the top of his virtue, so is it the root of his flaw. What goes up and stays up—too high, almost, for its own good, too certain of its Olympian presence— must perforce come down. Olivier's Othello commands the play by giving it a fatal calm from the start, a jocular arrogance and casual assurance that clearly hide as much from himself as they hide from others. A voluptuary in love and war, a foreign sensualist living in a peace that others—Desdemona's father, for one—would like to deny him, he is doomed by the power of his senses. Absorbed in them as he is, it remains only for time and the insinuations of Iago to turn absorption into anguish, to move consuming love into unquestioned hate.

Such an Othello demands a Iago away from custom. And this Frank Finlay, no doubt urged by the directorial sense of John Dexter, provides. The contrast with Othello could not be more striking. Where Othello is lofty, Iago is only haughty; where Othello commands in stately measures, Iago grovels and sidesteps. It is like the difference between the earth and a weed. Evil here is only an unplanned reaction, a way of being ruled by the smallest events. Touched with the tongue of a rough sergeant, Finlay's Iago is an ordinary man, and as such, all the more terrifying and credible. Charmless and arid, he persuades by presenting so little to beware. This may not be a popular way of playing Iago or of placing him in the fabric of Othello's tragedy, but surely it is closer to the reality of the play than a Iago of forced wit and open cruelty.

Perhaps more than anything else, this production suggests that the question of action in *Othello* has previously been answered only on surface evidence. Iago acts, it has been said, whereas Othello is acted upon. And so it would seem: the master pulls the puppet's strings. But neither Shakespeare nor existence rests so simplistically on such extremes. Othello, like so many of Shakespeare's heroes (Hamlet, Cleopatra, Richard III, Timon, and Leontes), is something of an actor, a man aware of role, a creature caught by the pleasure and fantasy of *acting out* an emotion upon the slightest hint. When the acting becomes real, however, he is finished.

It is this part of him, coupled with its corollary—his qualities as poet—to which Olivier rises with the most extraordinary, titanic force. With the invaluable support of Maggie Smith's Desdemona—sweet, delicate, yet with a voice that slices air, every inch a new woman—and of Joyce Redman's strongly assertive, passionately involved, and vocally ripe Emilia, Olivier rides the play as if he were on the crest of a huge tidal wave, now dipping, now soaring, but always holding fast to the heaving, forward surge. William Hazlitt felt that to play the part "to the height of the poetical conception," the actor must have the idea of "a majestic serpent wounded, writhing under its pain, stung to madness, and attempting by sudden darts, or coiling up its whole force, to wreak its vengeance on those about it, and falling at last a mighty victim under the redoubled strokes of its assailants."

Olivier's serpent, if we are to believe our ears, has the coiling power of a singer with three octaves in the voice, joined to the wounded majesty of a man whose nerves and senses, once exposed, can never be covered again. He seizes words and stretches sounds as if they were huge stones that had been waiting for centuries to be lifted from such a noble throat as his. From the resonant caress of his whisper to the towering commotion of his roar, he is never less than a splendid thoroughbred. But finally, it is his convulsive, strangled agony that hurts the most ("O Desdemona, Desdemona dead!" or "The pity of it, Iago"). Whether it be genius, instinct, planning or—as I believe—an indefinable confluence of all three, this Othello is certainly the summit of a great actor's vaulting art.

GR(December 1964)

What Would You Think If I Sang out of Tune?

Less than ten years ago, upon the occasion of Brendan Behan's *The Hostage,* Kenneth Tynan, momentarily exhausted by the categorical imperatives of modern criticism, heaved a breathless, aphoristic sigh, declaring that, "from a critic's point of view, the history of twentieth-century drama is the history of a collapsing vocabulary." Cleverness wedded to accuracy is not common in criticism. One might be forgiven, then, a short pause for the sound of one finger clapping. When a critic inclines toward confession, when he suggests a form of defeat, most readers have a right to feel faint heartbeats of triumph. The history of twentieth-century criticism, after all, will surely be the history of contrived vocabulary, the confrontation of real collapse by feigned invention.

Criticism, good or bad, has always required its special phrases, its apt categories, those molded chapter headings which seem to bring order into the persistently vagrant world of art. The reason for this condition is plain: digging into clay, listening to his voices, making line, color, and shape on a blank sheet of paper, the artist is playing Rhett to the critic's Scarlett; frankly, he doesn't give a damn. The critic, of course, does. Dialogue, clearly, is out of the question. Yet the critic, moved by objects, touched with an everlasting lust for reason, persuaded that nothing has quite happened until he has given it chronicle history, has to talk to someone, if only to turn the natural aggression of the artist into a rational defense of art. The measure of his success— always relative, always grudging—is the use to which he puts the inevitable greed for categories.

Tynan's tentative lapse into oblique confession was one of many gestures he had always been making toward liberation from labels. As he said in the same review of *The Hostage,* "I use the word [play] advisedly . . . the old pigeon-holes will no longer serve." (It catches one short to realize that he is referring to *The Hostage,* certainly an easy fit into the old pigeonhole today, not "well-made," perhaps, but very definitely a *play.*) All would have gone well had he not drifted effortlessly into the enemy camp. "Polonius," he went on to say, "did not know the half of it: a modern play can, if it wishes, be tragical-comical - historical - pastoral - farcical - satirical - operatical - musical - music-hall, in any combination or all at the same time. And it is only because we have short memories that we forget that a phrase already exists to cover all these seemingly disparate breeds . . . Commedia dell'Arte." Which is to say, Don't feel too uneasy, there's a phrase for everything, and if you can't find a new one for the occasion, just reach back for the old. He might just as well have called upon the word *tradition,* or, at the least, borrowed the thought behind Harold Rosenberg's ingeniously apt title, *The Tradition of the New.* Most of us are aware by now that we come from a very brief line of ancestors, all making an acceptance for every three or four rejections, yet all unwilling to be typed, titled, or bound in neat little boxes. The search isn't for identity, and surely not for identifications. It is for the liberty to be.

So much, then, for at least one critic. The artist, if he's any good, suffers such surrenders less easily. At the time *Marat-Sade* was such a popular success on Broadway, and after living through panel discussions and articles on the Beckettian in *Lear* and the Artaudian in Peter Weiss, Peter Brook was heard to say that he would be content never to hear of Jan Kott or Theatre of Cruelty again (Kott representing the label for Brook's production of *Lear*). To this, any of us at any given moment of frustration might wish to add the Absurd, Alienation, and without a second thought, all the old holes for all the old pigeons: Naturalism, Realism, Expressionism, Epic, and anything you might care to name. Brook's concern is with the implications of work, the open constructions that lend a mind freedom to touch itself, the inner life that reaches for form, any form, to express what is new within.

The most open construction available is theatre. One knows this intuitively by observing the compulsions of the other arts. At one time or another, successfully or unsuccessfully, with grace or clumsiness, the painters, poets, sculptors, and musicians try to join. Some element confining in their own discipline leads them, often with heads held rigidly high from condescension and noses cocked primly to the receiving aesthetic air, into the expansive spaces of theatre. Of late, the painters in particular have been declaring through their own work and their safaris into theatrical events, theatre environments, Happenings, and what-they-will that they have the answers. Theatre, as it has been known for centuries, a structure observing the unities of time, place, and action, is obsolete for the rather obvious reason that the mirror held up to nature shows no unity in time, place, or action. Character, like God (and, so it would seem, Love) before it, is dead.

One, like myself, who is not competent to preside over the corpses of God and Love, is nevertheless aware enough, and competent, to say that the painters are correct about time, place, character, and action. I would amend their assertion, perhaps, by saying that these elements are not so much dead as living differently. Unity, as such, is no longer possible, at least insofar as art is expected to reflect the cracked mirror of life. One of the primary modern sources of dramatic energy lies in the acknowledgment that fragmentation, speed, and refracted vision are present daily realities for everyone. A decade ago in London, just before Behan, there was a young American actor, married to an Englishwoman, who was continually in search of a job. It was his custom to make the rounds late in the day, admit early defeat, and bring himself languidly into the sandwich bar of the Arts Theatre Club, where actors he knew were sure to be congregating. It was during the hours between the afternoon closings of pubs and the evening's opening. One day, seemingly no different from the others, he wandered in, his neatly creased clothes suggesting Brummell, his eyes sagging from loss, and announced that he had been to the dentist. "You can build a whole day," he said, "on a dentist's appointment."

Shakespeare, Beckett, Ionesco, even the painters, would have understood the scene in an instant. Hamlet, for one, wished that he could be confined in a nutshell, counting himself king of infinite space. No less modern than Estragon, Hamm, or Krapp, he was made by his dramatist to see that real life occurred within the infinite spaces of his brain. The dentist's appointment is the activity, the action is in the responsive movements of the mind. The day is built around the unity of the appointment, yet the appointment itself does nothing to unify the day. When one lives as sovereign of infinite space, almost anything can happen, and often does: hence drama.

Theatre, however, is another matter, a twisted variation, or embellishment, of the same theme. Tangible, sensual, very much of the immediate moment, it occurs only for one reason: to bring a group of people together for a commonly received experience. Its spaces are infinite; its designs, both visual and polemic, intimate. The story it has to tell need not have a beginning, middle, or an end, but it must have a sense of story, that primitive urge within all of us to tell, demonstrate, mimic, or *act out* the events that most vividly concern us. Brecht, in yet another gesture that confounded the popular view of him as an austere propagandist, said something to the effect that first comes the narrative. When a man alone performs—either alone or in company—the events of a narrative, however fragmented, he is making theatre.

Drama and theatre are obsolete, then, only in proportion to their distance from the nutshell and the narrative. Without closeness to dream and the willingness to make play of it, there is nothing. That the painters, etc., are right, that the theatre commonly presented is obsolete, removed from current sense of reality, lodged firmly in the conceits of irrelevant forms, and slavishly enthralled by the old views of character, time, place, and action; that these premises are correct should surely be said, by now, without question. To say so, however, is not to undermine the possibilities of theatre. The theatres we enter today are almost always guaranteed to bore simply because they are so frantically boring from within, borrowing the old forms and styles, usually without skill or inventiveness, and playing mindlessly to a society of sleep-walkers. Communal experience is not possible without a community. More than that, even if there is a negatively inspired community, it must be willing to enter communion in the spirit of disclosure, in order to confirm, where necessary, its deepest fears, its darkest secrets. This, our theatre and its audience have been unwilling to do.

There are, of course, other ways of saying much the same. Obituaries of theatre customarily point to film as a more vital, relevant, and even theatrical form of art. Yet, even as this can be said to be true, it is saying more about some of the people who make films than it is saying about film itself. The medium is the message, and therefore successful, only insofar as it is willing to be itself, to use its own properties; and, in this respect, film has been making a more distinguished record than theatre. If the length and breadth of the community had anything to do with aesthetic success, then surely television would suggest even more of a challenge to theatre than film. But not even the wash from a thoroughly McLuhanized brain would be willing to say that. Theatre is lagging not because it plays to a smaller community than it has in the past, but because it is playing to an audience complicit in its own corruptions, an audience busily confirming outer illusions rather than inner suspicions.

It is lagging, too, because it is so totally embalmed in the quicksands of production; by which I do not mean *only* the business of business, but, more seriously, the business of mounting texts on a platform, whether shielded by the old fourth wall or surrounded (in part) by the audience. The shape of stages barely matters at a time when the experience on stages is so relentlessly remote from the experience of our lives. What do matter are the assumptions behind production. These are, very briefly, that theatre is the result of mating a text to a director, designer, and a group of actors, each of whom does his job. In the best circumstances, these people respect each other and simply get on with their respective tasks, meeting almost daily for a period of, let us say, four to twelve weeks, eventually presenting what they like to think of as finished work. Thereafter, if what they present seems to touch a lost chord in the collective unconscious of a group called audience, this finished work proceeds in its petty paces either nightly or, if circumstances permit, in rotating repertory, eventually coming to a finish in much the same shape or disguise with which it began its frozen life. In short, the assumptions and motivations of production both point in the same direction, namely to an unchanging event. How can this condition be changed? My first impulse is to say, I don't know. Yet for all the refreshing candor of such a statement, it would not be entirely persuasive, since I have pointed a rather scolding finger at the idea of production itself. The larger question might run somewhat as follows: are enough people sufficiently bored by the set of relationships defined by production and the formal hours of traffic on our stages so that a set of changes can be seriously initiated? To this, of course, I have to say, I don't know. It is possible,

nevertheless, to spy several clues in the dark underbrush of recent experience. If I say here, after what will be recognized as a siege of great personal
restraint, that one of the richest clues lies in a recent presentation of the Beatles, then I hope it will be possible to double back on my premises while developing the argument that theatre and drama are, as ever, here to stay. It is production that is the enemy, and the Beatles suggest one metaphor, among
many possibilities, for the necessary change.

One matter should be disposed of before pressing on with my suspicions.
Boredom, in current theatre, is not only an issue for the audience. On the contrary, the wiser audience, sniffing the smell of old bones in theatrical air, has a
very precise and easy action at its disposal; an action, miraculously, that is
really described by a noun: the exit. It should be obvious, in any case, that the
audience accustomed to making entrances into the lobbies of the land is not
the audience to which I am referring. My audience has learned not to enter;
the other audience keeps going back for more. John Arden, one of Britain's
more explorative and engaging young dramatists, once said that theatre can
never change society, all it can hope to do is confirm people in what they are
beginning to feel. Those couples swarming into the subscription seats of Seat-
tle's, Houston's, Washington's, and New Haven's theatres, and those proverbial weary businessmen who sink their heavy weights into the plush front
rows on West 45th Street are not going for such confirmation. Rather are they
seeking affirmation of their own solutions, and confirmation of their unshak-
able, though borrowed, convictions. Somebody once suggested that the place
for the tired businessman is in bed. Such a proposition might be usefully
amended by saying that the place from which the best audience is likely to
emerge is one where bed is more than just a place to sleep.

For the laborers in theatre, whether playwrights, directors, actors, or designers (not written in any particular, and therefore insidious, order), the issue of boredom, while it may not always be noticed by them, is central to their
imaginative lives. Actors, for example, give at least two performances every
night, the one on stage, the other in the dressing room. The routine in the latter, unfortunately like the routine on the former, rarely varies. Nominal success or failure has little to do with the predictable nature of the dialogue.

> "You were—well—as always—I mean, really darling . . ."
> "Well, thank you, but I wish you were here two nights ago. Tonight every-
> body was down."

Pushed further, warming not so much to modesty as to a melancholy
sense of loss, the actor is likely to suggest—particularly in the instance of
nominal success—that rehearsals had been exciting, inspired, etc., and that
performances, however well received, have never been the same. Without
exhuming the decayed remains of old arguments concerning the psychology
of the creative act, it is still possible to observe that the actor is very likely
privy, through his repeated experience, to a fact about creation which neces-

sarily crashes headlong into the professional arrangement of almost any artist's current life. He is expected to repeat an unrepeatable event.

This would be all very well if his concern were only with his personal
equilibrium or his sense of fulfillment. Neither of these depends, however, on
the mechanical arrangements of his working life alone. On the contrary, his
experience tells at least as much about the relatively new pressures within art
today as it does about his dressing-room disappointment. These pressures are
familiar enough, and can be described, remembered, and imagined by way of
one simple, reductive premise: art finds its meaning and forms today by waging a struggle against the repeatable.

For many, of course, the premise merely describes what is wrong with
modern art. Centuries of art declaring itself immortal, the experience of novels, poems, symphonies, painting, sculptures, *and* plays declaring themselves final, are enough to persuade any man that the peculiarly suicidal in-
sistences of contemporary art are fleeting aberrations, or in the case of
embattled old Marxists, passing fancies of a frivolously dying order. In terms
of both views, the total rejection would be valid were it not for the fact that
such totality is no longer possible. The muddle is too present, too real, too reflective, and finally, too internationally representative. The formula conclusions of nationalisms and political alignments break down over the sensitized
perceptions of the best, most organic, modern art. And among these are the
severe, often buoyantly expressed, reflections of a universe united by apoca-
lypse and divided by its own incapacity to accommodate the pleasures available from fragments, acceleration, and dissolution. It is an odd paradox, too,
that in the hands of the unyielding, the most evanescent experience in art—
musical or theatrical performance—is often wished into something rigid, mor-
tified *(definitive* is the more common word), and final. The last word, after all,
might be better left to the gods, not to the people who are challenging them.

To say this is not to condemn efforts for perfection. Yet, while it may well
be the dream of the performer, it is only possible within the framework of a
certain breed of surrender, the willingness to satisfy the impulse while moving on to a new one. Over every performer's head hangs the awareness that
the moment moves on. The cane that once hauled the seedy vaudevillian into
the wings before the tomatoes and eggs threatened to make the stage too slippery for the next trouper was an eloquent reminder not only of missing quality but of passing effectiveness. At the time, no doubt, it meant only what
was intended: get off the stage. Now, however, it takes on fresh reverberations, a symbol of the quickness by which men perceive. Getting off the stage
should be the perversely relevant goal of every performer.

One of the few directors in recent times who has instinctively known the
richer meaning of these suggestions has been Joan Littlewood, the tough,
bumpy little lady responsible, in fact, for the production of Behan's *The Hostage* that triggered Tynan into a search for old labels. Actors passing through
her company often describe an intriguing feature of her performance—not re-

hearsal—techniques. She will observe a performance, note its small perfections, and then adjourn backstage where she will tell an actor (or group of actors) that a particular moment, a singular gesture or inflection, was absolutely ideal, the quintessence, perhaps, of Behanism; at which juncture, she will then add, "Change it." The bumps and grinds of ready applause are not for her, not because she may be against the applause, but because she knows that it will not occur without the engaged enthusiasm, the spontaneous invention, of the performer. Life occurs on stage not when last night's life is imitated, but when tonight's life is freely released.

While this may be considered poor counsel, it can be no longer considered eccentric art. The modern temper insists upon recognition of change. In *The Hostage* itself, the besieged young captive is killed, only to rise immediately for a short chorus of "The bells of hell." Death here is no more sacred than an inherited artistic convention. One could see, from two performances of the Brook-Scofield *Lear,* that the actors had the liberty, where necessary, to fix their stares into space according to the shifting resonances of the nightly experience. (And this in a received, seemingly fixed, reverentially classical text.) Brook himself built *U S* on the foundation of acting experiments administered by Joseph Chaikin of the Open Theater and Jerzy Grotowski from Poland, very different gentlemen dedicated to the development of disciplined, yet highly inspirational, actors. The modern actor, in their separate hands, is a vibrantly tuned, supple, and available instrument; not so much a sounding board for the emotional lines of characters in plays as he is a trumpeting reminder that plays are more than character.

Today's inclination is not toward the perfect text, something finished, unbending, or marbleized, as it is toward the collaboratively suggestive, improvisational architecture of a fluid, open text. The least boring theatres today take on both the old and the new as if yesterday were indeed a matter of the past. The Royal Shakespeare compresses, rewrites, and often amplifies Shakespeare's *Henry VI* and *Richard III,* calling the "new" trilogy *The Wars of the Roses;* Grotowski reduces and intensifies the inner experience of Marlowe's *Dr. Faustus;* the Living Theatre takes on, of all things, Mary Shelley's *Frankenstein,* in order to cope with a suitable image for the nuclear freeze that continues to insinuate itself into good dreams; *America Hurrah!* was largely derived from Jean-Claude van Itallie's observations of a way of work—the adaptability of the Open Theater's actors gave him sufficient confidence in his own impulse for the crosscut, the sudden transformation of place and person, and the simultaneous action; and at this writing, Joseph Chaikin is at quiet work with many of the same actors on an approach to the dramatic actions of the Book of Genesis.

If the tumid breath of historical precedent seems to be breathing down the presumptuous necks of these experiments, it is only another theatrical illusion. Colley Cibber, it is true, shook Richard III into his own image, but it can be scarcely claimed that he did so for an idea, and certainly not for the reflection of a changing world; rather he adapted Shakespeare in order to shape a role more melodramatically appealing, he thought, for his audience. Equally, Nahum Tate's *Lear,* with its happy ending, is simply the refusal of one man and perhaps one period to accept the purgative reality of tragic vision. Neither can it be said that such inventions, in our own recent theatre, as the Living Newspaper were anything more than instant accommodations to both economic pressure and the need to shout clear messages to the home front. Salubrious intentions and results did not necessarily have anything to do with the inner compulsions of art, especially when artists themselves were moved more by the uncoverings of Joyce, Proust, Berg, Stravinsky, and Picasso than by the headlines of a world bent on territorial wars. In the thirties, when art addressed itself to outrage, it made direct assertions. Today, recognizing not only Hannah Arendt's banality of evil and its instinctively protective, spontaneous combustions, no less outrageous for all its omission of master plans, art makes oblique references, indirect assaults, cool withdrawals, and—most effectively—explosions of fun.

These, surely, are choices, very specific responses to the bubble permutations of genocidal societies. More than that, they are recognitions that these same societies stubbornly refuse to admit the discoveries of history, preferring instead the pretensions of righteous murder, the recasting of heroes, and the destruction of verbal meaning (war as a "police action," soldiers as "advisors"). It is almost as if governments have usurped the former roles of the artist, inventing phrases, shaping vision, playing dreamily (as the artist must) with possibilities. And naturally, since the business of even good government is banal, self-protective, self-conscious, and fundamentally mendacious, these modern rulers are proving to be bad artists as well as blundering fools. In turn, the best art has been able to preserve its dominion only by changing the rules.

The theatre, following its usual patterns, has only barely begun to do so. When Blanche DuBois begged Mitch (in Williams's *Streetcar*) not to "hang back with the brutes," she was referring to two images: the civilization of unfeeling, unthinking caricatures of men and women she thought she had known, and the dream of a better, more humane world. Her feeble ministrations toward domestic comfort and beauty, however, indicated only how far her imagination had yet to carry her. Oriental paper lamps, hymns to colored lights, a nod to the Pleiades, and a honky little pop tune were the extent of her artistic reach. The brutes, clearly, could not be far behind.

Blanche, sadly, was trying to change her world with what she had been given: faded objects, unreachable stars, steamy baths, cheap colognes, a shabby song, and a world of distorted memories. She could have no future because she was denying the present while lying about her past. Worse, she was relying upon the forms and choices of her inheritance. Similarly, the theatre, hanging back with the rules, is plunging deeper into limbo. But it is no longer sufficient to castigate its most common delinquencies—slavishness to orderly plot, character, and tidy solutions. What can be questioned now is the sweeping inheritance, that epic collection of assumptions upon which theatrical event almost everywhere rests. Theatre can no longer afford to imitate presidents, premiers, and generals. To be guarding bastions, to be enthralled by self during a period in which both experience and the other arts keep reaching intelligently and instinctively for the heady, sane, and bursting stratospheres outside the self is to be fatally exiled from the youthful spirit of the age.

By none of this am I neglecting the pioneer labors of those already liberated from so much of the inheritance: innovators such as Brook, Grotowski, Chaikin, Julian Beck and Judith Malina of New York's exiled Living Theatre, Roger Planchon in France, the Czechs, Hungarians, and even Russians who are constantly being brought to a specialist's attention. These people, fortunately, do not need critical essays to tell them where they are or where they are going; and it is reasonable to assume that they are currently shaping new surprises, some perhaps intimately related to what I have come to see as the touchstone liberations of *Sgt. Pepper's Lonely Hearts Club Band.*

Trying to bend theatre into an awareness of advances elsewhere might be more agreeably accomplished by citing its equally serious cousins in painting or music. Indeed, even to say "painting" is to shock oneself into a sudden attack of modern insecurity tremors, since "painters," as such, are not confined to paint materials. Equally, music can be silence. The serious—or rather, seriously intended—arts have made enough suggestions already to the laggard art of theatre for at least a dozen aesthetic revolutions. It may be, then, that all those uncollected messages from the serious arts are hopelessly alien to the formative impulses of theatrical action. Though I am by no means referring to the jungle roars of commerce, it can be still usefully asserted that theatre, if it is anything, is an elemental, and therefore popular, art. Which is not the same as saying that it must second-guess the populace, especially by imitating what has appealed before. Far from it. True popularity is lodged in more remote quarters—the huddling-for-warmth, often lonely regions where community is founded; where what is available for sharing is, in fact, shared. The groundlings, let it be recalled, apparently had the instinctive good sense to enjoy Shakespeare.

The Beatles enter where the groundlings left off. *They* are the audience. Poins, Fluellen, Davy, Falstaff, and yes, Prince Hal are being played by the groundlings, taking over center stage for the first time in history. Writing the poems, setting the music, choosing their impersonations, selecting partners, inviting others to play with them (engineers and technicians), they are actually getting on with the show, producing an occasion, guaranteeing, as they say, "a splendid time for all." That it is a basic experience doesn't make it less relevant or moving. Its deeply connected origins are, certainly, the wellsprings of its extensive reach. Slummers would not be welcome. The business of such fun is available for all, but all should be available.

In England, nostalgia is either a way of life or an internal pressure. *Sgt. Pepper* is textually based in both worlds. Yet it pushes beyond. The gallant little Club Band would have been familiar to Archie Rice's Edwardian father, Billy (in John Osborne's *The Entertainer),* but he may not have quite comprehended the change that had overtaken the young who can sing that they used to be angry young men, but "It's getting better all the time." Jimmy Porter, only twelve years old, is actually dead. For Billy, the good old days were roseate, always better than today. Here, however, is a thrust forward, an attempt outside of rancor, a gentle accommodation of small moments, fleeting tenderness, floating wistfulness, jaunty renewal. "The one and only Billy Shears" launches us into the kaleidoscopic world of a plausible modern music hall (would that it were so), in which there is a natural, performing progression from elementary appeals ("A Little Help from My Friends") to a coda ("A Day in the Life") where the casually obsessive spread of daily, detailed, indifferent experience is presented like an updated patient on Eliot's etherized table. In between, there are highs and lows, all of them individual, each fragmented from the same flinty dream: induced journeys for the imagination (the now legendary "Lucy"), determined surrenders to the imagination ("I'm fixing a hole where the rain gets in and stops my mind from wandering—"), abortive efforts to be released for imagination ("She's Leaving Home" is predictably rebellious until it becomes clear that the daughter has exchanged absent parents for a commercial hack—she's leaving home, fine, but to where and to whom?), and, as an interlude, a reminder both musically and textually that a good show uses everything—trampolines, hoops, garters, and hogsheads of real fire. One senses not so much that the show must go on, but that, good or bad, it is always going on.

From this point, it is all mixed rise and fall: contact with the imagined East, talk of the "space between us all," a tingling way station for meditative polemics ("We were talking—about the love that's gone so cold and the people, Who gain the world and lose their soul—"), good to hear musically, but otherwise a lapse—too insistent, uncharacteristically smug, and naggingly simplistic; then another return to English music hall ("When I'm Sixty-Four") where the joke is as much on our own sense of timelessness—all tunes will be nostalgic some day—as it is on the joyously crude flirtations of the young man; then a swing into a more pugnacious form of flirtation, singing the praises of a lovely meter maid who can pay the dinner bill and have a go on the couch with "a sister or two" (it hardly matters how many, since implicit agreement—very different from approval—is given to the implication that they're all having that splendid time guaranteed for all); then, before the reprise of *Sgt. Pepper* and the lingering coda, with all its crushing, resonant chill, there is a bravely resigned gesture to a "Good Morning" ("Nothing to say but what a day," etc.), casting, in its way, a sharp glance back at the hole-fixer who knew that it didn't matter if he's wrong, he's right, Where he belongs he's right where he belongs.

Once, several years ago, probably moved by the besieging question of filtered experience, I wrote a note to myself about the invention of the phonograph. It could have nothing to do, I said, with man's ingenuity; rather it represents a biological urge, a naturally selected means of survival amidst the industrial scream. Perhaps the theatre cannot compete. One had imagined that disc and celluloid were something like the final solutions for all performing experience, exhilarating and sensuous, perhaps, but ultimately unbending, unresponsive, not immediate and present dangers. The theatre, so it seemed, was still the citadel of color, light, immediacy, and sensual presence. Yet the change and the challenge are undoubted. Theatrical production, in its modes, its preparations, its tedious set of expectations, is too often less immediate, less colorful, less sensual than those endlessly intriguing compositions on records and film.

It needn't, of course, be so. The most open construction should stop closing itself off from the present. The material of this period suggests, as the Beatles suggest, that variety and invention need not be left to official killers with all their ingenious devices for new stress and new annihilations. It is too easy to be numbed, too soon to be lulled into living slumber. The forms we receive and the methods with which we work demand a kind of vigilance that will never let them rest unquestioned from day to day. Just as theatre, using people, need not bind itself to character, so, using space, it need not be bound by some prior idea of spatial relationships. Man doesn't move upstage or downstage. He just moves. Which is to say that the boundaries of imagination are the only limits on theatrical event. Performance need not be labeled work-in-progress, it need only acknowledge that it is work: this, like the pleasures to be derived from new sculptural, building, or painting materials, can be the current source of theatrical energy. If a pop recording can be a production, then a production need no longer be a record. There are no categories. There are only imaginations. "I read the news today oh boy."   *GR(Spring 1968)*

Living at This Hour

All innovative theatre in this mid-century has been fiercely political. There are no significant exceptions. Brecht in East Berlin, Joan Littlewood in East London, Roger Planchon in Lyons, Giorgio Strehler in Milan, Peter Brook wherever he is, Joseph Chaikin and Peter Schumann in New York—the Becks wherever they are. Moreover, they do not exemplify a range of political direction. There is no Nixon, Wallace, Harold Wilson, or de Gaulle among them. Neither is there any inclination toward the flaccid, insulting platitudes of Hubert Humphrey, or even toward—grudging sympathy notwithstanding—the graceful gestures-from-within of Eugene McCarthy. Only Brecht played politics directly, his theatre in the East, his bank account in the West; but that is because he was Left where the Left had already hardened into its own environmental Right.

What is remarkable, really suggestive about this information, is that it cannot be observed as such a fixed impulse in the other innovative arts. The theatre, so challenged, so fundamentally wrenched from its popular role, so distant from the groundlings, so dubious, therefore, as a public forum likely to inspire or produce political change, is nevertheless the only endeavor in Western art in which formal innovations are inextricably connected to political stance. And this stance, for all its shadings and different colors, is completely Left.

Jean-Louis Barrault was shocked into obsequiousness by the young Left and unceremoniously dumped out of power by the old Right. No mercy for the middle. (Or the middle-aged.) Jean Vilar, once of the Left, long bereft of a theatre and now a dead man, as a young French critic described him to me recently, was the mayor's big stick in Avignon, probably the first cop ever encountered by the Becks (who play Pied Piper to cops almost as often as they tootle for the young) who could club them over the head with dramatic literature. The lines, clearly, are being drawn. Theatre is rising to internal splendor again because, as "an exemplary action" (the Becks' phrase), it is rediscovering prophecy. It isn't changing the world. It is confirming a shift in consciousness.

Of course, the vibrations in a room containing, on one side let us say, the Becks, Brook, and Planchon, and on the other, Sam Shepard, Pinter, and Beckett, would surely be awful, terribly threatening to anyone caught in the mute crossfire. Beckett may be political to some blacks, a few embattled Poles such as Jan Kott, and even to Londoners retreating from the humiliations of powerlessness by way of the route between Carnaby Street and the King's Road, but he is not political, surely, to Beckett. A writer extends his reach vertically, not horizontally. He addresses us from other regions, from the past, yes, but most of all, from the reflective sanctuaries of his compulsively private mind. Deeply, of course, since he takes actions, he is really political too; but he is not likely (today) to be instinctively, automatically Left. He leaves emotive choices to the physical dramaturgy of the director.

Yes, I know the exceptions. But are they? Or at the least, what do they prove? I am describing patterns and developments, not immutable conditions, and certainly not moral positions. Alarm placed at the service of bridging the present gap between theatrical artist and dramatic writer represents misplaced energy. Astronomers don't argue with the stars, they merely note their changing positions. It is confoundingly plain: playwrights who have made politics their subject—Arnold Wesker, Peter Weiss, Rolf Hochhuth—

have not found a form; directors who have made political imagination their subtext have indeed found their form; and writers who have made mystery their subject—Beckett again, Pinter, possibly Shepard—have also found form. Innovative theatres are responding to two concurrent modern situations: the bombardment of the senses by unreliable words, and the absence of communally reliable sensual experience.

*   *   *

Mysteries and Smaller Pieces, the first event presented by the Living Theatre at Yale, comprises nine separate scenes or actions performed by a company of thirty-two. An actor stands rigidly down front and center in a hard burnished light. He keeps standing. He never breaks. There is every reason to suspect that he will stay in this posture indefinitely, all night, perhaps forever. Impossible, of course, but maybe they are just sane enough to try. Somebody speaks, not an actor. (No, *Time* magazine, you were misreporting again, she was a Yale secretary, not planted or hired, just responsively present; you're so accustomed to deception that you can't believe a spontaneously honest moment, you really can't presume to think that theatre of cruelty is as stupid and brutal as you are.) The provocation is working. Many possible messages, but one will do for now: Action in theatre can be more complex than what we have known; it need not occur only on stage; in fact, it is no longer sufficient for it to occur on stage alone; the audience is an actor anyway, whether it wishes or not; the visible stage is not the only authority; you can talk back to the candidate. Further: The theatre is not safe. Another: You can't supply instant meaning to any event. (In this case, the memory of the rigid actor reasserts itself during the last scene, an enactment of the plague concluding with the frozen forms of the dead raised in tearless silence to a giant pile. Only connect, said E. M. Forster. The audience, narcotized not by pot but by American politics, goes to the theatre to disconnect even more. So the scene, though remedial and didactic, has a suggestive subterranean life.)

A raga sung in darkness, again challenging the impatience of those who demand instant meaning, relief from reverberations. Next, an offering of incense (fire marshal permitting). *Street Songs* by Jackson MacLow, chanting hypnotically (the actor as priest or evangelist, the theatre as substitute drug) that change should overcome money, banks, police, the army, the state, prisons, and not surprisingly, the war in Vietnam. Members of the audience drift purposefully to the stage, joining the company in a circle, humming a chord (initiated as an exercise by Joe Chaikin and the Open Theater), making a connection. (Even an anti-connection is purgative: "Fuck you," said one Yale undergraduate after making the effort to confront the circle on stage.) In the second half, the actors form a series of what the British music hall used to call, in all its puritanical prurience, "living statues." No prurience here, only camera images, quick studies in human variety, sharp remembrances of animal reality.

Then another Chaikin exercise, the exchange of sound and movement between actors, performed here with more relentless commitment than the actors of the Open Theater give to it. (Joe's actors are liberated through exercise; Judith and Julian's are plunged further into the existential abyss; Joe's people grow childlike in an evening, J. and J.'s turn ancient.)

Then, finally, the plague. The actors die in agony. (The Yale secretary, suspending more disbelief than T. S. Eliot ever imagined, descends from the balcony to comfort and nurse the dying. A startling moment of total dislocation. Theatre is suddenly returned to its unpredictable origins. A group of blacks, either uncomfortable before or well beyond aesthetic suspensions, moves from hours of heckling laughter into a gentle spiritual.) The stiffened bodies glow in the circle. Purification for believers. Rest. A slow recall into a world where theatre makes its own images, unreproducible in any other medium.

Antigone, stretching across two thousand years of drama and human repression by way of Sophocles, Friedrich Hölderlin, Brecht, and Malina, is of course more textually rooted and, therefore, more theatrically confining than *Mysteries.* The theatrical argument is really more interesting than the political one; it may even be the same. Apollo vs. Dionysus, Brecht vs. Artaud, Antigone vs. the Chorus, mind into or against body; all useful metaphorical emblems for the company's evolving situation.

Every action of the Becks is grounded in metaphor, from the choice of material to the manner of presenting it. Here, as in *Mysteries,* the setting is the stage—cavernous, iron, brick, a Shubert stage of the twenties (in this case), a perfectly unnatural environment for a perfectly unusual, though exemplary, action. Again, the actors are actors; no disguise, the same people who float into the theatre to survey the stage and be technicians. Even here, they cover the aisles with their literal presence, touching people, shouting at them, begging not so much for physical attention as for personal acknowledgment—a very different matter. Greece couldn't be further away, though it feels closer through this agency than it has ever felt through the mimic togas and tuneless choruses of the Greek tragedies that have been bludgeoning us into oxlike indifference. (Prior to our innovative theatres, the antiquarian's Shakespeare and the curator's Greece derived from similar lies: the first from Victoria's England, smothering the coarse bursts of life with numbing gentilities; the second, from Max Reinhardt's bloated prussianism, oratorical solemnity masquerading as style.) Clearly, these actors don't speak the Greek's English, which is just as well, considering the chameleon origins of the present text. Where Brecht cools any sympathetic identification with character, Judith Malina (more than the others) goes him one better by figuratively snubbing a sharp, Brooklyn nose at any moment threatening to sink into dignity. Brecht's comment is, of all things, wittily commented upon. Actors turn into furniture and back into actors again. The chorus picks up the tongue-click of a rhythm and lets it take over—swinging, possessed, completely and confidently enthralled. It isn't very sad (hurrah), and it never finds total release from its demi-classical pieties, but it is more alive than it has any right to be.

*   *   *

The Living Theatre is now the most beautiful acting company in the world. (An exaggeration. The competition isn't keen.) Their bodies are supple and totally available to them, clean, sculptured, at ease, without the steel-spring hardness of dancers. Their presentational energy is boundless, their engagement in the smallest action total and large (with exceptions, of course). Their voices can be hoarse, but their breathing is open, expansive, loaded with reserves. They are more comfortable now in scenes with the audience than in scenes with themselves. They are radical, but they feel like a family. They play menace all the time, but their aggressions are deeply gentle. They keep reminding me of my vulnerabilities: the lassitude of my body, the protective clutter in my mind.

They are beautiful, I suppose, because they don't look like actors.

*   *   *

The Becks' theatre offers precious little fun, and it can be tendentious, insistent, selfish, and boring. But from inside the mounting hysteria of a nation-state that accommodates itself with such dexterity to the crushing choice of lesser evil, it is possible to say that their contradictions are better than most. Which is to say that, for all their frequent thoughtlessness, they are not outside the pressure of mind; that, for all their formula simplicity, they are not outside the spell of dense, complex experience; and that, for all their persistent humorlessness, they are not outside the realm of relentless irony, a heavy, though puckish wit that casts a sweet, seductive, even abrasive glimpse into that time forward when men discover the softening pleasures of felt experience and the gentle persuasions of active peace.

*   *   *

Art and life, as described implicitly by the Becks in their work, have reached us as separate nation-states. To suggest a merger is to suggest, therefore, another political action. The villain in this dramatic argument is not man in all his cumulative imperfections, not his aggressive response to that imperfection, but the structures evolved to bring order into chaos.

The first premise, then, in the proposed merger, is that man is better than his inventions. He can realize perfection, but only if he brings imagination to bear not upon refinements and decorations of what he has already wrought, but upon a complete change to—what?—other structures. No: to no-structures, no-form, no-states, no-orders, no-rules, no-inheritance. Art and life are one when, as words, they cease to suggest structural meanings. They are one when they cease, in effect, to be; or at the least, when they cease to be accountable to historical description, formal analysis, or definition.

*   *   *

"Be realistic, do the impossible." Thus Herbert Marcuse, quoting someone, and, in so doing, making the quote his own. It could have been Judith or
Julian. Robert Brustein once wrote that art is the politics of the impossible. As
a statement, it would appear to be no more than a variation on Marcuse's, an
assertion easily attributable, therefore, to the Becks. Yet, examining both, it
is clear that they are markedly different: Marcuse's is about action, Brustein's
is about reflection.

The Becks are different from almost all other theatre artists because they
make continuous, unrepeatable, assertive action. They talk just as ceaselessly as
the rest of us. But they *do* more. And so, we are angered.

(What they do could be, after all, much better, more refined, clearer, better edited—or just plain edited.)

*   *   *

Nobody, in accounting for the Becks' work, has discussed their Jewish-
ness and the pervasive importance of the drug experience. I suppose these
subjects come under the heading of the Unmentionable. It should be enough
just to place them in the Mentionable column. Even so, I shall surrender to
temptation in a small way, adding one modest observation to each category.
——The Jew wanders.
——The Head has more time for time.

*   *   *

"The theatre was for the people, and always should be for the people.
The poets would make the theatre for a select community of dilettanti. They
would put difficult psychological thoughts before the public, expressed in difficult words, and would make for this public something which is impossible
for them to understand and unnecessary for them to know; whereas the theatre must show them sights, show them life, show them beauty, and not
speak in difficult sentences. And the reason why the theatre is being kept
back today is because the poet is pulling one way, saying they should only be
given words, using the theatre and all its crafts as a medium for those words;
and the people are pulling the other way, saying they desire to see the sights,
realistically or poetically shown, not turned into literature. So far most of the
brainy people are on the side of the poets; they have got the upper hand. Still
the plays in the theatres are, artistically, failures; the theatre itself is a failure
artistically and commercially, and the secret of this failure is the battle between the poet and the people."

Not Brecht. Not Artaud. Not Malina or Beck.
Gordon Craig in 1905.   *GR(Spring 1969)*

THE
SEVENTIES

University Theatre: The Marble Wasteland

Not long ago, I was invited by a graduate-professional school associated with a large Eastern university to speak at a colloquium. The invitation was hastily invented by the dean of the school in order to place me forcibly before the faculty and students as a leading candidate for the position of Director of Performing Arts. A new building designed (in theory) to serve a new performing arts program was at that moment in the middle stages of construction, all the architectural and aesthetic decisions having been made by the dean and his associates in advance of any major appointment; indeed, in advance of any informed or agreed idea for a program.

The dean was likely to be in favor of anything that worked. Which meant anything that kept him off awkward hooks, pleased the largest number of people, and *incidentally* left his illusion of power unchallenged. There had been at least sixty unsuccessful candidates before me. They had submitted ideas, specific programs describing an alliance of professional theatre people with an educational structure, and they had provided budgets. One of them had even labored under the title of Acting Director for more than a year.

My proposal was called "A Natural Formation of Land," taking its central impulse from the appalling fact that yet once again the philanthropists, trustees, and their master-slaves, the faculty, were launching a five- or six-million-dollar building for the performing arts before considering the needs of the people who would be using it. In an extended preamble, I tried, immodestly, to offer a background that would seem radical only in a situation such as this one—where the same boring mistakes were being presented as if the Enlightenment had dawned again.

The American landscape is littered with the marble wreckage of good will badly contemplated. Awesome respect for surfaces, speed, and substitutes has given us travertine-stone from Italy that places a smooth skin over the acoustical hell of a Philharmonic Hall; trumpet-tongued publicity on behalf of instantaneous Great Theatre, as if it were possible in our embattled cities to build skilled companies, an imaginative and relevant repertory, or an enlightened, courageous audience outside the natural laws of creation. Fashion, as usual, was masquerading as Art, our table decorated with Wedgwood cups and saucers filled with freeze-dried coffee and cancer-producing sucaryl.

In the last twenty years this nation has begun to show some official embarrassment about art, if not always about artists. But always forgetting that the longest-running, innovative, aesthetically identifiable American theatres—Martha Graham's and the Becks'—have survived and sustained themselves without the aid of architects and contractors. The alarm that I was clearly sounding was directed at distracting impositions and false priorities; at hysterical balancing of budgets before making a long-range investment in balanced imaginations. The only virtue, I suggested, of the new building was its palpable emptiness. For all its errors, its misplaced plushness, those grievous confusions that lead to lobbies more sensibly imagined than wing space, the empty building could be, at the least, a place for work.

In the beginning theatre had been an assumed part of nature. But as it turned away from the sun, becoming, instead, a ceremony for night people and a mirror held up to the machine, it severed itself not merely from its origins, but from the echoes and metaphors suggested by those origins. Steps can be built for the audience, but the performer is expected to leap manfully into perfection. Only a handful of practical dreamers—Graham, the Becks, Stanislavsky, Brecht, and most recently, Grotowski—have succeeded in this century against the pressures of a culture insensitive to the real process of work. Indeed, process—the favored word of performers everywhere—is almost never included in the generous philanthropies offered to artists today.

Concluding my preface, I tried a delicate, far too oblique thrust at the university's obscenely imitative relationship to its parent nation-state. There is no evidence, I said, that the dishonorable surrenders of artists and managers—surrenders of needs and principles that many of them really comprehend—have any bearing on artistic or practical success. In any case—and here I was whispering where only thunder just might be heard—the university community is quite properly under fire today for similar surrenders. Even if it wishes to do so, it can no longer afford complicity with any part of a system that can be viewed as a microcosm of government today. If it does not place its new structures at the service of displacing old modes and discredited choices; if it does not give itself to the business of replacing inner structures, then it will reveal only the hollowness of a space not empty for work, but bare of ideas, passion, consciousness itself.

All this I called a warning and a challenge. As it turns out, it was no more than an educated prediction.

*   *   *

The proposal itself was lengthy, carefully argued, and, for all its subtextual anger, far too defensive. Somewhere in the middle of my presentation, I felt compelled to acknowledge the defensiveness. It comes naturally to the American performing artist, I said, plagued as he is by years at the untender mercy of amateur sports, those purse-bearers who pretend to know more about his needs and impulses than he does himself. A terrific tension persists between the artist's needs, obvious to him, and his deepest wishes: he needs trust, support, cash—and he wishes to be left alone.

Then, at this diplomatic crossroads of my report, I nudged my way into yet another overly oblique criticism of the university. My phrasing, though cautious, might easily have moved some of the academically experienced people to a second thought or two: It may well be, I said, that the attraction felt by the artist for the university is derived from his image of "academic freedom," some sense that it implies unencumbered study, minimal disruption, the liberty to make errors on the pathway to personal truth. The evidence might be to the contrary, but only the most confident explorer, or the rare man of independent means, can afford to look away from the university these days.

Which is probably the only significant, if obvious, point to emerge from my consultation: that academic freedom is, in fact, just another phrase manufactured by the great American Image factory. Freedom, academic or otherwise, is what the boss says it is. As George Dennison writes in *The Lives of Children,* a book describing the petty, brutalizing surrenders made by the faculties of American primary and secondary schools: "It was only too evident that in accepting their jobs they [the teachers] had given away their integrity, for the truth was they could not make moral judgments and implement them. . . . All that was left was the naked conflict of wills." Which, I submit, is all that is left for the teacher in higher education. He attains the illusion of academic freedom by giving up the citizenship of the self.

I say this now, but I was not to be stopped then from hoping just once more. It was possible in that situation to imagine conditions that were unprecedented; most particularly, that the absence of a theatre department corrupted beyond salvation by the naked conflict of wills promised opportunities for real innovation and concentrated experiment. There was no fixed curriculum that needed drastic revision, there were no tenured professors who needed artificial respiration, and since there was no reputation yet, there were no students—so it seemed—bringing with them only the most venial careerist impulses. In short, I was trying to address my remarks to a university theatre program that might possibly behave as if it weren't in a university.

Not that it could happen anywhere else. The proposal was clearly designed for an educational institution, or, at the very least, to the idea of a university that some of us had when we were very young. To any audience except the inner circle of academics, wearily holding up their heads with the help of the ever-present pipe planted firmly between the gritted teeth, the proposal would have spoken almost entirely for itself.

> The University and the Graduate School can and should become founders of the first research laboratory of theatrical performance.

But this was the inner circle, after all, a body of men and a few women conditioned to learn not from the patent evidence of personal experience, but from the heavy glut of lectured words. At this stage of our "negotiations," they required detailed descriptions of the obvious, at least two months of budget-hunting, and—as I soon learned—a lifetime's commitment to the defensive.

Here, I trust, I can be brief. The lab would be a source of entertainment in a manner and form entirely without precedent in this country: its performances unprogrammed, or, at any rate, never held in thrall to a schedule, a paying or subscription audience. Those who would visit its performances would be there as guests, participants in a phase of discovery, viewers of a process frankly and freely presented as process, visitors (if they like) to a simple act of work. Work, as lip service would too often have it these days, truly in-progress.

The lab would necessarily spin in many differing, unpredictable directions; but central to its actions would be a chamber theatre, or more accurately, an Exploratory Theatre group of some nine to twelve actors, two directors, several writers, at least one designer intrigued by flexible space and the wonders of light, and, when necessary, several managerial people—all of them in preparation for the eventual training of students. Devoted to experiments with words, without words, with and without music, film, movement, texts of the past and present, material invented *from* performance as well as *for* performance, this ensemble would be directing its attention not to any prior ideas we may have about good theatre, right or wrong theatre, classical or modern theatre, but to the discovery, through its own actions in special relationship to the local community, of a clear, visible, responsive performing identity. An identity, moreover, that can never be predicted or imposed by way of some messianic design, an identity that emerges from direct human relationships—an identity, finally, that requires time for its emergence.

The undergraduate students are, of course, the central reason for bringing such a laboratory into the university. But the proposal was conceived on the structure of a simple historical observation: namely, that *no performing arts school has ever given birth to a great performing theatre, while it has happened the other way around.* The Exploratory Theatre would be the natural core for a series of open learning situations—teaching by doing, sharing, engaging; above all, involving through interest, not merely teaching students to be teachers of students who are taught to be teachers of . . . Within three to five years, the profile of the group should be clear, and if this is the case, the company will very likely have a "Pied Piper" relationship to many students, acquiring followers and friends without pressure on either side for anything save a mutually needed connection. Or, just as likely, it will inspire negative reaction leading to the formation of imaginative opposition groups, more in tune for the moment with the lives of the young—thus keeping the Exploratory Theatre on its collective toes, rendering the patterns of habit a virtual impossibility.

Even in this attenuated version, the proposal clearly needs a word or two about its economic premises. First, of course, and for the ninety-ninth time, profit is not the motive. (One faculty member told me that there were officers of the university who, when the new library was erected, were seriously discussing ways in which to turn it into a profit-making operation. One can never be too cautious, therefore, about reminding such insensitive gentlemen that they are probably in the wrong business, an endeavor that is not, by any stretch of the imagination, a business at all.) Even so, because the new building contained at least two workable theatres, one large and one small, I suggested that the small theatre be the home of the Exploratory company while the large theatre might house guest productions, some of the most formative and dynamic performance work available on the international scene. Invitations might go to such theatres as the Berlin Ensemble (still unseen in the United States), the Piccolo Teatro, the Royal Shakespeare, the Open Theater, Merce Cunningham, an underground film festival, and so on. (I appended a full list covering possible programs and festivals for several years.) I had not reckoned, however, with the unyielding information that the large theatre was, nevertheless, too small to render any kind of return on the booking investments. So long as money was an argument, I was always vulnerable. In the American university, one hears more talk of money than in David Merrick's office.

Of course, the obligation for such a laboratory in a university setting should be *practical* only insofar as it serves study. It should be *businesslike* only insofar as it refuses to let business pressures interfere with the expansive, open pursuit of study. It should be responsible, first and always, to its own *informed,* experienced sense of need. Like any good lover, it can't be attractive or effective in love until it feels love for itself. Practical modes of business designed to support such an action can and must be invented. Business is an element of welcome concern so long as it places itself in service rather than command.

The most moving argument I know derives from Grotowski, one of the few theatre artists in recent history who has had the sustained experience of work supported by trust in its special rhythms, no questions asked, pride held for the process:

> Why do we sacrifice so much energy to our art? Not in order to teach others but to learn with them what our existence, our organism, our personal and unrepeatable experience have to give us; to learn to break down the barriers which surround us and to free ourselves from the breaks which hold us back, from the lies about ourselves which we manufacture daily for ourselves and for others; to destroy the limitations caused by our ignorance and lack of courage; in short, to fill the emptiness in us: to fulfill ourselves. Art is neither a state of the soul (in the sense of some extraordinary, unpredictable moment of inspiration) nor a state of man (in the sense of a profession or social function). Art is a ripening, an evolution, an uplifting which enables us to emerge from darkness into a blaze of light.

In simpler words, Art is a natural formation of land rising by steps and gradations . . .

                    *   *   *

Within the next two months, my anger surfaced from the subtextual to the melodramatic world of the thinly veiled. I had been advised officially by a committee of friends and colleagues conversant with the pleasures and anguishes of both university and commercial theatre. I had traveled to similar centers in California and consulted with men whose bitterness, by contrast, made me look and sound like Lillian Gish in her cushioned reminiscences of Mr. Griffith. My dean, of course, was no Mr. Griffith. Nevertheless, the campus wasn't big enough for both of us and he was already there.

I began my final submission with a quotation from Sir Laurence Olivier, and I concluded it with Oscar Wilde:

> If you wish to create a national or community theatre, begin by assembling your company, work with it, find out what's wrong and what's right, and then—and only then—build a new building for it. (Olivier)
>
> In this world there are only two tragedies. One is not getting what one wants, and the other is getting it. (Wilde)

That I provided more words, other pages, feeble efforts at reinforcing what everybody surely knew, is simply an indication that I have not been able to shed my links with the brainwashed community of scholars ever bound to the genteel illusion that Reason reigns in the university. Reason is just another name for Self-Interest; and if I am embarrassed about any part I played in this negotiation, it is for that part of me that muted necessary self-interest in favor of idealistic arguments. Not that the arguments were incorrect or misguided. It is just that they might as well have been spoken in Hungarian or the language of Fifth Avenue furriers.

Then came the argument that fully tested both sides. I cannot begin to say how many times I was reminded by the dean and his colleagues of what I already knew: that these are parlous times financially, that the university is under pressure for smaller classes, higher salaries, better insurance and retirement plans, larger libraries, and, most obviously today, contributions to the local community and Afro-American programs. To which I concurred, but then please stop flirting with Art, playing whoremaster to Theatre. Each of the socio-political-economic pressures deserves equal or greater priority than a performing arts building or program. But that isn't the way it is happening. The buildings rise—and so do their needs and the very real, fundamentally immutable, costs. Perhaps all performing arts centers and programs should vanish in favor of other community needs and pressures. But the albatross (the building) would still be hanging round the necks of university administrators who are not equipped to produce plays, build companies, preside over the quicksilver emotional lives of actors, directors, dancers, writers, musicians, designers, technicians, and theatre administrators, and, at the same time, make art.

If educational priorities are to be met, there is really no middle ground. Either the university initiates and strongly commits itself to a long-range, serious performing arts program, or it might just as well admit that the performing arts center, far from standing as the basis of a fresh approach to theatrical life and education in a university, is really just a group of additional spaces in which to book lectures, movies, and performances. As a glorified performance hall, the center will necessarily lean in the direction of box-office dependency. In that event comes what I have called elsewhere the juggernaut of production: a spiraling need to meet rigid schedules and the desperate need to sell subscriptions to a necessarily middle-class audience, thus effectively locking out the student for whom the whole damn thing was built in the first place.   *GR(Spring 1970)*

The Last Gentleman-Actor

The Gentleman-Actor is a disappearing breed, almost as extinct now as a lively production of a play by George Bernard Shaw. Perhaps the one cannot survive without the other—a bitter joke the century is playing on Shaw. Fortunately, Rex Harrison is still with us. Seen at the Kennedy Center in Washington, on his way to Broadway in Shaw's *Caesar and Cleopatra,* he was only beginning to pad his way into the cushioned suite in Claridges cleverly disguised by Shaw (if not by set designer Ming Cho Lee) to look like Egypt. I have no doubt that Harrison would be instructive about acting even at a first reading. In the middle stages of shaping a production, he is a textbook. Like so many Gentleman-Actors before him—one thinks of Clive Brook, Leslie Howard, Sir Cedric Hardwicke, Noël Coward, and Americans such as Claude Rains; as well as William Powell in movies, and, yes, Fred Astaire—Harrison does everything with an ease and grace that makes much of the public confuse his stage presence with real life. Even if the bones don't show, however, it is acting just the same, and very good acting indeed.

His range sets deliberate limits. Harrison will never be Lear, thank God. He might have tried a Benedick once, but save for the lapse of Pirandello's Henry IV, he has known his place and held his throne. Great actors of another type, such as Olivier, Gielgud, Ralph Richardson, and Scofield—though more versatile—have rarely, if ever, attempted Shaw. When they have, the result has been less than their best. Shaw doesn't descend to the mines, where grubby, domestic feelings might be found. Nor does he fly into rarefied, existential space. He was writing in this case for a gentleman who had, as Cleopatra tells Caesar, "a nice voice." All very well for Harrison, but for the vaulting, soiled, grainy voice of Olivier, the description would never fit. Sir Laurence's Caesar (to Vivien Leigh's Cleopatra) was muted, subdued, ever the well-tempered accompanist champing at the bit to play his dark, expansive, Mahlerian Antony-music. And he was anything but nice. Surely Olivier is the more prodigious, thrilling, and dangerous actor, but Harrison is the more naturally gifted.

He is also a better Shavian than when he played Higgins as glamorized by Alan Jay Lerner and Frederick Loewe. Abrasive, edgy, and not so wedded to charm, he would be more suited to Shaw's Higgins than to L. and L.'s. As Caesar, his face is a map of unanswered questions, weirdly resembling Bert Lahr's, the haunted clown inside of him at last permitted to emerge through lidded eyes and knobby nose. Hands calmly folded behind his back much of the time, even when he asks the big questions—"What have I to do with resentment?"—he sniffs the air impatiently, signaling a refusal to be trapped by useless certainties. Harrison is what Shaw meant by "a classical actor," referring then to Johnston Forbes-Robertson, for whom he was to create so many leading roles, including Caesar. "What I mean by classical," he wrote, "is that he can present a dramatic hero as a man whose passions are those which produced the philosophy, the poetry, the art, and the statecraft of the world, and not merely those which have produced its weddings, coroners' inquests, and executions." Harrison adds sensuality to statecraft, which saves Shaw from himself. Yet he also breathes intelligence, even into the one and only kiss he gives Cleopatra in their farewell embrace.

Harrison kisses his Cleopatra (Elizabeth Ashley) on the mouth, rather than on the forehead as prescribed by Shaw in the text. This might be his way of underscoring the softer side of Shaw, which was reserved, as a rule, for letters to actresses such as Ellen Terry and Mrs. Patrick Campbell (who, to Shaw's regret, performed the role of Cleopatra only in the copyright production in Newcastle). His advice to Mrs. Campbell was that his plays "must be acted, and acted hard." In Washington, the company was about as soft as they come, but it couldn't have been easy for the actors to find a Shavian profile for themselves when so much of the text had been cut by their original director. Since I saw the production, however, Ellis Rabb has taken over as director, and he is reported to have restored the lost material—a promising sign for New York.

Shaw knew what he wanted, and heaven help the director who lacks the bounce to make it happen. To Mrs. Campbell, he added that his plays "need a sort of bustle and crepitation of life which requires extraordinary energy and vitality, and gives only glimpses and movements of the poetry beneath." Harrison is master of the glimpses, and with Rabb to assist him and the other actors, perhaps he no longer has to go it alone. Shaw isn't really kind to modern actors. His bustle transmutes all too easily into fussiness, and his energy can be unintentionally made to look like peevishness. A company has to be robust in spirit and unscrambled in brains. Like Harrison.

Shaw isn't really kind to designers, either. He tells them to dress the stage and the actors for Cleopatra's Egypt, and then he fails to write *Aida*. Shaw makes room for talk, not crowds. Oddly, Ming Cho Lee didn't make room for either. The stage in Washington looked like a CinemaScope screen, all width and no dimension. It couldn't have been a matter of budget, since Jane Greenwood had designed a new frock (and I do mean frock) for every new appearance of Ashley, and Novella Nelson's Ftatateeta couldn't mount steps without gathering up what looked like the whole of New York City's garment center into her formidable arms.

Shaw wanted "a man with energy enough to bring up my plays to concert pitch." In the best—and I suppose the last—of our Gentleman-Actors, he has found his man. Concert pitch is something that Rex Harrison, as we know, can teach to musicians. By now, I hope, Shaw has also found his Gentleman-Director, someone almost as smart as he was, with at least half his grit, thrust, and passionate joy.   *GR(March 1977)*

Otherwise Obsessed

In Simon Gray's *Otherwise Engaged,* currently at the Plymouth Theatre on Broadway, the protagonist, Simon Hench (Tom Courtenay), is visited in succession by six people who not only stand in the way of his plan to listen to a new recording of Wagner's *Parsifal,* but who proceed to pummel him with insults. Simon earns the intrusions by wanting to be alone, and he earns the insults—whether from his tenant, his brother, his friend, his friend's latest lover, his own one-night-stand lover, or his wife—by not really giving a damn about them *or* their insults. He can give what he gets, though his insults are contained as much in his silences as in his words. Simon gets far and away the best of his playwright-namesake's wit. He also gets the best of Gray's feeling. The intruders report troubles, while Simon reveals pain. In short, Simon Gray gives Simon Hench advantage and game. Strange, then, that he doesn't really give him a play.

Instead, he gives him a well-oiled machine, a tidy arrangement of intrusions and insults that make their entrances and exits not from the mouths of people or the doors of rooms, but from the keys of a typewriter. If there is nothing startling about that, it is because most writers manage to conceal their little secret by allowing characters the illusion of choice. Gray dispels the illusion by so clearly reserving all the choices for himself. His leading character's leading characteristic gives the secret away. Hench is a man who wants to control his life as written by a man who wants to control Hench.

When Gray tires of an intruder's reminiscences or jokes, the intruder announces the name, and therefore the probable arrival, of the next intruder. "Did I ever tell you about Davina?" asks Simon's journalist friend Jeff, and sure enough, Davina rings the bell. The program informs us that the only character still to come in the second act will be Simon's wife, Beth, who is supposedly away on a job that afternoon. Gray can't resist announcing her entrance, too. Simon's brother, Stephen, informs Simon that Beth has been having an affair with Ned. Exit Stephen, enter Beth. That Ned never gets *his* entrance is because Beth's exit is the signal for Jeff's return, the two male friends alone at the final curtain, at last listening to Solti's Wagner.

The play buried under the avalanche of insults, entrances, and exits is the one about Simon and Jeff. Simon is remembered as the sexy little boy who slept with all the handsome older boys in his classy school. Jeff, in his turn, tells Simon, "I detest women, love men, and loathe queers." And it is these two cozy friends who share the ending with Wagner. If Jeff's statement means anything, it is that these two men, left alone and untroubled by the military maneuvers of their playwright, could really build a play. Simon tells Beth that "the worst thing to do about an important problem is to discuss it," which is precisely what Gray has them do.

Tom Courtenay almost rescues Hench from Gray's iron pen. He stops time long enough for a phrase to seem like *his* invention, not something planned relentlessly in advance, but something moved into speech by the actor's thought. Everything he does is vivid, plain, and exact. Who wouldn't wish to be otherwise engaged when faced with all those demanding, self-absorbed, hostile intruders? Hell *is* other people. And other actors. Courtenay is a marvelous intruder into Gray's unexamined world, but he would be better engaged in the plays by Heinrich von Kleist and Edward Bond that he did recently in England—or in the play that Gray has yet to write.

A playwright's control over his material is widely viewed as a virtue, alas, and nowhere more so than in England. David Rudkin's *Ashes,* also from England, produced in New York in December at the Manhattan Theatre Club and now moved to Joseph Papp's Public Theatre, is less crafty than Gray's work, while no less ruled by rules that give the characters little time or space for detours. This isn't playwriting, it's mapmaking. The problem is stated: Colin and Anne can't make babies. The problem is developed: Colin and Anne try harder, get clinical advice, and make it as far as the miscarriage, where Anne loses her womb. The problem moves predictably to Colin and Anne registering for adoption. They can't win that one, either, and they don't. But before the final meditations—"If we do not change, tomorrow has no place for us"—Colin does take a detour to Belfast, from where he returns with a message that speciously links his and Anne's troubles to Ireland's. The route is denser than Gray's, the map itself more bloody. Rudkin's feelings want to overflow the play's boundaries, but he can't let them make the crossing: he's too fixed on fine writing.

It is the fine writing that almost sinks the play, not least such lines as the moral uplift quoted above. Worse are the long, meditative passages, especially Colin's, where Anne is either offstage, or onstage and ignored. Rudkin keeps rubbing his Dylan Thomas bottle, but the genie never really jumps out to show him the difference between felt experience and fake poetry. "Suburban bellies bloated with the booty of the bed" would not have surprised me coming from the mouth of a certain disgraced vice president; but from an earnest, obviously intelligent dramatist, I expect some editorial grace.

Lynne Meadow has made smart directorial choices, facing the fake and the real with equal determination, taking the play at its clinical word. If the words are clotted, at least her stage is bare, her lights uncolored, and her own sense of economy intact. She could have used some Courtenays, actors more in touch with thought; willing to punctuate, phrase, and breathe, and, while so doing, to discover the density of the disaster rather than only its opaque, borrowed wisdom.

I have omitted one startling coincidence. Rudkin's Colin, like Gray's Simon, was also a practicing homosexual before his marriage. Rudkin lets Anne comment that what is unorthodox about Colin's sexuality is that he acknowledges it. But the play itself is otherwise engaged; indeed, it is otherwise obsessed with going it alone. Anne sits silently in the driver's seat in one scene, while Colin talks about Colin. He tells her that "the strongest feeling in the world is to be left alone," which is unclear enough to seem to mean that his strongest feeling is that he, too, wants to be alone.

In these two plays, the women are erased, and the loathed queers appear only in the footnotes. If the likes of Colin or Simon ever met a self-possessed woman or a contented gay man, much of British playwriting might cease to rely so much on control, craft, and the artful dodging of both experience and imagination.   *GR(March 1977)*

Tiny Albee

Edward Albee began by writing plays in which language joined fable to produce at least one passionate disclosure. His people lived and talked on the edge of a violence that occurred either in a physical action (Jerry prodding Peter to kill him in *The Zoo Story*) or in a verbal admission (George and Martha killing their mythical son in *Who's Afraid of Virginia Woolf?*). What survives in those plays is not the violence, but rather the motor energy of the language. It is a raw, elemental, insistent language, dragging its people from their guarded emotional lairs, compelling each to acknowledge the presence—the real life—of the other.

Albee's new short plays, *Counting the Ways* and *Listening,* performed on a double bill recently by the Hartford Stage Company under the author's flaccid direction, are about people without names, hiding behind a language without passion. True, Albee was always jabbing at the shadows cast by words. Even in *Virginia Woolf* he wanted us to notice that the blond, blue-eyed myth was also a metaphor. But he was not yet in the mortal grip of words as artifacts—crazy, threatening figures with lives of their own. Words have enemies in most of Albee's plays ("The plural is gone out of us," says the lawyer in *Tiny Alice*), and in these two plays the enemies are identified at last as other words.

Neither play makes much of plot or character. *Counting the Ways* is supposed to be "a vaudeville," a series of blackout encounters between She (Angela Lansbury) and He (William Prince). They are a married couple meeting twenty to thirty times across the dinner table in order to learn how much, if at all, they love each other. Over a gray space, with the table and two chairs in the middle, hangs a sign bearing the title of the play. This unfolds later to reveal another sign marked with the words IDENTIFY YOURSELF—at which point, She comes forward and says, "Good evening, I'm Angela Lansbury" (her only real moment all night), followed by a similar presentation from Prince. Still later, She walks into the yawning blackness of the backstage area, and He calls after her, "Where are you going?" To which She replies, "Off."

The territory is familiar: the brittleness of Coward, the allusiveness of Pinter, and even, to my surprise, the distancing of Brecht. Or is it Pirandello this time—two characters in search of their elusive author? Albee used to be available, but now he seems to be locked in a monkish cell populated only by theatrical quotation and decorative words.

First, there are the *words profound,* which, on closer scrutiny, say absolutely nothing: "There are two things—cease and corruption"; or, "Pain is a misunderstanding, it's really loss what it's about." Then there are the *words precious:* "We were still maidens—head and hood"; or, "Thousands have lived without love, but none without shirts." The latter, we are quickly informed, is a parody of a line by W. H. Auden, which—the playwright allows— some of us knew. Auden is, in fact, "one of the ones I cried when he died." And so we have the glory borrowed from Auden and the sentiment borrowed from another poet, Elizabeth Barrett Browning, both in the play's title and in an exchange that quotes the famous line: "How do I love thee? Let me count the ways." Finally, there are the *words self-congratulatory:* "We all had a bit of pudge—that's a nice way of putting it"; or the observation after a question that it was "good phrasing."

In *Listening,* Lansbury is The Woman, Prince is The Man, and Maureen Anderman is added to the cast as The Girl. This is a "chamber play" (allusion: Strindberg). Housman is the poet whose line nobody can remember in this play, and the encounter, while even more about language than the first play's, nevertheless ends in real blood. Real stage blood, that is. There is more deliberate mystery here, hence more words of the profound, precious, or self-congratulatory kind, especially the litany repeated monotonously by The Girl: "You don't listen—pay attention, rather, is what you don't do."

Some phrases don't try so hard to sound like writing. "I was surprised you turned away," The Woman says to The Man. "Many don't." But most of them made me long for *Counting the Ways.* What was symptom there grows into epidemic here. Did you ever think before about the "codpiece of the psyche"? Do you believe that "we all wish to devour ourselves, be the subject and the object"? Are you attracted to "the hot, moist, suffocating center" of anybody's "temporal being"? What would you say to someone who charged you to "get behind that sentence, find out what precedes"? Do you have any idea what it might be like to "hear . . . pupils widen"? I'm afraid there is more, much more, and I suppose that when The Woman says, "God, what a language!" we are meant to feel some relief about Albee's consciousness of, if not about his culpability in, the crimes against that language.

Is there anything lurking behind this awful fuss of words? Nostalgia, of course. When feelings don't show, can memories be far behind? Albee gives Lansbury one piquant recollection in *Counting the Ways,* about a dinner party given by her sister and attended by two men who do or do not know that one of them—but which one?—is dying of cancer. Albee has also released some tenderness between He and She that I don't recall in his other plays. Yet even as he brushes against a simple feeling, he wrenches himself away with still another preposterous verbal twitch. The Woman in *Listening* admits that she cried when her parents and cats died, when she turned forty, and when someone lied to her for the first time. All very genuine, for a change. But Albee has to add, "I cried when I died," which is plainly not true. And plainly not out of her mouth, but out of his. No wonder that he is agitating for people to listen. He talks so much and has so little to say.

David Mamet is apparently listening to America's lower class. The news he brings back in his new play, *American Buffalo* (at the Ethel Barrymore Theatre on Broadway), is that Americans living on the dark underside of small business and petty crookery speak of macho frustrations almost entirely in four-letter words. If the news doesn't seem new or persuasive, that may be because we have heard more antiseptic versions of it on big and little screens, where—with a little soap in their mouths—*American Buffalo*'s trio of charmless deadbeats would be more at home.

Robert Duvall's Walter Cole (known as Teacher) is the latest in a long line of Stanley Kowalskis trying to mimic the language they think businessmen use. Some of the linguistic turns are cleverly heard: Teacher-Kowalskis do like to say words like *averse, deviate, instance;* and they love to talk about planning, preparation, business propositions, and facing facts. Duvall's performance has as much body in it as it does dirty English, but it is more an expert impersonation of an archetype than an enactment of an authentic event.

How could it be otherwise? Mamet is imitating a hundred Bogart, Cagney, Robinson, and Brando movies, and he's not bad at the job. His dialogue has some of the vivacity missing from those movies. They were better at plot, however; and they didn't always treat Bogart and company like dummies. In *The Maltese Falcon,* Wilmer wasn't bright, but he had dignity. Mamet patronizes his trio: he is out to kill and get laughs. Modest ambitions, modestly achieved.

Albee's privileged agonizers could use a shot of Mamet's verve, while Mamet's sentimental slobs wouldn't be hurt by a touch of Albee's former gravity. Albee has read—and written—too many highfalutin' plays, and Mamet has seen too many lowbrow movies. With friends like these two, words don't need enemies.   *GR(April 1977)*

Long Night's Journey

Eugene O'Neill had the right pedigree for the role of serious playwright: a family freighted with misery, a series of boarding schools wrecking his intelligence, suspension from Princeton because of a student prank, a secret marriage dissolved early, an attempt at prospecting for gold in Central America thwarted by a case of malaria, and, after this, surrender to his actor-manager father by joining his company as an actor and assistant manager. As if the actor's life were not bad enough, O'Neill went on to restlessness at sea and in bars, then back to acting, on to journalism, and, finally, to a case of tuberculosis that led him to the most dangerous—and for him, most crippling—adventure of all: heavy reading in Greek tragedy and an obvious misreading of Strindberg. The Greeks appealed to his ambition and Strindberg appealed to his tormented image of himself. To make matters worse, he enrolled in a playwriting course.

Had he missed the Greeks and the formal education, he might have written the obligatory autobiographical play first rather than last; in which case, he wouldn't have written so many awful plays in order to reach sublime moments in *The Iceman Cometh* and *Long Day's Journey into Night*. The recent arrival of *Anna Christie* (1921) at the Imperial Theatre on Broadway is a useful reminder that the rules of playwriting are no substitute for absent feeling or instinctive technique.

O'Neill must have learned several inhibiting lessons at school. First, there was *exposition*: as *Anna Christie* opens, five characters are used to provide barroom atmosphere and information about two of the three protagonists. A letter arrives from Minnesota for Chris Christopherson. The handwriting, they say, looks like a woman's. Chris is supposed to have a daughter somewhere out west. "Come to think of it," says the owner of the bar, "I ain't seen old Chris in a dog's age." The dog's age, of course, ends immediately: Chris arrives. The atmospheric characters, their usefulness at an end, disappear into the wings or silence. Chris's woman, Marthy Owen, arrives. She will get longer shrift from O'Neill, but she is additional exposition nonetheless. When Chris is conveniently gone, his daughter Anna enters, supposedly to drink and converse with Marthy, but really to be recognized by Marthy as a whore. Marthy leaves when Chris returns. And just to be certain that she won't reveal the terrible truth about Anna (so that Anna can reveal it herself in a third-act confessional scene), O'Neill exiles Marthy from the stage forever. He ensures the credibility of her banishment by yet another mechanical device: sailing Chris and his coal barge to Provincetown and Boston for the rest of the play.

Other lessons learned by O'Neill were surely about *character* and *action*. Assuming he read it, he must have misunderstood Strindberg's sermon in the preface to *Miss Julie*, in which he described the "souls" in his plays as "characterless"—he wanted to avoid the immobile, fixed, and finished patterns so common to the middle-class stage. O'Neill fixed Anna in the death grip of the oldest pattern about the oldest profession. Her heart is tarnished gold and she hates men. Similarly, Chris is frozen in stereotype. A man who blames the sea for all his troubles, he will never let Anna marry a sailor. All of which brings on Mat Burke, a sailor who makes Anna feel clean in the same way that the sea makes her feel clean. Mat is Irish, which translates into "impulsive" and "romantic." Naturally, he likes his women clean.

Now, the *action*. Since a character in such a formula play is supposed to undergo a change of at least one characteristic, it follows that the action of *Anna Christie* will be directed entirely toward reconciling Anna to men, but not before the men turn against Anna. This is not only action, it is *conflict*. Anna falls in love with Mat. Mat goes on a binge after she tells Everything. He returns to Anna demanding an oath of fidelity on his mother's cross. (Could there be another?) And Chris agrees that gaining a son-in-law is better than losing a daughter a second time. The characteristics of the characters have been rearranged neatly for a happy ending.

O'Neill wanted to believe that "the happy ending is merely a comma at the end of a gaudy introductory clause, with the body of the sentence still unwritten," a wishful thought that makes sense only if one looks away from *Anna Christie* to the later plays. In them, the fix was broken. Messy, unarranged life was permitted to intrude. *Anna Christie,* however, is a mess in another way: it is a play about sex with sexual energy missing. O'Neill was hooked on chastity. Just before *Anna Christie* he wrote *Diff'rent,* in which the heroine is the one who rejects her lover because she knows he can't be a virgin. The other early plays also dwell on blame and fault, as if O'Neill couldn't push on with life or writing until an insurance policy could be taken out against the impurity of others. For a fleeting moment, he gives Anna her freedom. "Nobody owns me except myself," she says, and the play is suddenly threatened by life. But then O'Neill retreats to his textbook, reappearing with the mother's cross. The prig conquers the playwright.

Liv Ullmann plays Anna in José Quintero's faithfully antique production, and she has that "power of strength" in her that Mat boasts about in one misbegotten stage-Irish phrase after another. Her power is that she believes in her words and her actions. She isn't out to decorate the stage with shivering instincts and tremulous conviction; behind her reality lies a plan. Stage light will find her wherever she stands or sits; in it, her hair will glow and the whites of her eyes will tell all that need be known about loneliness. Neither is she a purveyor of conventions. Anna may have lived in "one of those houses," but Ullmann never plants her hands on her hips. Instead, she twists her fingers around fallen hairs or she clutches her arm around the bottom of her bag. In a voice shrouded in fog, she says O'Neill's clumsy words, but most of the time she makes us listen to her gestures.

Artful, clever, and accurate, she uses her own Scandinavian, vaguely Cockney English rather than O'Neill's absurd Swedish dialect. Yet Robert Donley, as Anna's father, listens to O'Neill instead of to Ullmann: "Py yiminy," he says, though she has already pronounced the *j* in *janitor.* Donley is otherwise as firm a believer in his tasks as Ullmann is in hers. So, too, are John Lithgow as Mat and Mary McCarty as Marthy. Despite their spirit, they can't crowd Ullmann out of her light; the play isn't crafted that way.

Anna Christie is one of the dumbest famous plays ever written, but it is smart enough to know how to shoot a star into orbit. When Charles Bickford played Mat to Garbo's Anna in the film, he told her that it was a "terrific vehicle for her," though a "bad one" for him. "I told her honestly," he wrote, "that I considered the character of Mat a mere human prop for Anna to play against." O'Neill escaped punishment for all those human props because his search for something big occurred just when the country was looking for a serious playwright. Grumbling about fate and hammering away at destiny, how could he miss? Bickford hated the film, adding that "if this be heresy, make the most of it"; so the pressures against dissent must have been daunting at the time. But must we suffer those early plays now? Mercifully, O'Neill's long journey into playwriting ended with moderate distinction. He, at least, was big enough to escape his history. Broadway, however, can't seem to let go.

GR(May 1977)

Musicals and the Unquiet American

The prevailing myth is that the best and most original theatre Americans have produced is musical comedy. I prefer to believe that the best and most original *American* we have produced is the musical comedy performer. Think about it. Who would be your desert island favorite? Helen Hayes or Helen Morgan? Ethel Barrymore or Ethel Merman? Can there be hesitation? On the one side, there is Hayes's and Barrymore's pious, deadly good taste; on the other, Merman's blowsy, vulgar, marvelously lively bad taste. The American musical comedy performer, at his or her best, is one of the few antidotes to such American (though not exclusively American) afflictions as righteousness, sentimentality, and murderous goodwill. A good tune, an insinuating lyric, and a shifting rhythm were all that Merman needed. She wasn't the mathematical result of a few studiously learned skills. She couldn't dance Giselle, and she couldn't sing Butterfly (though I have often thought longingly of her untried Brünnhilde); nor did she ever win contests for refinement of technique or subtlety of feeling. Yet she was always the most natural of American forces: not bigger than life, but better, every vocal inch of her a statement about the frontier spirit. Her world was whole, present, musical, and—as a dividend—vulnerably comic.

The myth has been, however, about the shows themselves. When Rodgers lost Hart and found Hammerstein, the musical comedy took a new course. The sound of music was still there, but the comedy gave way to the Big Idea, weighty messages about Hate and Fear, Love and Learning, Dreams and Illusions. We were told that Hammerstein had patented a new invention called the Musical Play, as if Hofmannsthal-Strauss and Brecht-Weill had not changed the face of musical theatre twice over years before. It is our custom, apparently, to be outside history or to be busily rewriting it.

All new musicals, of course, are trying to be history. If thinking could make it so, any new musical would easily dance into the books as an improvement on the Second Coming. Dizzy enthusiasts who find Beckett puzzling, Ibsen clumsy, or Chekhov slow can find the most amazing virtues in the trashiest musical. There is no way of knowing in advance why one form of rubbish might be luckier with the press and the audience than another. Years ago, a show called *Kelly* opened and closed on Broadway in one night, passing into legend as the flop to end all flops, but I am willing to swear that it was no worse than *Annie* (Alvin Theatre on Broadway), this year's hit to end all hits.

Annie tops *Kelly* because the dice were thrown at the right moment. It is supposed to be the first Carter musical, meaning it is the first show during Carter's presidency to reflect whatever it is that we think *we* know *he* knows. (A command performance of excerpts from the show was given at the White House during the Washington, D.C., tryout.) For me, on the contrary, it is really the first post-Nixon show. Thomas Meehan based the show on the comic strip *Little Orphan Annie*. He has crafted a new, occasionally amusing rags-to-riches story that follows Annie's journey from the orphanage to the Fifth Avenue mansion of Oliver Warbucks. The strip's neo-fascism has been laundered to suit the neo-liberalism of our time. Now it is the most accurate emblem of a country sick of its own sourness: a cartoon born again, celebrating cynical wealth, conservative optimism, spunky kids, and trained dogs. With all those elements neatly in place, it doesn't have to be good as music, lyrics, or theatre. *Annie* confirms what Nixon successfully covered up in his own devious person and what Jimmy has been assuring us: we *are* good, and since thinking can make it *seem* so, many of us are willing to return the compliment.

What *is* good, if not redemptive, about *Annie* are some of the performers, particularly Dorothy Loudon as Miss Hannigan, the mistress of the orphanage, addicted to *Ma Perkins,* booze, lies, and a remarkably sympathetic loathing of little girls. Loudon walks as if she were really two people, the first scouting for an ambush, the other waiting for word that the coast is clear. She learns that Daddy Warbucks is going to adopt Annie. "Wonderful news," she says. "My, my, my. . ." Then she asks to be excused for a moment. Taking a slow, almost dainty death march into the hallway, she can at last release the scream that has been locked inside of her. This is only one of many extended double takes lavished on a complicated woman who could so easily have become the cartoon almost everybody else is playing. Loudon offers the outrageous yell, the popping eye, and the bumping grind, but behind them all stands the distraught heart, numb with rage and heavy with unrepentant greed. That she is so special, so unapologetically funny and appealing in such an impoverished show—tunes going nowhere, lyrics discharging such astounding insights as "Tomorrow is always a day away"—is another sign that the Merman legacy is still alive and well, if not necessarily in the service of a smart idea.

One jarring moment in *Annie* occurs when Charles Strouse, the composer of the doodling score, seems to think it might be a smart idea to crib the rhythms, orchestration, and drift of a tune from the ample warehouse of Kurt Weill. The scene is in a Hooverville beneath the Fifty-ninth Street Bridge during the Depression, and the freshly washed bums and their mates, looking like early settlers in Levittown, sing "Who knew I could steal?"—not a question that a clever thief should ask.

Weill is one of the smart ideas largely missing from *Annie* (Strouse should have cribbed some more), but he is very much in evidence in *Happy End,* recently presented by the Chelsea Theatre Center in Brooklyn and later moved to the Martin Beck Theatre on Broadway. This is the 1929 collaboration between Brecht and Weill, presented then as a play by Dorothy Lane, a pseudonym for Brecht's friend Elisabeth Hauptmann; later, Brecht disowned it. By now the show has as much Brecht in it as *Annie* has, its book and lyrics adapted by Michael Feingold and its production "newly conceived and directed by Robert Kalfin with musical staging by Patricia Birch." In other words, a disowned child is producing a bastard. Brecht might wince at some of Feingold's improvements ("you rat" for "du Hund," or words like "creep" and phrases like "Can it"), but even he would have to admit that the Weill score is worth rescuing, especially as played with such jaunty precision under the musical direction of Roland Gagnon.

The production looked cramped, forced, and ugly on the Chelsea stage. Even so, some of the players—particularly Raymond J. Barry, Benjamin Rayson, and Tony Azito—were as direct, mercurial, and fundamentally honest as

Brecht actors must be. Lotte Lenya can't play Salvation Army lasses anymore, so Meryl Streep, a young American actress, made the leap into the bitter distance of the Brecht-Weill world. She fell, I'm afraid, only within shouting distance of the other side, even though her arrogant coldness might win browbeaten friends and influence slavish people.

Seen earlier this year as a Barbie-doll Dunyasha in *The Cherry Orchard* at Lincoln Center, Streep can do everything efficiently, but nothing really well. Her singing voice breaks into three equal parts: high, middle, and low, the top part pinched, hooty, and as empty as her cartoon Orphan Annie eyes. When she sings about water going up and ships going down, tiny invisible strings seem to pull her arms up for the one and down for the other. She seems not so much rehearsed as programmed. Perhaps she is the first Carter actress, always ready with a smile and a cop-out.

Some time ago, Brecht's widow, Helene Weigel, suggested Merman for the role of Mother Courage in the Broadway production of *Mother Courage and Her Children*. Such casting would have served Brecht as richly as the casting of Bert Lahr in *Waiting for Godot* served Beckett. It didn't happen, because most straight plays are cast with straight actresses, though there is no reciprocal trade agreement restraining straight and narrow actresses from invading musicals. Our best musical comedy performers, Loudon and Merman among them, belong in our best plays. But it may be just as well that they don't so appear: if they were in plays, some of us wouldn't have musicals to kick around anymore.   *GR(June 1977)*

The Very Little Mahagonny

Few people expect to find fun in the works of Bertolt Brecht. Yet fun is the word that keeps appearing in his own exhortations and the remarks of his friends and critics. Even in his frequently lugubrious 1934 conversations with Walter Benjamin, Brecht couldn't resist the subject, remarking about the answer he might give to a tribunal that asked if he meant to be serious: "Not quite," he would say. "After all, I think too much about artistic matters, about what would go well on stage, to be quite serious." *About what would go well on stage* . . . Meaning, and not obscurely, that Brecht wanted the audience to enjoy itself. Master dramatic strategist that he was, he knew that thinking can be fun. And in *Mahagonny* itself, the moment when music and text come most poignantly together is the Widow Begbick's lament that "there is not much fun on this star."

Brecht's poker face got the best of him, however, when he wrote about *Mahagonny,* the opera he and Kurt Weill fashioned in 1930 from the early songs in *Hauspostille* and *The Little Mahagonny* (1927). Operatic form and the operatic apparatus were "idiocy" to him, with so much reality and rationality "washed out by the music." He was happier with what their collaboration produced in *The Threepenny Opera* (written between the little and the large *Mahagonny*): tunes that could be spoken-against, plain speech shifting to heightened speech, and finally to singing, all of it producing what he called "a stubborn, incorruptible sobriety which is independent of music and rhythm."

Poor B. B. By now, even he might acknowledge that the pursuit of fun can be one of the most political acts available, especially in a compromised theatre so frantically, so mercilessly in pursuit of plastic realism, reductive homilies, tinned laughter, and earnest sentimentalities; a theatre, in fact, that doesn't "think too much about artistic matters." Whether he liked it or not, the full, operatic *Mahagonny* is not only fun, it is his best work.

Like surfers in search of the perfect wave, some people—myself included—have been crossing continents with alarming regularity in search of the perfect *Mahagonny.* The Yale Repertory Theatre has been more faithful than any other theatre in its devotion to the piece, this season producing its fourth version of what it calls "a work of Brecht and Weill with the name 'Mahagonny' in its title." This one is a chamber version "retranslated, rearranged, and otherwise altered" by its director, Keith Hack. And—bad news for surfers—it is the most funless *Mahagonny* to date.

Why? One need not cross Long Island Sound, let alone a continent, to find at least one of the answers. Turn to the Yale program, which publishes Brecht's remarks in 1926 about the traditional theatre with which he found himself at odds. "Take the actors, for instance," he writes, "I wouldn't want to say that we are worse off for talent than other periods seem to have been, but I doubt if there has ever been such an overworked, misused, panic-driven, artificially whipped-up band of actors as ours. *And nobody who fails to get fun out of his activities can expect them to be fun for anybody else"* [Brecht's italics].

I have seen Hack's work only once before, a London *Hedda Gabler* that seemed to be a rehearsal not for the smoky, insinuating encounters written by Ibsen, but for the Kentucky Derby. With *Mahagonny,* his taste for the gallop is held in moderate check by the music. His pressure on actors, however, is the same. Stuffing them into the confinement of the boxing ring used by Brecht for *The Little Mahagonny,* he paints their faces clown-white, smudges some of them with red cheeks, sketches cat's whiskers on his Jenny, loads them all with enough bolts of hideous, dark textiles to clothe an emerging Third World nation, and then has his prop man dump a clock, a bullhorn, a hydrant, a tire, a girdle, and the exhaust system of a car into the ring just to keep them hopping. Well, he doesn't shoot actors, does he?

But what does he do—for Brecht, Weill, for the text? If I say "Nothing," I mean to say only that nothing actually happens on stage, though there is plenty of noise, plenty of poses, plenty of—nothing. How could it be otherwise? This chamber version, this rearrangement, this "otherwise altered" thing ("altered" is good, really good, reminding one of fixed dogs and declawed cats) is not about fun, not about opera, not about dialectical wit, not about money, sex, anything. Hack is after the easiest game: a couple of hit tunes, cute show-biz attitudes, and a prolonged wink to the audience.

Throwing the cast of even this reduced version into a boxing ring is one way of throwing them into nowhere. The ring might have done service for the earlier "songspiel," but not for a *Mahagonny* where so much more is supposed to happen, where boxing itself is only one of four major pivots at the center of the piece. (The others are greed, love, and booze.) Mahagonny has to be a substantial place, a city of nets, a snare for fugitives from all continents. It is paradise found and lost again, where capitalism can be parodied but only up to a point, just as opera can be parodied but not quite all the way. The people who settle there, especially Jimmy Mahoney and his friends, the ex-lumberjacks from Brecht's very imaginary Alaska, must experience rich, full, counterpointing, *musical* events. A Mahagonny unthreatened by a typhoon, as this one is, becomes a Mahagonny unthreatening to the people in it, and unthreatening to us. In the complete version, Jimmy wants to go somewhere else almost as soon as he has arrived. "But something is missing," he says. In Hack's version, nothing much was ever there.

His city is without anything ominous in it, anything quietly seductive or sweetly ironic. There are no echoes of that "eternal art" remembered by the lumberjacks with such scented nostalgia when it is parodied on the player piano. This is a version without a past, and therefore, no present. Brecht and Weill's Jimmy is Tamino and Parsifal reborn, still on the same dumb quest for perfection that always gets tenors going. But if he's just another actor and not a tenor, then who can he be? Brecht's fear that reality would be "washed out by the music" couldn't have been more misguided: Hack's reduction demonstrates that the piece's reality can be washed out only by the absence of a musical *experience.*

Two cheers for Yale for its fidelity to the search, but no cheers to Hack for his meddling. We're all guilty, of course, a bunch of tenors dumbly questing. Next year, the Metropolitan Opera will be doing *Mahagonny,* presumably with tenors, sopranos, altos, basses, and something bigger and more varied than a boxing ring. If that one doesn't work, then I'm prepared at last to agree with Begbick that there is not much fun on this star.

GR(December 1978)

Stephen Poliakoff: Blind Anger

As the lights rise, a phone is ringing. Heavy breathing on the other end. Heavy, terribly Spanish accent accompanies the breathing. Filthy phone call. Clare recognizes the voice within moments. "Oh, it's you," she says, or something else that sounds like recognition. Of course, she's tense. It is easy to tell how tense she is because her hand grips the telephone as if it were the handle of a hammer. She is only moderately relieved to recognize the voice, whose accent has now changed to pure, incompetent American imitation of regional Cockney-Birmingham-Northern British-or-whatever. By God, it isn't an obscene caller, it's just another tense American actor pretending to be overwrought in still another American version of one of those British plays that is performed here not because it is a distinguished work of imaginative fiction, but because it is covertly sensational, mysteriously obscure in its plotting, vaguely metaphorical, and unhesitatingly British.

The British pedigree is important. Just as all things good, true, and tender are British on public television, so are most things harsh, grim, and grubby British in the theatre. With *Look Back in Anger* in 1956, John Osborne released a deluge of bitter humors, shabby bed-sitting rooms, and scruffy sweaters that were supposed to describe the story of an empire either blasted or betrayed. The politics were never clear. Was it nostalgia for a past never to be recovered, or nostalgia for a future that will never be? Later, we discovered that Osborne merely wanted to replace the sweater with a striped suit and an umbrella. If any metaphor remained, it was that Britain had fallen because women are a mess. This was so plainly silly that some of us snapped out of that British cultural trance and returned home to make theatrical truths from American sources.

Osborne lives, however, in those youngish British playwrights who must have been beaten into insensibility by the raging sixties and the dopy seventies. Stephen Poliakoff is more talented, I suspect, than *Hitting Town,* and surely he is more adept than the production he has been given by the South Street Theatre Company. Richard Hamburger's staging is pushy and loud, as if silence or pause might make his actors actually think about what they are doing or what is happening to them. Clare's telephone caller, Ralph, shows up chewing gum, chewing it so hard and toothily that for a moment it appears as if the play is mysteriously about a mouth. Ralph's hands are as jumpy and tight as his teeth. Clare is just as jumpy as he is. The stage is littered with the bare bones of actors' agitation, and if there is any story left to tell, it is difficult to know how these actors could tell it or how it could look half as pseudo-dramatic as these opening moments.

Hamburger must have been counting on the shocking disclosure that punctuates an early scene in this long one-act play: Clare is not merely an older woman about to be abused for an hour by her ineffectual Jimmy Porteresque lover; she is an older woman with a difference. "You've got to call our mother," she tells Ralph. And, weirdly, it is a moment almost lost in the playing. It is even possible to doubt that one has heard her correctly. Anyway, if one has heard her correctly, what difference will it make? The play has already been so obscurely tense in so many obscure corners of the director's mind that it hasn't really any place to travel, not even into the relatively rare—for drama—recesses of incestuous experience.

Ralph and Clare meet the only other character in the play at a hamburger joint where they go to eat. She is the off-duty waitress, Nicola, who demonstrates how she screams at bus stops when she is alone. This is presumably a footnote to Ralph and Clare's elusive story, designed to show how a zombie untroubled by incest can also be obscurely agitated. It doesn't take Nicola long to suspect that Ralph and Clare are no ordinary kissing couple, but when the incest is confirmed by Ralph—Clare is primly opposed to exposure—she rapidly loses interest. As do we.

Which is a pity, but something of a clue to what went wrong with Poliakoff's mechanics. Why must an audience be sentenced to an hour-and-twenty-minute session with a trio of tensile, jittery, relentlessly aggressive morons? Only if the morons are really touching in themselves, illuminating about moronhood, or if they are surrogates for some strange incisive concern. Poliakoff reveals that Ralph's agitation is derived as much from his minicareer as a terrorist as from his incestuous passion. But he never weaves these promising strands into the fabric of his play: they stand apart, isolated and unexamined. His scenewriting is always smartly terse, but his playwriting is curiously stuffed with extra words and flailing gestures, an awful mix of portent and pointlessness.

At his best, Osborne let his anger shape his plays. They took their form from his monologues, those great suspirations of loathing and invective. Poliakoff can't seem to breathe or grieve in that titanic mode. Clare and Ralph wrestle each other to the ground after he calls in a threat to blow up a bomb in London's Haymarket. Will she see him again, he asks? Yes, she says, or does she say maybe, or if? Whatever it is, it doesn't connect to anything before it. Poliakoff makes noises that want to sound like Life and Politics in a bang-up merge, but by the time he exhausts his resources, he can only end with a whimper.   *GR(January 1979)*

Liviu Ciulei: Murder by Concept

Liviu Ciulei cannot be blamed for the expectations aroused by his production of *Hamlet*. His credentials are precisely the kind that appeal to the lethal mix of generosity and self-contempt so characteristic of Americans easily impressed by credentials, especially European ones. A native of Bucharest, Ciulei has been associated with Rumania's Bulandra Theatre for thirty years as a director, designer, and actor. At Cannes in 1965, he won the Festival prize for his direction of the film *Forest of the Hanged*. His first production in this country was Büchner's *Leonce and Lena* for the Arena Stage in 1974; his only work in New York has been with Juilliard's students last December in a production of Frank Wedekind's *Spring Awakening*. If you missed it, as I did, you were led by the reviews and gossip to believe that you had missed an event equal to Brook's *Marat-Sade* or *Midsummer Night's Dream*.

Perhaps the Wedekind, the Büchner, and all those works in Europe were indeed such major events. But if *Hamlet* in Washington is representative evidence, they could not have been. Since the line between press agentry and criticism is now so blurred, there really is no reliable way of knowing anything about anybody in advance. Where imported directors are concerned, there is the further distinction between the production's visual appeal and what actually *happens* on stage. Ciulei, like Strehler, Zeffirelli, and Luca Ronconi, began as a set designer, graduating later to direction. At first, in fact, Ciulei was an architect. While such a pedigree is not a crime, it indicates what he is likely to stress.

In the production casebook for his Washington *Leonce and Lena* (published by *Theatre Quarterly* in 1975), Ciulei says: "We have to turn back to the autonomous means of the theatrical medium. Its most important quality and means are immediate contact with the audience." An unsuspecting reader might conclude momentarily that by "immediate contact" he must be referring to the live actor. But what architect in recent experience has been famous for his sensitivity to the people condemned to inhabit his structures? Ciulei's explanation gives away the game: "So, whatever ways and possibilities one is in search of, the audience has to be enabled to follow these ways and to take up the possibilities"—which are, as you may have guessed by now, "the scenery, the costumes, the music, and the masks."

Ciulei is, then, our old friend, the director with a *concept*. The premise is simple: the audience must be persuaded that what may appear to be an exhausted classic is really just another modern play in costume drag, as if the audience couldn't urge a few contemporary connections into its equally exhausted brain without the help of the director's visual signals. His interview in the program for *Hamlet* is a treasure chest of weighty concepts that, on close inspection, mean absolutely nothing.

First comes the observation that's supposed to make one's heart skip a beat: "The performance is an evening's event; a happening, like an evening newspaper." This is soon followed by: "A production today must answer today's questions." (It could be argued that some questions from yesterday are still lying around unanswered, but we'll let that pass.) These breathtaking insights are mere preparation for the explanation of *Hamlet* that has eluded scholars and other directors for several centuries; in this case, that "the central question is the recognition of disorder in the world and of the restoration of that order." This, come to think of it, is what a designer-director faces when he confronts an old play—a disordered world that has to be restored to order—by him.

Which brings us to Ciulei's Washington *Hamlet*. The setting and time? Well, it sure as hell can't be Elizabethan England. A Hamlet wearing the inky cloak assumed by Shakespeare "does not clearly tell today's audience what type of person this character is or what his occupation might be," says Ciulei. But a Hamlet living in—can you guess?—"a sort of Bismarckian world . . . is more easily recognized." By whom, you may wonder? The Hessians among us whose ancestors wrote the Constitution? Princess Grace?

A whacky, arbitrary, half-formed guiding image nonetheless might make itself felt in performance. The audience, after all, tends to embalm *Hamlet* in its reverential moments—all those familiar lines and Yorick's skull, for example. Any inventions that push the story forward would be welcome. Bismarck is not one of them. Instead of animating the story, the costume parade keeps bringing it to abrupt halts. Why, for instance, do all those late-nineteenth-century figures take so seriously that obvious nut pretending to be a ghost? And why doesn't someone stop to ask those other loonies, the strolling players, from what century or country they think they are straying? To say nothing of the peculiar pressures of language, to which Ciulei clearly can't address himself.

A less burdened intelligence might have placed more trust in *Hamlet*'s wondrous narrative. What Shaw said of Hamlet's passionate intellect and gift for self-criticism is also true of his story: "It is alive and thrilling as it can possibly be." Robust, unblushingly melodramatic, loaded with event, it is prodigal with danger. Yet the only visible danger in Ciulei's lugubrious dirge of a production is that the actors might trip on all those stairs they are compelled to mount and descend on their way to and from the black rampart on which all the action (or lack of it) takes place.

If the Bismarck image does nothing to light up the text, it does even less for the actors. Abandoned to the concept, they are lucky if they can be seen or heard on an arena stage that compels them into twists and spins just to get their profiles into view every few minutes. (From where I was sitting, the closet scene was really a minidrama about Gertrude's chignon.) They have been directed to be operatic where they might have been pensive, and strenuous where they might have been charming, witty, graceful, or just plain relaxed. That Kristoffer Tabori isn't Hamlet yet is not surprising, but he has an awkward, intelligent liveliness that is almost entirely suppressed by the persistent, holy darkness of this production. Richard Bauer is supposed to be Claudius, but he plays more like his own ghost. In *The Dybbuk* and *Landscape of the Body,* he was rarely conventional and always human. Under Ciulei, he is little more than beard and growl.

Ophelia's madness is the only scene in which the director's imagery is on the edge of accommodating his ambition. It is played as Gertrude, Claudius, and nameless guests are about to sit down to a quiet, stately, candlelit dinner. Ophelia's digressions are obviously disrupting and embarrassing. But even this momentary lapse into suggestive originality doesn't lend Ophelia's torments either focus or meaning. As Gertrude rushes down those steps once again, one can think only of the uneaten paté and the unconsumed wine.

GR(May 1978)

The Unfinished Theatre of Joseph Chaikin

The best questions in Joseph Chaikin's work have always been the ones that neither he nor anybody else could answer comfortably. There are always questions in his work: questions about how we live, about how we work, how we play, how we die, and how we mourn. Beyond those, however, there are the questions about the work itself: how it, too, lives, works, endures, develops, and meets its end. It could be argued that these questions are the most pressing, the ones that finally give the work shape, texture, and identity. Chaikin is certainly obsessed by issues that cut to the bone and the soul, but he is obsessed equally—now unfashionably—with his medium itself, its possibilities and its uncomfortable limits.

Re-Arrangements is the first work of this kind that we have had from him for many years. As an actor, he tried *Woyzeck* two years ago, placing himself in the hands of a director who tried to answer questions buried in that myste-rious ruin, as if they could be accurately unearthed. With such heavy certain-ties surrounding him, his bewildered soldier, owl eyes starkly rejecting the claims from his own mouth, could not possibly seem convincing. It wasn't Woyzeck who had strayed into the world unwanted, it was the actor.

As a director, he wrestled in recent years with texts such as Chekhov's *The Seagull* and Ansky's *Dybbuk.* The questions kept coming, of course, but he seemed subdued. The dramatists were not only framing too many con-straints, they were also insisting on solutions that Chaikin's inquiries were never designed to make. His medium is the actor at war with domestic reality. It would be characteristic for him to help Nina look and sound like a seagull, just as Nina might have wished in her delirium. The point of the play, however, is not the image of the bird; it is the leaden, denatured, untalented reality of the girl. His productions of these fixed texts were less interesting than his earlier collaborative works with the Open Theater, because the actors had to sacrifice ecstatic imagery to word, place,and architecture.

Four of the six actors in *Re-Arrangements* were collaborators with Chai-kin in several Open Theater works: Joyce Aaron, Ronnie Gilbert, Tina Shep-ard, and Paul Zimet. Their presence may account, in part, for the fact that, whatever else this frequently hilarious inquiry may be about, it is also about nostalgia. Set in the form of a series of interviews with the actors (called sim-ply "The woman with red hair," "The woman with gray hair," etc.), the work appears, at first, to be gazing at those little upheavals in the heart that distinguish most personal relationships. Abruptly, somewhere in the middle, the questions turn away from cardboard romance, and the sexuality that keeps invading our reluctant hearts, toward what has haunted Chaikin's work for years—the bleak, suggestive charms of death. Not the unanswerable fact of death itself so much as the lively, animating nature of it as an artifact and a guid-ing image. The work seems to be leaning forward and backward at the same time. Death may be with us and ahead of us, but in *Re-Arrangements,* there is a fascination with it as a moment behind us.

The work begins with a growling, *agitato* accompaniment on a double bass, suggesting that the hour or so ahead of us will be grimly fraught with tension and hysteria. Instead, the agitation is followed immediately by the sound of laughter. Ronnie Gilbert is sitting behind the center drop-curtain (there are two others on each side of the large, open space), which is raised by the first two interviewers, dressed in the hats and gloves of vaudeville come-dians. Gilbert's laughter is warm, enveloping, convulsive, halted only for a moment as she tries to remember the answer to the question, "Is there any joke that makes you laugh every time?" Through her laughter, she tells a joke about Mr. and Mrs. Beethoven (which is already a joke, since Beethoven was never one-half of a couple), a wonderful performance and a joke that are squarely in the tradition of music-hall entertainment—both of them hard acts to follow. The setup is clear: there will be perturbations and disturbances, but nothing too charged, nothing too dangerous.

Replacing danger are the risks, all kinds of them: the risks of jokes, images, or moments that don't quite look like what they seem to be saying or
say what they seem to be indicating; the risks of banality when what is
sought is mystery and wisdom; the risks of borrowings that are less eloquent
than their originals—borrowings from the silent world of modern dance when
neither the actors nor the staging possess the sculptured energy that makes
the best dance so pointed, clear, and startling. The paradox here is that there
would be no meaning at all without the risks and failures. When actors are in
rehearsal, talk and analysis yield much less information than their attempts
to visualize something in action. In *Re-Arrangements,* those attempts *are* the
story.

The most successful are gestural and small rather than dancerly and
large. Moving from one couple to another, the eye is drawn to Gilbert caressing Zimet's knee while he is caressing her shoulder. Meanwhile, the man with
the blond hair (Will Patton) is caressing Aaron's foot under the breakfast table,
which is sitting on a tiny platform revolving slowly like one of those foolish
restaurants on the tops of skyscrapers. The piece rests its case on quiet and
languid humor, as if tranquillity might turn out to be the last possible weapon.
After a while, it is easy to see why Chaikin had to shift toward death from
meditations and sketches about love and sex: just as actors' inventions are
the ephemeral art, so is the work itself something like a rehearsal for oblivion.

Completion or satisfaction would be alien signals in such a world. Even
so, Gilbert, Aaron, Zimet, and Patton manage to offer oblique images that occasionally look like fullness and victory. Gilbert sings a song written by Richard Peaslee to a poem called "Then" by Muriel Rukeyser (the nostalgic
centerpiece of the entire work), rescuing it from the glutinous sentiment that
hovers around the edges of the lyric by the elemental force of her presence
and conviction. Her stillness and breathing are better than the poem.

Meanwhile, Aaron and Patton seem to be emissaries from a world of sexual experience that has actually been felt—she with her matter-of-fact directness and gift for rapid transitions; he with his undulating coolness, like a serpent in heat, a vivid representation of sex as a force that can obliterate
personality. He doesn't distinguish between strangers and those who are
close to him, nor does he think that suffering is necessary; a succession of observations that would carry much less weight were they in the hands of an actor who merely said them. Between them, Patton and Chaikin have made
those words visible.

Similarly, when Zimet is asked if he believes in life after death, his rigid
body wants to say what it finally does manage to say—namely "I can't say"—
but before that, he erupts into spasms of high, low, squeaky, stentorian
voices that overtake his thoughts. And this, too, is one of those moments in
which a satire on actors' vocal equipment merges seamlessly into a satire on
the little accommodations people often make with thoughtless, daily life.

Chaikin and his best actors are burrowing for a linguistics in acting that
can uncover layers of eloquence, hitherto elusive in ordinary narrative the-

atre. If they fail as often as they succeed, it might be because some risks aren't worth taking. Chaikin too often urges his actors to settle for the illustration of expressiveness. At the same time, he reveals distrust in the painterly beauties and clarifications that emerge when a director collaborates with an organizing, elegant, and expressive design. There is something parsimonious in his vision. He is always making images while disdaining the eye.

The actors are compelled, also, to supply too much of the text, and while their facility and intelligence are never in question, their phrasing rarely matches the subtle immediacy of their acting, nor should it be expected to do so. Like the denial of the eye, the denial of the shaping word and governing shape are losses that the piece need not have suffered. The pleasures in Chaikin's theatre derive from the evidence within each moment that nothing will happen that is entirely predictable. The cost, however, is high: in a theatre of barely written moments there can be no sustained intensity. *GR(March 1979)*

Max Frisch: Drama of Footnotes

Max Frisch doesn't write plays, he writes dissertations. He means well, thinks strenuously, and sometimes even turns a clever phrase. What he can't do is write a play of ideas that makes the ideas live in people. Arguments are buried under an avalanche of references and citations. In *Biography: A Game,* written twelve years ago and only now produced in New York by the continually enterprising Chelsea Theatre Center, he has a heroine who did her doctorate under Theodor Adorno, and a spokesman who keeps reminding us of the headlines. Autumn 1959 means Cuba and the U.S.A., Nigeria's independence, Eisenhower's welcome of Khrushchev, Somalia's independence, and the Soviet Union's crash landing of Lunik II on the moon. Just in case you have forgotten, he adds that the moon rocket was 160 pounds. When in doubt, write a footnote. When in doubt about the footnote, add another.

Some of the citations are supposed to be funny. Early in the play, Kuermann, the professor who is given a chance to relive or reenact his life in a way that might make it possible for him to live or enact it differently, asks Antoinette, the Adorno scholar who will become his wife, what she thinks of Wittgenstein. He isn't really interested. He is asking because he has to say something, he wants to be polite. His life has been recorded by an actor-person called the Recorder, who reminds him that the theatre can go well beyond whatever reality permits. Yet their exchanges are cluttered not with vibrant choices but with lists: the Recorder tells Kuermann that he could have talked to the young lady about Hegel, Schoenberg, Kierkegaard, or Beckett.

Frisch says in his "Author's Note" that he "intended his play to be a comedy." He also says that "the play does not set out to prove anything." If only both were so. The doctor treating Kuermann for cancer leaves him in the hands of his assistant, Dr. Fink. But Dr. Fink immediately corrects the older physician, reminds him that his name is Funk. And, of course, this slip is repeated moments later. Kuermann's son is a gifted scholarship student majoring in film technique. You get it: only in America . . . gifted minds . . . scholarship . . . all devoted to something trivial rather than to Hegel, Wittgenstein, Schoenberg, etc. Kuermann is surprised to hear that once he said, "We only live once." The comment of the Recorder, confirming the embarrassing truth, is that it was "trite, but heartfelt."

Biography is not, in itself, trite. Rather, it is a painfully overcrafted specimen of High Art that cannot resist the impulse to trivialize the heartfelt. Writing plays about people who are constantly questioning their reality, or who are asking uneasy questions about their superiority and/or inferiority, might have made sense for Pirandello. But smarter people than Frisch have recognized that it is one matter to be Pirandello; quite another to attempt the Pirandellian. Frisch has no ecstasy, and so he assumes an easy advantage over the people in his play. He *knows* he is superior because he *knows* that only he is really pushing them around. *Biography* isn't comic and it isn't really serious. It is just *This Is Your Life* in highfalutin' theatrical drag.

The idea, like so many ideas stillborn in the theatre, reads better than it performs. The play has no motor energy. It is like the little engine that could, but won't: all steam and no motion. It sweats, strains, puts twenty actors through the paces of forty roles, makes actors look like stagehands or stagehands look like actors, and above all, it never shuts up. Frisch doesn't like the language of the theatre, the image of people saying what they have to say because there isn't anything else to say, or the spectacle of wondrous silence and breathless repose. He likes words, buckets of them, not because the people he dumps on the stage are thinking them, but because he himself is thinking them. He wants to write a play about a man who might seize the chance to reconstruct his life, but he is a writer who won't let that man build anything without his permission. His is an intelligence that keeps outsmarting itself. Frisch acknowledges the astonishing truth that real life has an infuriating way of being better than plotted theatre, offering "something far more exciting—a series of actions that remain fortuitous." However, he can only offer planned arrangements, a series of benevolent despotisms masquerading as freedoms. He likes playacting, but he doesn't really like the unmanageable truths that liberate drama from plot.

His games with language often betray him. He can think of a startling phrase, yet he can't always place it in the mouth of the person who can make it live. Kuermann shoots his wife, and testifies that he did so because she was on the point of saying that she was going to spend the afternoon in the library. "As I knew this sentence already and was sick of it, I fired at this sentence, so to speak, in order not to hear it again." A blinding, splendid construction, but in the play, not actually spoken by Kuermann, but reported *to* him (and us) by the Recorder! Frisch seems to prefer the assertion to its enactment.

Could the play ever come alive in production? Perhaps, but only if the stage were shimmering with glamour. In a play that presumes to review a man's life, the man himself ought to look like a man worth reviewing. Frisch's Kuermann is said to be "under suspicion of wanting to change the world." But, in fact, the Recorder patronizes him immediately by adding that "no one will suspect that you merely want to change your biography." Merely? The difficulty with the role as written is that it possesses all the energy, soul, mystery, and fantasy of an IRS agent on the prowl after a bookkeeping error, and George Morfogen is practically bug-eyed with modesty, self-effacement, and mereness. His is a performance almost too honest to be true. An actor with weight, resonance, and demons inside of him might have made a more interesting lie out of Kuermann, but Morfogen is probably closer to Frisch's dispiriting asceticism. Similarly, Pamela Burrell tries to make Antoinette look educated, sexy, and liberated, but Frisch doesn't really give her much playing evidence for all those good intentions. She is so busily employed in Kuermann's biography that she doesn't get much chance to build her own. Antoinette is trapped in Kuermann's play, and Burrell keeps looking—quite sensibly—as if she wants to be somewhere else.

The Lunts might have fooled us in those roles, and if Noël Coward had both played and written the Recorder, maybe this play within a play might have looked like a play. Casting in heaven can't be done, but surely it might be possible to find a less landlocked actor than Paul Sparer for Coward's part. Lubricating his voice, pampering his eyebrows, massaging his ego, and applauding his own cleverness, he may think he is the image of his playwright. It is an image, however, that no play really needs. Besides, it isn't really fair to Frisch, who for all his miscalculations, possesses a dark, exploring wisdom that an actor's diaphragm can never truly replace.   *GR(April 1979)*

Clone Theatre

Oscar Wilde's famous observation that it is only shallow people who do not judge by appearances trips off the tongue almost as if it had always existed, a thought any one of us might have had and then uttered. But with Wilde, art doesn't conceal art, it positively flaunts it, and this thought is no exception.

The phrasing has both muscle and grace. Heard or read instantaneously, it actually seems true. But what is so astonishing about it is that it wants only to adopt the appearance of truth. Wilde makes his case not for inarguable truth, but for inarguable style—the means that persuade, the moment in which the breath catches itself, when despair can be suddenly tempered by wit. For Wilde, complexity is the only available comfort. He embraces it as source and inspiration. And then, just to fool the slobbering, melodramatic tragedians among us, he dares to make it funny.

Wilde was not the first homosexual writer to liberate his personality through plays. By now, we know there were others, not least Christopher Marlowe, who found the obsessive affair between Edward II and Gaveston fair game for his real subject, the rival claims of power and responsibility. The Elizabethans knew that the rival claims of sexual choices could provide narrative threads for issues that push beyond the boundaries of story—ethical encounters that exclude no one. The Macbeths are as sexy as any heterosexual couple that has ever hit the stage, but the play is not a document about marriage, pro or con. Sex keeps getting people into trouble, but the trouble rarely has anything to do with sex.

Wilde had the guts to place his sex in the witness box while putting his passion for paradox into his plays. Would it have been better for him to have done it the other way around, as undoubtedly he might be tempted to do in today's allegedly freer climate? Perhaps, but more likely the boys he shared with Bosie and the humiliations to which he found himself irresistibly attracted were no more than blueprints for those astounding transformations that can occur only when imagination is not enslaved by fact.

"By a dextrous transvaluation of words," says Richard Ellmann, "Wilde makes good and evil exchange places." With equal dexterity, and like Miss Prism checking the baby rather than her manuscript in the cloakroom of Victoria Station, Wilde exchanged abject fact for funny fiction. To paraphrase Lady Bracknell: to lose his heart to Bosie might be considered a misfortune, to lose it on stage would look like carelessness.

Most playwrights today who also happen to be homosexual are getting very careless, indeed. Mistaking a moment of politics for a moment of truth, they are showing bedrooms, bodies, kisses, and embraces, but precious little felt experience. Reacting wisely and firmly to the dumb surrenders in early gay fiction when protagonists were expected to kill themselves or somebody else, they have for the most part turned to comedy; not, unfortunately, with either the wit or individuality possessed by Wilde (and later, also, by Noël Coward). Instead, so thrilled do they seem to be with apparent political freedom, they are falling over each other—almost literally—in the race to laugh with Neil Simon all the way to the bank. I do not mean to suggest that any gay playwright is or is likely to be as popular as Neil Simon, only that many of them are imitating his putdowns, insults, and phrasing. In so doing, they are also betraying their experience.

Two of the plays in what is billed as the First Gay American Arts Festival are Robert Patrick's *T-Shirts* and Doric Wilson's *Forever After.* Meanwhile, outside the festival is a musical comedy called *Fourtune* that has the pleasing audacity to make two women in sex look as if they're having fun; more fun, certainly, than the men are having. If only the songs didn't keep interrupting Bill Russell's frequently dippy and unpretentious dialogue (not all of it putdowns), then *Fourtune* might easily stake a claim as the first gay comedy not gagging on its own gags. The songs keep trying to say something, however, and their interventions, while not fatal, keep pulling both the male and female couples away from the sensual territory they keep starting—and failing—to explore.

Russell is less enthralled by insult than are Patrick and Wilson. Yet much of his phrasing could be lifted from or inserted into their plays. "Get off my back," says a Russell character. To which the other replies, "Is it your turn to be on top?" Russell's people talk about "making it" as often as any other American heroes. But one of them is put down with the observation that "making it for me is making it all night." This is only a little smarter than Patrick's playwright-protagonist (played by Patrick himself) who says that he writes what he knows—"hardly likely to make it on Broadway." Wilson, in his turn, has his tragedy queen (yes, a male in drag) insult the comedy queen (also in drag) by saying that if she wants happy endings, she should get her "butt up to Broadway." They all like to play with words, not in order to delight in epigrammatic paradox, but for the benefit of assonance, creepy puns, or smart-ass show-business allusions.

Only a hiccup separates dialogue that might have been cloned from one play or another and characters who *are* clones of one another. The handsome young men in all these works don't always look alike, but they are certainly viewed alike by their playwrights: they are Marilyns in tankshirts, blue jeans, or the raw; objects of lust, of course, but also targets for the more bitter thrusts. They are usually dumb, craven, and naive. Bright people are never as beautiful. They get their kicks from campaigns against the studs. "One nice thing about being ugly," says Patrick, "is that it doesn't get any worse when you're old." Wilson's boys are referred to as "a couple of Christopher Street clones who seem to think love is a substitute for crazy glue." Few of these echoing mouthpieces really believe that sex itself is half as good as anticipation. Unlike the bamboozled boys, the gallantly gag-ridden protagonists seem to be committed to disappointment. "There are times when I wish I could satisfy you," says somebody in *Fourtune.* "Who does that for anyone?" says the other.

The trouble with most of these works—charming as they can be sometimes—is that they insist on traveling in only one direction, relying upon the hocus-pocus that loud voices and declarative sentences can take the place of real, separate, complicated declarations of independence—independence from lifelike routine and theatrical routines, from the imagery of the crowd, from hysteria, self-pity, self-contempt, and dopy jokes. Unlike Wilde, who risked his life in the dock (which probably seemed easy), but who also risked his intelligence and imagination on stage (which was not), they rarely take any kind of risks at all.

At the risk—indeed, the likelihood—of misunderstanding, I must cite, finally, the example of Morton Lichter's *Morandi's.* We have been companions and colleagues for many years, and I directed the play last January at the Theatre for the New City; I cite it also because my production didn't reveal all its contours and mysteries. Working within the gestural framework of playwrights such as Rainer Werner Fassbinder and Franz Xaver Kroetz in Germany and Jean-Paul Wenzel and Michel Vinaver in France, Lichter took chances with a story about a young man's quest not for identity but for ambiguity in a series of gay bars. This alone is heresy enough. Even chancier, however, was the mix of epic progression with harsh images that were at once realistic and painterly. Lichter was risking the use of an environment that is now (and I hope only now) sensational, deliberately casting it in the epic form whose purpose, as described by Walter Benjamin, is "to make what is shown on stage unsensational." There is no reason why gay theatre need settle for less. As Richard Gilman wrote of the play—*not* my production—*Morandi's* is "quite daring in both structure and theme . . . resists all temptation toward flamboyance and easy emotion in order to work subtle effects . . . delicate, ironic, from the heart, but not straight from it: a keen intelligence has been at work here."

Which is what seems to be missing from most plays, gay and straight. Or perhaps it would be more accurate to say that *authenticity* is missing. Lichter's work draws its pain from the pressure of real experience. Inauthentic trash such as *Bent* borrows its pain from the authentic experience—unspeakable and still unknowable—of Nazism's real victims. Unearned, expropriated seriousness is probably worse than imitative frivolity, especially in this political moment, when authentic gay experience can provide so many emblems for the way people are living others' lives rather than their own.

GR(June 1980)

Peter Brook: Ubu Raw

During a recent performance in Milan of Alfred Jarry's *Ubu* under Peter Brook's direction, a little boy of four or five strolled from the audience onto the playing area, and was eaten instantly by a bear. Soon after, the bear disgorged him, returning him to his mother's side. The boy was still squealing with delight as the bear, Papa Ubu, and Mamma Ubu went on with the play.

Later, during the trial of the Ubus in the production's second part, drawn from Jarry's *Ubu enchaine*, the little boy was still edging his way into the action. By then, he had become the active surrogate for an audience enchanted with the genial freedoms offered by Brook's company. Mamma Ubu had found her buried treasure under someone's seat, a shower of pears and oranges pelted the audience as the second part opened, water was sprayed everywhere, while the great hulk of Jarry's marvelously goitered French was continually sprinkled with instant translations into Italian and even English. The little boy was merely the least self-conscious figure in a group that had successfully breached the barriers customarily separating actors from audience.

It had been a slow, casual, almost unnoticed crossing. Brook, with his usual distaste for categories, had said in a program interview that "collages" had become a cliché: "One can take a play and make it a trampoline," he said, and "I see absolutely no need for making a trampoline out of Ubu." As Part One of *Ubu Roi* began, it was clear that there would be no central, demanding, guiding trickiness to the work—no trampoline, no singular design image whatsoever; just space, actors, unchanging bright light, some useful props, and movable objects.

The Ubus bustled on stage unannounced, catching the audience by surprise. They were in the middle of their lives. Our presence was just another one of their oversights, no more than that. If we must eavesdrop on them, so be it. Meanwhile, the other seven actors dropped in for a scene, did it fully and directly, ambled or ran off, only to return soon enough in another hat or jacket, as earnestly as ever, pretending to be someone else. Their appearances were more like insinuations than statements. Take them or leave them, they seemed to be saying. Life is cheap, anyway, and we're just doing a job, and for a moment it's not so bad. In fact, if you bother to notice, it can be fun. The actors weren't falling over each other to be impressive. Technique, like everything else, was theirs to use or ignore. They didn't gush, they didn't demand attention, and above all, they made no threats.

That is, not until the little boy went too far in the second act. He wasn't doing anything that he hadn't done before. It was just that life on stage was shifting to another realm: Ubu and company, no longer mock royals, were now enslaved to liberty in France. This was Jarry the ferocious, writing—as Brook put it—"with an apparent lightness that pushed violence to its limits." If he couldn't quite manage to destroy everything, at least he could try a few earthquakes.

The little boy had apparently not noticed the change. The pears, oranges, and water were part of the same game. Rubber or plastic bricks, like so many of the props, had become many things: sometimes the food the actors ate, perhaps a miniature house, or a tiny hearth, or—most breathtaking of all—the stepping stones bridging a precarious river crossing. Nothing really harsh in this world, only irreverence, outrage, toys. It is true that Andreas Katsulas, the actor playing Ubu, seemed to be growing more and more gigantic with each scene, though not with the aid of padding, boots, or anything external. The loss of even mock power had diminished his soul. He was consumed now by bitterness, a freezing grief that was expanding inside of him. Think of Groucho suddenly caught off guard, his biography spread out before him, unapproachable, a bit mean, preparing to write another letter to the author of *The Wasteland*. What little boy could have known that the rules of this particular game had changed?

For that matter, could the rest of us? The boy was just an accident that night. Without him, it is always possible that the adults—audience and actors together—might simply conspire to keep the earthquakes infrequent and undelineated. With him, Katsulas had an opportunity that a less courageous actor might have missed or blunted. Could the trial of the Ubus continue in a room so crowded with cheerfulness? Only if this were the usual kind of *Ubu* production, where a mad world is presented by madly literal, frantic, gagging, arch, winsome, and winking actors, all of them racing headlong for cartoons and caricatures, a world where nothing ever really matters.

Katsulas-Ubu was getting annoyed by the little boy. Suddenly he switched from French to English, whipping his body toward the mother squirreling her son by her side on the floor. "Keep that kid quiet, lady, or I'm going to throw him out of here!" he shouted. Maybe the kid didn't understand English or the sound of Katsulas's voice, but everybody else did. And with a brutish speed that can occur in a theatre only when all the choices have been made with natural, yet contained, authority, a ghastly pall descended on the space. Nothing could save any of us, except perhaps the kid; mercy for him was not to have lived his life yet. In the end, Katsulas drew him quickly and gently into the curtain calls as sweet, momentary peace crept back into the theatre to the accompaniment of the actors' voices and kazoos. We had wandered into hell and had all decided to come back.

The meeting of Brook with Jarry had seemed unlikely, and even, perhaps, a little unnecessary. As Brook himself said, outside of France he had seen many *Ubu* productions. Why another? Partly because his company of international actors based in Paris could rescue Jarry's language while leaving room for other languages, and partly because this was a moment when Brook could demonstrate uncontroversially that the only way to treat a classic with respect is to stage it unrespectfully: *Ubu* is in fact a classic, he says, but as a classic, it insists on not being subjected to the "severe criteria that the word 'classic' habitually evokes."

Brook has rescued Jarry from Jarry's own terrible logic. Making art from his ridiculous life required not only the fragmentation of art, but inevitably, the dissolution of life itself. Everything Jarry did had a way of turning in on itself, not only his life, but these ordinarily unmanageable *Ubu* plays. To his contemporaries, Jarry was a *potache,* half brat, half prodigy. Gide thought of him as a "nutcracker," using the word to define Jarry's uninflected speech, his way of placing equal stress on all syllables, including the silent ones. For Yeats, he was "the Savage God," while for Apollinaire, he was "the last sublime debauche of the Renaissance."

Many of these Ubuesque qualities find a place, too, in the Peter Brook we have known. Unlike Jarry, Brook tempers them by a questing intelligence that resists the temptation to defile itself. Brook can miscalculate, but he never betrays the quest. In him reside Ubu-earthquakes that might yet frighten little boys, but for the moment, what he presents are the hard work, the tenacity, and the broad reach of theatre respecting itself.   *GR(May 1979)*

The Merits of Obscurity

Remarkable how often the word "viable"—as in "viable alternative"—turns up in all the anthologies of plays produced in spaces once called Off-Broadway, and for the past twenty years, in looser arrangements Off-Off-Broadway. For the serious playwright, there has been only one place to go in the last few decades: as far away from Broadway as possible. True, like Edward Albee, whose first viable alternative (for *The Zoo Story*) was Berlin in 1958, the playwright might once again be lured back to the big Broadway crap game; God knows those high stakes and occasional victories might well be a much

more viable alternative to the pitiful handouts from public and private foundations. Still, the wise playwright is likely to press for the more modest and less
lacerating gamble found on East Fourth Street or—why not?—the Kurfürsten-
dam.

However one dates the birth of Off-Off-Broadway—was it actually O'Neill
at the Provincetown in the twenties, or the combined forces of the Becks, Ellen Stewart, and Joe Cino in the fifties and sixties?—there is no doubt that the
wheel keeps coming back full circle. Last year, it was Berlin again, this time
for Robert Wilson (a playwright, yes), whose costly vision stretches too far
beyond the impoverished improvisations in the Village. As with many artists
before him, he finds the cash needed to develop his images only in exotic cap-
itals where the links between good business and nontraditional art have never
been obscure.

The British, haughty as usual, but less hypocritical, have always called
their Off West End theatre the fringe. To where else do you consign work that
is deliberately engaged in confounding expectations? The fringe is probably
the best, if not the safest, place to be, even if American playwrights still yearn
for the center. Perhaps the British are in touch with a less corruptive wisdom:
by letting Peter Brook disappear to Paris for research into his Rough and Holy
theatres, while nonetheless inviting him back for the occasional star-crossed
Shakespeare (last season with Glenda Jackson as Cleopatra), they are, in effect, issuing a bulletin about where new, intransigent, fugitive visions ought
to be housed. Leave popularity, the kitchen sink, and the drawing room to the
traditional storytellers, they are saying. Above all, don't confuse the issue. If
the theatre wants to draw the boobs from their tubes, then make that big proscenium up there look as much like a tube as possible. Make it real, simple,
noisy, and imitative. Put the real dramatists on the fringe where they belong.

When an Off-Off-Broadway playwright, such as Sam Shepard, wins a
Pulitzer, it doesn't signal popularity, only token surrender. The prize usually
goes to the lame, the sick, the deaf, dumb, blind, and the dying—the more
sentimentally viewed, the better. When still another Off-Off-Broadway veteran
wins, such as Lanford Wilson, it has to be for his most ordinary work, and
then only when it captures Broadway's flinty heart. Clearly, the lines were
drawn long ago, and only a fool and his mother would wish for anything more
than the glory of twelve nonprofit showcase performances on New York's
fringe. In obscurity lies safety, and probably the only assurance of good, representative work.

So what has Off-Off-Broadway yielded in the past twenty years? Energy,
tenacity, and vision, certainly. Also, futility, chaos, and the inevitable trivial-
ity of even a fringe marketplace. In one of Off-Off-Broadway's early stages, it
was the fine writer, especially the poet, who was promoted as the alternative
to mundane realisms by Miller and Inge. Think of it: the Becks began with Picasso, William Carlos Williams, and Paul Goodman. Meanwhile, the Artists'
Theatre, under the direction of the late Herbert Machiz, produced plays by
Frank O'Hara, John Ashbery, James Merrill, and Robert Hivnor.

Robert Hivnor? Whatever happened to *The Ticklish Acrobat* (1954), a play admired even by traditionalist critics such as Gerald Weales? In Hivnor's disappearance lies the true history of Off-Off-Broadway. Nobody can make the effort forever. The American Place Theatre brought Robert Lowell into the fold, but soon enough it became clear that linguistic facility and intelligence are no guarantee of respectability, even on the fringe. What is more likely to survive for a time are sensation, the illusion of the new, and—with Papp as Godfather—a fleeting, tasteless, and arbitrary promotion of power images.

Despite this history, women have shown Off-Off-Broadway that there is more in heaven than is dreamt of in Lillian Hellman's philosophies. Some of the best playwrights of the past years have been the women: Maria Irene Fornes, Rosalyn Drexler, Julie Bovasso, Rochelle Owens, Megan Terry, Susan Yankowitz, and—the most eloquent black dramatist of her time—Adrienne Kennedy. Surely this, too, says something about the necessity for critical distance from the standards set by Broadway and the majority of reviewers. Can there be any doubt by now that without Off-Off-Broadway, there would be absolutely no visible women playwrights in America?

The darker truth is that, if an alternative didn't exist, it would have to be invented again and again. Actors' Equity—always quicker to bully its members before taking on the Shuberts, Papp, or Alexander Cohen—is currently engaged in assaulting playwrights by asking them to hand a percentage of zero royalties to their actors. Absurd theatre was never welcome on Broadway, but absurd tactics continue to be one way of sending American playwrights even further away than Berlin.

Nicola Chiaromonte said that the theatre should enjoy its unpopularity. It was never meant to be anything else.   *GR(June 1980)*

THE
EIGHTIES

Those Dancing Feet

When Broadway plays and musicals sound serious, it is easy to think they're joking. Arriving, usually, in a cloud-cover of blameless innocence, wishing to teach and please but not to shock, they continue to be the most sophisticated purveyors of what one of their sages once called the impossible dream. All they want is the best of several worlds: the magical and dreamy laced with homiletic instructions for living better, wiser, more responsibly, nicer (but firmer), more true-to-oneself; uplifts with no letdowns; tears halted by jokes, otherwise known as laughter without pain; and quantities of heartstopping excitement that stop short of pressuring the brain.

These greedy combinations carry only the sound of seriousness, not the sense. They are salable to a public, true. But that doesn't really say very much either about right or wrong, the shows themselves, or even the public. The latter, after all, used to buy snake oil and Richard Nixon. It seems to know that deception *is* the name of the game, and—like Rhett Butler—it doesn't give a damn. Perhaps there was a moment when real seriousness was possible, or even happened. I'm not certain that I remember it. Serious playwrights— good, less good, even near-great—have been produced on Broadway, but their presence is not associated automatically with either the shiver felt in the audience before the Broadway curtain rises, or the Broadway experience charted in the history books.

If today's seriousness on Broadway seems to be even less noticeable than the seriousness of the past, it may be that today's seriousness lacks the courage of its emptiness. It tries so hard to be convincing. The public may be easily deceived, or just plain dumb, but it doesn't want those secrets to be leaked. It comes to Broadway because it is bored by the box and has an instinctive consciousness that German films—for just one alternative—are probably dangerous for the health. Besides, Broadway, unlike the other possibilities, represents that marvelous specimen known as the live experience or the shared response—the community that every Essalened and ested clone needs in order to feel alive once or twice a week after the thrills of dancing alone in discos have ceased to weave their spell.

Broadway, at best, used to be charming, starry, and bright. Now, if it is lucky, it is only charming. Starry almost never, probably because the stars can't afford it or Broadway can't afford the stars; bright not at all, because most of the clever people who used to write for Broadway are dead. (If alive, like Tennessee Williams, they're simply disdained, ignored, or discarded.) In the last scene of *42nd Street,* the stage is covered in bulbs advertising the shows of 1933. What catches the eye and upstages the production number is the list of stars such as Edith Evans, Tallulah Bankhead, and Helen Hayes. And *Playbill* tells us that in 1930 Bogart, Bette Davis, Tracy, Leslie Howard, Sydney Greenstreet, Cagney, Claude Rains (in Shaw's *The Apple Cart!*), W. C. Fields, Jack Benny, Fred Allen, Victor Moore, Paul Muni, Jane Cowl (supported by Hepburn!), Fred Astaire in a flop, and Ethel Merman making her debut were all on Broadway. Clearly, seriousness and maybe good sense were at a minimum even then, but in their place was a tactile, sensuous glamour that is neither attempted nor achieved any more.

Broadway producers follow the formulas that used to work, they push their characters into the right crises, they pull them out in time for still another one of those earsplitting production numbers that always ends with a sea of arms flung above the heads, or a moment of truth (in so-called drama) when somebody weeps, shouts, or locks a jaw, and still they can't be sure, still they don't always wake up one morning with the shouts of Sardi's gluttons ringing in their ears. What keeps going wrong so much of the time? It can't be a question of sellout, since the formulas and the audience are probably well matched.

Perhaps the flaw lies less in the formulas than it does in the tonalities with which they are repeated. Something always seems a little flat, sharp, or just plain sour. When the director in *42nd Street* implores the heroine to "think of musical comedy, the most glorious words in the English language," it is clear that he doesn't really mean it. Or does he? Probably just a little, since the phrase is surrounded by so many other joking, charming truisms that smell, finally, like propaganda for the show itself. This could have been a genuinely funny line, but the one element of humor from which it is retreating is wit. If, as one song says, "every situation has a sunny side," and if—as is likely—no one really believes that any more, the seriousness of any momentary wit has been irretrievably lost. Does the public really want—as the director says—youth, freshness, beauty? Perhaps, but the public doesn't really know that the director—or his creators—really thinks the line is funny. It doesn't know because it has been tugged everywhere except into the realms of what the makers of the show truly feel, think, or even know.

One line in this year's pseudo-serious hit, *Children of a Lesser God,* reveals the philosophical surrenders of Broadway's makers as nakedly as any heard in recent years: "It *did* come out of a textbook, but I think it's true anyway." Something borrowed, something blue—that's Broadway seriousness. It's like saying that clichés should be pitied, so helpless are they, suffering from a truth that nobody believes. Broadway is the nation's treasury of received and obsolete wisdom. If I were a candidate for national office, I'd take my basic training on 42d Street. And I don't mean with the junkies and the whores. They just went into the wrong business.

As a candidate, what I would be doing is imitation. Not just imitation alone, but imitation of an imitation. First, like the teacher-hero of *Children of a Lesser God,* I would reveal my pain by cracking jokes. Then, like the play's director, Gordon Davidson, I'd imitate John Dexter's staging of *Equus* by moving benches even more deftly than I move people. Then I might arrange a series of encounters, called debates, for my second act, in which the rules were set by previous productions and my characters were overwhelmed by complications that I didn't feel I had to explain because I knew already that nobody really wants to know.

The *New York Times* says that Carter's recent press conference covered nine topics. On Broadway, I would be certain that my play covered at least one topic. Not an idea or an issue, certainly, just a topic: the maimed, the dying, the dead, the almost living, the wounded, the ugly, the sick, the afflicted, the unhappy, the oppressed minority, the misunderstood majority—it wouldn't matter which, so long as it was perceived as a topic. Then I might let my heroine say—as she says in *Charlie and Algernon*—that she wants "no surprises." Of course, I wouldn't let my hero be upstaged by a mouse. Better to make him look beautiful and sexy—like an elephant.   *GR(October 1980)*

The Shouting Epidemic

Acting is the cruelest art. For a start, it can't be done alone. Like Sartre's Hell, it is always Other People. Not merely the experts in the audience who know nothing about it but know what they like; also, those other actors who prefer classes to rehearsals, and can never agree if the action or the emotion comes first. For Eleonora Duse, the only possible happiness would have been "to shut one's door upon a little room, with a table before one, and to create; to create life in that isolation from life." But how could she do it on the stage?

Monologues, perhaps. Yet they wouldn't really do. The great perorations in Marlowe and Shakespeare, those snares for actors who believe that vivacity need happen only in the throat, are only a small part of their plays. After they are over, the actor still has to face the other actors. The best dramatists (B.B.—Before Beckett) love a good crowd.

So Duse didn't have a choice. Unlike most actors, however, she could choose her roles. Even then she wasn't satisfied. Gabriele D'Annunzio, Alexandre Dumas, Hermann Sudermann, even Ibsen, just weren't good enough. She wanted "beauty and the flame of life," Rome and Athens, rather than the "children and spirits" she was doomed to perform. Her power to command didn't seem to give her the power to choose the art and the drama she wished to celebrate. In utter despair, she assaulted both audience and actors in one breathless paragraph, loathing the first for treating the theatre as after-dinner sport, and the latter for their bad taste, playing not drama, but what she called "pieces for the theatre."

While acknowledging acting's cruelty and dangers—the misery of the marketplace, the failure of the profession to agree on technique, and the unutterable sorrow that one would feel for a piano virtuoso condemned to play "Chopsticks" rather than Schubert most of his life—it is difficult to forgive the surrenders and corruptions made by so many gifted actors in recent years. I don't mean only Welles selling wine (Gallo!) and Olivier selling cameras, or the willingness to spend half a lifetime on television opening and shutting the doors on cars and refrigerators, or the relinquishing of so much power to directors, especially directors with Big Ideas. These are perhaps forgivable on the grounds of survival.

Less forgivable is the epidemic of shouting that seems to have bewitched the actor's art. In the past, American actors were scolded—usually with some justice—for making a meal out of mumbles. But surely, repentance has been carried far enough. Now, in big theatres already fitted with systems that amplify the voices, and even in tiny spaces where the actor's mouth is only inches away from the public's ear, the art of conversation has been truly lost. Romeos hurl endearments at their Juliets as if words were footballs, simple domestic exchanges often sound like declarations of war, meditations are turned automatically into immolation scenes. And is it really necessary for John Rubinstein in *Children of a Lesser God* to keep yelling at both the deaf and the hearing people as if gentle persuasions had gone out of style?

When American theatre started going classical with a vengeance, everybody began to take the most ordinary, mechanical, routine British actors seriously, snobbishly confusing accent with talent. The young Olivier was scolded by James Agate for gabbling, and had he kept it up, he never would have become the prodigally inventive actor who could slice the air with one word out of a hundred, while never shouting (a distinction understood by pianists who play *fortissimo* without pounding). Guinness always purred on stage, Gielgud has a *viola d'amore* in his mouth, and the incomparable Edith Evans, asked to explain her amazing vocal technique, said that "it's just that my voice runs up and down more or less naturally, and I let it." As she put it, even Shakespeare is "ordinary talk really." She would use emphatic words as springboards, she said, leaning on them a bit whenever she might wish to slow up. "We don't emphasize every word when we talk, do we?" she asked.

On our stages, we do now. Poor Irene Papas, in *The Bacchae* at Circle in the Square, arrived at her opening-night performance with a voice gasping for resonance, begging for nuance, a voice sacrificed to the director's lunatic whim that size of emotion and style in drama can be measured in decibels. The exceptional quiet of the clever Philip Bosco seemed to be there only to confirm the new rule. Because he wasn't shouting, he didn't have to rush. A word here or there could actually catch him by surprise. What he did was rarely individual, illuminating, or intimate, yet in such a soundscape, it couldn't fail to *look* different.

All the people who don't know a thing about acting know, of course, that the Greeks and Shakespeare are supposed to be shouted, despite Hamlet's warning that the groundlings' ears should not be split by actors tearing a passion to tatters. When Jonathan Miller was rehearsing Irene Worth in Lowell's version of *Prometheus Bound* at Yale in 1967, he called down from the balcony to say that he couldn't hear her; the same Irene Worth who could undoubtedly fill Epidaurus with a sigh. True, he didn't ask her to shout, nor did she ever do so; but obediently, politely, she raised her voice, and was never again so rapt, so inward as she had been before his interruption. Similarly, the Circle in the Square is not a space that requires rant: in *The Lady from the Sea,* produced there in 1976, Vanessa Redgrave proved, unsurprisingly, that a totally engaged, committed, entranced performer can make thought tangible in a whisper.

In great actors, such as Redgrave, Worth, and Dame Edith, there is always what Stark Young found in Duse—"something withheld." At the top of the lung, one is listening neither to oneself nor to others, and there is no true acting without true listening. Actors today, whether by default to directors or by their own design, are drifting into selfishness. Those boring one-man shows in which actors pretend to be great writers reveal themselves quickly as celebrations of the self. Perhaps, they are shouting out of desperation after so much unemployment. Sounding their barbaric yawps to the rooftops of our theatres, actors rarely give themselves a chance to learn what Michael Redgrave learned from Edith Evans—that you don't act for yourself or the audience; you act for your partner, which is the only way to turn Sartre's Hell into Actor's Heaven.

"You don't start acting," she told him, "until you stop *trying* to act." To which she might now amend: You don't start acting until you stop shouting your act.   *GR(October 1980)*

Jukebox Theatre

Plays about teenagers don't have to be bad. The great ones, surely, are *Romeo and Juliet* and Wedekind's *Spring Awakening.* In these, the agonies of the young, the poetics of early wonder, and the patterns woven from their bewildered ecstasies are seen entirely from within the framework of true experience. There is size, but no exaggeration. Life *is* awful for the adolescent. Wedekind and Shakespeare have memories, but they don't brood, swoon, or celebrate. Neither do they mourn. They simply see, trusting in precision, a cool eye, and a warm head.

Even a lesser, second-hand work, such as Carson McCullers's adaptation of her novel *Member of the Wedding,* possesses a tight hold on adolescent reality, saved from its inclination to dissolve in pain by its awkward humors and its distinctive, genuinely heard language. So many of the kids racing across screens and stages today are viewed only as figures in a crowd, living not their own lives but the images thrust upon them by a show-biz assault that is always selling them to themselves. Not McCullers's Frankie. She is eccentric, freshly imagined, and above all self-contained. It doesn't matter she is often silly and irritating, like so many real people, young or old; what saves her is that her actions take flight from an author's imagination, not from a committee mind looking for formulas and hard sells.

The latest committee mind is called David Rimmer. His play, *Album,* now at the Cherry Lane Theatre, is about the high school years of Peggy, Trish, Billy, and Boo. Rimmer doesn't bother with precision: the town, the state, the high school are never named, possibly because he knows that with names like Peggy, Trish, Billy, and Boo, you don't need to know anything more. The town is Hollywood, and the state is Blah. Not surprising, then, to see that the producers are presenting *Album* in association with Twentieth Century-Fox Productions. When you go to *Album,* you aren't a live-theatre audience anymore, you're just a Sneak Preview.

Album is not the worst of its kind. The worst is yet to come. Make no mistake: a trend is sneaking up on us, and there will be no escape. Not that all the evidence is in. Teens have always been making it in the movies, from Mickey and Judy to Travolta and the cyclists of *Breaking Away,* and what they've done or represented has often been sharply observed and fun. But this trend, as it insinuates itself into theatre, has a different aroma: desperate, empty, a backward glance that is aggressively regressive, and charmless, harshly insisting on America's right to stay girlish and boyish forever. An actor I know called his agent three weeks ago, asking if any roles were coming up in the theatre. "If you were seventeen, there would be," he was told. Agents may not know much about art, but they do know what they like about money.

Hal Prince and Stephen Sondheim, a committee that ought to know better, have just announced their intention to backdate George S. Kaufman and Moss Hart's *Merrily We Roll Along,* recasting its adult characters as teenagers. Why? They don't really say. Or rather, they say what is obvious and doesn't really mean anything—"that the whole emotional thrust would be different if the story were told by kids." The same would be true if the emotional thrust were given to old people—not a bad idea—or nurses, lawyers, or even monkeys. Prince and Sondheim are too smart to be arbitrary: they've spotted a trend and they're planning to race to the bank with it.

Prince adds that his wife has been nagging him to do a musical showing teenagers. They have a couple of kids in their house, and it seems that the kids need representation on stage. Producers like to dress up their venality as democracy. Barbara Tuchman, in her tortured, selective lamentation about the decline of quality, included Senator Hruska's plea for representation of the mediocre on the Supreme Court, but she omitted the theatre. Either she noticed it had declined light years away from quality long ago, or she had forgotten that commodity theatre is always one step ahead of the latest shoddy fashions. When the crippled and the terminal found "democratic" recognition in the theatre (in a country hostile to national health insurance!), a stage set didn't seem complete without a walker, crutch, or deathbed. Now, so it appears, we are programmed for a rash of Beatle memories, picture albums, and record albums embraced by an army of Dorian Grays in their thirties.

Teens themselves rarely go to the theatre. So why so much fuss about their tastes? Possibly because the theatre has become the rubbish dump for television's discards. What works there is perceived—isn't that the latest fashionable word?—to be workable on stage. Any minute now my own generation will make musicals out of Corliss Archer and Henry Aldrich. Or have they already done so? Backward reels the mind, and reels and reels.

To where? Bonzo in the White House. The oldest American teenager. Trends are not without logic. The road to the bank is, after all, the same road to Washington. Tuchman is still puzzling over Gresham's law, as if the bad driving out the good was an issue anymore. She hasn't noticed that today it's the bad driving out the bad.

What ever made me think I was living in an adult world, a world that learns from experience, that cares for anything but its own corrupt, blasted illusions? Yes, the mirror is being held up to nature, but it isn't Shakespeare's mirror. Waxed, like one of those stage mirrors designed to reveal shadows without dimension, it sees only what little it wants to see. Not Juliet's courage and heartbreak, Romeo's passion, or Mercutio's gallantry and wit. Only Peggy, Trish, Billy, and Boo on their way to the banks of America, never having read a book, never curious about Mozart, and blind to Vermeer; zonked-out wanderers in a sexless wonderland turning leaves in family albums while trying to remember a Dylan tune.   *GR(November 1980)*

The Set Is Half the Job

If you're rich and foolish enough to spend $25,000 next summer on a house rental in Southampton, don't rent one designed by Oliver Smith. What you'll get is what Jean Kerr's marriage counselor gets in *Lunch Hour:* a house with a front entrance only inches away from a raised sundeck, the sundeck itself off a landing that has two staircases leading to a sunken living room that doesn't have a view of the sea, a hi-fi unit blocking the view from the landing, and a mingy kitchenette that doesn't have a window. Surely the rent is too high.

Smith is not saying anything sharp and dreadful about the taste of the rich. *Lunch Hour* is not that kind of play. It isn't even about the rich. It's about how the rich behave in plays. Meaning: they flirt with forbidden relationships for a few hours, they talk about warm and cold hearts, they get angry, drunk, hysterical, embarrassed, and lovably clumsy; and finally, they go back to where they were in the beginning.

Smith's angles and levels are peculiarly careless and unlikely; they don't even pretend to spill into unseen spaces suggesting a world surrounding the action of the play. The bedroom seems to be through a door off the landing that first opens into a corridor that may have some steps leading to a space above the kitchenette. It must be painfully small, but where else can it be? The landlord lives in what appears to be a flat below, which suggests that his split-level dwelling may have a spectacular view of a dune. Meanwhile, the action moves from blazing sunlight to caressing moonlight while a white curtain keeps waving in an unchanged, gentle wind. Smith can't deliver a habitable house, but he sure offers reliable weather.

In John Conklin's gargantuan version of a Main Line mansion for Philip Barry's *The Philadelphia Story,* the weather is what Barry ordered—something sweet and benign for which Tracy Lord and her mother can keep thanking God. No doubt Barry knew his models, and there is even a chance that he might have recognized Conklin's rooms, sofas, and verandahs. To get to downstage, a CinemaScope spread that is just about the only staging ground available to directors in the misbegotten Beaumont Theatre, the actors have to run a one-minute mile. Ellis Rabb makes the most of his giant, cluttered spaces by cutting the run down to a stroll as often as possible, staging a stately, butlered saraband before each scene as the actors move flowers on and tea-cups off. Gallant and futile, it serves only to remind us that the play is leaving all that space behind unused.

Strange, too, that Conklin's amplitude is just as imprecise, finally, as Smith's confinements. The butlers come from a kitchen that doesn't seem to serve a dining room, but must be on a collision course with the hall upstage through which Tracy marches to her wedding in the final moment of the play. The verandah wraps itself around a part of the house that ought to lead to the front entrance, yet the unseen guests at the wedding seem to have arrived from somewhere else. The rich in Barry's world are probably so privileged they can defy gravity, but surely they don't go to parties through the ser-vants' quarters. Why, too, do they use so many plastic potted plants and flowers? With so much space and luxury to play with, can't their vines grow real, tender grapes? This is, after all, a three-D version of a black-and-white movie, and it deserves to be in Smell-o-Vision.

Andrei Serban spares us the smell of sulphur that stops Konstantin's symbolist play in the first act of *The Seagull* at the Public Theatre; but he is generous with imprecisions, not least in the design that he has urged from Michael H. Yeargan. His permanent Japanese floor, with its reeds in the cen-ter and its graceful footbridge at the top, is lovely to look at and crippling to think about. One moment the servants climb down to the lake upstage; the next moment, everybody is looking at the lake where we are. Does Sorin live on an island? Or a peninsula? Or is this merely the license of a design that doesn't care what country it is in anyway?

Chekhov on the modern, open stage doesn't yield to clean, open spaces without a struggle. When the late Sean Kenny set Laurence Olivier's 1963 Chichester production of *Uncle Vanya* on a stage like the Beaumont's, he solved the distinction between exterior and interior scenes by a simple change of light and with only the most economical change of furniture. Still, he had to omit Yelena's piano, and the loss was felt at the end of the second act when Yelena and Sonya are so anxious to make music together. Yeargan and Serban are even further away from serving the wondrous, small details of the play when they choose tableaux, silhouettes, and choreographed sprints across the footbridge instead of the actions plainly described in the text.

It isn't a matter only of the difference between the inside and the outside of Sorin's house. Two years pass between the third and fourth acts, and what Stanislavsky's designer, Simov, wanted to show in Act IV was "the stamp of impermanence." In a design prettily made to show nothing but transience throughout the play, there can be no effective contrast after those two years.

The people are living in a travel poster, rather than a world, always attractive and mostly untrue. Konstantin burns his manuscripts in a stove that has never shown signs of flame or heat until that moment. The sudden burst of fire is so alluring, you want him to stay longer and burn some more. Then, too, where is he going? Chekhov had him leaving through a door unused and locked until then, thereby making it clear that he isn't off to play Chopin again. But with Yeargan-Serban, there isn't any door, and the fatal, deliberate tremor cannot be felt.

"Until you have the right design, you cannot begin to plot the action," said Stanislavsky. "The set is half the job." A simple, approachable truth, one might think, but apparently not simple enough for many of today's designers and—to be fair to the designers—their directors. Sets that distort the reality of the play (not necessarily the real world's physical reality) and that overlook prosaic details do not automatically capture some otherwise elusive poetry. Serban keeps illustrating lines with literal gestures, such as Masha carrying a long scarf behind her when she says she is dragging her life around, or when she tears a sheet as she declares that she is ripping out her heart. Quick enough to make snapshots, he is laggard with larger commitments. It isn't a question of one "ism" or another. In theatre, both nature and fantasy are served by the details surrounding them. The prose *is* the poetry.

GR*(November 1980)*

The Ravages of Modishness

Alone, and in conversations with Brecht, Walter Benjamin wrestled with contradictions aroused by political theatre. He couldn't escape his own argumentative intelligence. For every "on the one hand," there was always "on the other hand." He kept hoping that he could make himself clear, but he never fully did so. He would try to prove that "a work which exhibits the right tendency must, of necessity, show every other quality as well." On the one hand: the good or "right" idea without the "right" form won't go anywhere; on the other hand: quality without commitment is not worth pursuing. Worse: the right idea captured by fashionable form will be conspiring toward its own ineffectiveness.

He found some hope in epic theatre, particularly if it really stimulated thought. He had noticed, however, that the best weapon on behalf of thought was laughter. "Spasms of the diaphragm," he said, "generally offer better chances for thought than spasms of the soul." There was no suggested "other hand" in this instance.

Benjamin might have been pleased by the first act of Dario Fo's *We Won't Pay! We Won't Pay!*, which is as funny as *Duck Soup*. That it doesn't sustain itself is a failure of form: on the one hand, Fo begins with a superbly invented character; on the other hand, he doesn't let her take over the play. Antonia is neither hothead nor spokesman. She is a clever, witty, energetic agent not so much for change, but for responsiveness, telling lies that are much more effective—and much funnier—than the truth. One never doubts that she will prevail and survive. Like the play in which she lives, she isn't really political. Rather, she is reactive, alive, competent.

Fo, unfortunately, is less competent than she is, possibly because he is so firmly lodged in politics and timeliness. When the second act begins, Fo stays at home with her much less interesting husband and his friend. Antonia returns, yes, but not soon enough to rescue the play from its detours. Fo has been hoisted by his prior commitment. Multiplying events without adding anything to his farcical energy, he demonstrates that political consciousness is not necessarily a substitute for the consciousness and presence of an extravagantly imaginative central figure. Antonia persuades by giving pleasure. The play drops her and becomes a pain.

Antonia is instructive in several ways. Either Fo or his translator and director, R. G. Davis, has her say to her husband that "indignation is the real weapon of the asshole." Until that moment, it had appeared that she was claiming food as her property because she, too, was suffering from indignation. Perhaps, however, she was claiming her right as a sentient person, bored with routine, caught in the passion of her own inventiveness, bewitched by the joy of living improvisationally. Sure she's angry, but that doesn't mean that she wants to be as boring and inactive as everybody else. The asshole broods, feels sorry for himself, and usually does nothing. If he is in a play, he weights it heavily with his indignation, telling us what we already know—that life out there is scary, awful, unjust; and then because he is in a play, he tells us what we already know not to be true—that it is redeemable.

Fo, like the asshole, tumbles into seriousness. His characters converge around the table in the play's final moments, exchanging platitudes about some kind of a better world. But it is too late. Antonia was the better world. Besides, if the play was written in 1974 and has now been revised for 1980, hasn't it noticed that inflation is worse, nothing has changed?

Why is political theatre so frightened of irony, so seduced by its own voice, so assured that everybody is listening? Benjamin found one aphorism in the works of Lichtenberg that provides a clue: "It is not what a man is convinced of that matters, but what his convictions make of him." For the sake of comprehending what keeps going wrong with political theatre, this might be revised to say: When a man doesn't let his convictions make something else of him, then perhaps his art stands a chance.

Political theatre keeps sinking on the shores of good intentions. Athol Fugard's *A Lesson from Aloes* is one long brood. Fugard is a journalistic novelist in search of a play. Like a novelist, he organizes the behavior of his characters, standing above and outside them, omniscient, telling them what to think, what to feel, how to *resolve* their experience. The journalist is the fundamental Fugard, however, the reporter of South Africa's bad news. But the news never becomes a theatrical image in *Aloes*. It just sits and suffers. Which isn't clear enough.

Joanne Akalaitis is certainly gifted with more clarity about her indignation in *Dead End Kids,* but it doesn't help her make either a persuasive statement or—and this is the same thing—an organized theatrical event. Where Fo cavalierly throws away his strongest theatrical weapon in favor of politics, and Fugard demonstrates that the theatre can't contain his experience, Akalaitis shows that she really wants to make a movie. (The clearest, most sustained moment in her presentation of the case against science and nuclear power is the hilarious film Mabou Mines has arranged from Atomic Energy Commission documentaries about the bomb, shown as part two of *Dead End Kids* begins.)

Mabou Mines makes most of its considerable impact through its organization of technology rather than of ideas or actors. The latter are mostly subsumed by the more urgent call of the visual and aural images. Akalaitis engineers her material so that intelligence placed in service to destruction is seen precisely for what it is—intelligence hopelessly corrupted. But her targets are muddled, mixed too casually into the nightmare realities of her lights, sound systems, and movie screen—her basic distrust of theatre as the workshop of good actors who can do all that stuff better than machines. On the one hand, she damns science. On the other hand, she celebrates its inventions. Her means keep arguing with her mind—a fascinating quarrel—but whatever she wishes to agitate here is undermined by the propaganda of her form.

If indignation doesn't automatically confer eloquence on the imagination, neither does it necessarily arouse the beholder. Letting a work discover its subject, as Ibsen, Chekhov, and even Brecht in his best plays kept doing, may be the most political act available to theatre. Uncorrupted intelligence does, in fact, exist, even if it rarely finds space in our institutions. Benjamin warned against "the ravages of modishness." He was concerned that "the struggle against misery" is often turned "into an object of consumption . . . converting revolutionary reflexes into themes of entertainment and amusement which can be fitted without much difficulty into the cabaret life of a large city." Political theatre too often fails to identify the problem because it is so much a part of the problem.   *GR(December 1980)*

Phrase Slinging

Have you noticed that we live in a period of extraordinary masterpieces? No matter that language has been evacuated of meaning: while you're racing from one masterwork to another, crowding your heart with expectations of wonders never known before, you can hardly waste a moment on the miseries of words gone haywire, loonily climbing into stratospheric ecstasies that offer something better than caviar or sex. Once upon a time, our teachers cautioned us to avoid comparisons between apples and oranges. Distinctions were made, genres defined, actions described, and, above all, masterpieces didn't collide with destiny every other week.

A random sample of theatre and movie reviews during December reveals that history is bestowing blessings that make Shakespeare look like an underachiever. One play is "a masterwork." It is also "remarkable," and it "floods the theatre with light," suggesting to the unwary that some experimental lighting designer, prompted by his director, is reminding the audience that we are all guilty. (You know how it works: light on the audience means objectivity, stark truth, harsh reality; in short, guilt.) Meanwhile, if you still have doubts about the occasion, you are assured that the play is the recipient of " a perfect production." If there is any justice, all involved should soon cop a Nobel Prize.

Achievements have a way of blending into the hyperbolic scenery. Any play or movie that "literally dazzles" or "swamps the senses" doesn't leave much space for *The Importance of Being Earnest* or *Tristan and Isolde.* Lanford Wilson is gifted, yes, but has he earned an enthusiasm that expresses itself in a vocabulary that might easily embarrass Chekhov? Has he really written something that is both "hilarious and heartbreaking"? If *Fifth of July* is "sharp, witty, riotous," why isn't the whole town laughing, why aren't there riots outside the theatre?

In November, most serious plays "soared." By December, the flight patterns had apparently changed; plays went back to stationary positions, "towering" instead of "soaring." One reviewer, probably recalling the time that a colleague invoked Mother while shrieking over the rooftops of our brains ("Mama, mama, mama, what a helluva good show!"), called upon the Lord: "Glory, glory be!" he yawped, capping it, of course, with the obligatory exclamation mark. (In other corners, movies were alternately "stunning," "mesmerizing," "inspired," and "incredible.") One show—*Brigadoon!*—was "a miracle," making it difficult to know what God can do for an encore. Somewhere else there was a "stunning powerhouse drama," also known as "a pacesetter." And, as if the reviewer was still unsure if he would be welcome on first-night lists, he added these assurances: "a riveting, blistering, provocative drama."

Plays that rivet are popular these days. If you feel uncomfortable riveted to your blisters, you can always shift to a musical such as *Really Rosie,* where one reviewer insists that the score is so lively "you can't sit still." (He was probably confused by all the kids in the audience heading for the toilet.) It's nice, also, to be faced with something called a "colossal entertainment." How big is colossal? You may not find out from the show, but at least you know you've spent your money on something bigger than you are, if not necessarily better.

Comedy "smashes" are sometimes "delicious" or "infectious." Theatre, it seems, can please the tastebuds, or just to confuse you further, it can bring disease. At other times, it can even threaten electrocution: one play that opened recently is said to possess "high-voltage scenes." It is reasonable to deduce that if you aren't smashed, flooded, stunned, knocked out, run over by a play as powerful as an express train, or carried on a rendezvous with greatness, you can't be sure you have lived. Surrounded, as we evidently are, by so much monumental magnificence, what point can there be in making love, reading a sonnet, or humming a favorite tune.

Reviewing was not always a media event. True, Max Beerbohm was obviously haunted by William Archer's inclination to call every Shaw play a masterpiece. About *Mrs. Warren's Profession*—"a powerful and stimulating, even an ennobling piece of work . . . a failure with elements of greatness in it"—he cried, "With all due deference to Mr. Archer, 'Not a masterpiece, no!' " (Note the cunning placement of the exclamation point here.) Shaw himself advised a young would-be critic not to call Charles Warner's performance "perfection." He congratulated the same critic for actually describing what he saw: "Don't you feel how much better it is than mere pompous and unmeaning phrase slinging like 'Undoubtedly it is one of the finest things he has done &c'?"

Theatrical achievement *and* the language deserve tender respect. Ibsen's *John Gabriel Borkman* is surely the best play in town now, directed by Austin Pendleton without fuss or muddle, and performed by Rosemary Murphy and Irene Worth, especially, as the great piece of chamber music that the play most resembles. It took courage for Pendleton to give such good actors time and space for weaving their unconventional patterns. Each section finds its own weight and measure. Here, for a change, is acting caught in the warm embrace of thought. Those flashes of sardonic comedy and the gorgeous sustained outbursts break through the hush so forcefully because the textures from one moment to the next are so diverse, so plain, clear, and individual.

In fact, this *is* a masterpiece, for the most part masterfully directed and acted. Yet it won't find its audience because neither play nor production concedes anything to that journalistic need for ingratiating experience. The language that tumbles all over itself in gleeful homage to *Lunch Hour* finds words for Ibsen's flaws but shrinks from urging you to confront his vision and energy.

There was a language once, a language that not only describes the achievement of *Borkman* with precision but also provides a model for a criticism that sometimes finds cause for celebration without putting funny party hats on its prose. Henry James—yes, Henry James!—said all that needs to be said about Ibsen's play:

> In the cold fixed light of it the notes that we speak of as deficiencies take a sharp value in the picture . . . sunset over the ice. Well in the very front of the scene lunges with extraordinary length of arm the Ego against the Ego, and rocks in a rigor of passion the soul against the soul—a spectacle, a movement, as definite as the relief of silhouettes in black paper or a train of Eskimo dogs on the snow. . . . Never has he juggled more gallantly with difficulty and danger than in this really prodigious *John Gabriel* . . . in which the whole thing throbs with an actability that fairly shakes us as we read.

Sunset over the ice is good, really good. Language and a major theatrical event have been rescued by that rarest of creatures, a master.

GR(December 1980)

Boxed Stages

An unwritten agreement among theatre critics is to pretend that the theatre is not already dead. Statistics are always at hand to confirm the premise. Corpses don't sell tickets, not even to Japanese businessmen who recognize that musicals don't offer any language barriers. At its worst, the theatre is just our old friend, "the fabulous invalid"; a little sick, perhaps, but only awaiting patiently its next Elizabethan age. Meanwhile, profits don't lie. If actors under the command and control of sound-mixers seem to have neatly moved one sidestep away from a live event, you can still give them a standing ovation (very "in" these days) to prove that at least you, the audience, are really there.

The theatre's suicidal bent can scarcely be denied. Once the public smells the sitcom rat on almost every Broadway stage, it won't bother to leave the reassuring comforts of its own sitcom kitchens and living rooms. No need to weep in the company of a thousand over *The Shadow Box* when you know you can see it unabashedly alone (and much more cheaply) three years later on the home screen. Then all those clever trumps of the eye foisted on the stage by design-happy directors—designed, especially, to cover up the work they haven't done with actors—will be seen for what they are: something the movies do better.

Has anything ever brought to the theatre by technology really given the event more presence, more liveness? Arguably, one can sound two cheers for the electric light, but even that is used only rarely by directors and designers to illuminate the mobile, responsive face and body of the actor. The "best" invention has more to do with the inventor and with profit in some part of the system than it has to do with the art. Meanwhile, there are those mixers, those screens, special effects, and the most haunting threat of them all—the televised "live" event.

Make no mistake about it, the latter is the Future, and in its eerie, moderately disgusting way, it works. Which would you choose, for example: An expensive outing at the Metropolitan Opera to see lighting tricks for *Tristan and Isolde* that take your mind off the under-rehearsed, half-sung performances of unqualified principals assembled to assist James Levine as he once more learns a score before a paying audience? Or a version of the opera presented in your living room with a hand-picked group of visually stunning singing actors who sound vocally fresh throughout and have been rehearsed so thoroughly that even the loudest passages emerge from their throats as if they were the most natural, most relaxed forms of communication available? Furthermore, the stress is on them, on the orchestra, and—not surprisingly—on the conductor (Leonard Bernstein).

Not a difficult choice, is it? Bernstein, wisely participating in the packaging of a media event, has embarked on this *Tristan* in Munich. Last month I attended a concert version of the first act, performed before a large audience sweating as much as the musicians under the banner lights flooding the Herkulessaal for the cameras. The first act only. And thereby hangs the tale: in April, they will do the second act, and in November the third. Could the principals, Hildegard Behrens and Peter Hofmann, manage the whole work in one evening? Probably not, at least not yet. Meanwhile, television is paying for rehearsals spread over nine months, Bernstein gets thirty-six hours to prepare the prelude alone (did Levine get that many for the entire opera?), and one day, we shall see the results at home. There will be a recording, of course, and some buzzing around the house suggested that Ingmar Bergman or Franco Zeffirelli would use the singing stars and this pre-recorded soundtrack for a film of the opera.

There are amusing dangers in such a development. Somebody crucial to the event might die between the acts. Certainly, members of the audience will either pass on or pass out. The strain of getting tickets for each act or of sitting under the harsh lights might wipe out dozens, or even hundreds. No matter: what counts is the living room, theatre from the box.

Surely this is only the beginning. While there is not much point in resisting, it is still not too late to examine some of the more elusive causes leading to this particular annexation of the theatre by the tube. For a start, managements and directors have been pushing too hard and long for spectacle; smart-assed Bright Ideas in each new production of every old work. For them, new production does not refer to a new reading or to extended preparation with performers, but to a new collaboration between directors and designers (this is also true of *Hamlet* and *The Cherry Orchard* in most regional theatres). Did I say Bright Ideas? Wrong: Visual Conceits that fill the space where a production's brains ought to be.

The futility of this kind of enterprise was once more demonstrated in still another opera house last month, in Florence, where Luca Ronconi and Pier Luigi Pizzi are continuing their collaboration on Wagner's Ring cycle begun several years ago in Milan's La Scala. The years have passed, and they have changed their minds a bit, no doubt because Patrice Chereau and Pierre Boulez at Bayreuth made so much more out of the "idea" that the Ring is about the ravages of industrialism. What director-designer can compete now with the hydroelectric dam from which Chereau's Rhine maidens emerge? When I last left Ronconi's Brünnhilde seven years ago in Milan, she lived with her sisters in a museum housing giant machines, and Wotan put her to sleep leaning over a dinner table. In last month's *Siegfried,* conducted by Zubin Mehta—still another New York Philharmonic fugitive playing with Wagner away from home (which says something about cash available abroad)—Brünnhilde woke up in a hall of mirrors mounted above an incredibly hazardous staircase lifted from Gordon Craig's dreams sixty years ago. Siegfried had found the dragon earlier in a forest that looked like it had—surprise!—real trees. In the first act, Mime's workshop revealed a toy bear and a few skyscrapers or factory chimneys in the background, virtually the same constructions seen in the second act of Andrei Serban's *Cherry Orchard* at the Beaumont some years ago. Ronconi's singers were in mortal danger on those steps, and they showed it in their tensile, frantic duet. (MGM made better and safer steps for the *Stairway to Paradise* number in *An American in Paris.*) It wasn't easy to figure out what was going wrong for everybody on the way to Valhalla, because the visual choices had become so arbitrary. The work was pale, undefined, listless, just sitting there being visual. The dimension and presence of theatre were only a memory.

Bernstein's *Tristan* flies a painted Turneresque sky over the organ loft of the hall, and the singers stand above and behind the orchestra, not in evening dress, but in rudimentary homage to the notion of costume—Tristan and Kurwenal in turtleneck sweater-suits, Isolde and Brangaene in "timeless" gowns. The cameras will undoubtedly be monitored to provide heartstopping close-ups of the Marlene-Neff-Garboesque Behrens and the Guy Madisonesque Hofmann. And they will look so animated, so at ease, designed not by a desperate team of theatrical directors and designers, but by nature.

Can the theatre survive? When Robert Wilson directs *Parsifal* in Kassel next September, perhaps making it longer than even Wagner intended, then a blow will surely be struck once more for the theatre-theatrical. For the moment, however, the threat is real and the irony is tremendous. Wagner's dream of Total Theatre is about to be contained in a nineteen-inch frame.

GR(February 1981)

Sir Joseph Papp

When Sir Joseph Papp began his press conference on February 20, 1981, he seemed confident about his stature and importance, but diffident in his suggestions. He offered some background—he had recently returned from several rounds of meetings in the White House about the version of *A Chorus Line* presented last week in the East Room for the Governors' meeting, and he had discussed the proposed cuts in the National Endowment for the Arts budget with Reagan's aide James Baker—but the conference seemed to dwindle rapidly into mini-stories. As the conference staggered from one ramble to another, it was possible to speculate about dramatic pause. Sir Joseph reported an exchange with Baker in which he questioned the proposed cut of half the NEA's budget. "Why only half?" asked Sir Joseph half-mockingly.

Could this be the headline we were awaiting? Baker looked up quizzically from his desk (my decoration, of course, since I want to give someone credit for a Shavian twist) and replied, "Are you suggesting we cut more?" And some of us stopped a beat, only to be dropped once more into the uncertainties and unassertiveness with which the conference had begun. It seemed to be a case of No, but not quite Yes, not Really, but perhaps Something Else.

The pause kept being dramatic. Sir Joseph offered his views on the proper role of federal funding, announcing that he withheld any ideas about the spiritual importance of the arts, suggesting only (to us, not to Baker) that for New York, at least, the arts were its tobacco industry, responsible for millions in the residual economy, etc., and so on, blah-infinitum. Where could a mind wander for both comfort and fun?

My own headlines popped into view: Papp Refuses to Let *Chorus Line* Play the East Room. Subheading: Ties White House Performance to Decreased Military Budget. In fine print, he would add that he was holding *Chorus Line* as hostage for the new administration's guarantee to stay out of El Salvador.

Or: Papp Calls for Nationwide Artists' Strike. Subheading: Nation Will Discover Importance of the Arts. This will be followed by amplifications: hotels, restaurants, taxis, and tired businessmen respond by asking for bailout for artists. What's good enough for Chrysler is good enough for us, says Papp.

Or: Papp Sends *Penguin Touquet* to White House, Replacing *Chorus Line.* Subheading: Revenge for Arts' Cuts. Amplifications: Reagan to find out what new acting is all about. Papp announces that Wolfgang Hildesheimer's *Mary Stuart* was first choice, but with all respect for Nabokov and none for the president, he didn't want to suggest an invitation to a beheading. Offers mercy, however: *Penguin Touquet* will be seen in cut version.

In the end, Sir Joseph had to be asked a direct question requiring a direct answer. Was he saying, asked one reporter, that the National Endowment for the Arts should be liquidated? "Yes," he said, adding that he was in favor of a smaller cut in the actual funding, the money distributed instead to states and municipalities, most of them already furnished with agencies better equipped and less expensive to administer than the funding agencies of the Feds. (The NEA sets aside $10,000,000 annually for its own administration.)

At last—predictably—the press had its headline, and so it appeared the next morning in the *New York Times.* Livingstone Biddle, Jr., head of the NEA, called it a "bizarre suggestion," and that, to date, is where the matter rests. Sir Joseph will meet with groups affected by the proposed cuts, no doubt a position paper will emerge, and Reagan will continue to think that what he used to do can be covered by the name of acting. As opposed, of course, to what he is doing now.

Meanwhile, though not as important as El Salvador, the theatre, too, is burning. Has anybody really noticed that funded theatres, most of them charged with fiscal responsibility by the NEA and the New York State Council on the Arts, are faced with imminent extinction precisely because of their mandated fiscal good sense? Theatre Row on 42d Street has eight theatres, seven of which are faced with closing because of the high cost of real estate. The NEA has just announced grants to fifteen arts groups, including several theatres, *not* for the work of creators, but for more "fiscal responsibility," for development of "efficient fundraising," for "better marketing strategies" (let them eat fake), and for "stronger boards of directors."

Could there be a better illustration of the NEA's distance from practical reality? Only weeks ago, a perfectly strong board for the Chelsea Theatre voted to close down the theatre's creative operation, giving Robert Kalfin time, presumably, to prove himself again while the theatre is rented to outside productions. The American Place Theatre is also renting to outside producers, unable to do much of its own work, weighted heavily by such costs as $60,000 per year for Con Ed; and the administrator of the AMAS Repertory Theatre on East 104th Street reports that, despite their success as the originators of *Bubbling Brown Sugar,* they are "in serious danger of closing for good." So much for fiscal responsibility. Real Estate stands while actors, writers, and directors are driven from the temple.

Performing artists, however, are crying too much too soon about the NEA. The announced cut of fifty percent doesn't hit until 1984 (that year again, though Orwell was after bigger game). Besides, the arts are only one program out of thirty-six slated for a similar slash. Who among us would say that a play or concert is more important than Mass Transit, Health Care Regulations, or Fossil Energy Research? We're lousy lobbyists anyway, usually failing to make the most convincing argument. Such as: one figure trundling around Washington now is that while Reagan plans to cut the NEA budget to $88 million, the insatiable Pentagon allocates $52 million to military bands for the current fiscal year. In Germany, the federal subsidy to theatres was about $630,000,000 in 1979, contrasted with the U.S.'s $154,000,000 now for *all* the arts. It's true that we lost the war in 1945, but did FDR mean us to be quite so abject about it thirty-five years later?

And Sir Joseph? I've given him an honorary knighthood because he tries harder, even if he does blow the big moments, the grander possibilities, and the available comic inventions. He did make one definite suggestion, however. Let the federal government honor at least one artist each year. (He seems to have missed those Kennedy Center occasions when medals were given to Astaire, Bernstein, Cagney, etc.) We need the equivalent of knighthood, he declared, and a stipend of not less than $50,000 should be attached to it.

Well, I can't offer him the stipend, but I can easily bestow the knighthood. I'm still not sure why he called a press conference. But the issue of knighthood will have to do. The British gave their first theatrical knighthood to an actor (Sir Henry Irving); it is only logical, albeit sickening, that Americans should find their first theatrical knight in a producer. Ronnie already has his honor, and Lord Lunt, Sir Frederic March, and Sir Paul Muni are not available for comment.   *GR(March 1981)*

Nothing Fails Like Success

American actors, oppressed by disorganized and muddled training systems, by their supply so far ahead of demand, by awful producers, mean directors, dopy agents, and a union that protects them from developing their craft, are perhaps even more oppressed by reviewers who love them. It takes luck to be born great and time to achieve greatness, but in America the real danger is to have greatness thrust prematurely upon you. Or to put it another way: William Hurt may be lucky, but he certainly needs time.

Greatness could lie ahead, but there is no assurance that it can happen to Hurt any more than it happened to Orson Welles, Marlon Brando, or John Barrymore. You don't need to be a conspiracy theorist to know that nothing in American arrangements conspires to make an actor as good as his first efforts. The path isn't merely thorny, it just isn't there.

Brando studied with good teachers—Erwin Piscator and Stella Adler—but even their flaming intensities didn't drive him into roles that might have tested his capacity to make sounds beyond the woodnotes wild which sustained him in the movies. The medium became his message before he had a chance. Odd that the only neo-classical roles he ever tried publicly were Marchbanks in *Candida* and Sergius in *Arms and the Man*. The brute Kowalski was his one-way ticket to Hollywood, but he must have had some idea when he tried Shaw that the gift of tongues was within his grasp. There wasn't a theatre in this country to pick up his hint.

Welles was in a wheelchair the last time he was seen on stage in New York. During the rehearsals of *King Lear* in the late fifties he managed to break one leg and then the other, finally barreling down steps and ramps in a performance that became the perfect visual metaphor for the American actor's reluctant expeditions into the serious classical repertory. John Barrymore's Hamlet had impressed the young Olivier with its athleticism, but it never led Barrymore to Malvolio, Iago, Benedick, Macbeth, or Lear—the latter a role he might have made eloquent even in his cups. Whether it is to be the wheelchair, the drunken stupor, or exile in Tahiti, the usual motion of the actor in America is not so much *to* the silver screen (where the gold lies) as it is a passionate withdrawal *from* the great challenges of the stage.

It may be stretching the point before William Hurt has even begun to stretch his talent to place him in such promising—which is to say *un*promising—company. But that is what reviewers are doing. What keeps making them damn a young actor with so much great praise? Probably, they need to demonstrate affections, to prove they are not bottled only in vinegar and acid. The young actor, however, should be wary of fickle friends bearing hyperbolic gifts. Reviewers are surrogate salesmen. He, in his turn, is buying time to find something within his talent worth selling.

Hurt's talent is sturdy and momentarily salable to a movie public that eats personalities for breakfast. Where the stage is concerned, however, he could not possibly be ready for all markets. Now playing Byron in Marshall Mason's cocktail party trivialization of Romulus Linney's *Childe Byron,* he reveals a quirky, eccentric imagination and a gray, humming sexuality caught in body, voice, and performing habits that keep collapsing into convention. He seems to have heard about heroism, but he's too down-home, even folksy and charming, to let it fly with flags unfurled. When he does, he lets his voice pitch him into gabble and rant. He has yet to make the big decisions, the ones that distinguish between poetry and prose, letting the ordinary speak through the verse and the remarkable sing out from the mundane. He looks alternately terrific—big-boned, sculptured, unselfconsciously handsome—and lumpish, whitewashed, drab. The mix is not as volatile and attractive as it might be, no doubt because his presence is finally so indecisive. He can make sharp turns, quick about-faces in his emotional directions, sometimes with astonishing ease. Even so, those gifts of repose and unpredictability are constantly sabotaged by tensions in the voice, arms that don't quite know how to accommodate the air.

How could it be otherwise? Hurt is thirty and has had a bash at Hamlet. At thirty, however, Ralph Richardson was playing Brutus, Iago, Toby Belch, the Ghost and the First Gravedigger in *Hamlet,* and also General Grant in *Abraham Lincoln* and Ralph in *The Knight of the Burning Pestle.* In the two years before that, he played twelve major roles at the Old Vic, and four odd-ball parts in the Malvern Festival. Michael Redgrave played Laertes when he was twenty-nine during two seasons at the Old Vic when he played eleven other roles, and tried his first professional Hamlet when he was forty-two and his last when he was fifty. This, I take it, is what critics used to mean when referring to a "seasoned player." Hurt's seasoning has been Milan Stitt and Lanford Wilson. Think of Maria Callas, not in *bel canto,* but in *The King and I.*

Hurt is being told that he is great by people who hate history, difficulty, and process. The quintessence of acting, as Shaw said about Ibsenism, "is that there is no formula." A demon in Hurt's acting impulse knows this, but there is no obvious way he can give it release. Producers and audiences alike invest nothing in actors. Easy come, easy go: a well-behaved actor is a disposable one, especially one who can be recruited by an advertising agency to sell disposables.

William Hurt is hardly alone within the threatened species. Women, as usual, have it worse than men, not only because great roles are scarce, but also because the critical establishment views them sexually rather than artfully. Heresy to say so, but Meryl Streep simply has not been tested: on the evidence of her *stage* performances, she is proficient, but not nearly the Duse of critics' sentimental dreams. High cheekbones and frozen eyes are not really substitutes for challenge and hard work. To escape their formula destinies, actors such as Hurt, Streep, Al Pacino, Lindsay Crouse, Sigourney Weaver, and Robert DeNiro will have to find a world elsewhere.   *GR(March 1981)*

Class Unconsciousness

Probably nothing can be protected from the whims and frequently inventive wisdoms of modern directors. Beatrice and Benedick will continue to be presented as cowgirl and cowboy in Texas (Stratford, Conn., many years ago), the Agamemnon clan will plunge down sanded chutes to their inevitable fates (Luca Ronconi in Spoleto, mid-1970s), and Russia's cherry orchard will transform itself into Louisiana's wisteria trees (Joshua Logan in the 1950s). Similarly, plays from other languages are presented now in "versions" rather than translations, the translators themselves (such as Thomas Babe in the Brooklyn Academy of Music's current *The Wild Duck*) almost proud to declare their ignorance of the play's native tongue. Nothing should be sacred, of course, but modern theatre has a way of taking profanity into a realm beyond intelligent provocation and into plain and stupid shock.

Most transgressions are as easy to spot as wisteria in full bloom. Since the new disguise is precisely what the directors wish to proclaim, they do nothing to hide it. Seeking a passing relevance and a fashionable theatricality, they are frank purveyors of aggressively inauthentic events. They wear their lies pugnaciously. They present their frauds in style.

More difficult to notice are violations in productions that possess external signs of fidelity to the text. Plays by Shakespeare and Chekhov often appear to be dressed according to period, yet they are as often naggingly wrong in some central, guiding way—the notion that Polonius is just a foolish old man, for example, or that Nina is a talented actress. Minor crimes, however, can lead to major misunderstandings.

Such a crime has led several reviewers—not least, Michael Feingold here two weeks ago—to misconstrue Franz Xaver Kroetz's *Request Concert,* still playing at the Interart Theatre in Joanne Akalaitis's apparently faithful production. Feingold finds that the director meets the text as an equal, and he seems convinced that playwright and director create "an impact twice as powerful as either could achieve alone." But this confidence must have its source in an illusion shared not by director and playwright, but by director and critic. When Feingold declares that "Kroetz's play is a simple and carefully sequenced naturalistic anecdote," he is falling into the trap of mistaking production for play.

Kroetz is rarely simple and never naturalistic. So astounding is the new image, sustained for more than an hour, of a woman alone who never utters a word, that it is easy to assume that the enactment is a fragment from nature; or at the least, an extended glimpse into a "real" activity. But it isn't. Like the great deceptions in Ibsen's and Strindberg's plays, the actions presented by Kroetz are selected to unearth a vision of experience unrelated to either conventional realities or theatrical conventions.

In Richard Gilman's irreplaceable and brilliant introduction to Kroetz's *Farmyard, and Four Other Plays,* the mysterious connection is joined between the plays' "simplicity of incident" and their actual distance from what has been called naturalistic drama. These are plays, as Gilman says, that refuse to judge or argue, that deny or repudiate "authorial bias," that are nothing like Zola or Hauptmann, in no way enslaved "by what Delacroix called 'the fetish for accuracy that most people mistake for truth.' " The details in Kroetz's plays are lures into the unseen and unknowable. They look like behavior and indeed they *are* behavior, but they are arranged by Kroetz to reveal not themselves—which is, anyway, very easy to do—but the otherwise invisible motions of mind under pressure.

If Kroetz's text is viewed as a "scenario" (Feingold's word), then Akalaitis's choices would seem to be logical and representative. Certainly, they are painstakingly executed by all involved: the details in Manuel Lutgenhorst and Douglas E. Ball's set are especially breathtaking in their thoroughness; the fundamental commitments by Joan Macintosh to the successive behaviors arranged by Akalaitis represent a trust and bravery rare in most actors.

The text is not a scenario, however. It is a play. Which means that if Kroetz had wished to "say" some of the things chosen by Akalaitis in her restless urge to amplify the text, then he would have undoubtedly chosen to say them.

These amplifications seem to spring from the initial wrongheaded decision to take the play out of Bavaria and into New York. (The title means nothing in its adopted country: Kroetz's woman listens to a popular German radio program not given a counterpart in the American radio programs chosen by Akalaitis.) Surely, this is still another replanting of those wisteria trees, inspired by the crackpot notion that most of us are too dumb to make identifications with foreigners and their local customs. It may be, also, that Akalaitis was really attracted to the play because it seemed to open itself to mixing media again, this time using "real" television and radio to give added weight to the illusion of "real" reality. Yet, in one long moment almost fatal to Kroetz's vision, Akalaitis interpolates radio melodrama that is at once too talky for the play proper (since Kroetz is presenting an experience where nothing is, in fact, articulated) and much too literal. The melodrama has a line that could be misinterpreted easily by the woman and the audience as an inducement to her eventual suicide: "something wasteful in spending the rest of your life in prison," says Akalaitis, but most assuredly, not Kroetz.

Behind the conceit of this "version," however, lies what may be a snobbery more abiding than attraction to illusory naturalism or media games. Akalaitis presents a play about a nameless American woman, rather spicily attractive in a once-upon-a-time Rosalind Russell way, coming home from a presumably hard day at the executive or secretarial desk, living in a kitschily plastic flat, yes, but one with all the amenities. Kroetz, on the other hand, writes of a Fraulein Rasch, a woman with a dark complexion, "what one might call dirty," offering a "plain, average impression." Her flat has "an industrial and worker's atmosphere," and she herself tends to envelopes in a "stationery factory." She has no hot water. In short, she has class, albeit "lower" class, a status Akalaitis may believe few in her audience might recognize.

See it anyway, if only because it is a suggestion about a great play yet to be seen. But what a distance we have come from genuine sympathetic consciousness. It's bad enough that the smart, talented Akalaitis seems to have surrendered to the view that foreigners don't exist. What's worse is that, in an America currently bent on proving that the working class doesn't deserve to exist, an educated, serious theatre is already prepared to agree.

GR(April 1981)

The Meyerhold Train

Lofty, imperious, easily caricatured by Mikhail Bulgakov in his hilarious novel *Black Snow*, Stanislavsky was nevertheless a lucky man: lucky to be rich when he first dreamed of theatre, lucky to have a first-rate talent for publicizing himself, lucky to have his theatre travel abroad (his disciples carrying his iconography of the actor's soul into cellars from London to Manhattan), and lucky to die in bed. His renegade pupil, Meyerhold, was less fortunate.

Meyerhold, for all the reports of his constructivist creations, his stress on grotesque behavior, and another method with an impossible label—Biomechanics—barely rated a footnote in the consciousness of American actors. He was obviously too difficult, a recalcitrant, stubborn martinet allegedly obsessed with visual invention. Murdered by Stalin in 1940 at the age of sixty-six, his "crimes" were against that monstrous construction, Socialist Realism. Crates labeled Moscow-New York were left behind in the theatre closed by Stalin: no Meyerhold production ever reached New York.

Despite excellent books by Edward Braun *(Meyerhold on Theatre* and *The Theatre of Meyerhold)* and Marjorie L. Hoover *(Meyerhold: The Art of Conscious Theater),* it has seemed impossible to rescue the great actor-director-teacher from the clutches of his own slippery history. Accounts of productions and of political strife left only the image of an embattled romantic, who gave legitimacy to conceptual directors and illegitimacy to inventive actors. If the symbol was a hard nut for Stanislavsky to crack (as he said once), then the symbolism of Meyerhold has been an even harder nut for the world to crack.

Until now. Paul Schmidt has edited just the kind of book that passes by the generalized sweep of history in order to unearth its truly critical details. *Meyerhold at Work* collects what Schmidt calls "the memory of a community." These are the notes and letters of Meyerhold himself; perhaps more importantly, of those who worked with him and loved him. The other books point the way to some of these documents, but they remained untranslated until Schmidt and his colleagues, Ilya Levin and Vern McGee, set to work. It may be true, as Schmidt admits, that Meyerhold continues to escape "our grasp, moving ahead of us as he did in life," yet it is also true that the book demystifies a legend. Meyerhold deserves a major revision, and this inspiring book should initiate it.

For a start, the slander that he turned actors into puppets can be given the indecent burial it has long deserved. He was a superb, inquiring actor himself, and other actors adored him. One speaks of his "scrupulous attention to the interplay between actors, his search for the most varied actor's choices." Another says: "He trusted his actors and did not like to drill a scene endlessly once it had become lucid, organic, and alive." He depended upon actors' "creative initiative." It was "their skill and individuality . . . the living spark of their presence" that rescued his work as a director from becoming lifeless.

As for concept, well yes, he may have been among the first to stress the word, but he didn't mean imposition from the outside—as many contemporary directors do—so much as he meant an incarnation of the playwright's world. "I am not inventing any approach to *Boris Godunov,*" he said, "I am trying to understand Pushkin—what it was he wanted to accomplish with this piece." His creed "is a theatrical language, simple, laconic, that leads to complex associations . . . a concept in constant motion."

His complex associations astonished other artists in and out of Russia. Fernand Léger worshiped him, Gordon Craig and Louis Jouvet were great admirers, and Sergei Eisenstein insisted that, without Meyerhold, there would have been no Eisenstein. But none was more astonished, apparently, than Boris Pasternak, who "never imagined a metaphor could be realized in theatre" until he had seen a Meyerhold production. Pasternak had not liked the theatre much, accepting Swinburne's cockeyed claim that Shakespeare was meant only to be read. But the encounter with Meyerhold's theatre persuaded him, at last, that "as an art . . . theatre . . . was indeed conceivable." A poet had, in fact, discovered another poet.

Pasternak, like most of us, would have been moved by the production of *Hamlet* that Meyerhold was able to develop only in his imagination. He had always dreamed of a theatre with only one play in its repertory—*Hamlet*, directed by Stanislavsky, Craig, Reinhardt, and himself. But even his own was never to be, thanks in part to Stalin, and perhaps in another sense, to the poet within him who still had far to go. Speaking with utmost care and delicacy of the scene in which Hamlet meets his father's ghost, he describes not a concept, but an experience. There would be the sea and a midnight sun. The ghost approaches Hamlet from the distance. When he reaches the shore, Hamlet embraces him: "He sits his father down on the rock, and then, so that he won't be cold, he takes off his cloak and wraps him in it."

This tenderness, this gestural reality surely touched Pasternak and might have made him realize that the stage could be worthy of Shakespeare. When Pasternak wrote his extraordinary letter to Meyerhold in 1928, telling him that his "train is genuinely gathering speed and moving off, not standing with brakes frozen by petrified formal habits," he could not have known how far that train would carry both of them—deeper into their work, yes, work that would never be finished, but closer to the fate of all those who insist on eluding definition.   *GR(April 1981)*

More Beckett, But Less

That great disarmer of the critical act, Samuel Beckett, has done it again. Having given the theatre its only undeniable masterpiece in this century, he continues to deny the theatre another image of equal weight, preferring instead to go out with eloquent whimpers. Verdi and Shakespeare approached the end differently, the one in an explosion of comic reversals, the other in sublime, valedictory statements. If anything, their work was more command-ing at the end than ever. While *Falstaff* and *The Tempest* don't travel in the same rhythms, they are supremely energetic, confident in their choices, loaded with invention and mischief. With the end in sight, there wasn't time for nos-talgia. In both works, there are laughter and relief.

Not with Beckett. It may be his last cosmic joke that, while his audience keeps waiting for another *Godot,* he presents instead a series of short works that resemble only themselves, brief encounters with mortality in the form, essentially, of monologues. Man, woman, or mouth, the image is much the same: conversation turned in on itself; not mind over matter, but matter ab-sorbed completely by mind. For a long time now, this image has exerted a strange force on his idea of what theatre can or cannot do well. With mind alone as his subject, Beckett has refused to give theatre its confrontations and many of its customary sources of playful energy. He has been saying No to ev-erything, in fact, except theatre's looming presence.

Rockaby, directed by Alan Schneider, and seen recently at La Mama with Billie Whitelaw as the Woman (W) in a chair and her recorded voice (V), is only the latest in the series. Lasting little more than fifteen minutes, the play charts the waning moments of W's life as she rocks in her chair in the usual half-light ("hellish" as Beckett called it in *Play*), asking her mind to continue the recording of her voice describing the thoughts and actions that brought her to this last repose. If there is any humor in the event, it lies in the repeated "More" that she says aloud, dividing the recorded passages neatly into four sections. That "More" is the only verbal life left in her; indeed, the only phys-ical life, since Beckett directs the rock of the chair to be "controlled mechani-cally without assistance from W." It isn't explosive, desperate, or anything like an appeal for sympathy. But it *is* amusing, partly because it is so isolated, so deliberately stressed; perhaps, too, because it exposes almost breathlessly an extravagant and ridiculous greed for living, whatever the evidence may be. A small word emerging from an increasingly attenuated sense of experi-ence. In these brief, tapered suspirations, Beckett has found the form that successfully releases his theatre from the banality of his obsessions.

Earlier, with *Godot* especially, the obsessions were also about existence, surrounded, however, not only by void, but quite playfully, by relationships. Didi, Gogo, and to a lesser extent Pozzo and Lucky were terrific people living in a marvelously precise, yet textured, theatrical universe. Peering beyond that tree and mound, one could glimpse a naturalistic past that captured these four as they crawled from one Dublin pub to another, but Beckett's ingenious move into a theatre ripe with imagistic possibility rescued them from a prac-tice and tradition that might have stranded them in photograph and carica-ture. He scraped his tramps not only into essence, but into vibrancy and re-newal: life never seen in quite this way before. *Godot's* people lived in a perpetual present, despite the pressures from waiting and a shadowed past. They never really looked back, they simply contended with each other. The play had scope because Beckett seemed determined to make theatre bend to imagination and ambition.

Not incidentally, *Godot* was also more fun to live with than the current series. *Rockaby* offers less and *is* less, even though it is far more than it would be if it allowed its pervasive nostalgia to be more audible, more sustained. Most recent naturalistic plays drench their characters in wet dreams of a past that had to be even more ordinary than the present we are compelled to share with them. A play called *The Vikings* at the Manhattan Theatre Club earlier this season presented the lives of a grandfather, his son, and his grandson in a language and situation so debased by formula that only banality could emerge. The play *was* what it says: "Reminiscing is a large part of what I have left," says the old man; or "My years have been fine and full"; or "The aging of the body only hides the child within"; or—and this, too, is *Rockaby*'s story, but with quite a difference— "Life is one long story of loss." Beckett's W, on the other hand, rocks and listens to incantations that have shape and rhythm. For all their bareness, they drop into the air as uniquely theatrical utterance:

> so in the end
> close of a long day
> went down . . .
> into the old rocker
> mother rocker
> where mother sat
> all the years
> all in black . . .
> till her end came
> in the end came
> off her head they said.

The concern and ambition may be smaller than *Godot*'s, but it is awful to think where Beckett would be now if he had only his quotidian intelligence to offer: the long story of loss would be as long as most naturalistic plays, and no doubt just as blithering.

So in an odd, refracted way, these sketches are a blessing. Whitelaw read a Beckett short story called *Enough* to make something like an evening out of the new play, and it served, at the least, to make *Rockaby* look more like the fragment of theatre that it really is. Young, vigorous, real actor's blood pouring through her veins, she was forced to illustrate the story with literal gestures and moves around the reader's lectern designed to fool listeners into thinking that something theatrical was going on up there. But it wasn't. This was undisguisably a short story meant to be read alone without help from an actor. Too many words for theatre; beautifully patterned words, surely, but not in urgent need of theatrical space or Whitelaw. Neither, in its cruel, stark way, does *Rockaby* need her. But she was boldly there in voice and body, submissive to orders from the text. She was serving the best dramatist the century has offered, one who disappoints, it is true, but not half as much as he must disappoint himself.   *GR(April 1981)*

Brecht in a Cold Country

In *Brecht Chronicle* by Klaus Volker an entry for July 1945 finds Brecht in New York, where "he sees Elizabeth Taylor on Broadway, in an idiotic piece." Anyone in search of existential show-stoppers might well stop right there. You and I know that it couldn't have happened. Elizabeth Taylor had only recently hopped off Velvet. She was officially thirteen and had never been near a stage. Meanwhile, Brecht was in his prolonged American exile, but why would he choose a play with a nymphet movie star when he could just as easily catch a performance of *Oklahoma?* (Which is precisely what he did in 1946.)

On the other hand, why not? Brecht plundered history for rearrangements of facts that had a way of making reality more persuasive. As for maps and time, he had no respect at all. His China, Florida, Chicago, and his centuries were all Weimar and Berlin between the wars. Assaulted by dislocations that would cast most people into catatonic rage, Brecht escaped the ravages of history by making history useful to his work. He could probably make a play from Volker's error, and he wouldn't be so far wrong. It was, of course, Laurette Taylor he had seen in what he labeled cruelly and obtusely an "idiotic piece" (*The Glass Menagerie*), but since time has no dominion in Brecht's work, he might just as easily be with us today to see Elizabeth in what would be, for him, an equally idiotic piece.

The real America was never so much fun for Brecht as the America he invented in *Mahagonny* and *Arturo Ui.* Yet where else could he go? A born survivor, he was not about to disappear into Stalin's huge belly, where poets and directors either killed themselves or were murdered. With customary dispatch and adroitness, he crossed that icy continent on the trans-Siberian express to catch the S.S. *Annie Johnson,* landing one month later in San Pedro, California. He had managed to slip away from Russia just before the Nazi invasion, and he crossed the Pacific just before Pearl Harbor. Characteristically, he wrote a poem suggesting that his was the last crossing before the war. It wasn't, but then again, why not? Certainly he was the last distinguished artist-fugitive from Hitler to make California—and Hollywood, naturally—his first American home.

The others had been luckier; at least, they were more accommodating to American ways. Most of them were working at their work and some were getting rich. While he probably didn't care about affluence, Brecht wanted to work. If Fritz Lang, Peter Lorre, Oscar Homolka could manage in Hollywood, and Weill on Broadway, surely he could do as well, or even better. But America—and Americans—had an obstinate way of being either repelled by or uninterested in the dialectical hat tricks he had been able to pull off in Europe. As James K. Lyon says in the prologue to his useful, overstuffed account of Brecht's American years, *Bertolt Brecht in America,* these were not to be an "exile in paradise." The *Annie Johnson* had carried Brecht to "one of the most difficult periods of his life."

Lyon's book is indeed valuable, but since it is hell-bent on academic completeness, it tends to have facts where its brains ought to be. All sources, details, quotations, documents, and letters are given equal weight: the book is a junkheap of unselective information. A detached yet sympathetic collector, Lyon could probably tell you where to find a Ming vase and a new brass bed, but he couldn't tell you why you ought to consider either one of them. Still, he offers facts that seem to be more reliable than Volker's, though he thinks Paul Muni played Chopin in the movies and that Eva Le Gallienne was a Method actress.

Accidentally, perhaps, the book discloses more about America than it does about Brecht. No doubt the playwright was as "obdurate" as Lyon describes him, politically dextrous, and clever enough to create at least fifty situations that might have led to finished screenplays (only one, Lang's *Hangmen Also Die,* ever reached the screen, and then without credit for Brecht); then, too, his determination to succeed on Broadway (more blindness than obtuseness, surely) led finally to Laughton's worthy Galileo under Joseph Losey's direction (which didn't really succeed). It can't be said, however, that many Americans behaved as if another Shakespeare had landed on the West Coast for a visit. Of course, most of them would have sent Will back to his desk to revise *Antony and Cleopatra;* nobody here would accept a play divided into seventy-two scenes; besides, the lovers never kiss; and those double suicides are a downer.

When Brecht wasn't fighting American inflexibility, he was fighting American uplift, especially the kind represented by liberal writers and the left. He argued with Orson Welles, who found him "shitty," with orthodox Communists who found him "arrogant," and with playwrights such as Odets and Donald Ogden Stewart, especially the latter's "consoling references." "We have fraternized too long with ignorant decency," he was saying while nobody here knew that the Holocaust was going on. His taste was beyond the comprehension of the mindless and the Marxists. Finding virtues in American musicals (but not Weill's) and loathing Paul Robeson's *Othello* was an assured route to fitting nowhere. In Hollywood, he met Chaplin *and* Groucho Marx at the same dinner party: two Azdaks at the same table, and none, including Brecht apparently, thought of producing a *Caucasian Chalk Circle* that might even have found an audience.

He was a prodigious miscalculator, jumping from one aborted project to another, getting minimal help from fellow exiles, most of them having left their art and politics in Germany. Lyon fails to unscramble Brecht's disastrous encounters with show business and politics, except to observe the obvious in a tone altogether too neutral, even naive: "Brecht was probably too far ahead of his time and too uncompromising in promoting his kind of theatre in his own way to have succeeded in an alien environment like America."

Compromise was never a real issue. America wasn't alien for Brecht, it was another planet, where idiotic pieces were the rule and idiotic people couldn't recognize theatrical genius swirling in smelly cigar smoke, laconic wit, and a subversive intellect.   *GR(May 1981)*

The American Way of Theatre Death

Fifty years ago, June 8, 1931, the Group Theatre left New York for Brookfield Center, Connecticut, to rehearse a play for fall presentation on Broadway. It was only eight years since some of them had been galvanized by the appearance in America of the Moscow Art Theatre. The three pivotal organizers were Harold Clurman, Lee Strasberg, and Cheryl Crawford, all of them employees of the Theatre Guild, a producing unit which—according to Clurman's account in *The Fervent Years*—was presenting plays that were pretty but wanting in passion, point, or individual drive. Moscow became the model instead: long rehearsals, a concern for truth in acting, and, said Clurman, "a sense of theatre in relation to society." Six years later, Strasberg and Crawford resigned, Clurman accepting their resignations with a kind of "friendly fatalism."

Four years after that, the tenth and final season of the Group Theatre began and ended with Irwin Shaw's *Retreat to Pleasure,* the story of a young woman pursued by many men. As always, the play had a message, in this case that youth should have fun before the war absorbs and annihilates them. An ironic, unlikely conclusion to the Group's stormy life and its gallant experiment: point and passion had given way totally to individual drive.

Clurman finally attributed the Group's attrition and dissolution not to financial troubles but in part to its lack of humor. Has anybody except Clurman ever noticed that group theatres—in America, especially—suffer from the importance of being too earnest? Now, on the eve of the Group's fiftieth anniversary, still another attempt has bitten the readily available American dust, choosing to disperse in an explosion of seriousness—albeit fake, pompous, and unconvincing. The Brooklyn Academy of Music Theatre company, after two dreary seasons, has just announced its dissolution, declaring that "financial considerations left us no choice." Harvey Lichtenstein refers to "tremendous effort" and "first-rate work." David Jones, BAM's artistic director, speaks of "ten major productions at BAM over the past fifteen months," skimming past histories of other companies that might have cautioned him to do less more effectively; not least the Group's ten major years, in which they did only twenty-three variable, though usually provocative, productions.

American theatre peddles its humorless and intellectually impoverished groupings in prose dripping with optimism, not unlike colleges that keep insisting kids can read, critics who say that graffiti can be beautiful, and presidents who proclaim a "new spirit" in the land. A skunk by any other name is supposed to smell like a rose in America, so it can't be surprising that Lichtenstein and Jones should be expecting us to deny what we know and feel. "Actors and audiences have committed themselves to the idea of classic repertory," says Jones, giving new meaning to commitment.

If only as much invention had gone into building the company as seems to be going into reinvented language and rewritten experience. Jones is surely right in applauding "enthusiasm, perceptiveness, skill and dedication," at least for some members of his team. Can this be reconciled, however, with the claim that follows; namely, that these virtues "exceeded all expectations"? If so, then why such a conclusion? If Jones and Lichtenstein expected less and actually got more, then what kind of "con" were they committing with their financial sources? Surely they didn't raise money on the basis of low expectations. And just as surely, they should not be dissolving the group just as its expectations have been "exceeded." They claim that "BAM will return to" this "type of theatre," but only the dumbest foundation would surrender to so much doublespeak so artfully and witlessly presented.

Against this background—and also the pause for a year during which the Vivian Beaumont will be reconstructed physically (which is, of course, no guarantee of artistic reconstruction)—it is easy to see now that the Group Theatre's failure was really a success. Its flaws were always closely allied to its virtues: passion bred war in the membership, none more devastating than the war between Strasberg and Stella Adler, with Adler finding his unhappiness and "lack of cordiality" infecting everything, while Strasberg retreated to his now-familiar defense that his theatre had won a Pulitzer and, anyway, the Moscow Art Theatre "had gone downhill." Yet the assembled talents were remarkable, especially when measured against BAM, Lincoln Center, or for that matter, most regional theatres and Robert Brustein's imperious claims that mini-Royal Shakespeares have been created in New Haven and Cambridge during the abject seventies.

Is it too much to say that something in the American theatrical character was wrong then, but something worse is wrong now? American theatre people continue to make alibis while unmaking theatres. How much better it would be to admit that we don't really want them, that we like our chaos, our timidities, our commitment to an "excellence" that has nothing to do with convictions or ideas, our refusal to pay for development and process (otherwise known as rehearsal), our insistence on imitating television while ignoring advances in painting and music, our taste for Book-of-the-Month-Club stories and entertainments, our loathing, in short, of the art.

"We are the problem," wrote Clurman in his 1974 reassessment of *The Fervent Years,* "we and our ignorance of theatre's very nature." It need not be so, and there are some survivors who keep striving to find the form that might return the theatre to its nature. Perhaps in a history crowded with wound and retreat, nothing is more ironic than the persistence of one not-very-humorous American theatre that never bent conviction to the banks, foundations, or even its natural friends—the Living Theatre, still alive, producing, and at last report, well. Not in America, however, but in Rome.

GR(June 1981)

Theatre der Welt Discovers America

The huge World Theatre Festival in Cologne, held between June 12 and 28, was a demonstration of many quirks and strains within the theatre, but most of all, it was a demonstration of its own quintessential loneliness and distance from the other arts.

Theatre is the only performing art that doesn't travel often enough to prove it can travel well. Leaving aside the usual and unconvincing excuse of language barriers, the only explanation is that theatre finds comfort and safety in its isolation. Remaining on home ground most of the time, it doesn't test itself in the world as the other arts must; more seriously, it doesn't view the world nor does it find many moments to learn from the world of other theatres. Europeans are wounded less by theatre's persistent immobility: since their borders are so close, they travel more, and they spend more money regularly on invitations to other theatres. America, however, is as far from other theatres now as if it was connected to Europe only by the *Niña,* the *Pinta,* and the *Santa Maria.*

Cologne could mark the beginning of a change in this condition, not only because, of the fifteen countries represented at the festival, the U.S. sent the greatest number of companies or individuals (seven), but because the American presence was so visible in the work of the Europeans. Not some kind of marketable aesthetic presence; rather the presence of American popular iconography, myths, and images gathered from Hollywood in the past sixty years.

Somebody once said that America is sexy to Europe, and Cologne was as clear a sign of that allure as any I have ever seen. Perhaps this isn't really news: we've been colonizing Europe with gadgetry and credit cards for years. But placing so many different theatres in one place at one time is a way of revealing succinctly how successful we have been in colonizing Europe's dreams.

Not only Europe's, but also—and this may be news—the Soviet Union's. The Russians sent only one production to the festival, the Moscow Satire Theatre's version of Brecht and Weill's *The Threepenny Opera*. At first, this gesture appeared like so many coals being sent to Newcastle. At the press conference for the company, however, the Germans made it clear that Brecht in Russian was not a problem or an issue, since *The Threepenny Opera* is, said the German host, "rather an antique for us by now."

The production stood on its own, then, as something more than the usual ambassadorial image of a nation's official art. It seemed to be there in order to prove that Russians, too, have a popular theatre, one that not only moves gracefully among Chekhov's white birches, but also can belt, tap, and high-step with the Rockettes' pizzazz. The director, Valentine Plutschek, dodged the issue of American influence by insisting that he didn't have our musicals in mind, anyway. "Musicals were not born in America," he said. "Brecht and Weill came first." On the other hand, he wasn't claiming some kind of Brechtian authenticity: one could almost hear the Western groans diplomatically silenced when he added that "each generation has the right to do its own version of the classics." As if he had to run as far away from the American taint as possible, he unleashed the names of Eisenstein, Chaplin, Fellini, Gorky, and Mann as images for his work; also such masters of the grotesque as Cervantes, Shakespeare, Hoffmann, and Gogol. Plutschek was not only trying to elude American influence, he seemed to be auditioning for a book reviewer's job on the *New York Times*.

Meanwhile, the show itself was as American as he and his actors could make it. This was neither Berlin in the 1920s nor London at any time. The stage was crowded with skeletal panels rolled in and out of place by stagehands. Each panel was lined with colored bulbs surrounding giant lifelike dressed mannequins, as if Edward Kienholz or even George Segal had been let loose in a star's dressing room. One giant photograph of Chaplin's Tramp loomed over the rear part of the stage throughout the show, fixed in position—indeed, the only fixed statement within the design.

While the gloss of the show recalled Richard Foreman's moving panels in his *Threepenny Opera* production at the Beaumont a few years ago, this could be simply the coincidence of chic directorial invention. Both directors have ravenous appetites for personal statements, and both couldn't care less that the big numbers—especially for the women—were merely excuses for rolling the panels into position for the next scene.

Direct quotations from American movies, however, came with the casting and the clothes. Mack was weirdly old and puffy for the part, perhaps by design, which seemed to locate him somewhere between George Sanders's suavity and Peter Lorre's creepy menace. The women wore those semihooded gowns popular with Carole Lombard and Garbo whenever they were supposed to illustrate the life and times of the Vamp. Strangely, the Russians still do those stage slaps that used to be popular in vaudeville; one actor swings while the one getting hit makes the noise. And just to prove how contemporary, "liberated," and bigoted they can be, one of Mack's gang was a sinuous, mincing queen, not unlike Hurd Hatfield's Dorian Gray.

The performing style was grand, leisurely, confident, broadly conceived, and luxuriously easygoing—most emphatically un-American. But also un-American was the consistently dull, arbitrary lighting, or the moment when the lights were choreographed to the rhythm of the song. The sound was Big Band 1930s, suitable for Louis Armstrong's Mack, but heaven help them, without a Louis in sight or sound. In short: a big statement about not-very-much, almost as long as *Tannhäuser* and just as stately.

If Alexander Haig's cold war were really about the battle for men's minds rather than the battle to reline the pockets of the rich, then Cologne's festival would be sufficient evidence that he—and we—can relax. I couldn't stay long enough to see all fifteen countries and some thirty productions at work, nor did the festival management make it easy for anybody to see enough in a day or for the companies themselves to see each other's work, since almost everything was scheduled within the same hours. But just as I saw a lot of America in the Russians, I know I didn't see any Russia in the others.

*   *   *

By coincidence or design, Cologne has been running a giant show of contemporary painting and sculpture at the same time as its theatre festival. Called *Westkunst,* it is a retrospective attempting to isolate and display all the major art "isms" since World War I. Costing millions, taking years to organize, and presenting more than one of everything—nine Magrittes, an entire room for Joseph Cornell, still more from the Picasso factory—it seems to have been built upon a theme placed prominently at the entrance: Joseph Beuys's statement that "Everybody is an artist."

Fair enough for the art world, perhaps, but it couldn't be proved by the theatre festival. Not that such a gathering could ever insure goodness, or even attempt to be representative. Every theatre person is not even an artist, good or bad. Many are simply merchants who strayed, perhaps foolishly, from the car or fur business. Others are merely surviving, walking a tightrope on the way to either Andy Warhol's famous fifteen minutes of fame or a life in movies, commercials, the classroom, or—most commonly—oblivion.

Cologne's festival director, Ivan Nagel, went further than most in bringing together an enormous collection of theatres and nations, but he couldn't expect to make discoveries, since most of the invitations had to go to those whose reputations have already been made.

I can't speak about the Turks, the Javanese, the Chinese, the Dutch, or the Belgians, but I can say that official England looked awful; France seemed witty and sentimental; Hungary-America (Squat Theatre) was incisive, hilarious, political, and original; and Germany offered—with Pina Bausch's Dance Theatre of Wuppertal—the best long evening in the theatre I have had in years.

The British have long been an artistic law unto themselves, at their best good for eccentricity, rhetorical splendor, and discipline. They are the best of actors and the worst of actors. The National Theatre sent some of the worst in *The Passion,* a selection from the medieval mystery plays arranged by John Russell Brown and Jack Shepherd, directed by Bill Bryden with the assistance of Sebastian Graham-Jones, and featuring a noisy, overmiked rock group called the Albion Band. If there are still any brain-damaged sociologists around bewildered by Britain's street riots, they need turn only to *The Passion* as an emblem: the work is a strenuously arch definition of British pomposity, quaintness, and condescension to practically everybody—the avant-garde outside of Britain, rock, actors, religion, mystery, the lower orders, and real passion. Performed in a beautiful old Cologne church dressed to the nines to look like a theatre, it should have taken place where it was really born—under a Thatchered roof.

This was history as Morris dance, the group ever-so-freely creating false joy by having the audience clap rhythms, putting God and Lucifer on elevator chairs, speaking in carpet-thick English country accents while substituting "I wiss" and "I wean" for "I know." The lighting was an impenetrable dark orange mist throughout, except for the occasional glaring follow-spot on God, the devil, or Gabriel. The Noahs squabbled as a British sitcom couple, candles were given to the surrounding audience for the birth of Jesus, God wore suspenders and a beret, the shepherds wore tweeds, and—God should really help us now—Adam and Eve were born clothed, either with body stockings or stage mud. Medieval? No, this was the Dark Ages.

If the British event viewed history as a preface to their puritanical assumption of power, the French event chose to present history rather cleverly in the shape of popular ballroom dances since the 1930s. Jean-Claude Penchenat's Théâtre du Campagnol, an offspring of Ariane Mnouchkine's Théâtre du Soleil, is touring Europe with its wordless piece, *The Ball.* Beginning slowly with the arrival of each of the nineteen actor-dancers at one of those anonymous dance halls where the unattached meet and change partners, the piece moves gradually into scenes of the war and Paris liberated by GIs and

Jerome Robbins's navy. These are cartoon sketches, scenes occurring simultaneously, others flashing by like lightning, some of them sharp and tensile, others precious and self-conscious. (But there it was again: America abroad, this time with France beginning to see the light through a Glenn Miller fog.)

I missed *The Ball*'s second half in order to catch Pina Bausch's version of Stravinsky's *The Rite of Spring*. Bausch was the unmissable, unmistakable, unbeatable experience of the festival. Seven of her "pieces" were scheduled and my only regret is that I could see only two. The *Rite* was the more conventional work, neither "ballet" nor "modern," but danced with a savage clarity that makes the Netherlands Dance Theatre, acclaimed here recently, look like the prim and proper finishing school it really isn't.

Bausch's *1980,* a three-and-one-quarter-hour theatre piece, revealed how she defies categories: she is Graham (and even looks like her, too) with a smile and without severity; Hermes Pan guiding Freds and Gingers into the dying falls of foxtrots accompanied by Beethoven; Robert Wilson with time and space, but without the unedited text and department store window grandeur; Mabou Mines with more intelligence and less machinery; her melting-pot company of dancer-actors having the supple physical beauty of the old Living Theatre and the swift, transitional brilliance of Chaikin's groups. Only Grotowski seems to be missing: Bausch can be funny and harsh about the way men treat women and women fight back, but there isn't a Catholic moan or sadomasochistic urge in any scene or gesture she invents.

1980 is opera without a soprano in sight, an epic study of memory and childhood, never bending to the nostalgic winds that, in most hands, would blow the actors into the wings. The stage is covered by an enormous carpet of green turf. Bausch stops the parade of images once to place a large sprinkler hose on the grass: for about five minutes, a girl dances in and around the jets of water. By this time, Bausch has so clearly defined her territory that what might otherwise seem irrational looks logical, right, even sensible. Sometimes the reflected images, Magrittean cross-references, thematic variations and reprises come close to the cutting edge. Bausch isn't afraid to show hurt, to slash into conventions and sentiments, but in the end she rescues herself (and us) with laughter. Having played the soundtrack of the young Judy singing *Over the Rainbow,* she soon plays the old Judy with Carnegie Hall's hysterical applause: on stage, however, the actors are sunbathing in seventeen different ways, one of them covering up his back and his legs to reveal only his ass. The past, one might say, is put where it belongs—under a blanket, dodging a sprinkler, just an object littering a lively, genial present.

If I've neglected Squat's new piece, *Mr. Dead and Mrs. Free,* it's partly a matter of space; also, we are privileged to have these startling satirists of American mindlessness and violence among us. They are just as sharp, just as gifted, just as important as Bausch and her group. Cologne, however, was not only about America's invasion of world theatre, it was also—for an American—about how few world theatres we ever see.

GR(July–August 1981)

Bentley's Brecht

For about forty years, Eric Bentley has been the best critical friend—in English, anyway—that Bertolt Brecht has had. There have been other friends, of course, but none so rigorously willing to meet Brecht in so many roles: the playwright, thinker, polemicist, innovator, and master of contradictions. Critics such as Kenneth Tynan were always flashier than Bentley, capturing those moments in the theatre when Brecht's directorial dazzle and clarity illuminated a text without placing theoretical landmines in the path of an audience's response. For Tynan, Brecht was simply the best director of actors he had ever seen. As for the theories, they could go hang themselves, and in Tynan's spun sugar prose, that is precisely what they tend to do. Martin Esslin's book about Brecht is the work of still another enthusiast, albeit one literally mesmerized by Brecht's ambiguous expression of political certainties. In England, Esslin's book has the subtitle *A Choice of Evils,* thus betraying his anxiety and doubt. Esslin wasn't prepared to meet Brecht's quixotic Marxism with challenging language or argument. Instead, he merely deplored, leaving behind an ashy aftertaste. Attraction and repulsion have always spread themselves across the Brecht landscape, but it was odd that anyone should take the trouble to write a book about them.

What may be odd about Bentley, however, is that, for all his genuine enthusiasm, he has never written a book about Brecht or the plays. And even now, with the publication of *The Brecht Commentaries* he is not really presenting a "book" in the sense of a singular, developed argument; rather, what he calls "a collection of interim reports, a record of periodic soundings."

In the past, Bentley offered a brilliant study of Shaw, and for years now, he has been unsurpassed in his analytic travels through the territory occupied by intelligent modern playwrights—particularly Shaw, Ibsen, Pirandello, and Brecht. Surely, he has been the most tireless and versatile theatre critic this country has ever known. Has any critic before Bentley examined so many dramatists with such broad perspective and so much analytical detail? Has any critic produced so many anthologies, so many arguments, so many essays and introductions, letters to the editor, to his colleagues and his friends? Bentley seems to have been writing criticism the way Schubert wrote songs—on any piece of paper flying by the breakfast table. Such abundance and concentration are not normally part of the American theatre critic's trade.

For that reason alone, his "periodic soundings" of Brecht always seemed to be leading to a summing-up. The Shaw book was one model, of course, but that was a young man's book—portrait of the critic swept into broad river currents cunningly arranged by the subject himself. With Brecht, the soundings probably have to be different. He's so slippery and tricky. Perhaps Bentley didn't write the big, thematic book because he knew that his own prodigal soundings were sufficient. Where Brecht is concerned, the river would be a lie; only the inlets and undercurrents point the way.

Which is what *The Brecht Commentaries* do. Random, discursive, sometimes informal or journalistic, at other times grander and more historical, these articles and essays finally organize themselves into a real book—one that keeps renewing itself on every page, never gathering dust over a guiding idea that would limit its scope. Bentley is enthralled by Brecht's particular, austere magic, his capacity to reveal what he knows by trusting his senses, even though they may often get in the way of traditional, ideological good sense. Brecht said in 1949 that Bentley was virtually the only person with whom he discussed intransigent, political issues aroused by his plays; referring, it is clear, to Bentley's way of grasping Brecht in the thicket of argument. Bentley is so much more convincing than Brecht's nominal friends because he never dismisses Brecht with praise. Neither does he waste time on blame. When he grapples with Brecht's *Galileo*, for example, Bentley says, "It is a work that goads me into talking back." All these pieces demonstrate not only that Brecht's best work always goads, but that Bentley is the most educated, eloquent back-talker Brecht ever met.

One of the book's best features is that it, too, inspires back talk. Bentley even refutes himself at times, correcting an early judgment of Brecht's *Private Life of the Master Race* that had made it look like a masterpiece. Meanwhile, it is possible to argue with Bentley's view that Brecht has arrived in America, even twenty-five years after his death. Bentley is as clear as anyone has ever been about Brecht's failure to capture Broadway, but he keeps imagining that the mini-industries in our universities that have kept some plays alive in (usually) poor productions are signs of a Brecht conquest. Brecht was more accurate when he observed to Bentley in 1945 (on the subway!) that he would have been more popular here had he been French. And not even Bentley can persuade me that *Mahagonny* is better in the hands of actors than in the throats of singers such as Teresa Stratas.

But Bentley does open doors to Brecht's plays that keep revealing spaces nobody else knows so well. Bentley keeps uncovering the "essentially solitary . . . disenchanted revolutionary" artist that Brecht really was. Like Brecht's Azdak, Bentley's Brecht is an outsize comic tragedian who "comes out of solitude and returns to it." Brecht was lucky to find a critic in America willing to embrace the solitude that comes from loving Brecht.

GR(September 1981)

Shaw vs. Shaw

George Bernard Shaw thought about practically everything that might affect his reputation, yet he neglected to be clear about one element that continues to be a threat: the way his plays are acted. A master publicist, especially for things Shavian, he tried to tell both the theatre world and his public what he liked and loathed in acting, but he kept bumping into contradictions and paradoxes that turned his arguments upside down. For example, among his favorite memories was the great Italian Othello, Tommaso Salvini; all very well if he didn't also cite the French actor and theorist Constant-Benoît Coquelin in many of the same phrases. Salvini was on record in opposition to Coquelin, particularly Coquelin's "cool" or "mechanical" approach, but Shaw didn't seem to be able to see their differences. Which is undoubtedly why Shaw's unsystematic, offhand references to acting styles offer so few clues about acting in Shaw's plays.

But there *are* clues, even if the only way to unearth them is to plunder Shaw's provisional remarks and the history of Shavian productions. When Shaw was publicizing his work, acting was not yet either a codified craft or a public sport. Nobody went to school to be an actor. As Shaw said in his tribute to the work of Herbert Beerbohm Tree, Tree's legacy was the establishment of the Royal Academy of Dramatic Art. Before that, neither he nor anybody else had anywhere to study but the stage itself; obviously a good, perhaps the best, teacher, but not exactly what anybody, including Shaw, had in mind when praying for a trained actor. Shaw's allusions to the actor's art and craft are based, therefore, on momentary wishes for his plays rather than on conclusive means to make them playable.

He was returning, he said, "to Aristotle, to the tribune stage, to the circus, to the didactic Mysteries, to the word music of Shakespeare, to the forms of my idol Mozart, and to the *stage business* [italics added] of the great players whom I had actually seen acting, from Barry Sullivan, Salvini, and Ristori to Coquelin and Chaliapin." Describing himself as a "roofless pavement orator," he seemed to be suggesting that to act in his plays, one must be in command of words and musically sensitive elements that make words come alive on stage. Shaw is too loose with his allusions, yet it is possible to see that his broad sweep wishes to embrace something that can only be called *rhetorical variety:* coupling the "circus clown" to the "ringmaster" and adding the

"Greek tribune" as a confounding afterthought means only that Shaw saw acting as a grand, emphatic, startling art; above all, perhaps, as an art undaunted by words, words, and more words. He was expecting too much from those words: they were to do for actors what Mozart's tunes, harmonies, and rhythms presumably did for singers.

He liked to pretend that acting was really very simple. After all, he merely began his texts with plots unknown, putting his characters in place, then expecting to "let them rip." But what if on stage the ripping didn't happen? Shaw covered the absence of a ready answer with an even more wishful description: he "went back to the classical style and wrote long rhetorical speeches like operatic solos, regarding my plays as musical performances precisely as Shakespeare did." (His "precisely" is a wonderful dodge: that Shakespeare might have had other things in mind, such as not writing like Shaw, doesn't fit Shaw's argument.) It is as if he is trying to make his plays "actor-proof," using the analogy, false as he above all knew it to be, that operas can be "singer-proof" because so much is directed by the music itself.

One can share his wishfulness if not his conclusions. If Shaw's reputation is under a cloud—and I think it is—it is precisely (why not?) because he wished too hard for what cannot really be. The strongest evidence for this is that so few modern actors have chosen to play even his most appealing and challenging roles. In the most important theatrical sense—getting one's plays on with the best possible casts—Shaw has barely arrived.

It can be argued, in fact, that Philip Bosco's latest appearance in a Shaw play, this time as Tarleton in *Misalliance* at the Roundabout, is a reflection of the fact that only nonstars—albeit talented and obscure—love Shaw. That production makes it easy to understand why: boisterously loud, replacing energy with fuss and frenzy, rarely pausing for a breath, pounding out words like human printing presses, the actors are unable—most of the time—to grip what many of them clearly know about life, credibility, and even the pursuit of beautiful music. Two of the men are so tall and so paralyzed by the need to look stylish that they turn their scenes into problems about walking, both of them giraffes caught unaccountably in a Surrey drawing room.

On occasion, Shaw dropped a clue that really helps. He loved Beerbohm Tree most because he "always seemed to have heard the lines of the other performers for the first time, and even to be a little taken aback by them." Bosco is not yet up to that, partly because he falls too easily into still another trap often cited by Shaw—the temptation to pick up rhythms and inflections from the other actors. But one actor, mercifully, rescues the entire production just as Shaw cunningly may have suspected he would: Anthony Heald as the Gunner comes in to assassinate Tarleton halfway through the play, and through his grasp of surprise, spontaneous response, and just plain marvelous unpredictability, he lifts the performance to that realm of theatrical reality that is always the best argument against theatre in thrall to mechanics and rhetoric.

Shaw knew the difference between Salvini and Coquelin, of course. How ironic it really is: Salvini was the favorite of both Shaw and Stanislavsky, and in New York for a moment, only a young, unknown actor named Heald seems to know how to make that unlikely reconciliation come alive in a clownish, ringmasterly, superbly Mozartian way.   *GR(August 1981)*

The Old Virtuosity Shop

Where English actors used to be thick in the middle, overweight with resonance, layered with eccentric gestures or inflections, slow in response and avuncular in confrontation, they seem now to be darting and swift as birds on the hunt, undernourished, eager, and ready to survive. The older generation—Ralph Richardson, Michael Redgrave, Paul Scofield—have become grand seigneurs, ruling over an acting territory of limitless dimensions. Everything they did and do is about space, size, ease, and resonance. The younger group, if the Royal Shakespeare Company's *Nicholas Nickleby* is representative, stands for something else, not less talented, perhaps, but surely less rich in texture, less defined, less personal. Nothing they do is really uninteresting, and everything is done with polish, finish, joy in the task, and a great wash of energy in the execution. It's a curious exchange: the unpredictable, dotty, humming dissonance of the past has given way to the direct, foursquare, buzzing harmony of the present.

Dickens found what Emlyn Williams has called a "blessed release" in the readings he performed from his novels. He had claimed that he "was an actor and a speaker as a baby." Is there any doubt that, had he been born earlier or later, he might have written plays? David Edgar's adaptation of *Nickleby* exposes—not for the first time—the born dramatist, that great, incisive, divine storyteller for whom the stage was an obvious instrument. He didn't possess a theatre, so he had to keep inventing one in his novels, meanwhile insinuating a second career for himself as the narrator-actor of his stories and his characters.

E. M. Forster was right when he said that "those who dislike Dickens have an excellent case." The characters were flat, but "his immense success with types suggests that there may be more in flatness than the severer critics admit." Why? Because he had a compensating "immense vitality" that caused "his characters to vibrate a little." Which is precisely what the RSC actors do for an astounding, riveting, untiring eight and a half hours.

That flatness in Dickens is perfect for the thin British actors of today. Characterization comes easy to them. Most actors from other countries have to reach for dark thoughts and bleak psychologies to justify an action, but these actors have only to press class or regional buttons to find their prey. They chew up Dickens's types alive, vibrating, shivering, gulping down ticks, gestures, mustaches, red noses, shakes, bumps, grinds, a thousand shameless visual pleas for the public's affection.

The adaptation gives them unequal opportunities which most of them seize with equal zeal and skill. With only two exceptions—Roger Rees as Nicholas and David Threlfall as Smike—the actors play more than one role, all of them as a narrating chorus from time to time, and some of them in as many as six roles. Sometimes the doubling of roles seems to cast a shadow on the previous relationship in either Nicholas's or Kate Nickleby's experience: Lila Kaye plays the nasty Mrs. Squeers and then reappears as the wondrous, Mary Bolandesque-Margaret Rutherfordish Mrs. Crummles, all double-taking chin and eye. Surely this is a deliberate, unabashed coupling of Dickens's dual visions: loathsome horror and lovable silliness absorbed into the same acting vessel. Other doubles fail to connect: Christopher Benjamin's Vincent Crummles and Walter Bray are simply splendid technical feats, like the wonderful show itself, not artful or cunning at all. Suzanne Bertish gets a double that works well for the play, offering the ugly Fanny Squeers, frustrated by unrequited love for Nicholas, and the elegant, sinewy actress, Miss Snevelicci, also doomed to lose him. But when she takes on the hideous Peg Sliderskew, all her acting judgment falls to pieces: bent, raving, and fake-Scottish, she howls her way into unbelievability, a curious sign that mimicry and etching don't always build a character.

At least she has a chance to be superb. Yet the entire project would have slid askew had it not been for the emotional resonance of Edward Petherbridge as Newman Noggs, John Woodvine as the granitic Ralph Nickleby, David Threlfall as Smike (perhaps too much in love with his own pathetic transformation), and—more than anyone—Roger Rees as Nicholas. He is the binding force to everything that works magically in this production—the sweep of the piece, its sweet humors and delicate sentiments, the worry in a bleary eye, and the panic that haunts almost everybody. He is all the strings on the fiddle, a beautifully tuned, masterful actor who vibrates a lot.   *GR(October 1981)*

The Management of Management

When Joseph Chaikin's Open Theater was launched in the early 1960s, there wasn't a management team in sight. Each actor contributed five dollars a month toward the rental of rehearsal space. And that was it. No system for development, no plan for building and maintaining an audience, no tortured schemes for staying alive as a group had been envisioned. The Open Theater kept doing its best work in sanctuary, sometimes responsible for an Off-Broadway success such as van Itallie's *America Hurrah!* (produced by a traditional management), but otherwise retreating to monastic, laboratory conditions; experimental in a framework understood by scientists, though not by those who make and break theatres in America. Chaikin was lucky: the great assault of management consciousness had not yet brought performance research to a virtual halt.

America's limitless capacity for absorbing adventure and experiment into the traditional economy calls for a vigilance that few artists could really exert while inventing new work and new forms of survival. Yet who could have predicted that American foundations and theatres would develop a system of interlocking directorates determining repertory, personnel, and standards in ways which make an Open Theater (or a Living Theatre or a Free Southern Theatre) in the eighties more unthinkable than the dodo bird? By now, management teams are graduating from some of our universities in alarming numbers, most of them guaranteed a job in regional theatres or in the foundations that support them, all of them sharing a vocabulary that has little or nothing to do with creative spirit or process.

What are they saying? Insuring their own perpetuity, they are advising artists to stay alive by hiring management teams. Theirs is a remarkably closed system, permitting little air or space for the development of new ideas about art or even new strategies for survival. Their language determines reality and describes the fix: it confirms worthiness not by what is done in the theatre, but by how much income can be earned at the box office and in related community services.

A manager's idea of purpose and success requires limited literacy. Only a few phrases are needed, and repetition of all of them is guaranteed to fulfill their conviction that the artist in theatre is probably the most expendable member of the team: first, there is *fiscal responsibility,* followed soon by *effi-*

cient marketing strategies, the same for *fundraising,* a *strong board of direc-tors,* long lists (unknown, by the way, in Europe) of *patrons, friends,* or *do-nors,* and those magic talismen—*matching funds* and *audience development.* Finally, there is the finger wagging away at all artists: when *public funds* are being spent, then they have to be aware of fiscal responsibility—thus closing the circle while insuring the locking of the directorate.

Where patronage is concerned, of course, a sinister motive cannot be far behind. Few of us would be willing to trade our foundations and management teams for a trial relationship with the Medici, Prince Esterhazy, or Ludwig II of Bavaria. But then few of us are as marvelous, extravagantly gifted, or quite so aggressively committed to our own work as Michelangelo, Haydn, and Wagner were. What is sinister now has little to do with conscious deviltry and conspiracy. The American way is quite different. Those who fled Europe and conquered this territory were not searching for a better place to produce art. Theirs was a commercial venture with a lot of piety about freedom and reli-gion thrown in for good measure. The Constitution must be the most sophisti-cated afterthought in the history of complex societies.

Our systems of patronage have created a gigantic network of pernicious controls over what is actually produced by making fiscal responsibility and overconsciousness of the audience into the central measures of success and failure. We don't possess a developing theatre art. Instead, we are possessed by theatre buildings too costly to maintain, most of them inflexibly designed, and run by managers devoted to selling subscriptions, planning seasons years in advance, declaring finite numbers of performances, and, thereby, fix-ing dates for openings that have little or nothing to do with the way a particu-lar play might be developed in rehearsal. America has always wanted the-atres with the prestige and reputation of Stanislavsky's and Brecht's, but it never wished to foot the bill for the time it takes to make such productions and build such companies.

Experiment cannot be fiscally responsible. Small groups may not always be in a genuine artistic vanguard, but they are always constructed to be in the vanguard of what can never be anything but a cottage industry. Managers don't know what to do with experiment any more than they would know how to handle a small farm.

Blame need not be allocated and predictions would be foolish. There are few saints in the avant-garde, and even fewer sages positioned to give advice about balancing books while doing the hard, lonely labor of crafting an art in the theatre. A new Open Theater must keep Steven Marcus's wise observa-tion constantly in mind: "In America," he wrote years ago, "nothing fails like success." If the Reagan administration has any lesson for young dream-ers (are there any left?), it is that the eighties means going it alone; which is, after all, what the Open Theater was doing anyway. An incorrigibly mean and puritanical nation that only feels alive when a cowboy has his finger on a trig-ger is not likely to pay for art in a peaceful, disinterested way.

An artists' strike might help, but I doubt that artists are up to it. Theatre is surely the least well organized of the arts to defend itself. Bustling from coast to coast with motives no less mixed than those held by other Americans, theatre people get sloppily sentimental about their fellow workers when the cameras turn on them at award ceremonies. The truth is, however, they don't really like each other that much, and few of them know how to work well together. If they knew how to serve their interests, they might be able to demonstrate that classrooms and Open Theaters are just as essential to the big, productive movie and television industries as the forging of steel and making of wheels are to Detroit.

But isn't this the wrong approach, still another polemical surrender to the standards of the enemy? Too many of us keep apologizing for art, as if America's managers shouldn't be on their knees to the rest of us. Certainly, it is Them rather than Us who ought to be accountable. Right now, we are paying the bills for their ghastly presumptions in Vietnam, for their flirtations with tyranny, for big oil, and for a system that can't deliver ordinary services but persists in living on military hardware and wheels. If Americans can't really live without the drug of big entertainment—and I'm sure they can't—then that means they can't really live without the small groupings where occasional hits and future stars are born. I go further and insist that they can't really live without the dark, complex visions of real theatre. If art, like the Constitution, continues to be an afterthought, there won't be much point in this nation anyway.   *GR(September 1981)*

Malle Treatment

There aren't any laws about it, but for the most part, movie directors make movies and theatre directors do plays. When there is movement from one medium to another, it is usually the stage director who breaks into films. Money has been an obvious inducement; still, there have to be reasons for the unequal exchange rooted in the forms themselves. Apart from Ingmar Bergman, directors hold to what they know most intimately.

Odd, then, that three movie directors—Louis Malle, Robert Altman, and soon Karel Reisz—have chosen to make the shift to theatre in this season alone. Are they bored with movies? Tired of montage, jump cuts, the roving, meandering authority of the camera? Even if their interest in the stage is more coincidence than trend, it still may be viewed as an affirmation of the special magic that always resides in the theatrical event despite the frequency with which many of us broadcast the rotten news that most theatre is more boring than movies.

But the crossing from one form to another is not necessarily magical itself. I don't yet know Altman's or Reisz's work in the theatre, though if Louis Malle's recent journeys reveal anything aesthetic at all, it is that inclination for one medium provides no assurance of success in another. Malle has been flirting with a curious geometry. With John Guare's screenplay for *Atlantic City,* he is where he has always been—in movie space where the viewer is led to believe that anything can happen but where in fact nothing happens that the camera and director don't choose to see. With *My Dinner with André,* a text provided by two theatre people (André Gregory and Wally Shawn), Malle has actually staged for the camera conversations and monologues that might otherwise reside quite comfortably in theatre space. Movies have looked long and hard at talkers before: Robert Bresson, Eric Rohmer, and Bergman have often seemed to be concerned only with mouths in motion. But in *André,* Malle is really announcing that he feels ready for the stage. As a project, it's too zany and unlikely to mean anything else. The camera willing to dwell with such tenacity on the monotonous landscape of Shawn's and Gregory's faces is an instrument in flight from its natural versatility.

For Malle, perhaps, the next move—to Guare's play *Lydie Breeze*—might have seemed easy and logical. Working earlier with Guare, Shawn, and Gregory, he was already well on his way to text as a way of life. Great stretches of *Atlantic City* couldn't, of course, quite happen on stage: exploding hotels, a chase up and down a parking lot elevator. But most of it is just two or three people in a room talking, some of it droll talk, shifty and unpredictable as, well, a play by John Guare. ("Teach me stuff," says Susan Sarandon to Burt Lancaster, to which he replies, "You want information or wisdom?") Then there is the irrepressibly bug-eyed, self-conscious stage-space performance of Kate Reid, heaving theatrical shouts from her bed as if rehearsing for the General's wife in *The Waltz of the Toreadors.* Malle's camera, too, seems least at ease when it is charting violence—an admirable awkwardness, yes, but strange to find these days.

In *André,* Shawn and Gregory not only come from theatre, they talk about nothing else, even though Gregory has a gift for dressing his obsessive theatrical concerns in fly-blown philosophical speculation. Malle includes some street scenes and other frank interpolations, but they are loose and sketchy, because Malle is really more interested in luring us to listen rather than watch. Watching, in fact, doesn't reveal very much: Gregory tells one tall tale after another, the camera sometimes catching his profile in a mirror behind the table, but his face rarely connects to anything he is saying. Perhaps this too is meant to be wit and drollery, like Guare's texts in the other two works, but it isn't easy to know what Malle really means or feels. Gregory speaks of fascism, Poles dancing and singing in a forest, a Japanese monk, the Sahara and Montauk as if they're all the same "wild" thing, the same collision with the same despair. At one moment, Shawn's eye twitches involuntarily. It's a lucky twitch that would be lost on the stage, funny because it punctuates one of Gregory's assertions with the kind of Mount Rushmore intensity only available to movies.

If *Lydie Breeze* had been in movie rather than stage space, then perhaps its huge cut-out Nantucket house set would have assumed less importance. Where an accidental twitch on camera can slice through miles of narrative detail, fixing meaning or humor in an instant, a stage set can rarely be anything but itself; sometimes—as in this case—pretending to be real, but despite its skeletal nature, all too literal, unyielding. Guare may be going through a murky phase in his work where he can't fix his places or his narrative in any economical, orderly way, but he isn't helped by Malle's imprecisions, those glossy, movieish moments when the soundtrack is used to suggest that what is seen and said doesn't have to be clear. On stage, Malle flip-flops into cinema. He can't suspend Guare's humor with a leap into another place or time, but he can *dissolve* everything into something he deems poetic. Fake poetry at that.

Most of the actors in *Lydie Breeze* aren't on Nantucket, they're at sea. In movies, Malle doesn't really have to know much about acting, especially since scenes are rehearsed rapidly and nothing has to be sustained. He can trust his clever camera to pick up the occasional, eloquent twitch. Ben Cross, so vivid, clear, and flexible in *Chariots of Fire,* is reduced to pose, blurred choices, and rigidity in *Lydie Breeze.* Malle gets the worst staginess on film from his theatre actress and the worst vapored filminess on stage from his movie actor.

Why theatre, then, instead of movies? It isn't easy, after all, to master one form in a lifetime, and Malle, surely, isn't claiming that he has mastered either. All three works are really fairy tales about privileged people positioned to ask Big Questions and even take Drastic Actions without always suffering Dire Consequences. If they don't exactly live happily ever after, at least most of them are living. Malle uses theatre itself as his private fairy tale. Maybe the movies, for all their financial rewards, don't seem as aristocratic and distancing an art for Malle as the theatre of Guare, Shawn, and Gregory. He's not wrong, but he's muddling the forms. The theatre can still be the place where Big Questions can go comfortably unanswered so long as its idioms are used with freedom anchored by precision. Used as a surrogate movie, however, Malle's theatre finally looks like a privileged whim.   *GR(April 1982)*

Vanessa Redgrave Is Not the Enemy

Blizzards in April, Reagan the recipient of a humanitarian award, a British armada hurtling to the South Atlantic, and Mrs. Gandhi's daughter-in-law asking to come home: all these incongruous events fall into place when you realize that the enemy all along has been Vanessa Redgrave. Or so it would seem in Boston, where the management of the Boston Symphony Orchestra has canceled Redgrave's appearance this month in New York and Boston as narrator of Stravinsky's *Oedipus Rex.* The reasons given were devious and obscure: threats to disrupt the concerts from the outside, musicians in the orchestra granting Redgrave's right to political opinions but charging the orchestra's management with "lack of sensitivity" in hiring her, and "causes and circumstances beyond its reasonable control." In short, the BSO has behaved like a passport agency in a banana republic—or in Washington or Moscow. Despite the evidence that most lethal and stupid decisions originate in the dangerously empty heads of politicians, statesmen, and other unprosecutable criminals, the BSO has found the time and energy to punish a performing artist, the public, and the Constitution in one breathtakingly distracting, lethal, *and* stupid action.

Distracting, of course, because neither Vanessa Redgrave nor any other artist has ever been the enemy, even though many of us—including me from childhood—have been conditioned to think otherwise. The first actor I was supposed to hate and boycott was Victor McLaglen, who had apparently formed a private vigilante army with a view toward marching on FDR, though so far as I recall, he never did so. It was easy to be on the right side of that one: had he realized his bellicose dreams, most of us would have defended our right to oppose and even jail him, if necessary. Meanwhile, however, I was not allowed to see *The Informer* or *Gunga Din,* thus missing some enlightenment about the Irish Troubles, some obscurantism about imperialism which might even have impressed me with its badness, and not incidentally, some fun.

After that, I was distracted from the big targets by warnings not to read crusading Christians and alleged anti-Semites such as T. S. Eliot and Evelyn Waugh, to stay away from Walter Gieseking's concerts and from Kirsten Flagstad's infrequent, sickeningly controversial reappearances at the Met after the war, and to protect my ears from the heavenly recordings of Wilhelm Furtwängler and Alfred Cortot. Even when I was well past the tyrannies of the home itself, I was urged not to see Stanley Kubrick's *Paths of Glory* because Adolph Menjou was so clearly a certifiable McCarthyite shit. Like so many Americans, left and right, I was trained from the cradle to check the political credentials of an artist before confronting his or her artistic reality. There were real murderers out there in the world, but since I couldn't do much about them, I was expected to vent my indignation by banning some artists from my experience. How futile it was politically, and how harmful to me: I couldn't see and hear Flagstad in *Tristan and Isolde,* but nobody warned me with prophetic wisdom to avoid Ronald Reagan in *King's Row.* As a carrier of the banning disease, I deserved to live outside political reality and inside my own soap opera.

That I escaped from such imprisonments I owe to England. It was there in the fifties that I heard Furtwängler and Cortot. Flagstad was appearing almost nightly in the Mermaid Theatre's *Dido and Aeneas,* and for the first time, I was enchanted by such young musicians as Elisabeth Schwarzkopf and Herbert von Karajan, then under the cloud of their alleged wartime associations. Surely Britain had more cause than us to despise those who in one way or another had been on the side of the Nazis, yet all these artists were popular *in their work* and, to an American, noticeably unpicketed.

I had been missing all the important nuances: Thomas Mann had been rightist in the 1920s, but he became a good guy in the thirties; Shaw flirted with Mussolini in the twenties and with Stalin almost forever; some artists had views, some didn't; some who had good ideas were good or superb, others kept doing lousy work. I was an American caught for too many years in the undertow of a righteous politics that was finally unpolitical because it didn't know how to locate distinctions, how to make the most of what might be passionately ambiguous in art, and how to target the real enemy. Knowing what I liked in politics didn't mean that I knew anything about art.

Then I met Vanessa Redgrave. In her late teens, she was studying acting at the Central School while helping me and other unpaid zealots to edit a small theatre magazine called *Encore.* Looking like an ungainly sunflower punctuated miraculously by the clearest blue-green eyes ever made, she seemed to be consumed by the need to be better at whatever she did, whether it was acting, editing, or just helping all of us to organize and direct our passions about theatre and the rude world. One day she was pushing her father to write a marvelous analysis of the actor's craft, or joining our efforts to save an obscure theatre group in Dublin from the censors, or struggling alongside Vivien Leigh in *Encore*'s and Leigh's vain campaign to save the St. James Theatre from wrecker-developers, or marching down Whitehall after Suez shouting—and what an early Brechtian Joan she made—"Eden must go!" At Central, she finished her studies with the first glimpse of her Nina in *The Seagull*—sunflower transformed into red, yellow, and white roses, aromatic, spiky, and seductively dangerous. She couldn't be any *one* thing because, as Ellen Terry said of the twelve-year-old Olivier, she was already a great actor.

Which is all that counts. The BSO impoverishes all of us, not least because it is an artistic organization denying an artist her vocation. In the long run, it is guilty of association with the most destructive political positioning available. The *New York Times* reports accurately that "Miss Redgrave has been engulfed in controversy for years . . . prominent in the antinuclear-arms movement . . . a leading activist against American involvement in Vietnam." Meaning that on some issues, she shares the same views as many of those in the orchestra who would now banish her because they're "sensitive" about her passion for Palestinians. There is only one way not to get "engulfed"—as they have—by the ambiguities, and that is to get as absorbed as she is in both passion and art.

When those same musicians who would murder Redgrave's right to work show equal passion for turning down Reagan's next State Department-sponsored tour of countries acceptable that minute to Reagan Inc., then perhaps they will have earned the right to turn political fury on a bystanding artist. It is time to make distinctions.

*   *   *

When banishment occurs, the public and profession are denied an experience that might be not only enjoyable, but also nourishing to the art itself, sometimes in ways that can be neither predicted nor imagined. Few people today know, let alone care, that years ago Brecht's great theatre, the Berlin Ensemble, was effectively banished from a New York appearance by members of the Phoenix Theatre's board of directors who wanted nothing to do with a company based on the other side of the ridiculous Stalinist-Churchillian curtain. No matter that the Russians themselves were coming in droves, and not all of them by way of leaps into the loving arms of American ballet companies: the Bolshoi became a regular visitor after 1959, and in 1964 we were graced with four productions by the Moscow Art Theatre, two of them exquisite, exemplary renderings of Chekhov.

Keeping New York safe from Brechtians while giving space and hurrahs to Chekhovians is precisely the sort of bogus distinction that guardians of one faith or another, such as the Phoenix board, are always making. The Soviets never liked Brecht either. The MAT's "political" play in New York was *Kremlin Chimes,* socialist realist hackery that brought Lenin on stage, a cozy, wise, and charming Lenin, no more upsetting to any body politic than *Annie*'s FDR. That may have been a clue about how the board reached its rotten decision: Russians and Americans, as Polish history has recently confirmed, frequently share similar interests; Mother Courage is no Santa and Brecht will never be an American middle-class or Soviet bureaucrat's saint.

His American banishment, however, can be ascribed also to his liberating skills as a theatre artist. When his company appeared in London shortly after his death in 1956, the galvanic effect on British theatre was astonishing. Styles in plays and performances changed almost immediately. For a time, the dividends wrought by the ensemble's visit were clear and secure. Shakespearean production became less fussy and vaporous, more precise in its outlines than before, more austere and resonant. Quite simply: more intelligent. New plays were suddenly about people transformed by experience instead of romps around the tea tables of a stately England that didn't want to show the casualties strewn on the bloody path to stateliness.

True, only some of these lessons were absorbed for a sustained period. British theatre took on new subjects, new characters, and even new ideas about how to mount plays, but the politics of the country, the pathetic nostalgia for a past that never was, and the accommodating impulses of theatre people who are, perhaps understandably, only too willing to please, didn't help the Brecht effect to prevail. Brecht's most besotted critical champion, Kenneth Tynan, later became the producer of *Oh! Calcutta!*, a work that didn't need the ensemble's visit to release its dubious freedoms. Still, the effect was tremendous for a time. If nothing else, when the British respond even today to Brecht's plays, many of them are responding to a specimen that was permitted to come alive in its best and most accurate incarnation.

We were less fortunate. All kinds of Brecht reached our stages, even on Broadway—Jerome Robbins's clean-cut but sentimental *Mother Courage,* Lincoln Center's cuddly *Caucasian Chalk Circle* and stuffy, rhetorical *Galileo*—but never Brecht's Brecht.

If I am less visibly outraged when I read of the gaps in a Soviet citizen's experience—whether Dostoevsky, Akhmatova, or Stravinsky—it is because I recognize that we too continue to cultivate our own deprivations. We don't kill poets but we do share with Russians similar gifts for revising all kinds of histories. Losing the real Brecht was no small matter: as is our habit, we didn't find out what long rehearsals and attention to detail can yield; neither did we help our actors extend their vocabulary to accommodate fierce realism within a highly disciplined, elegant, aesthetic vision. Finally, we were denied access to plays and productions that never trivialized experience. Brecht's was a political theatre that was actually fun to watch, a cool, beautiful object too hot for us to handle. What we didn't know, as always, really hurt us.

Redgrave's BSO appearance is a loss that will not cast so long a shadow, but the darkness is no less suggestive, no less ominous. Has the human condition been improved by canceling Stravinsky, replacing him with Berlioz? Has Israel come closer to solving its problems by not listening to Wagner all these years? If not Wagner, then why those arms to South Africa or that congenial trade with Argentina? How, indeed, can the mind absorb all those dips, turns, and logical declensions? Delighted by Casals's stand against Franco, yet disgusted by Cortot's performances for Nazis, we would have to throw away our Thibaud-Cortot-Casals Trio recordings, or ask an engineer to remove the piano part, thereby mutilating Beethoven, but victimizing ourselves even more. When the cause is even ambiguously good, it cannot be served by slamming down an iron curtain on the brain.   *GR(April–May 1982)*

Kantor Seen and Not Heard

Idle to pretend that *Wielopole, Wielopole,* a seventy-minute work by Tadeusz Kantor, can be understood as total theatre by anyone who doesn't know Polish. Not that Kantor's Cricot Two Theatre is concerned with language or narrative. Born in 1915, Kantor came to directing by way of stage design, a route common to many—perhaps too many—theatre directors in Europe. When he formed an underground theatre during the World War II German occupation of Poland, it was with a group of painters. He has worked with plays by Stanisław Witkiewicz, Witold Gombrowicz, even Shakespeare, created innumerable Happenings, and issued—as so many theatre visionaries before him have done—manifestos obsessed by questions of theatrical purity and possibility. From the beginning, Cricot Two wandered around the world more than it stayed at home, and *Wielopole, Wielopole* had its 1980 premiere in Florence, sponsored by Italian regional and city administrations. Meanwhile, Kantor has been exhibiting his paintings in Europe and South America. As an artist, he can't be boxed into theatre or painting alone. Similarly, he can't be confined to Poland.

Yet his theatre and his manifestos are in Polish. Unlike Grotowski's works, which drew so much power from actors' physical and vocal athletics, only rarely using a recognizable Polish, Kantor's non-linear scenes are not in gibberish or derived from great echo chambers buried in the actor's gut. Many words and phrases are deliberately repeated—that much is clear—but presumably the actors are saying something that adds dimension to the experience of the work. At La Mama, no scenario is provided, no simultaneous translation is offered, and only a group of "texts" by Kantor are printed in the program, "texts" not of the work itself, but of thoughts that inspired it. Kantor's work is not dance, mime, or music; and even "pure" theatre makes connections with words, so it would be presumptuous to respond as if it were a work by Brook, Chaikin, Foreman, Wilson, or even a Chekhov play performed by the Moscow Art. A theatre audience cannot live by images alone.

The images help, of course, especially as they accumulate, repeat themselves, and provide evidence that Kantor has looked into his past and found terror and solace. Much of what I report is inference rather than fact: at the press conference after the first performance I learned that the experience presented is from a child's point of view; recollections of an older man, the characters in the work bearing the names of Kantor's family but not necessarily their biographies. There is no child on stage, only Kantor himself, playing the role of director, or perhaps simply viewing the piece from a non-performer's middle distance; not really redirecting it before our eyes, but simply presenting himself as authority for the evidence.

Is it just inference or fact that Kantor is really using actors as a painter uses paint? There they are—released by Kantor from an upstage confinement to which they keep retreating, usually under the silent but direct orders of Kantor himself. Sometimes he adjusts a door or window, or points with his marvelous drooping hands to the sound engineer or above to—whom?—the gods of theatre art who love to play with light and sound. (More playing with sound than light in this case.) At other moments, he seems to dismiss an actor from the image, or he looks like Solti trying to rip more sound and energy from those instrumental wombs.

Nothing that happens from one scene to another is quite as resonant or forceful (at least to an outsider) as the presence and activity of Kantor himself. Painter or conductor, he is demonstrating one man's hold on life, a way of impressing himself on events, an insistence that the family, church, or army can not finally resist the imaginative power of the artist. At first, his presence jolts, even moderately offends; in time, however, it becomes the link to those elements of playmaking that have been otherwise discarded—story, character, development. It is moving to see an intense, committed man coping with his enemies, presiding over their disgusting violence, their parodies of power, prevailing over their mockery of spirit and invention.

But it is painting and music animated into theatrical assertion; a series of panels Chagall might have done brought into substance and flesh: twin brother actors playing against others who find their twins in giant, inanimate dolls, almost everybody—except Kantor—masked by a yellowish-gray parchment makeup, responding not to impulse but to the insistent and loud music of an army march, or a psalm recorded by a church choir in a Polish mountain village. A fragment of the C-minor Scherzo by Chopin, distorted, flat, but mercifully quiet, is played by the sound engineer whenever Uncle Stasio, the family deportee (but what does this precisely mean?), appears staring into the distance while cranking the handle of a broken hurdy-gurdy. Aunt Manka (a splendid performance by Maria Kantor) plays a chanting Rebbetzin who is killed repeatedly, but she also plays Judas at the grotesque version of the Last Supper, a provocative but unexplained doubling. For me, a Jew several generations removed from Polish-Russian origins, her appearance late in the work is the first image and sound that suggests a memory other than Kantor's. With patience and time, I can let his painterly slashes and symphonic designs impinge upon my experience even though I must be denied the fullness of his imagination.

A case can be made for such a denial, though I don't think it lies behind the decision to give us so little help with the text. Another distinguished Pole, Czesław Miłosz, has described the war as something "lived in a dimension completely different from that which any literature or experience could have led us to know. . . . What we beheld surpassed the most daring and the most macabre imagination." For too long we have been intimidated into believing that ordinary forms can carry the news when, in fact, it is only maverick artists who can begin to make the essential translations. As Kantor says, "The baby defends life, sets its terms. The artist does the same."

Please see his work in the few days remaining, but don't be stampeded by a reviewing establishment thriving on inflated language to believe that the artist in this case can be wholly known. On opening night, the company and Kantor received what has now become the obligatory standing ovation. If, like me, you don't normally stand for either national anthems *or* artists, you can still comprehend why an audience here has to feel gratitude for a tenacious act of pure theatrical art. Yet such a response in this context has even less meaning than usual, especially in view of the hysteria drummed up these days by reviewers who write in high gear only, whether loving or loathing what they see. A terrible irony that those who abuse their own language might commend Kantor's individuality and intensity to you without understanding a word he said.   *GR(May 1982)*

On Not Attending Theatre

There are two ways to know what I am missing when I don't go to theatre: one is to stay away from it most of the time, the other is to go. Staying away means theatre is displaced for a moment by pleasures and disappointments found in private retreats, such as kitchens and gardens, or in quasi-theatrical haunts (books, concerts, galleries) which touch the imagination obliquely. Perhaps less of me is invested in the book or garden, so I can put expectations gently to one side while accepting less—as I can't in the theatre—as quite enough. At such moments, I remember theatre at its most vivid, those peaks scaled by artists who let it speak in its own voice rather than the voices of other media, other rooms. Staying away, I remember the best work of the past, retrieving it from the muddle into which it falls when too many bad plays and productions insist on defining the art itself. Staying away reminds me to look more carefully the next time I go.

When I go, however, I am not always there. In 1939, E. M. Forster wrote two brief essays, "Not Listening to Music" and "Not Looking at Pictures," referring to woolgathering at concerts and "a laugh or a sigh or an amorous daydream" in galleries. At concerts he kept finding himself thinking of the soprano's chins, or the plainness of the audience. Roger Fry loved to see paintings with Forster because he was intrigued by "someone who scarcely ever saw what the painter had painted." Forster was clearly more at ease with music or paintings than I am at theatre, because he was never really doing them. He wasn't gathering wool; rather, he was gathering material for novels, stories, and essays. He was not listening or not looking because he needed distance for his real job.

Going to theatre but not attending to it means, for me, that I may actually be doing more than what my real job requires. When I work as critic, I'm not supposed to be "making" theatre. Instead, I'm instructing myself to respond to visible and audible intentions, accounting for their presence or their disappearance. Yet, even if I succeed in following those instructions, which may be all that is asked of me, I can't help not attending in ways more fundamental to my conscience. When someone—dramatist, director, designer, or even actor—tries to maneuver me into agreeing with what I already know rather than patiently and plainly using the space and time to uncover what may be unknown, then I turn to active resistance. Which means attending only to ways in which they maneuver, and no longer going where they wish to take me.

Theatre that keeps me away from theatre is usually the play or production that is trying too hard to be impressive, calling attention to one startling element so that attention can be distracted from an emptiness within. In Milan, for example, Giorgio Strehler has by now redefined the director's art as some kind of strenuous search for the color-of-the-year—black for *Lohengrin,* gray for *Falstaff,* white with a shock of red for *The Good Woman of Setzuan*—leaving the internal suggestions of the text or music to fend for themselves. Strehler doesn't direct works, actors, or singers, he merely positions them into his eternal back-lights where faces need never be seen. He or one of his colleagues tells us in program notes what we are supposed to be seeing, while on stage there is either a parade of stately silhouettes or (as in the Brecht) an actor screaming or crying for attention. For Strehler, the play is definitely *not* the thing.

He has been impressive, however, especially for those who expect or want nothing more than animated store windows when going to the theatre. But impressiveness such as Strehler's, which is about nothing, is not really more offensive than the play that borrows its impressiveness from the news of the day. MASTER HAROLD . . . *and the Boys* had me dodging its BIG moment— the young man under stress suddenly revealing to his black friends that he's a white South African after all—when it finally came because I had to gather so much wool while waiting for it. And waiting for it.

After the play was over, I finally noticed that the actors had undergone something called "stage movement." Athol Fugard, directing his own play, seemed to sense that the first hour had to produce energy because the conversations were only pretexts for the *MOMENT* that had to be held for the end. So the actors don't walk, they stride or slide. Neither can they use an arm emphatically without thrusting an outstretched finger at the actor opposite, repeatedly and therefore—impressively—alluding to Michelangelo's God and Adam on that truly impressive ceiling in Rome. These people can't tell a simple story about flying a kite, they have to perform it, gesture for gesture; just as illustrative and didactic as that phone on the bar that will surely ring once or twice to push the plot into another place. And then, too, there is the usual fake poetry common to impressive plays with *TOPICS* rather than ideas on their minds: the boy, otherwise remarkably inattentive to his homework and only a hop, skip, and a slide away from a well-earned couch, is quick to observe that the kite was "sad, lying on the ground, like something that had lost its soul." Get it? That's really the kid striding through the land of playwriting on the way to his own lost soul.

Transparent maneuvers of this kind ought to keep more people away from theatre than high prices. Theatre that knows its limits while searching for shapes and language that distinguish it from the other arts may be the only form left that doesn't really have to bully an audience into attention. If I don't always find my mind staying in the theatre while going to the theatre, it is probably because my intelligence has barely been solicited. The giantism of Strehler and the schoolmasterism of Fugard are soliciting us and their material to submit to one idea, an idea that is usually monochromatic, reductive, and predictable. Calling attention to oneself is not authentic theatricality, though if you are Laurence Olivier you may just be able to get away with it. When Fugard has his spokesman on stage say, "Do not confuse art with entertainment," he succeeds only in reminding me that self-conscious, teacherly entertainment need not be confused with art.   *GR(October 1982)*

Bold Coward

The special triumph of George C. Scott's production of Noël Coward's *Present Laughter* and his own performance in it as Garry Essendine, "one of the world's foremost romantic comedians," is that with apparent ease and explosive good humor, a guiding idea keeps shining from the waxed surfaces of the text. It isn't always that way with Coward, partly because Coward's public performance imposed a fixed image of what theatrical performance might reveal. A poor lad who learned quickly how to charm the wigs off royalty and other rich, oppressive upstarts, he placed his wit and intelligence continually in a jester's role—café society's reigning courtier between the wars, jaunty, brittle, caustic, meltingly patriotic when needed, and despite his quick tongue, dependably safe. Marvelous as his stage appearances in his own plays must have been (I saw him only once, as a glittering, unabashed farcical King Magnus in Shaw's *The Apple Cart*), they were too often seen as mere extensions of Coward's offstage daily life.

Scott, of course, doesn't come to the play with such biographical luggage. Broadway's first production of *Present Laughter* in 1946 was apparently less fortunate, since Clifton Webb was one of those American actors who thought that imitating an accent while stressing monochromatic nastiness was all that was needed for translating Garry to the American stage. He knew Coward, it is true, but Coward—according to his friend and biographer Cole Lesley—disliked the performance intensely. "Garry," Lesley reported, "is quite funny enough as he is, without adding venom that is not there." Webb was dead wrong, clearly, but it must have been difficult to get at the truths of the play, since so much of it came directly from Coward's life: not only Garry, but the Scandinavian spiritualist maid with her cigarette hanging from her mouth, the secretary, the business partners, all of them passed through Coward's suites in much the same form as they are in the play.

Scott's version rescues the play at last from life, removing the waspish bitchiness that Coward loathed in Webb's performance, and adding many more layers to the "likable charm" that Lesley offers as Coward's overly modest intention. Scott is quite naturally more dimensional in every way than Coward or his imitators would ever be, bringing to Garry a physical bulk, a fullness of spirit, and a weight of emotional history that become more and more funny and even touching as the play rolls forward. With a less physically challenging performance, the play could seem to be mainly about Garry's dressing gowns and the telephone.

Scott's is, indeed, a performance about performance, the continually astonishing ways in which a ravenously passionate man tries to bring his appetites under control. Those repeated half-truths in the text—"I'm always acting, watching myself go by," or "Complete naturalness is my strong suit," or "No one can accuse me of being emotional"—are vividly seen for the complicated half-lies they really are. Scott's mask isn't as pretty as Barrymore's, but he's just as enormous and attractive in scope—that long left arm reaches for help from the unyielding heavens and can find agitated peace only from the span of his roman-coin face. When he dashes and jumps across vast reaches of the arena space, clutching a teddy bear in his arms, he is like a whale who has just discovered flight. Sure it's "just a comedy," but what a terrific one. Seriously funny because so much is at stake: this whale has to fight off all the sharks around him, eager for his glory or his cash, and when a whale can finally be so graceful, it's a great event indeed.

Scott has grace as a director, too. Otherwise this production would not be so clearly the best conquest of that awful Circle in the Square stage that I have seen. As usual, when people on the other side are laughing, I wish I wasn't gazing at a zipper or an upswept coiffure, but Scott is just as generous in his sweeping, fluid use of the space as he is when working with himself and the others as actors. Even those performances that don't quite persuade because of too much effort or because the British accent has slipped out of focus find their own reality and breath.

Most of the actors keep meeting Scott on his own inventive and dangerous ground, especially Dana Ivey as Garry's secretary, the image of Maggie Smith, but with her own soft grit and suppleness that have the right phrasing and high-pitched pause; and above all, Nathan Lane, as the intruding loony young playwright with the powerful handgrip that everybody quickly and hilariously learns to avoid.

Lane and Scott together are virtuosi in service in the most amusing and understated adaptation from Coward's life—his gentle treatment by Shaw when he himself was a young dramatist cribbing unashamedly from Shaw. In *Present Laughter,* the young playwright Roland Maule is unstoppable in pursuit of his proud, willing, though horrified victim. Their scenes together are a brilliant parody of Chekhov's ambivalent presentation of actress-mother and would-be-playwright-son in *The Seagull,* the tough commercial professional covering up his confused respect for the theatrically infatuated amateur. Lane is Scott in miniature, tiny, darting, wrapping himself around furniture the way Scott drapes himself around words, the embodiment of a comic idea and a comic relationship that is as funny as anything in the language since *The Importance of Being Earnest.*

If anything, Coward became a consistently better playwright than Wilde, despite his absorption into a society that gave him his material while denying that he could be anything better than an inspired craftsman. In fact, he was much better than that, and with George C. Scott as his spokesman now, he can be viewed finally as the great playwright he really was within his genre and range. *Present Laughter,* in Scott's production, is one of this century's funniest plays (with all respect to Beckett, Pinter, Bond, and other gifted heavyweights), and should seize and hold its place as the best play of 1982.

GR(July 1982)

Shall I Compare Thee?

Hyperbole comes in strange disguises, but none so boggling as praise lavished by reviewers on plays that are supposed to be good because of the season or weather. I recently surrendered to a friend's challenge that I write at least one phrase that might be used in the *New York Times* ad for George C. Scott's production of *Present Laughter* (Circle in the Square). Having enjoyed the play and Scott's performance, yet unaccustomed to the translation of those pleasures into the linguistic equivalent of an Italian soccer fan's delirium after the World Cup Final, I set about writing my review in the only way I know, keeping my friend's challenge in mind. Anybody ought to be able to write a phrase or two that might easily leap into a press agent's dream without corrupting the thought or the language.

More than halfway through the review, I had to admit that I wasn't really trying. Describing Scott as having "a fullness of spirit, and a weight of emotional history that become more and more funny and even touching as the play rolls forward," is not precisely adaptable to the hard sell. "More and more funny" might work, but any fool can see that it immediately invites inquiry about how it got to be funnier than the unnamed something else. Later, I was getting even less quotable, actually suggesting that the play and Scott's performance were "seriously funny." Worse, while I wanted to be clear about my admiration for Scott's direction, I couldn't help adding that it was "clearly the best conquest of that awful Circle in the Square stage that I have seen." By now, it was clear that I was a master at uncovering an enemy under every friend I might make.

The happy ending to this episode is that the undaunted press agents did indeed find a way to bend some of my phrasing to fit their advertising needs. By restructuring, and the inevitable addition of exclamation points, they put me squarely in the circle of those enthusiasts who always sound as if they had checked their brain cells with their coats when entering the theatre. Of course, to do so, they had also to make me look like a grammatical idiot, having me call "Scott's *production* one of this century's funniest *plays*" (my italics), but who was I to complain? Without really trying, I had met the challenge, the winner of a point though a loser of a war.

The more obvious way for a reviewer to win a place on those huge ads is to work for one of the real powers in print or broadcast journalism. Lacking such position, then, I could have borrowed from those reviewers' tested, infallible formulas. What I had never considered was that *Present Laughter* wasn't just a play, it was a play appearing in summer!

Mama, mama, mama, how could I have missed it? There I was, examining the public Coward against something revealed in the play of the private Coward when what I had not noticed at all was that *Present Laughter* was, in the words of four reviewers, either "perfect summertime fun!" or "a perfect summer romp!" or "a summertime frolic!" or simply welcome to Broadway "on a summer night." This last remark really stopped me in my critical tracks. Did it mean that Noël Coward would be welcome *only* on a summer night? What was meant to happen to him in winter? Are playwrights and audiences destined to romp and frolic only when the sun is hot? Should there be a new course in college playwriting, "Drama 110 (in the shade): Playwriting for All Seasons"? Where, as any oppressed dramatist has a right to ask, would it all end?

It's not surprising, under the circumstances, that the craze for new ways to say the same old praise might lead theatres to plan productions deemed suitable for May or September. Summer theatres, especially, are awful much of the time because they don't know how to ignore the only season they have. Were it not for summer, for example, Philip Barry's *Holiday* would not recur quite so often, nor would his inept *The Animal Kingdom* have earned a revival at the Berkshire Playhouse in Stockbridge last July.

The ideal summer play is about the rich—at play. But, of course, they should have a few problems. Writing lovingly and respectfully about some of the dumbest people who ever lived—the 1930s filthy-wealthy who refused to notice that a sound economy had gone on holiday in 1929—Barry has to have his obtuse, witless hero barrel his way through a hundred sentimental hoops before arriving at one of those preordained conclusions reached by us in the fifteenth minute of the play. In the quintessential summer play, the audience is always fifteen minutes ahead of the hero and light years beyond the playwright.

Not that it is always so bleakly sunny. A more sophisticated summer theatre, such as Williamstown's, can yield to an audience that keeps demanding the popular return of *Room Service,* but that doesn't stop Nikos Psacharopoulos from offering them Gorky and Chekhov too. Perhaps that is because he is giving serious summer work to strong, seasoned actors who want something more than just a romp and frolic in the summer hay. Underrehearsed, sketchy, but bursting with charm and energy, the Williamstown production in August of Arthur Pinero's *Trelawney of the Wells* featured Blythe Danner in a role far more challenging and credible than the sub-Hepburn effort she was asked to drag out for Barry's *Philadelphia Story* at Lincoln Center several seasons ago. A theatre that respects actors, whether operating in summer or fall, is a theatre that respects audiences, too.

The *Times* ad won't have it that way. To join my colleagues there, I should have to speak of Danner as the "perfect summer date," revealing myself as the perfect reviewing nut. *The Winter's Tale* would have to wait for a December opening, and *A Midsummer Night's Dream* could never be played in March. Where will it all end, indeed? Judge for yourself in coming months as hyperbole swings with the thermometer: *Cats* will be as perfect for a cold winter's cuddle, *Plenty* might turn out to be bracing as a ski run, and *Good* could be the best inducement for plowing out your driveway. It may be true, as Shakespeare's Rosalind says, that "men are April when they woo, December when they wed," but I can't imagine any reason within the history of drama why reviewers have to be July when they write.   *GR(October 1982)*

Beggars Must Choose

Poor sportsmanship though it may be to knock American theatres when they are more out than down, I cannot really say that I mourn the passing of the Phoenix Theatre any more than I grieved over the end of the Brooklyn Academy of Music's brief, feeble attempt at making a theatre company several years ago. It may be that just as we get the leaders and wars we deserve, so do we get our theatres, especially those that keep producing plays without ever revealing any particular passion for doing them. Everybody is so busy filling forms these days, writing grant proposals, sitting on panels that dole out coffee money to abject artists, and generally clotting the phone lines and airwaves with appeals for charity, that it isn't any wonder so little time or energy remains for making rousing theatrical events.

Theatre isn't on or off Broadway any more, it's on the Bowery. While actors wait on tables for a living, their would-be bosses—producers, artistic directors, and rude flunkies—are always waiting for the next opportunity to polish a bureaucrat's boots for the privilege of a handout. Along with ideas, pride and dignity were tossed into the wings years ago when theatres began tailoring their programs to fit into the dreamless schemes of the non-writers, non-directors, and non-actors who run the public and private foundations. Some, like the Phoenix, moved dizzily from classic-eclectic to contemporary-eclectic, neglecting to shape a profile along the way. Others made a habit of declaring that whatever they were doing—old or new plays—was just what the public wanted, as if artistic success could be elected in the same way as presidents.

Why can't it be admitted at last that America is not likely to subsidize anything less than the latest bomb, missile, or space ship with grace or generosity? When hardware is god, can stupidity or indifference be far behind? With all respect to innocent Shelleys who still want to believe that artists are the legislators of mankind, the truth is that legislators are the legislators. Poets, dancers, and musicians may be wheeled out for the occasional inauguration or even for a ceremony-broadcast honoring them for growing old without fuss, but they have never been and never will be heroes and heroines to Americans. We simply don't have the will, imagination, or tradition.

Worse, when artists submit their hopes and fantasies to the legislators, they are making an awful admission that they really believe those elected and appointed paper-people are competent to evaluate their work. The evidence is plain enough that government knows even less about managing money than the most humble citizen, and a properly unhumble citizen such as a playwright or performer is usually a master of budget and survival. The Nobel Prize for Economics should have gone to an actor long ago. It's absurd and demeaning for theatres and other artistic institutions to hand over the governance of their lives to experts who are always wrong about everything.

If the financial stakes were higher, then perhaps a case might be made for standing on cultural breadlines. When Chaplin's modest murderer, Monsieur Verdoux, was asked if he had anything to say for himself before the guillotine, he said that he should have gone into munitions. In Germany, where the tradition of subsidy was probably born, it makes sense for theatre to feed at the public pigpen. Peter Stein, director for the past fifteen years of what has become arguably the best theatre in the world, the Schaubühne, said in 1971 that "all who work here at the Schaubühne—even if they believe that capitalism should be changed or destroyed—stand as individuals within the contradictions of the capitalist system. We carry them with us and we are a part of them. I therefore see no problem in accepting subsidies from the Senate." Which is precisely what he and his colleagues have done, on a scale that would have thrilled Ziegfeld or Barnum. *Variety* reported that in 1979, when German theatre audiences had diminished, the states and cities nevertheless raised their support by seven percent. As Beckett once said, he knew Roger Blin was the director for him when he saw so few people in Blin's audience. A sense of irony or humor is not what we have come to expect from our subsidizers—or, sadly, our theatres.

What we get instead are cost-accounting from the subsidizers and courteous, uninvolved, imitative, unadventurous repertories from our theatres: plays about psychological basket cases and the tears and cheers to be found in hospital corridors, aimless stories about the unaware in languid pursuit of the unaligned. Referring to money, the Phoenix Theatre's co-founder, T. Edward Hambleton, declared that "it's not just us alone that are in this trouble." But it's also not them alone who have been producing so timidly. Everybody's doing it and nobody cares. The survival game in America is not about selective nonsupport, it's about the right to destroy at random. Does Hambleton wish us to pause for a moment of silence in commemoration of the Phoenix's good intentions and frequently good work? Why should we, when we know that the great publicist in the American sky has finally declared that our lives are defined by the survival of the shittiest?

The German theatre has been rewarded for its government's cynical wisdom, its capacity to recognize that theatres with guiding ideas might actually gain a particular, if narrowly based, audience. Stein has produced an impressive range of work: twenty-three pieces ranging from improvisation on Greek theatre, a theatrical introduction to the age of Shakespeare; German classics; a French farce; the most spectacular Ibsen (*Peer Gynt*); early and late Brecht; two Edward Bond plays; a play by Peter Handke; some Russians, Irish, and plays that move from realism to romanticism in one easy, unselfconscious leap. All this and politics, too; a theatre that makes investigation its primary purpose; presenting itself frankly as a metaphor for democratic collaboration while insisting on its right to use its money in its own way—for no more than four productions each year. Stein can say what no American has thought of saying: "It is incorrect that we must confine our artistic expression in order to get state support—*We can really do whatever we want* [italics added]. That's what the state is proud of—that they dare to allow this."

Whether the American state is called the National Endowment for the Arts, the New York State Council on the Arts, Rockefeller, or Ford, it has certainly never shown pride in daring work. In the end, it justifies only itself and its multiplying hordes of droning executives. Has anybody noticed that while the Phoenix falls, leaving gifted creative people without employment, there is still no shortage of managerial monsters in the arts foundations? Their employment goes on forever. Stein can say luxuriously that "starting from the hope that perhaps everything can be achieved in the theatre, we have of course arrived at the conclusion that not so terribly much has been achieved." But, as Stein's theatrical biographer Michael Patterson says, "that 'not so terribly much' consists of a series of almost entirely successful productions, of a consistently clear and precise style of direction, of the restoration of beauty to committed theatre, and of the beginnings of synthesis in the divergent strains of modern theatre. Most important of all, Stein the explorer clearly has no intention of stopping where he is."

Whereas in America, the Circle Repertory in its infinite whitherdom has invented a meaningless new term called "lyric realism" to account for the television plays it keeps putting on stage, the Living Theatre lives in Rome, Papp plays with whims and imports, many of the others play with themselves, strong plays remain unproduced, and good actors give their best performances at union meetings. Let the managers congratulate each other, keeping those guidelines and regulations floating up there in the swamp between their ears. The rest of us will have to go on working without guidelines in smaller frameworks—the only way anything good can happen here anyway. Let 1983 be the year in which beggars refuse to beg, the end of a world in which grant proposals outnumber the plays that are produced.

GR(January 1983)

To a Hare

If David Hare has made any miscalculation in his brilliantly arranged, epically bleak, anti-romantic *Plenty,* it may be in the way England appears to be the subject of his play. Good, bad, ordinary, and indifferent English people float through his account of Susan Traherne's passage from the peace she found in war to the war she made of peace, so it can't be denunciation alone that drives the play forward. Yet the language Hare gives to so many of his characters (not only to Susan) is so ripe with bile, so energetically, pungently furious with England that it is sometimes difficult to uncover the play's other territories.

In a second viewing, however, this time in a territory—Broadway—that would have surely driven Susan to mass murder, the play's cleansing intelligence is miraculously clearer. Hare's targets loom large indeed: passion trivialized by those who value forbearance more, traduced by those who refuse to put it into their work, and twisted by lies to others that are only a little less corruptive than lies to oneself. The subject isn't England, it's the mess made by hypocrites who hide feelings and by hypocrites who hide themselves behind feelings that run aimlessly all over the place. It's the Western world—feelings and romance untempered by awareness, the inner world untouched by work or politics.

"Don't creep around the furniture," says Susan to Raymond, the man who will become her husband. "Just look at me and make a judgment." Which is what the play lets us do in a cool, dispassionate, selective manner uncommon in most modern drama—or at least, in drama pretending to be modern most of the time in New York. Susan is smart, but she's rarely very nice. Like Hamlet, she feigns madness and begins almost to enjoy it. "The only dignity," she says late in the play, is "to live alone." That's what her quest has been all along—to express pain better than anyone else (which she does) while passing on the responsibility. When she finally admits her weakness, Hare is studious about letting her acknowledge not that she loses control, but that she *likes* to lose control. Susan is the West sick of its privilege yet privileged to be sick.

The play's patterning is ingenious, so that Susan's dream of the postwar future isn't actually stated until the last scene, back again in France, 1944, after we have seen what happened to her from war's end until 1962. Hare's peacetime England is a succession of burnished rooms surrounded by tapestried darkness. Suddenly the darkness lifts and Susan is a girl again, rejoicing in victory, believing with fierce conviction that all the days to come will be like this from now on. But we have just seen ten of those days, and Susan could scarcely have been more misguided. Why? Because she was infatuated with that countryside, and probably adored the idea of that rough French farmer also looking at the light, the sun, and the air. But she neglected to hear him when he remarked upon his status—"shit . . . the lowest of the low . . . the harvest not good this year." She wasn't even listening when he casually said that he "must work every moment of the day." She was listening only to her illusions.

A pitiless play, then, one that keeps dashing traditional expectations on the shores of a masterful technique: scenes chosen because they advance the play's circumstances rather than the plot, so that effects are cumulative and what is left out gradually assumes as much resonance as what is seen; images, therefore, of people who drift seamlessly through experience without experiencing much change while people like Susan change clothes and hairstyle frequently but can't find the route to another dimension; words used as weapons, yet each character possessed by personal tonality; and finally, the punctuating afterthoughts of those bitter, witty, disruptive voice-overs between the scenes. Hare may be bringing bad news from the existential front, but he does it with a buoyancy and heft that give the play lightness and elasticity even in its most charged, tensile encounters.

What may be more remarkable than his playwriting, however, is his direction; not, after all, something that most playwrights do very well, especially when their own plays are the specimens. Hare gets all the details in place while never losing control over the architecture of his text. The production isn't afraid to shift from lushness to iciness with startling elisions. Actors find their places and often stay there within what seems like an alarming circle of danger. The space between them invariably suggests meaning rather than arbitrary staginess. Eloquence is found in distance, sudden closeness, furniture, even the gorgeous dying fall of a white parachute in darkness. This is a harsh, unforgiving production that has the courage to place some faith in quiet, intense beauty.

Obviously, much of that beauty derives from Hare's splendid collaboration with his responsive, imaginative designers: John Gunter's swiftly changing, apt, complicated, but useful sets; Jane Greenwood's clothes, defining two decades with simple clarity; Arden Fingerhut's lighting, which is illuminating in every respect; and even Andrew Reese's marvelous "hair designs," additional clues to the care and sensitivity that are crowded into every moment of this distinctive production.

As it should be, however, Hare's casting and most of the performances finally make the best possible case for the play. Even if Susan cannot find another dimension for her life, the actors have found shimmering, vibrant life within the dimensions of their roles. Working within small, gestural frameworks, many of them find some uncanny way of suggesting that we are seeing only a fraction of their souls. The great confrontation between Kate Nelligan's Susan and Edward Herrmann's Raymond has so much unforeseen whiplash power and sorrow in it because both actors have been so discreet earlier: architecture again, a musical gift for placement, an awareness of the difference between *mezzoforte* and *forte,* an appreciation of *crescendo* and *ritard.* Nelligan can come into a room with raging energy, only to expire slowly into a taut whisper, but always with a ping to everything she says that gives resonance to the thoughts below. They are both of them actors with reserves, armed to the teeth to break our hearts, like the plentifully gifted play they inhabit.   *GR(January 1983)*

Sontag in the Park

Milan Kundera knew that it couldn't be done. Adaptations of extraordinary novels are "reductions," he says in his introduction to *Jacques and His Master.* "The more the adapter tries to remain discreetly hidden behind the novel, the more he betrays it." Even so, it is not entirely surprising that, as a banished writer in Prague in 1971, he should make a version of one of his favorite novels, Denis Diderot's *Jacques le fataliste.* A work done mainly for his "private pleasure," he never really imagined that it could be produced in a Czech theatre under his own name. Officially unpersoned, suspecting that *The Farewell Party* was his last novel, he chose eccentrically to write for a theatre that didn't exist. Silenced, he rescued his writing voice by choosing drama, the most public platform of them all. And for this he was willing to risk the reduction of Diderot.

Or was he? On the evidence of the American Repertory Theatre's production, directed by Susan Sontag in her English-speaking stage debut (she has directed Pirandello in Italy), Kundera has not reduced Diderot so much as he has reduced the possibilities of theatre. A strange lapse from a writer who is surely one of the smartest in the century. In his novels, no character, least of all his apparent protagonists, can escape the cubist limelight into which he lets them fall: his men, especially, can see angles within angles even as they try to live and think in the singular dimension of the moment. Thinking is

Kundera's splendid obsession, thinking as an object, the only reality. The novel may indeed be his natural form, the realm where thought can find continual breathing space, where it can refract, split, and subdivide itself without threat or violation.

It is his natural form, however, only because in his "variation-homage" to Diderot on the stage, he is unwilling to allow theatre the same liberty as the novel, and in this he has made an astonishing, if common, miscalculation. "The theatre," says Kundera, "has never had its Laurence Sterne." Which is to say that the theatre still does not have its Milan Kundera. For some weird, only partly plausible reason, Kundera believes that "the form of a dramatic work has always been a good deal more rigid and normative than that of the novel." That this might be news to Shakespeare, Brecht, or Beckett doesn't seem to occur to him. Therefore, choosing to write a play that would assault what he calls the "laws" of dramatic structure, he finally does nothing of the kind.

True, he goes some distance toward freedom, evidently aware that he can put his characters on an empty stage, moving them from place to place without going anywhere, allowing them to talk, argue, and tell stories that are then enacted in place of the play that is not really happening. All this is modern enough, and even very promising. His is a deliberately opaque version of Diderot's eighteenth-century world and characters. Even in English, the language locates itself in today's idioms, albeit in words and phrases that cast a misty sensuality around the contours of the stories told by Jacques, his Master, and the Innkeeper they encounter on their travels.

The three stories are about sex and betrayal, each one ringing changes on the other; more often, revealing similarities. The basic relationships are familiar: the Goldonian servant, Jacques, cleverer than his Master, and the Doll Tearsheet-type Innkeeper, sprawlingly sexual herself but quick to be used by Kundera-Diderot as an actress showing the story of the Marquise de la Pommeraye, who manipulates a mother and daughter into becoming the instruments of her revenge on a young Marquis who simply won't tumble into her marriage bed. Jacques shows how he lost his virginity by betraying his friend, and his Master shows how his best friend, the Chevalier de Saint-Ouen, betrayed him. Above these stately enactments (stately, at least, in Sontag's production) hovers the spirit, even the hope, of violence. In the text, there are two such moments: the young Marquis literally kicks the daughter out of his life when he discovers that he has been duped by Pommeraye into marrying a whore, and the Master duels and kills his friend, Saint-Ouen.

Sontag's Marquis doesn't kick the daughter, he merely pushes her away petulantly, a boyish gesture that scarcely disrupts the sexless proceedings, already suffocating from so much polite and decorous behavior. To be fair to Kundera, his homage to Diderot did not include an equal homage to eighteenth-century theatre: his surrenders to convention are of a different order, revealed by his self-conscious digressions about the great author "on high" and by the

Master's repeated complaints that he is walking rather than riding horses "because of a stupid theatre." To be fair to Sontag, she has respected Kundera's instruction that the play should not be shouted: it is a particular pleasure of this production that the largely lightweight company rarely forces and pressures the words, endowing many stretches of the text with a gentle, sweet energy that gives the audience a chance to think.

Kundera's other wishes, however, are ignored in that conceptual directorial manner to which we've become so lazily accustomed: where he asks that "the set avoid all ornamental, illustrative and symbolic elements," Sontag has Douglas Stein devise not an empty stage with a playing area for the storytellers and a platform for the enactments, but a white Styrofoam version of Piranesi's engraving of a Roman ruin. Further, Jacques's luggage contains a bust of Diderot that occupies center stage most of the time, as if it could lend resonance and meaning to an action that is never permitted to become complex. Kundera wants intelligence to explode into violence, even though he doesn't have a clear, respectful idea of how to make that happen in the theatre. Sontag, unfortunately, wants to subdue both intelligence and violence by decorating the play with pretty pictures, the lovely but helplessly unilluminating lighting of Jennifer Tipton and the aimless diagonal crossing of one character in front of another.

Jacques refers to the Master being cuckolded and he actually places four fingers above his head. Like the Piranesi quotation that stands in the way of the travelers, the actors are always illustrating the text, entering and exiting with the same languid stroll. Priscilla Smith's doubling of the Innkeeper who performs the vengeful Pommeraye is the most mannered version of the show-and-tell disease. Her Pommeraye is not much different from her Innkeeper, and her Innkeeper has only the most monolithically monotonous acquaintance with that Tearsheet sexuality. Her face never reveals anything—not thought, humor, or pique. Her hands and arms float around her like fugitive punctuation marks. Every fifth syllable invites an arbitrary stress. Forever looking down at the stage as if trying to find a lost bug, she is the perfect illustration of Sontag's fatal picture-book approach. With at least one character caught by the giggles, much of the production feels like *Amadeus* in collision with *Barry Lyndon,* a static painting called White on Wet.

Jeremy Geidt's Saint-Ouen, however, suggests what Kundera himself has only attempted to master. Finding a hundred overtones in the word "friend," he is the one actor who seems to enjoy Kundera's smoky verbal penetrations, sensually uncovering the insinuations lurking behind so much of the thought in the play. The problem is that neither Kundera in his doubts about the form nor Sontag in her reliance on concept have faith enough in the play that can be derived from thought.   *GR(January 1985)*

A Rosemary for Remembrance

Rosemary Harris is the best reason for seeing Hugh Whitemore's *Pack of Lies*. The story she tells through the architecture of her performance is much more intriguing than the story-from-fact told by Whitemore. His tale is about Barbara and Bob Jackson, a stodgy British couple living in a London suburb who seem to have learned behavior from movies or plays. Harris's story is about a woman discovering anguish for the first time in her life. True, Whitemore gives her the markings for such an experience, but he never really acknowledges much more than her surfaces—her apparent mousiness, her husband's charge that she always takes blame on herself, and, in Clifford Williams's soberly detailed production, all her dowdy skirts and cardigans.

Harris's gift is to make the familiar strange. It may be that British mystery plays don't all have an Inspector calling on complacent suburban families, but when Patrick McGoohan enters as the impeccably suave Mr. Stewart, describing himself as just a civil servant, the echo is loud and clear. The Jacksons are being asked to lend their daughter's room to the British secret service, hot on the trail of Helen and Peter Kroger, the Jacksons' Canadian neighbors and dear friends. In an instant, it is clear that the Jacksons will be living a disrupted life for two acts, that Stewart will divulge the truth about the Krogers' link to a Russian spy ring, and that the Krogers will be caught. Since there wouldn't be a play without suitable delays in revelations, many of the actors seem to be trapped in the tidy timings of playwriting rather than the undertow of real, unsubmissive, messy experience.

But Harris takes her character into realms barely imagined by Whitemore. For a start, she is almost always in motion, padding from kitchen to parlor, touching objects along the way, almost as if she isn't quite certain she belongs. A sofa cushion is enveloped by her arms as protection from the eruptions of her conscience. Unsuccessfully, she tries to pull a loose strand of hair that escaped her effort to put it in place. In the beginning, she seems to be as neatly packaged as the play, but by the middle of the second act nothing she does is quite right, even as her voice begins to suggest a developing strength, the glimmerings of a previously unimagined purpose. Harris doesn't wait for the play's arrangements; instead, she lets them catch up with her while she submits to the undertow.

This isn't acting about one or two big moments here or there, it's acting about line, weight, and structure. What we see is seamless thought in action. Harris listens masterfully, somehow making a distinction between what she hears for the sake of conversation and what she is taking in for future reference and decision. Not that she's hiding anything from the audience. Part of her style is precision and articulation: what she says is phrased with staccato clarity; what she does emerges from a spirit clearly hearing itself at last.

A pity that the play is so clogged with predictability and freighted with good manners. Why are the British so enthralled by their spies? And why don't they dramatize the questions that can't be answered by commitments to good citizenship and proper form? *Pack of Lies* inevitably challenges E. M. Forster's continually misread essay, "What I Believe," in which he says that "if I had to choose between betraying my country and betraying my friend, I hope I should have the guts to betray my country." Forster didn't mean "my friend, right or wrong." He actually began that famous sentence with the phrase "I hate the idea of causes," meaning he hoped he might protect his friend whenever his country might be on the rampage with a rotten, murderous mission draped by the flag. Ibsen said much the same when he wrote that he had no "great liking for symbols," especially flags. "Remove the sign of prejudice," he added, "of narrow-mindedness and wrongheadedness and slavishness and the groundless belief in authority, so that the individual human being can sail under his own flag."

Whitemore, sadly, is light years away from the company of Forster and Ibsen, not only ethically, but also dramatically. His play never grapples with issues or even with something so clumsy as an idea or a point of view. He always seems to be warning himself away from the consequences of the real story, shrouding the events with premises shared only by governments and dumb citizens. Everybody is explained by a single motive: The Canadian spies are really Americans who left the U.S. on the heels of the Rosenbergs' trial and who became Communists because they were revolted by the homeless seen in Riverside Park during the Depression. Stewart is merely "very good at his job." He tells a good story about how he knows more about his Soviet counterpart than he knows about his next-door neighbor, but despite the fact that Whitemore gives his leading characters one or two personal monologues, Stewart never really examines the weird truths behind such information that might well haunt both a better man and a better play. This is official British art, I suspect, a tame, deliberately modest, small-minded pack of hemi-demi-semi-truths that don't generate much drama.   *GR(January 1985)*

Rosalyn Drexler: Theatre Whirled

Rosalyn Drexler's barely hidden agenda in the two plays collectively called *Transients Welcome* is to present hilariously serious theatre criticism in the form of lunatic comic fables. In the first play, *Room 17-C,* Linda Loman falls in sex with a giant cockroach while on the road, now that Willy's been retired with a gold-plated watch honoring his masochism. In the second play, *Utopia Parkway,* a man sitting in a Beckett chair in familiar half-light, muttering a sepulchral incomplete sentence, is quickly surrounded by fugitives from or allusions to official performing art (Balanchine and the woman who *is* ballet), Broadway whimsy (*Harvey*), and Broadway seriousness (*Of Mice and Men*). For good measure, Harpo's horn joins the punctuating Japanese tinkle-sounds heard continually offstage. Only a sheltered fool would ever imagine that anything might be sacred in Drexler's world. For her, all art is fair game, but theatre art enthralled by its own perceived importance hasn't got a chance.

Utopia Parkway, unfortunately, keeps spinning out of focus even as Crystal Field's marvelously earthbound ballerina, oblivious to her eternally flat feet, keeps trying to whirl some sense into the proceedings. Unlike *Room 17-C,* the targets are scattered and the story is quite deliberately not a story at all. If it is about any one thing, it is about abstract art; as usual, Drexler can be trusted to provide her own critical perspective: at the end, someone says, "One can only extract from the abstract what one puts into it," which is not finally a criticism of the audience alone. The mix here is understandably messy, fun to watch because John Vaccaro's production is blithely in charge of each fleeting moment. At its best, the play seems to be suspended in a delicious void, unconcerned with order or sensibility, refusing to mean anything that can be reduced into words by the traditional critical act. It simply dances with unashamed clumsiness while flinging out miniature observations that either say everything or nothing, but always with momentary, quickly disappearing, precision.

Mildred the ballerina says that she has been pink and she's been blue. "Pink is better," she says, bringing back news from the frontiers of performance. The play is just like that—as if to demonstrate that floating on pink clouds has to be better. Neither Dada nor doodle, *Utopia Parkway* passes swiftly through brief episodes that leave behind confident overtones, touched by a divine, but durable, ecstasy. The absence of center or Drexler's customary verbal dazzle may be the price paid for dealing so honestly with abstraction. In an odd, but not funny enough way, Drexler has been true to her subject while surrendering some of her natural wit.

The deconstruction of *Death of a Salesman* in *Room 17-C* finds Drexler on much firmer and funnier ground. Linda's encounter with the roach doesn't even require knowledge of Arthur Miller's play or Kafka's *Metamorphosis,* since it stands well enough on its own as the story of a women who—unlike the husband she talks to so often on the phone—loves life and is splendidly prepared to let sexual impulse be her guide. This means noticing that a roach who "revels in dung and bird-droppings" may actually have "a romantic nature." What is even more romantic is the refracted image of a playwright willing to borrow characters and transform their destinies, liberating them—for the moment—from the snares of rigid dramaturgy and stuffy ethics.

Drexler's Lomans have fallen through a Lewis Carroll rabbit hole, only to emerge in a world where Willy is admonished by Linda not to kill himself because "it'll be anticlimactic," surely the most incisive criticism ever leveled at that ponderously obtuse play. It is Linda, in fact, who dies this time, in a hotel fire which the roach, of course, survives. Before dying, however, she manages to answer the phone, telling Willy that she never loved him—still another variation on the critical mode. Best of all, she finally lets us know that Willy sold all kinds of brushes, one of those details omitted by Miller as he marched toward his own idea of universal abstraction.

Crystal Field's Linda would never have lamented the absence of tears at Willy's grave: she's been thoroughly de-Millered and Drexlerized, full of sassy asides that match her glamorous spike heels. Will she be able to give up her initial repulsion for Bill Evans's charmingly bug-eyed roach? Of course she will, since she's a free spirit and a free actress in an equally self-possessed play. Vaccaro's direction encourages the actors (not the least George Bartenieff's uplifting Mr. B) to listen with a third ear—indeed, to show themselves listening as if in gigantic close-up, letting their roving eyes and moist mouths reveal every rude corner of their secret lives.

Wonderful to see so much certainty at work—the victories over production poverty displayed by Abe Lubeski's half-elegant designs, the bold patterns of Jeff Nash's lights, and the antic eloquence of Tavia Ito's costumes. Point for point, Drexler is served well by the controlled anarchy of John Vaccaro's production. It may be news to *Biloxi Blues,* but our best comic dramatist is alive and well on Second Avenue.   *GR(April 1985)*

No, We're Not

Frederick Lonsdale's 1923 play, *Aren't We All?*, has two sets. In such comedies of mostly bad manners, this means there will also be two sofas and two plush armchairs, all of them facing the audience—which automatically becomes if not a fourth wall, at least an invisible fireplace. It is characteristic of plays like this, not so much written as upholstered, that there will be plenty of time for the audience to ponder questions about interior design, and the eating, drinking, and dressing habits of the rich; if none of that proves sufficiently nourishing, there is also the weather.

Lonsdale's rich are so devil-may-ga-ga, it doesn't really matter that he sets them up to look like eccentric decorators as well. Since it isn't the kind of play intended to arouse anything so vulgar as a thought, it may not be cricket to think about furniture turned away from a mantelpiece that is plainly on stage. On the other hand, it's equally strange that when the play moves to Grenham Court in the country, the sun seems to be shining all the time over a garden conveniently situated so that characters can wander on and off stage without always bumping into one another in the corridor outside Rex Harrison's—I mean Lord Grenham's—sitting room. Perhaps, like so many colonialists in his time, Lonsdale believed that he could protect the sun from setting over the Empire by pretending that it was rising regularly over England.

Where there's a Lord, of course, there will always be a Lady, an Honorable So-and-So and maybe even an Honorable Mrs. So-and-So, and, remembering the gentle mileage Wilde covered with Canon Chasuble in *The Importance of Being Earnest,* a suitably dopy Reverend. Lonsdale never stints when it comes to presenting the expectable, but he's a stingy provider of Wildean wit. Weirdly, he turns out to be a premature ageist, scoring most of his jokes at the expense of Lord Grenham and Lady Frinton (Claudette Colbert). In this production, Lonsdale's cruelties are tempered by the *moderato cantabile* playing of Harrison and Colbert, never on stage long enough at a stretch to betray weariness, but always quietly perky and alert. These marvelous survivors turn the joke on Lonsdale: Colbert, draped in silver and black lamé, showing more leg than the younger ladies in the cast, and dripping in diamonds, is told that she's looking younger every day; to which she replies that she's "glad of that, because it takes most of the day to become it." Even if we know it took decades and cash, her glowing presence is enough to make Lonsdale sound like the cad he would never wish to be.

Harrison's face seems to have disappeared into his eye sockets, but that doesn't stop him from demonstrating that even this development can be used by an expert minimalist to show character and intelligence. He shoots out the whites of his eyes no more than three or four times, a signal always that he's awakened to something like a decision, or, at the least, a resolution of some idea that has been lurking protectively behind his cornea. He may look old, indeed he *is* old, but he makes less mean more almost as if he were Merce Cunningham turning two fingers into a subliminally momentous saraband.

When the tempo shifts to Lynn Redgrave and Jeremy Brett's vigorous *allegro*, it becomes even clearer that Lonsdale is the lucky recipient of a gift only indestructible actors can bestow on a play that deserves destruction. Lonsdale supplies one of those soap-bubble stories that is meant to hide a multitude of nasty grins: returning wife catches lonely husband in a kiss with vamping ingenue; clever father discovers that returning wife had done the same on her Egyptian holiday; wife tries to cover her tracks; husband concludes somehow that her escapade, like his, proves their love; father is tricked into marriage with Lady (Colbert); and "bloody old fool" Reverend elicits comment from father: "Aren't we all?" Fools, that is. All very neat, sweet, discreet, and a cheat.

It's probably fitting that a bad play from 1923 should turn up in these regressive eighties, soliciting suggestions that they don't make plays like this any more (i.e., with prissy butlers, wardrobe changes, champagne, tea, cakes, bonnets, brooches, and the comfortable lie that high-toned deceptions are the only protection of happiness). Better Lonsdale's version of truth than Reagan's, I suppose, even if they are really the same. When Harrison's Lord observes that someone thinks they are all "useless people," it's difficult not to feel that the observation is right and the play is still wrong: such useful actors should be doing something better.   *GR(May 1985)*

Bill Irwin's Dumb Show

When one of the many judges in Bill Irwin's work-in-progress-silent-film-semimusical-comedy-tap-breakdance-mime-show, *The Courtroom,* asks an attorney to present his case with "clarity and precision," the lawyer juggles three white balls for two or three minutes as if bewitched by magical powers. With an apparent life of their own, the balls rise, fall, displace, lure, and repel each other—articulate dancers in what is finally the most inarticulate satire I have ever seen.

There is no reason to suspect that Irwin would want it any other way. His language is the body clothed in baggy pants, oversize checked jackets, funny hats, and, sometimes, gigantic, goggle-eyed, dark-rimmed glasses. If he has an enemy, it's not likely to be American law or any other social artifact. Peering around a door before entering a room, he seems to be looking only for the most visible form of imminent disaster. It might be the space itself, or a particularly eager vacuum cleaner pulling him through a hidden door, but in this case the greatest menace happens to be a courtroom. Because his theatre's only mission is to be insubstantial as a barely remembered dream, the courtroom—designed by Loren Sherman with the most accurate eye for absurd grandeur—is a crescent ring of seven shiny mahogany doors flanking a giant judge's bench much larger than the large witness box and other bloated courtroom clichés.

Irwin's querulous, wandering witness, looking like an overgrown child crossed by some mammoth chemist in the sky who couldn't separate the genetic vapors of Monsieur Hulot, Truman Capote, and the speechless dancers of *Le Bal,* finds all the provocative menace he needs. In a work that seems to be haunted by an undigested past, only Groucho is missing. Replacing him are zany lawyers marching in and out to the tune of a daffy drummer; judges who become corpi delicti as the lawyers knock them off and take their places; a court clerk playing an invisible piano while playing Edgar Bergen to a red-haired dummy; a tweedy stenographer reporting proceedings with Ann Miller taps; and a four-person jury that includes two rubber-faced puppets by the remarkable Julie Taymor.

When there are words instead of movement, dance, juggling, or antics, they still don't point to anything resembling a plot or an idea. One judge remarks that he thinks "it's just jurisprudent to tell you . . . ," but the thought fades out with the feebleness of the joke. Irwin may be protecting his intentions wisely when he has a judge suggest that a counselor should "rough it out" so that the jury will see his case as a "work-in-progress," but he isn't finally protected from the consequences of so many soft, elusive, and repetitive targets. He and his nine lyrically clownish colleagues make fifty minutes pass like forty-five not because they aren't fun to watch at their trickiest, but because they seem interested only in being fun for three or four minutes at a time. It's an exercise in brief attention spans, each of them anticipating more than the work wishes to deliver.

The best part of Irwin's creative world is its apparent simplicity, a naive conviction that arms, legs, and hats make talk look cheap. Good enough some of the time, but not good enough when it falls flat-footed into racial caricature: two lawyers are announced as coming from "a relatively new law firm," and they emerge as a break-dancing black man and his pot-bellied Stepin Fetchit partner, who later becomes a judge fully decked out in sunglasses, hand-held mike, and rock number. With so few words in the evening, that "relatively new law firm" sounds like trumpets and drums. Wordlessness, in the end, may not be next to godliness; like Irwin's suspiciously innocent mask, it may just be hiding an unspoken, but articulate, fear of the wrong menace. Irwin won't make a sustained and satisfying theatre work until he finds a true, indignant voice in his mind.   *GR(May 1985)*

Neil Simon for President

Looked at one way, Neil Simon's comedies offer the most provocative public experience currently available. With jokes clocking in every ninety seconds, rhythmically predictable and utterly void of inner logic or real humor, one is left in a delirium of pure thought, carried irresistibly into realms where anything seems plausible. For example, during the latest rerun of *The Odd Couple* (now about Florence and Olive instead of Felix and Oscar), I began planning the next Democratic presidential campaign.

The women on stage were playing Trivial Pursuit. In the 1965 version, Simon had the men playing poker, and it's just possible that the change of games had an even more momentous effect on his word processor than the change of genders. Can we infer that Big Men wouldn't be caught dead in the eighties playing Trivial Pursuit, or women playing poker? (You see how Simon gets you thinking, really thinking.) Anyway, the first joke, emerging with air-blown ease from the game, is about penguins. It seems that the answer to the penguin question is that they "do sex only once." Naturally, one of the women is astounded. After all, that's her role in life, first to be arranged by Simon, second to be astounded. "Once?" she cries, winces, or blurts. (My way of getting you ready for the laugh.) "I married a penguin."

Now: the important, horrible fact is that Simon hasn't really let us know her yet. Indeed, he's not about to let us know anyone. Certainly, the women's husbands—so the program reveals—will remain offstage phantoms or unheard voices during convenient phone calls. In a world where characters possess only one-liner histories, nothing could be funnier than a woman revealing her husband's impotence. Moments later, however, the oldest gameplayer turns up the question, "What's the oldest known vegetable in the world?" only to be told by the penguin's wife, "You are."

Retreating to myself, I thought: If Simon loves insults so much, why hasn't anyone thought of nominating him as the next Democratic presidential candidate? Even if he is really a Tory, surely he's more famous than Jimmy Carter was three years before running. His jokes, too, are in the automatic tradition set by the current Master of Ceremonies in the White House. Hollywood has had its chance. Why not Broadway? Think of the headline: The first Jewish presidential candidate! Or the subheading: A real man whose ass can't be kicked by George Bush! Best of all, like the emcee himself, Simon never tells the truth, only what the bridge-and-tunnel crowd wants to hear.

Bridge-and-tunnel crowd? Simon keeps pushing all the buttons that bring out the worst from everyone. Including me. Surrounded by an audience screaming with laughter when Florence, kicked out of her fourteen-year marriage, is suffering two minutes of the most unutterable psychic despair, I can think only of how much I loathe those suburban slummers. Simon, of course, has more acceptable targets: incompetent men (all of them), libidinous women (almost all), linguistically ignorant Spaniards, gays, and Miami vacationers. A perfectly democratic bigot, isn't he perfect presidential material? Laughing against their own interests, the crowd can be trusted to vote, as always, against themselves.

Not that they're practicing the willing suspension of disbelief, which would be fair enough. Instead, they are willfully believing in jokes—and therefore, realities—that simply couldn't be happening. People who know at one moment that Rembrandt was Dutch might surely be expected to have heard of El Greco in another. Furniture reupholstered in two weeks is no more credible than those rescue-the-plot telephones. And if one woman admits to mistaking a statue for a security guard at a museum (a uniformed statue?), is it really possible that another will do the same? Was Simon born in a test tube or a pilot show? Has he ever met a woman? Has he ever met himself?

His alleged competence would surely look better in Washington, where, as the Gravedigger in *Hamlet* might say, he won't be noticed because they are as mad as he. A pity, however, that Gene Saks, capable of uncovering detail in an eggshell, should allow his frequently inventive company to settle much of the time for glances at the audience rather than glimpses into each other. Only Sally Struthers's Florence emerges with original instincts intact, looking like a depressed Mae West whose dancing limbs have been ripped untimely from her central nervous system. A natural realist, she threatens to invest her scenes with the sorrow and kindness that Simon disdains.

If you hadn't already guessed, I want him in Washington for the most selfish reason: to rescue theatre criticism, if not the theatre, from the trivial pursuit of Neil Simon.   *GR(June 1985)*

Nathalie Sarraute: Fighting Words

"Vocables, so to speak, with their fingers to their mouths." That was how Mary McCarthy described the "peculiar world of Nathalie Sarraute" in 1969, calling her novels "auditory pantomime." It is plausible, then, to find theatre in Sarraute, even if her hushed obsession with language does not at first appear to be theatrical or dramatic. Sarraute's characters, living in shadows and mist, confront words more than each other, yet those words emerge from some of the most titanic conflicts of all—defining the self when life is continually *telling* you to be like everybody else. Words are signs and weapons for Sarraute, but they are also traps—inherently dramatic, in fact, because traps are set by the self and others.

Bringing Sarraute to the stage, however, Simone Benmussa has set traps of another kind for herself. By presenting her adaptation of Sarraute's memoir, *Childhood,* with a forty-five-minute curtain raiser, *For No Good Reason,* a radio play by Sarraute, she offers a dangerous contrast between Sarraute as conscious dramatist and Sarraute as interior monologist. Naturally, the more conventional dramatist wins the conventional battle.

For No Good Reason may have been written for voices alone, but Benmussa's staging gives it a riveting, almost touchable profile. In a gray and black world, a padded cell with light dimly streaming through a skeleton window frame, two gray-suited gentlemen are first seen with their backs to one another. They pause, talk, pause again—a familiar, Pinteresque illusion, perhaps, but not fraught and menacing; rather, a place where separations are the only known vocabulary, separations primordially filled with bleak suspicion.

Coming from the same class, they are supposed to be best friends, yet their words finally disclose nothing but distance. One, played by Max Wright on the edge of terminal splutter, the seams of his face threatening to explode over verbal indiscretions, has been arrested for "being the kind of person who breaks with people for no good reason." What is enacted, then, are the very good reasons why Wright will break with Stephen Keep's tensile, apprehensive, quietly loathing friend. Wright is too transient, insubstantial for Keep, who in turn makes Wright feel claustrophobic and inert. Sarraute's intelligence is icy here, almost unforgiving to both characters. Even so, it covers the stage with warming detail, an almost supernatural respect for precious moments, a loving grasp of interior experience that comes alive with special intensity in theatrical space. In short, a play—and a good one at that.

Childhood, on the other hand, is a reduction of Sarraute's remarkable evocation of the years before 1914 when she was shifted from Russia to France by her divorced parents. Adaptations are always asking for trouble, but particularly here: Sarraute's return to her past is a brilliant reminder that memory is itself vulnerable, that what can be recaptured are fragments only, themselves glimpsed through accumulations of language and consequent sophistication. Benmussa was probably tempted by Sarraute's intermittent and deliberate dialogue with herself, brief passages woven into the memoir where the old woman questions the child's memory. Thus, on stage, Glenn Close—woman and child in one—frequently converses with the taped voice of vintage Sarraute, an aromatic voice crowded with experience, ready if not eager to be resigned.

These exchanges suggest a courageous form of adaptation that Benmussa evidently doesn't trust. Most of the time she moves panels and reveals tableaux in which Mother, Father, and Father's second wife appear. Sarraute, however, had carefully withheld specific images of characters, preferring instead to remind herself (and the reader) that corporeal re-creations are probably a lie. Another fatal trap, then, for Benmussa. Where the book trusts imagination, the theatre version insists upon illustration; in effect, it denies the floating, uncertain realities that give the book its atmosphere and substance. Inevitably, Benmussa must be selective, and, inevitably, she omits some of the most vivid and dramatic episodes—the step-grandmother who gives the child so much uncritical attention, or the wonderful moment when she tells her stepmother that an uncle has called her "stupid."

Glenn Close is a daring actress, at her best when poised for what seems like flight. She, too, sadly, is another Benmussa trap. In body and person, she is as far from the time, places, and spirit of the book as she could possibly be. Sarraute as a child is cobblestones shining in the rain, nettles in the garden, or cream at the top of milk bottles; as a writer she is silver-green olive trees, gray stone houses, samovars and plum pudding, the onion in a crisp dry martini. Close, however, is irretrievably in an American present, an America nourished by eagerness, good will, and money. Wheat fields just before harvest, ski slopes, cherry blossoms, and champagne in Venetian crystal, she is the embodiment of what is admirable and wrong about the entire production—a good heart doing a misguided job of what doesn't have to be done.

GR(June 1985)

Lillian Hellman's Bad Trouble

Famous for pride and bullish indignation, Lillian Hellman was an expert entertainer who seemed, in fact, to know her limitations: she could get the plot right, give her characters marching orders into preordained corners, and occasionally pitch one against another into a scene bristling with cruelty and righteousness. If she revealed anything fundamental about herself, it was by way of slavish attachment to the melodramatic well-made play, the one genre calculated to crush the natural will of protagonists and antagonists alike. A Hellman play—any Hellman play, even the elegiac, pseudo-Chekhovian *The Autumn Garden*—is like a visit to an imaginary, dramaturgical prison in which the inmates are controlled by an exceptionally crafty warden.

A visit to *Lillian*, alas, is not much different, even though memory plays and monologues are free to ramble. William Luce's play is Hellman's conversation with herself, a monologue standing in for the truly personal drama she never wrote. It would take a special kind of useless homework to mark the differences, if any, between Luce's Hellman and Hellman's Hellman, but as one of them conveniently lets her say, this monologue is "all out of order here, as most memories are." *Lillian*, however, never relinquishes tightfisted control: like its sources, *An Unfinished Woman*, *Pentimento*, and *Scoundrel Time*, this enactment has a highly selective memory, telling us always just as much as she wants us to know—or rather, just as little.

Mostly there is Lillian the cutesy little Southern daughter of a lordly Papa and ditsy Mama, a Hollywoodian white pickaninny under the influence of benign Negro-retainer folk wisdom ("So shut the shit, Lillie," says Sophronia Mason, her wet nurse and "first love of my life," always warning her about being "bad trouble"). Then there is the querulous, quasi-religious Lillian. Brought in for heroism—but only for an instant in the first act and for a climax to the second—is political Lillian, the defiant lady who stood up to the House Un-American Affairs Committee without taking the Fifth Amendment. Major other Lillians, such as heroic Lillian defending her honor against Mary McCarthy's accusation that even her "and" and "the" were lies, or political Lillian who thought the Moscow trials were just, rate either nonappearance or one passing line. Drinking Lillian is heard about repeatedly, but never seen. Jewish Lillian is almost entirely avoided here, as in life. And angry Lillian, the one we all heard about for years, has to be taken on faith.

Occasional, forgivable insults notwithstanding ("Norma Shearer, her face unclouded by thoughts"), *Lillian* is finally a portrait of tasteful Lillian, the woman who called herself unfinished while trying to present a finishing-school version of brave little Lillian in love with an even braver Dashiell Hammett. I have a dreadful premonition that the public and its surrogate-sentimentalists, the daily reviewers, will be buying and selling this brazen advertisement for herself as some kind of hard-edged but charming love story—a New York subintelligentsia Antony and Cleopatra boozing while America burns.

This is, after all, a quintessential New York occasion: the celebration of a theatrical and public life, possibly not worth knowing, as if it were some kind of golden avenue to a promising land. Good old Lillian—tough but vulnerable (she cries when Hammett dies!), hurt but gallant (she has to sell her farm one month before testifying to HUAC!), and blunt but feminine (not knowing what to do with herself before the hearing, she goes shopping for a Balmain!). Privileged victimhood has never known a more sophisticated, self-absorbed, or insensitive mouthpiece.

Nor has there been in recent years a more quintessentially self-conscious display of Acting (!) than Zoe Caldwell's impersonation of Hellman. When she isn't sharing digs and barbs by casting sly, knowing smiles at the audience, she is pausing . . . and pausing . . . for pregnant effect. Unwittingly, Caldwell seems to confirm McCarthy's charges by making every "the" or "I" into a stretched vowel ("theee" or "I-eee"), thus preparing phrase after phrase as if it might contain truths easily missed or cleverly hidden. Meanwhile, she seems to be Lillian—and actressy—proud of that gorgon's nose and iced, rat's nest coiffure, to say nothing of the way she and her director, Robert Whitehead, keep playing *moderato cantabile* on those Lillian cigarettes and her smoker's wheeze. When the light from Hammett's hospital room floods the stage and Lillian jumps to the door, Caldwell's hand grasps the edge and pulls her back on stage as if Lillian had suddenly been captured by an irrepressible desire to play Phèdre. Holding her left arm on top of her right hand, or playing her Papa, Sophronia, and, of course, Tallulah, all in Tallulah's blah-blah British baritone tempered by Southern drawl, she always sounds closer to Land's End than Martha's Vineyard. Like so many British-trained actors, she thinks all Americans have a nasal twang, or that we pronounce nine*t*een as a soft nine*d*een. Never concealed for a moment is her extravagant pleasure in herself: Look everybody, I'm so Brilliant, so Technical! But it's a form of glossiness and technique that can't disguise the absence of reality.

Like Hellman, of course. Which is no excuse for Caldwell. Quintessential, yes, but not essential for anyone but the half-baked writer and the over-cooked actor. *Lillian,* finally, looks, feels, and sounds not like the writer honorably furious with herself, but like the story of an undeveloped woman caught by her own design in an unmade play.   *GR(January 1986)*

Lost Shepard

Sam Shepard's America certainly exists out there—troubled, stupid, vainglorious, battered like Jake's wife, Beth, in *A Lie of the Mind*—but it doesn't fit neatly into his improvisational, hallucinatory scenes, which always seem to be in desperate search for a play. That desperation, fortunately, is always acknowledged as part of the process. Shepard may not have conquered drama so much as he has conquered drama's inhibitions about what it might dare: a fearless national treasure, he has become a playwright willing to be big, epic, demanding, and ironic without ever quite knowing how to contain his visions and desires in the recalcitrant limits of theatre. *A Lie of the Mind* keeps reaching for Homeric passions, yet the imagery, finally, retreats into what this century knows best—seductive, technicolored simplicities masquerading as ideas.

The play is loaded with divisions and symmetries colliding with one another at almost every turn. Two American families are linked by the marriage of Jake and Beth. As the play begins, Jake is telling his brother, Frankie, that he has murdered Beth in a jealous rage, imagining that her amateur acting partner has become her lover. Beth, too, has a brother, Mike, comforting her in the hospital where she is coping with the damages to mind and body inflicted by Jake's failed onslaught. Both families, naturally, have fathers and mothers: Beth and Mike's are Baylor and Meg, living four miles from the nearest grocery in Montana; Jake and Frankie's father is dead, but their mother, Lorraine, is very much alive, ignoring both Frankie and her daughter, Sally, in favor of consuming attention to Jake, the hapless image of the unheroic alcoholic Air Force husband who long ago abandoned her.

Each family is also linked by failures of memory: in a deliberate exaggeration of reality, neither can quite remember the names or faces of the other; by forgetting what they don't wish to know, they can obliterate their own histories. For the greater part of four hours, Jake's family lives on one side of the stage while Beth's lives on the other. Shepard seems to be abandoning center stage, as if he were any one of his characters abandoning civility, sanity, and each other.

Seen as an arbitrarily patterned map of America, the play is consistently enthralling and explosively funny, even as it keeps running into detours and dead ends. Like a gigantic Georgia O'Keeffe canvas—skulls in the desert—invaded by a Duane Michals narrative, it can't seem to decide whether it wants to be painterly vision or documentary photograph. At its best, the dialogue erupts into bitterly reflective humor. When Lorraine, for example, hears Jake say that the leather box containing his father's ashes is heavy, she immediately speaks the unspeakable—that "he's a lot lighter than he was." At its worst, however, the words seem to be branded onto the characters: Jake referring to the fear that "swarms through me," Lorraine not hearing "no revelations," Baylor (the monolithic hick, Mr. Dumb America) talking about "the boys back there with diplomas tall as a man," or Meg reflecting philosophically that "the male one—doesn't really need the other." Meg was better and more accurately seen when Baylor, once again quietly astounded by her detachment, commented that "there's got to be a borderline between polite and stupid." But even Baylor's subliminal wit can't quite persuade, since it seems so detached from how he talks and thinks before and after.

That the production is so alive, peculiarly quick (in spite of its length), and continuously suggestive is a tribute more to Shepard the director than Shepard the writer. His characters' profiles scarcely differ from one another and almost never depart into development. Caught more in metaphor than in Henry James's fact, they rarely escape from playwriting control. Most of the actors, however, find color, light, shade, and bewitching physical realities, giving the production a drive and form that too often eludes the writing. Geraldine Page's Lorraine may be too shrewd for her story, but her puffed-wheat face and wind-blown slobbishness finally seem like design and order, only because Page is so rooted in the moment. Like Page, Harvey Keitel's Jake is always there, even when he has become a protagonist who has lost his play: his brief monologues when he is suddenly expected to be wise and contemplative could be slow dissolves into Shepard murk; Keitel, however, manages to set them apart from character without giving them more weight than they can bear.

Karen Young's Sally discreetly pulls away from the temptation to be intense before her time, so that when she finally tells the story of her father's death, in the play's best, most coherent scene, she has at last found her voice. (Page's capacity to let her character change is splendid here: drawing Young to her, she seems to dabble in her daughter's hair, almost as if recovering an infant once known and loved.) Will Patton moves from infinite gentleness to dancerly hysteria with remarkable presence and precision, even though the character as a voiced, envisioned person hardly exists. Much the same can be said for Aidan Quinn's Frankie, trapped by Beth's lunatic family in a frozen landscape almost as much as he has been locked by Shepard into the role of passive, helpless observer. James Gammon's Baylor is the most amusing cartoon, laconic, specific, unremittingly literal, and ghastly: Gammon, alone among the actors, chooses an American drone, chanting his phrases in a blatant, dark wheeze that sets him apart. Ann Wedgeworth's Meg could easily be the mother of Amanda Plummer's Beth, sharing her daughter's inexplicable descents into twitchery, but she rescues the part by listening well. Plummer, however, can't resist the self-conscious invention of muddling subtexts: if she picks up her father's plaid shirt, it has to become a momentary infant in her arms, though there isn't the slightest suggestion in the text that this wounded woman wants or needs to be a mother.

Plummer, in fact, is one sign of Shepard's failure to define and select the story or stories he might possibly tell. As a director, he lets a man complaining of cold feet walk casually and barefoot into the snow. As a writer, he can't decide if he wants to tell a tale about people or a parable about the nation; similarly, he wants language to be both plain and symbolic, or he wants to be bitter about American dreams while pushing the last moments into improbable tinkle-tune embraces around the flag. His characters, brutishly working-class with plenty of time to travel and talk, have no visible sources of income. Does he know America or does he only know its myths and movies? Even as he embraces a larger sense of theatrical possibility than almost any other American dramatist, one wishes that he might soon discover how to shape, omit, and choose—or, as Beth might say from her blasted intelligence, that he might become "more better."   *GR(December 1985)*

Crying Steppenwolf

With all the clutter onstage in John Malkovich's production of Harold Pinter's *The Caretaker,* it would be reasonable to assume that space might be cleared for Pinter. Malkovich is obviously a great multiplier: give him a stage direction calling for a "mound" of oddball items that might be collected by Aston and his brother Mick, and Malkovich can't resist additions meant, no doubt, to improve on Pinter's imagery. "A few short planks of wood" become six or seven long slices of timber artfully crisscrossed against a gigantic back wall.

(To be fair, any cramped room would have to look like a palazzo on that impossibly elongated oval called the Circle in the Square.) Pinter calls for the clutter, certainly, but he's suggesting insufferable claustrophobia, not the crowded, vaulting precincts of Kane's Xanadu.

Malkovich can't stand unadorned significance. Mick's sudden destruction of Aston's precious Buddha is an act on its own, the one that will really hurt: Malkovich, always blurring details, sends Mick flying around the room, breaking up everything. His freewheeling directorial approach with Chicago's Steppenwolf company—body thrusts and raucous slambangery—may be popular these days with television-dried brains impatient for the next explosion, but it's no substitute for the eerie intelligence behind Pinter's gorgeously austere mystery play.

From the first moments, it's suffocatingly clear that Malkovich is headed for disaster. Not only because he's locked into a proscenium staging within that resistant oval (good enough for the small part of the audience viewing the stage head-on), but mainly because his actors can't make a move or sound that isn't riddled with falsehood. Where Pinter describes the opening moments with Mick (Gary Sinise) looking slowly "about the room at each object in turn," finally sitting "quite still, expressionless, looking out front," Malkovich lets Sinise glare at the space with glinting eyes flinging daggers at the audience.

When Davies (Alan Wilder) comes in with Aston (Jeff Perry), he's shuffling rather than walking, a dead-giveaway sign that Wilder is a young actor desperately trying to look old. Tossing wise-guy glances at Aston, stumbling on words, his head bedecked in a white fright wig, he's unable to hide the news that he'd rather be playing Dracula. Perry's Aston is only moderately better, possessing a completely abstracted repose, intriguing to watch at first. Finally, however, he melts into his own drab, uninflected phrasings. Malkovich isn't directing Pinter, he's finger painting all over the place; despite his supercharged fussiness, the play emerges stenciled, undimensional, gray.

Pinter had intended originally to end with Davies's violent death. He discovered, however, that the violence he had relied upon in earlier plays could at last be "largely eliminated in a physical sense." No longer did he need "cabaret turns and blackouts and screams in the dark." Malkovich, unfortunately, can't resist cheap laughs and even shocks in the dark. If he has any commitment at all, it is to outbursts and physical threats—all derived from Pinter's situations, but meaningless without the interior flow that has carried them to climax. Pinter composes, constructs, restrains, and withholds; Malkovich and his actors lurch from one moment to the next. In between lurches, they stretch those famous Pinter pauses, but never fill them: for all the surface energy, the production groans to a thousand halts, finally clocking in at a few minutes under three hours.

Peter Hall—the most experienced Pinter director (though Donald McWhinnie was the man behind the great 1961 production in New York featuring Donald Pleasance's Davies, Robert Shaw's Aston, and Alan Bates's Mick)—cites Magritte's "hard-edged, very elegant, very precise style" as the visual equivalent of Pinter's manner. He suggests that "you have to construct the mask of the character . . . though it's no good having a mask unless you know what's underneath it." Forget underneath: Malkovich's actors aren't even in raspy shouting distance. Instead, they are more eyes than mask, staring, gazing, and flashing pupils from one side to another, never suggesting an idea or feeling about life before the play's events or outside the room. Coming from a dim-witted notion that all plays can be subjected to the same physical anarchy or—sadly—the same limited techniques, they act like every high school kid trying to play Everyboy in every play.

This is what journalistic puffery has enshrined as a Chicago style—one Chicagoan calls it "broad-shouldered"; Sinise sees it more accurately as "ass-kicking . . . somewhere between gutsball realism and wide-open sarcasm." In the past, they "didn't understand Stoppard," he says, "but knew he was funny."

Now it's Pinter's unlucky turn. As Peter Hall warns, "Pinter's audiences get off the hook and laugh at people as objects if you don't control them." Malkovich and company, smugly satisfied with their pseudostyle, mistake sinister lunges for mystery. Some in their audience seem to agree, responding to what they're given as if it were an off-the-wall sitcom about those wonderful zanies, the poor and the dispossessed. In the end, the most ass-kicked object may be Pinter, but the most broad-shouldered and demeaning assault is on the actor's responsible, analytical, complex art.   *GR(February 1986)*

Peter Sellars: Auteur Hauteur

The life of conceptual directors can't be easy: every day a new and merciless pressure to invent, program notes that must be written to justify those inventions, performers rebelling against disbelief ("To be or not to be" in a mound of quicksand?), and finally, the stubborn resistance of those who insist that Shakespeare, Bizet, Chekhov, or Handel may not really need a rescuing conceptualist to enliven their allegedly inert plays and operas. The rewards are real enough—fame, jobs, foundation grants, and the solacing sound of "genius." If self-doubt intrudes, they can always point reassuringly to innovative productions, from Meyerhold to Brook, where the light cast upon a play was usually stronger than the shadows that occasionally obscured a moment or two. Perhaps, like Orson Welles, they might bring their dazzling "auteurism" to the movies rather than theatre, yet it can't have escaped them that Welles remains a dangerous model in every respect—not least, that he's mostly out of work.

To be fair, most conceptualists appear to love the works they plunder for new ideas. Peter Sellars, in what may well be the most elaborate instructional program notes ever written by a director, tells the audience for Handel's *Giulio Cesare* that they are about to attend "a remarkable evening of opera, just over four hours of gradually deepening comedy, romance, and intrigue." Comparing the work to Wagner, calling it a "masterpiece," adding that Handel "was one of the greatest theatre composers who ever lived," Sellars would seem to be backing away from any impulse to fit the opera into a modernist scheme. He even says, "I myself detest updating," following this, however, with the cautionary phrase, "as a rule." Meaning that *Giulio Cesare* would be updated after all—"cheap and gimmicky" though it may seem to be. His hope, however, is that the updating to today's Middle East, with Caesar holding presidential press conferences and Cleopatra playing with rubber toys by the swimming pool, will be seen only "as a base camp in preparation for the ascent to far, far higher terrain."

Base camp? Is Sellars a secret ironist, pulling all legs—his, Handel's, our—or did he just slip subliminally into that revealing phrase? His *Giulio Cesare* is never irretrievably base, but it is certainly camp. Sellars leaves not an aria or moment unturned, evidently convinced that committed listeners went out with the dinosaurs. Surely this is the fussiest, most restless production in history. Guns, plastic glasses, toys, chairs, rubber snakes, a hand mirror, a lipstick litter the stage throughout as if Handel had been writing a metaphorical treatise on dropped objects. When violins play repetitiously with a note, Ptolemy taps his head with each staccato repetition. Cleopatra apparently saw Chaplin's *The Great Dictator,* because she can't resist imitating his dance with a balloon globe. Equally, Caesar can't resist a photo opportunity at almost every entrance. When Cleopatra's lady-in-waiting silently mouths the words of her mistress behind Cleopatra's back, one leaps inevitably to the conclusion that (a) she doesn't like her, or (b) she's heard all this before, which suggests that (c) Cleopatra is a routine fool, making one wonder (d) why Handel bothered to write such stunning music for her. Add to this two non-singing Dobermans, unaccountably omitted by Handel, His and Her robes for Caesar and Cleopatra at the end, and it's possible to doubt that Sellars would ever reach that higher terrain from his prodigiously decorative base camp.

Yet, amazingly, he does, if only intermittently and briefly. Handel threatens boredom only if director and singers doubt the inner movement of the formal *aria da capo,* so Sellars keeps pushing them along with all those breathless cartoons, no more convincing or musical than most of what passed for interpretation in Disney's *Fantasia*. But when faced with a real relationship— Cornelia grieving over Pompey's death with her vengeful son, Sesto—Sellars suddenly finds himself at liberty to respond nonliterally, yet tenderly and logically, to the undulating ecstasy of the music. In one of the most exquisitely realized scenes I have ever known in lyric theatre, he directs the heavyweight mezzo-soprano Mary Westbrook-Geha (Cornelia) to perform an unselfconscious, supple, and delicate body-and-hand duet with soprano Lorraine Hunt's Sesto, herself momentarily stepping away from the obsessive passions that consume her in most of the work. Bending, shaping the air with their palms, barely touching one another, they sing quietly and possessed, alive in a realm reached only through music, enthralled by theatrical time and possibility.

Clearly, Sellars can do it—by which I mean he can respond to the life, rhythms, and formal tensions invented by the composer or playwright. That he perversely places Cleopatra's most beautiful and gentle arias in almost utter darkness is an admission that his decisions are often more "political" than "directorial." Sellars doesn't like modern leaders, and who can blame him? It doesn't follow, however, that Handel can be maneuvered convincingly into the same disdain. Relentlessly literal about actions, Sellars illustrates every thought with a picture-book gesture. Yet we are expected to ignore the fact that the Italian word for sword is always illustrated by a gun. Cleopatra croons over Caesar's eyes, but again, neither she nor we can see them. Sellars keeps betraying not only Handel, but himself. "The essence of the Baroque," says one Handel specialist (Christopher Hogwood), "is to stretch the forms but not break them." Sellars is good at soliciting the best possible stretch from his performers. Irresistibly drawn to mischief, however, he can't stop breaking Handel's back.

*   *   *

Breaking Bach turns out to be not very different. In Sellars's second event at Purchase, he linked Brecht and Weill's brief 1927 songspiel, *The Little Mahagonny,* to excerpts from five Bach cantatas and *The Christmas Oratorio,* calling them *Conversations with Fear and Hope after Death.* In still another program note, this time provided by Sellars's musical collaborator, Craig Smith, the provocative doubling is explained as an effort to resolve the "murder and judgment found in the *Mahagonny Songspiel*" with "some kind of redemption."

But it is really some kind of superfluous mischief once again. Sellars's version of Brecht-Weill is plain, direct, undecorated, and consequently begging for more Brecht, not Bach. For once, he seems on home ground: since *Mahagonny* is more theatrical space than literal place, his cavernous opening of the entire stage so that giant shadows of the singers can be cast upon the brick walls is all that is necessary to reflect the epic desolation of the words and music. He too often repeats effects, disclosing a limited gestural vocabulary, but when the gestures spring from situation—as they do in the *Alabama Song* when two women simply stare at the glass each holds outstretched—they reveal a trust in the event, a true yielding to musical line and suggestion.

The Bach looks similar and is therefore no kind of redemption at all; since it has no organic need for narrative or staging, it doesn't even redeem itself. For the most part, these evenings show Sellars as an urgently creative author of scenarios working in a medium that can offer only partial relief to his exploding imagination. When Bach supports an idea that emerges finally as a glacial, High Art music video, something has gone radically wrong. Sellars is failing to imagine that Bach—and Handel—are self-contained in their own forms, no more in need of his less-than-divine interventions than we are.

GR(August 1985)

John Guare: Bananas Republic

In John Guare's *The House of Blue Leaves,* Artie is a failure, his wife may be schizophrenic, his son wants to kill the pope, his best friend steals his mistress, and four characters die, one of them murdered before our eyes. Naturally, this is a comedy, since Guare knows that nothing is funnier than the clash between American dreams and the American ways of death. Presented first in 1971, the play's reappearance is a useful reminder that an extravagant comic imagination can indeed keep up with the headlines. The only event likely to be funnier than Guare's twists, turns, and explosions would be the Marcoses and Duvaliers forced to eat dinner every night with Idi Amin on a St. Helena's in the Pacific, near where the French are testing the bomb.

There is something breathtakingly tonic about a play that almost never lets family and community values have a respectable moment. Guare lapses only once in the course of a brilliantly conceived series of unlikely—therefore likely—episodes: when Artie's wife, Bananas, addressing the audience, tells about her effort to stuff Cardinal Spellman, Bob Hope, Jackie Kennedy, and President Johnson into her gypsy cab, she finishes mournfully with a question that momentarily dislodges the play from its deliriously unsentimental moorings—"Why," she asks, "can't they love me?" Guare has to know that his theatrical vocabulary can't accommodate the voicing of conventional solutions: what he is continually unearthing is the thought normally left unspoken, the horrible decision made when hypocrisy no longer works. *Blue*

Leaves is not about the failure of love, it's about the failure of wisdom and the absence of conscience.

Like the best comedies, then, it is a play in touch with darkest intelligence, unsparing in its fundamental concern with public lunacy. Bananas may have retreated into certifiable madness, but it's clear by the end that she's the only sane person in that Sunnyside, Queens, apartment. Artie has fallen for Bunny, an ambitious blabbermouth with starfuck in her eyes, who wants him to clap Bananas into shock treatment so that she can marry him. Pressing him to call his old pal, Billy Einhorn, now a Hollywood producer whose work—as a fugitive nun says later—means "quality," she is a Greek chorus gone haywire, leading a pack of characters all driven by the mindless ideas in their hysterical heads. Artie's son, Ronnie, wants to blow up Pope Paul VI in Yankee Stadium, visiting nuns want to see the pope in person, Billy's starlet girlfriend, Corrinna, wants to get her hearing back in Australia, and Artie wants Billy to make a musical out of his rotten songs. (Only Bananas recognizes one song as a direct steal from *White Christmas*.)

Oddly, the play is delicate, not always clear about its own brutal consciousness, or rather, clear about its brutally American world, but less clear about what it feels. Artie and Bunny's cruelties to Bananas could easily call for a bomb dropped on all their shabby dreams. Guare doesn't make it easy: even as he kills off some of his characters with remarkably little effect on anybody remaining, he seems to be suggesting with the most Cheshire leer that most of them are better off dead anyway, especially because they're killers at heart. Keeping those thoughts and images alive while letting the whacky details careen into place must be a director's nightmare, but Jerry Zaks is not only a master of bang-on comic accumulation, he's also a vigilant guardian of actors' freedom—meaning he gives them a chance to fill in the spaces, play their reveries, act out plainly and with dignity their absurd, terrifying obsessions.

Perhaps the production could be less splendid, and less realistic: that panoramic Queens behind the apartment suggests a musical called *Sunnyside-Up*, while the kitchen-living room suggests an Odets scream-up. But the actors are buoyantly superb, even Stockard Channing as Bunny, always on the edge of impersonation or a weird detachment from the others. John Mahoney's Artie, with his failure to ingratiate and his shit-eating grin while singing, has a vacant charm which never disguises his pain. Julie Hagerty is a lanky dreamscape as Corrinna, good will and desperation sprinkling from her creamy surfaces. Ben Stiller's Ronnie, left eye twitching, his body pummeling the air like his own choreographed explosive, is an impressive presence at the play's epicenter.

Best of all, however, in the most completely realized comic performance I've seen in years, is Swoozie Kurtz as Bananas. Like a stray gazelle, legs splayed, eyes gazing on memories of a sweetness that never was, she strolls in and out of these proceedings as if she ought to belong. The brutal fact is that the trance she is in can't save her. When she tells Artie and Bunny how lucky

they are—they're going to California, she to "the loony bin"—one wants to
tell her to go as fast as she can. Bananas is inhabiting a wonderfully private
world that can't, finally, offer protection: only a wonderfully public, open,
uniquely centered actor could make such a clear distinction between lucid nut-
tiness and the other kind. She may not be able to save herself from Guare's
cold-bloodedly accurate plot, but she stands there nevertheless as the emblem
of his cool departures into realms reserved for the best and the lightest.

GR(April 1986)

Chekhov with Wings

If acting is the art of confounding expectations, then Vanessa Redgrave is indisputably the best of the best. Those who know her on big and little screens
know only a fraction of her power. In movies, her giraffe serenity propels her
from one jump cut to another as if the camera were actually following a continuous life. Like Garbo, her face wants only to be viewed. It doesn't really
care who's watching, though this is merely the lucky side of her remarkable
talent: the camera is there in the same way as momentary experience approaches her for answers, metal to her magnet. On screen, then, she is always a reckoning, furiously quiet presence.

On stage, however, she is more. As Mme. Arkadina in a London production of Chekhov's *The Seagull*, Redgrave shows how the stage can solicit from
an actor a palpable, disruptive presence unavailable to the camera. Where
film maneuvers relationships, quite literally calling the shots, the stage is
finally a more neutral instrument, despite the dramatist's selective scenewriting.
In *The Seagull*, Redgrave isn't patched into life, she is there with all her history
and even her future stretched like the most detailed mural across the widest
possible wall.

Hers is the only Arkadina I have ever seen who clearly had a husband,
the father of her subdued, sweaty, unformed son, Konstantin. Like so many
of the people surrounding her, that husband clearly didn't share her energy,
nor could he ever know whether she would be seducing him one moment with
laughter and deliriously sensual movement, or if she would be punishing him
with a sigh or a slap. In her middle forties, she is less a mother, sister, land-
owner, and lover than she is a practicing, dazzling actress. No wonder Kon-

stantin's feeble little abstract play, starring the haplessly naive Nina, is such a dud for Arkadina: the plays she performs that bring her fabulous receptions in towns like Kharkhov are about people as substantial, overdressed, and electrically charged as she is. Later, when changing Kostya's bandage after his suicide attempt, she can't help falling into a fit of laughter at the turban round his head. Pushing him down, poking him in his face, she tells him firmly, "I do not act in bad plays." It isn't that she doesn't love him, it's just that she likes life—her life—so much more.

Redgrave sparks an intelligent production by Charles Sturridge that unearths all those little brutalities that people do to one another, most of them overlooked in productions enthralled by languid entrances and wandering moods. She's tight about money, so of course she pinches Trigorin's cigarettes. When Masha is feeling sorry for herself for the ninety-ninth time, Redgrave's Arkadina stops listening, studying her own boots. Suddenly, she makes Masha stand up, tosses a pillow at her, asking the others, "Who looks younger?" A moment later, after beginning to put up Masha's hair, she quickly sweeps away in a whirl of ballerina poses, declaring that this is how she keeps young. Attempting to get horses from Masha's father, Shamraev, she drops to her knees; when that doesn't work, she jumps up, slamming him in the face. Later, having conquered Trigorin once again, she is pleased enough with herself so that she can kiss Shamraev, reserving still another impulsive slap for the servant-girl who is desperately trying to help her put on her coat. Murmuring about how her conscience bothered her when Kostya abandoned his play after her derisive remarks, she turns on her chair, bellowing "Kostya" in a voice undoubtedly reserved for great, madly passionate, vulgar stage scenes. Trigorin, of course, doesn't stand a chance: when she wants him to come with her, leaving Nina behind, she simply chases him around the table, tackling him on the fifty-yard line of the door. As he says, he doesn't have a will of his own. The scene miraculously offers a glimpse of them as they might be in bed together, facing each other on their knees, Arkadina locking him in her grip, his arms unable to withhold a submissive embrace. Chekhov has been saved from melancholic slop: if Trigorin doesn't stand a chance, neither does Nina, Kostya, or anybody else.

In the last act, she is older, her face more rouged, hair up in a Lautrec knob, wrapped in a fur rug that she relinquishes eventually to her brother in his wheelchair, an act of gentle kindness amid the mercurial cruelties seen countless times before. Redgrave is the first among several actors who give performances that defy convention. Jonathan Pryce's shaggy, bewildered Trigorin gets an idea for a line by watching Nina spoon some jam. Peter Wight's Medvedenko is cracking nuts while declaring that nobody would want to marry a man who can barely afford to feed himself. Natasha Richardson (Redgrave's daughter, almost as sublimely pensive and alive) plays Nina as an actress-bird out of air and water: she, too, can be hard, wanting "earsplitting fame" which she uncharacteristically shouts to the trees.

By the time Konstantin actually succeeds in shooting himself, it is possible to imagine precisely how Arkadina will react when they finally tell her. She will howl like Lear, pummel Trigorin's stomach, hug Shamraev to her bosom, distract herself by braiding Masha's hair or drinking vodka with an upraised little finger, living and acting until the ultimate brute force finally knocks her senseless.   *GR(October 1985)*

Manifest Fo

Dario Fo is ideally suited to make comedy out of hungry people consuming their gluteus maximus, testicles, and intestines, since his own insides and limbs are made of rubber springs, exploding balloons, and pogo sticks. Even if he wanted to be sacred about priests and presidents, his body wouldn't let him: the words would always be subverted by the independent drift of an arm hanging itself over his forehead like an apostrophe gone haywire. Coming to us as a clown who drives church and state into periodic spasms of revenge, Fo is, if anything, even more of a threat to comedians laboring under the heavy weight of stolid bodies and empty heads.

Like all great comics, his humor disgorges itself from dark wellsprings of pity and terror. Fo seems to have seen it all—hypocrisies, lies, grotesque injustice, the pompous, dispassionate greed of those who live only for the ceremony of their self-proclaimed innocence. Letting his plays leap out of headlines, he never releases them from history. The past is his serious playground, a place where he can uncover homely truths and divine confirmations of his current suspicions. As a writer, he stands unsquarely in a mixed tradition of overflowing Elizabethans such as Ben Jonson and the more furious conceits of Molière. Eclectic, at war with God and at peace with himself, he is, in a word, Italian.

Or rather, a modern Italian. "Poor Italy," one hears over there all the time, while everybody continues to eat, drink, and laugh. The laughter, especially, is about themselves as victims who still know how to outsmart the victimizers. Their great protector is doubt, their great secret is play. Unlike Americans, they are excitable, but never hysterical. Wise enough to be cautious about each other—after all, they're playing the same game—they are smart enough to be afraid of us. In practical terms, this means that daily life is simply a matter of momentary survival: mistrust of the powerful is the only way to enjoy real power.

Which is what Fo enjoys in the theatre. Alone on stage in *Mistero Buffo*—or almost alone, since here he shares the stage much of the time with his fluently genial interpreter, Ron Jenkins—Fo chats *buffo*-style about Italians, banks, capitalism, America, doges who don't believe there are so many hungry people in Venice since it must only be a matter of telling them where to find the garbage cans (but we can laugh, he says, about this, because it was so far back in the fifteenth century), French nobles trapped in miles of lace, which was a disaster when they wanted to pee (the origin of aristocratic walks and court dances), stories of women whose heavy breathing and butterfly eyelashes were "provocations" for rape, the present pope's insatiable passion for kissing ten babies a day while fielding them to basketball players disguised as priests, and a television announcer who got fired for reporting that the pope's sphincter was shot. In one of those flights of verbal wizardry that would be clear in any language, Fo declares that you can't say the pope has a sphincter, you must refer instead to his "sacred conduit."

When Jenkins leaves the stage, Fo moves from these stand-up routines into the "mistero" part of his performance—unholy monologues evidently derived from the hand-me-down literature of the *giullari,* comic tales and virtuosic performances in which he throws body and outrageous soul into a series of gorgeous impersonations. His language, translated on a screen above him, is *grammelot,* an invented gibberish capturing in one scene the guttural grandeur of peasant Italian, in another the haughty adenoids of the French, and finally, the stiff upper-glottal shocks of the British at their snobbish worst. Nobody is safe from his slashing maximalism: like an expert cartoonist, making one sharp line or curve stand for a thousand sins, Fo dips and sweeps about the stage, collapsing into his gut, spreading his mouth into his chin, turning his eyes into glowworms, his red socks and moccasins into flashing tentacles, and his voice into whatever it must suddenly embody, not least the bubbling grotto of that famished stomach. Fo may be sixty, but he puts to shame our youth-centered theatre crowded with dancerly athletes who have the energy of snails. In two and one-half hours Fo never stops, unflagging in his gusto for the moment, for the wry ironies that burst like bombs into his tales, and above all, for the extravagant fun he is having with ideas, the game of performance, and us.

Certainly he could use an editor and perhaps the eye of another director; perhaps, too, it might have been more strategic and less exhausting here to have shared the program with his wife, Franca Rame, rather than giving them separate evenings. But such doubts threaten to tamper with what may be more precious in Fo (and Rame, too)—generosity, scope, and savage, merciless, hilariously political sweep.   *GR(June 1986)*

Jesurun and Fabre: Perchance to Dream

When I was six or seven years old, I believed that the giant images on billboards were real people flattened into an advertisement because they had been naughty. I had not yet learned that the naughtiest people were the advertisers behind the billboards. While I cannot recall the precise moment of liberation from that terror, I can remember that my freedom carried with it a sense of loss: would I ever again be able to believe in life blown up on billboards? The giant film screen, equally fascinating as an escape from real dimensions, would always have allure, but I would never again believe in it as I choose to believe when life is enacted on a stage.

Young performance artists such as John Jesurun and the Belgian director Jan Fabre (both twenty-five) have faith in the singular reality of their own self-referring images, turning the live stage event into a continual restatement of the theme that belief in screens, blow-ups, repetition, and the almost corporeal reality of dreams can be self-sufficient and sustaining. Jesurun has the provocative wit to make the tension between screen and stage reality his actual subject; Fabre, on the other hand, having almost nothing on his mind except repeated destruction, succeeds only in presenting his evident boredom with High Art as a license to bore the rest of us.

Boredom may be a necessary ingredient in performance art, if only because the best of it (Robert Wilson, Pina Bausch) deals so sensitively with time. Even then, while one is pitched inevitably back to the self, the work generally acts an an inducement to enjoy boredom—or rather, to turn it into an activating sport. If, suddenly, I am at liberty to receive images from a performance while nonetheless thinking about myself, the actual time of the performance automatically drifts into the most unconstrained, stratospherically free moments of my day, far better than the routine daily activities so easily perceived as reality.

Jesurun doesn't play with time in this manner, but in *Deep Sleep* he does play with reality. What's more, he never bores. Partly this is because he takes only a bit more than an hour to stage his "melodrama" about five live characters under pressure from four filmed characters to join them on two screens opposite one another. Fabre—an aggressive promoter of himself as the heir to all the avant-garde—might appear to be using time as Wilson and Bausch do, but in fact he's only killing it. In *The Power of Theatrical Madness,* he takes four and a half hours (I stayed for four!) to present fourteen actors in repeated assaults either on each other, on Wagner, Richard Strauss, Mendelssohn, and Verdi, or on Renaissance painters (washed-out color slides blown up on an upstage screen). Fabre brings new tonalities not to art, but to the idea of repetition and the word "excruciating": nothing he does disappears easily from his stage and everything he does can be predicted.

Where Jesurun has a modest idea in his head—that seductive, hypnotic signals from the screen might lure us away from quotidian commitment—Fabre has only his immodest, spoiled tantrum about artistic heritage, as if art were a threat greater than his own tyrannical sway over actors and audience. His obsession with repetition has nothing to do with time or any form of meditation; on the contrary, it is only about an arrogant, demanding director fighting battles already won.

Jesurun's work suggests that the screen has plunged us into a relatively new primal reality—whatever we may think of our daily lives, we are also being defined by dreams. The act of dreaming doesn't question itself, yet awake, the dreamer begins to reshape what seems to have happened, while slowly the dream recedes into a system of memory lacking line, shape, or even shadows. So, too, does the act of viewing film. Jesurun's ingenious conceit is to imagine what it might be like if we were suddenly engaged in conversation with screen images. He has the boldness to state the problem directly: his characters on both sides of reality are asking how they might bring "rationality to bear in an entirely irrational situation." Not surprisingly, they can't. The alluring, commanding, scolding filmed figures succeed eventually in capturing all but one of the live characters—the one seen in the beginning on screen arguing about whether he is Sparky or if Sparky is the boy "over there," that is, on stage.

In a theatre, naturally, it is possible *not* to suspend disbelief, especially when—as here—it is obvious that the screen characters were filmed earlier and are merely coordinated with the stage characters and their dialogue. It is impossible, moreover, to ignore the pressure on the live actors: they have to keep moving, especially when questions from the screen characters are scheduled. Jesurun, however, is also willing to be loose and just a bit silly. Our belief in his conceit is subverted by images of the screen characters playing music on several instruments not on the soundtrack, or by moving lips that do not match the sound, or sound coming from the "wrong" screen. When the screens go white, the live characters still have to rush in order to be poised for their next encounters with the interrogating screens. Disbelief notwithstanding, the continual reappearance of screen reality reinforces the paranoid fantasy that real people might just be projections after all. "No one," as one of the screen characters insists, "asked you to believe."

A splendid reminder, this, that only in the theatre are we free to choose what we see; film, in fact, is always directing us like *Deep Sleep*'s screen characters, telling us how and where to live. Jesurun may be fascinated, even obsessed, with screen reality, but his world is spacious enough to include other possibilities.

Jesurun is careless about women, turning one live woman into a filmed candle while making three of them his screen villains, but it isn't surprising that his most vivid and best-acted character is Sparky (Michael Tighe), the nine-year-old junkie who believes, questions, and fights the hardest. Tighe's intensity, his furious reading of a Lou Reed lyric about "smack," driving himself in a circular prowl around a center table, is the indelible imprint of Jesurun's eccentric yet passionate engagement in the two realities. Tighe crosses into territory unavailable to the grown-ups. I've seen nothing more vividly realized this year nor more poignant than young Tighe's insistence on his own reality.

If only the same could be said for the older, not wiser, Fabre. His company of ten men and four women is handsome enough—when they can be seen. Most of the time, they are ghostly presences under the dim light of hanging bulbs, or simply zombiesque stiffs moving in clock-work time to unvoiced orders. One young woman turns her back to us for an hour while repeating ballet positions. Earlier, another woman had been brutally denied her grunting wish to join the others on stage. Meanwhile, frogs appear, only to be captured by the actors under white cloths, eventually stamped on and (so we are to believe) obliterated. If there was one spontaneous, gratifying moment in the entire event, it was that wonderful frog who jumped gloriously into the wings. Oh for the wisdom of frogs!

Eight actors jogging fifteen minutes while chanting the years marking notable avant-garde theatrical events, a toneless baritone bravely attempting the *Liebestod* in notably sharp or falsetto moans, two naked actors wearing crowns and carrying scepters (get it?), a ritual smashing of white dishes followed much later by the inevitable half-hour taken to sweep up the shards— these and not really much more make up Fabre's spectacular misuse of everybody's time. This is one of those historical moments when there isn't any doubt that the rear guard has taken over.

In the end, there is only unexamined time, the frog's heroic example, and the self. Jesurun's play keeps the faith, unabashedly theatrical, dramatic, and cinematic all at once. Fabre's solemn self-congratulation deserves nothing less than the walkouts he was getting the other night or (as in my case) the total return to oneself: I think about my day. I watch the person across the aisle putting her pen away. I think about my day. I notice a friend dozing, his pen and notebook sliding off his lap. I think about my day. I watch, I notice, I think. Finally, I take off my mind and show it to the audience. I hold it up to the dimmed light. I put it back again. I keep wishing for amplified, repetitious music to accompany my review.   *GR(February 1986)*

Richard Foreman: Internal Gestures

Hovering like a warning or an admonition over the tiny space in which Richard Foreman's *The Cure* moves through its subdued meditations is a sign saying NO SECRETS. As usual with Foreman, the words don't slip easily into a category or conclusion: most of the time, he has set up oppositions and unanswerable questions which act as a dialogue with the self. This time, however, with NO SECRETS hanging over the proceedings, he does something new and ironic—a confrontation of the most private theatre artist we have with the impulse to tell everything he knows and feels.

It isn't probable that Foreman's privacy can be breached even by Foreman himself. That he's theatrical is, I suspect, his personal salvation: using a voice and iconography all his own, he releases himself to open struggle, a continual play of words and energies that probably make his bad dreams bearable. In *The Cure,* what is seen and heard most certainly must be all we need to know. While there may be a temptation to cast interpretative veils over his signals and images, it is sufficient to take the journey as given—no more, no less than what it looks like or seems to be at any passing moment.

Designed by Foreman, the set looks like a fun-house funeral parlor. Gray curtains with black lace trim hang over the bottom half of the side and back walls. Most of the objects and props are various shades of black and gray, all of them surrounding or placed on two tacky pseudo-oriental rugs. A black box with unlit candles on its four corners awaits the actor who will climb into it for a time. What appear to be black-curtained election booths stand on either side of the stage. On upper shelves in the back are a box of Kellogg's Corn Flakes, some empty soup bowls, and another bowl of fruit. On a shelf above them, a curved scimitar sits as impassively as all the other objects, another thing to be used, even if that use can never be palpably clear. A dark thronelike chair sits to one side of the back wall; on its crest is an inlaid photograph of Tchaikovsky. Intruding on all this rational gloom are still more hanging mechanicals—a series of colored discs that are eventually set in circular motion by an unseen hand. Foreman gives his actors a space that is deliberately unsettling and only pseudocomic. Yet one thing is clear: unlike most imagistic theatre, *The Cure* is not trying to paint pretty pictures.

The pictures here are almost accidental deferences to the theatrical mode. Foreman's biggest open secret is his passion for words. Placing the three actors—Kate Manheim, David Patrick Kelly, and Jack Coulter—in a hermetically sealed parlor, Foreman gives them nothing to do but enact or present the story of a writer possessed by language and argument. At one moment, as if summoned by a sudden glimpse into ecstatic realms, the men dash and shake their bodies into staccato riffs; at another, they suddenly clap their hands repeatedly on their knees. Kelly is imperturbably cool; Coulter leers and lurches, trapped in his own strenuously induced steam heat. Meanwhile, Foreman spreads a glistening pattern of questions, observations, and half-answers over almost every move and tic. "Can the truth be conveyed in a story?" he has an actor ask, and we know implicitly from the work itself that Foreman finds stories a lie.

Wearing body mikes so that their voices are heard over speakers, the actors are further distanced by the continual accompaniment of alternately ominous and whimsical music, that too scored by Foreman. Can it be an accident that the tunes and rhythms have an effect not unlike the scores for Chaplin's silent films, a kind of tinny, filtered, music-hall quality suggesting paranoid games? Consider, too, that *The Cure* is also the title of one of those films. (With Foreman, some of the fun lies in playing the games.) With one of those old-fashioned radio signals denoting the hour or the announcement of the station, each section is halted and a new one begins. Foreman's theatre is a conspiracy on behalf of words: these orderly, marked divisions are designed to convey us into a listening mood; the text may be densely packed, but Foreman makes it unavoidable.

With po-faced intensity, the actors move from one object to another while speaking their litanies. "Here is an important dream," says Manheim, telling us that she "woke up one morning and found the world was all I desired of it." She doesn't, however, tell us what those desires were. Another section begins with the demand to find out something—"how to punish a man approximately five feet eight-and-a-half inches tall." And again, nobody finds out how to do any of it. In still another section, the actors declare that nobody knows much about them, but repeatedly they conclude that they don't care. Further on, they are implored not to guess or analyze. Warned later that "it's not wise to talk about things that scare you, make you cry, make other people mad at you, or jeopardize your economic security," Manheim replies that she "never does—such things are private." Yet she can't avoid her own subversion: "Sometimes I talk about them without knowing."

Toward the end of this one-hour ceremony of the half-alive, Foreman flirts dangerously with what looks like a conclusive statement: "The cure," we learn, "is in the pain." This is turned quickly, however, into its opposite— "There is no cure." And then again, it becomes another question: "The pain of the cure is the cure?" The danger has passed just as swiftly as it emerged. Foreman is no more likely to provide homilies than any other inquiring artist. If a man thinks he's eating normal cornflakes, someone is bound to tell him that he's wrong. "You'll never solve it," says Manheim.

If he can't solve it, at least he can share some of the pain. Manheim's brittle presence—limping wrists and high heels conveying her over territory that never quite explodes under her focused assaults—is the walking-talking emblem of Foreman's quizzical distress. In one of those lines that keeps escaping into his own prepared oblivion, he has her say that she heard the "glacial cracking of her own emotions." Quoting Alfred North Whitehead's "nothing in excess" as "the motto of the philistine," Foreman provides an excess of vigorous speculation that is as glacially cracked as Manheim's elusive emotions. *The Cure* may remain private at the end, but if you can bear its solemn fun, it offers the gift of what theatre does better than the other arts these days—what Foreman calls here "an internal gesture of the mind." Glacial, yes, but uninsistent and deeply felt.   *GR(June 1986)*

Martha Clarke's True Danube

Vienna is not the city of dreams for nothing: even now, when the news is grim again, when ghastly political realities—reborn anti-Semitism and Kurt Waldheim's shame—cannot possibly be subdued by a waltz or a Sacher torte, the noises coming from Vienna are crackling with rage and denial. Despite their share of horror, the Viennese can say that they have earned those dreams, though the credit surely must go to their astonishing writers, artists, and musicians. That convergence in fin-de-siècle Vienna of unprecedented talents in all the arts is unmatched by any other city at any other time—even Paris, Berlin, New York.

It is no exaggeration also to say that Vienna has always been on the edge of one form of death or another; momentary relief, a pause before the inevitable, could usually be found in art. As Carl Schorske says about Gustav Klimt: "The painter of psychological frustration and metaphysical malaise became the painter of an upper-class life beautiful, removed and insulated from the common lot in a geometric house beautiful." Later, Schorske refers to "the image of the garden" reflecting "the changing outlook . . . as the ancient Empire approached disintegration." Whether in house or garden, Vienna has never stopped dreaming about itself.

Few of those dreams could ever have been more ravishingly beautiful than Martha Clarke's integrating visions in *Vienna: Lusthaus.* In little more than an hour, Clarke moves her dancers, actors, and musicians through a succession of scenes and images that drift with unassuming grace through a kind of history. It is a history without faces or names, all the more suggestive because of its refusal to lecture or describe. Every stance, every turn of a hand or foot, even the shadows of chairs or bodies on the white walls seem possessed by a passion for discretion, an almost supernatural devotion to detail. Disintegration and death have never looked more alluring. Clarke is a visual poet daring to release a lurking beauty she finds in the darkest corners of human experience.

If the texture comes from Clarke, the precise historical richness comes from Charles Mee, Jr.'s equally dazzling text. Marvelous to see a dancerly work so at peace with words: Clarke fills her meditation with those *Luftpausen* so beloved of Mahler and the Waltz King; into them she lets Mee supply actors with anecdotes and memories that nudge the piece into more reverberant territory. In between Clarke's swirling couples, her solos and duets about officers making love with girls, girls making love with each other, an officer gathering momentum as a Lipizzanner stallion, another with shoes on his hands going through every possible permutation of sexual play, Mee inserts tales about a startling moment on the banks of the Danube when rain covered half of the silky river while sunlight poured blindingly on the other side, or about Kraus's nephew dashing across a theatre to pull out two of the taleteller's teeth, a story repeated later as in a litany, with the added question, "Why would he want to do that? Is he a Jew?"

In still another pause, a girl with spectacles, wearing a man's jacket, lists what she doesn't like, starting with Johann Strauss. Still later, a bearded gentleman, top-hatted like a shadow of Freud, lists the names of girls and the number of times he has had them. The same man, rigid with frustration, tells of a rat he couldn't manage to kill: he sees himself caught "in some sort of Greek fate—to be left forever trying to choke a rat." A sick mother tells her daughter, "We don't want to live any more."

Yet Clarke's Viennese live indelibly within ghostly patterns, ephemera seen through the white relief of a scrim, under the magical beams cast by Paul Gallo's haunted lights; not least, they live in the fluent bodies and voices of Clarke's gifted company. Robert Israel has set them in brilliant designs that are as useful and stunning as anything I've seen in years, none of them slavishly imitative of the golden Klimt or any other Secession painter. Israel's high walls, giant doors, shimmering uniforms, tall and feathered hats, his jackets, skirts, and chemises for the women, all blend seamlessly into the grand fluctuation and flow. Richard Peaslee's score casts an insinuating, supportive fragrance over Clarke's inventions: how cool and restrained he is in allowing some of the waltzing couples an unexpected silence. In the opera, Vienna usually inspires only size, weight, and vulgarity. Clarke and her collaborators are commanders of depth, resonance, and the most liberating sensuality.

If Vienna could produce love scenes as natural and respectful of both sexes as we see here, if it could disarm and disrobe as unalarmingly and tenderly as Clarke manages when a beautiful muscled young man caresses the body and hair of a beautifully squat old woman, then perhaps those obsessions with disorder and death might find a happier end. It is Clarke's genius, however, to have uncovered Vienna, city not of dreams but of what Schorske calls "long-gowned dreamy spirits" where "wish is king; encounter is avoided." The whole is a miraculous summation of all its parts, a great theatrical event where intelligence, bitter reflection, quiet wit, and an enveloping discrimination have conquered what Mee describes as the light pink, red, light blue, deep blue, purple red of death. *GR (April 1986)*

In My Mind's Eye, Horatio

Among the brilliant series of provocations initiated by Heiner Müller in his *Hamletmachine* is a moment when an actor slowly and methodically tears Müller's photograph in half. With Müller, one learns quickly to postpone questions until the provocations have multiplied. His ground rules are plain enough: he prefers drama to other forms because it enables him to "say one thing and say the contrary," and he isn't suggesting self-destruction; rather, Müller is offering himself stripped to essentials. The torn photograph is like the text itself—stripped, blasted, divided.

Nothing in *Hamletmachine* can be taken as found, least of all our dramatic expectations or our experience of Shakespeare. But if this were its only innovation, it would be just another version of the fragmentary, nonlinear forms that have been disrupting drama since *Woyzeck*. Müller, however, is extending the vocabulary. His recent plays—*Hamletmachine* goes back to 1977—are histories with a difference, gathering into their explosive energetic fields a remorseless sense of loss and destruction. *The Task* (1979) is subtitled "Memory of a Revolution," because he is less interested in the French Revolution as such than he is in "a revolutionary model that had an especially large arsenal of theatrical forms." About *Landscape with Argonauts* (1982), a text which "presumes the catastrophes which mankind is working toward," he says that "the theatre's contribution to their prevention can only be their representation." He might mix different periods into his text, or pieces from his own biography. Unlike most American playwrights, however, he is using the stage for public discourse rather than private confession.

Müller's discourse, then, is embedded in his confrontation with theatrical possibility. Still an East Berliner, but freely traveling in the West, he is calling a plague on all our houses. If theatrical texts can act as public documents, they can do so only as they are willing to deny the truth of history as normally reported. Müller's plays are such denials, suggesting an exhaustion that can be overcome only by theatrical process itself. In the absence of coherent ideology and leadership, the playwright addresses us from unexpected, dislocating barricades. "The political task of art today," says Müller, "is precisely the mobilization of imagination." And so he does what little he can do.

Which turns out to be a lot. *Hamletmachine* is a six-page scenario in five parts that stands, like most of Müller's plays, as an artifact waiting for a director whose imagination can be mobilized. Taken literally, the text appears to be little more than Dada scribble: Ophelia's heart is a clock; Hamlet begins by saying "I was Hamlet," but later says he was Macbeth; the third part is called a scherzo and takes place in the university of the dead; the actor playing Hamlet is not supposed to notice that stagehands are putting a refrigerator and three television sets on the stage; and in the fourth part, Hamlet splits the heads of Marx, Lenin, and Mao with an ax. Even if any of this could be literally embodied, there would be no point. Müller's ideal mobilizer has to be more cunningly theatrical—more provocative even—than Müller's wildest dreams.

Who else but Robert Wilson? In Wilson, Müller has found the perfect director for unearthing the form behind the scribble, and in Müller, Wilson has at last found the dramatist who can give textual weight to his stunning, impalpable visions. Once seen, nothing could be simpler than Wilson's ingenious, rational, cubist solution, but it isn't likely that anyone else could have thought of it.

Müller's five scenes are preceded by a dumb show in which fourteen actors perform ritual actions in an elongated, yawning rectangle surrounded by a white screen on the left side and black curtains on the back and right sides. A woman in a swivel chair, her back facing us as she moves, turns and utters a silent scream, the powder from her frazzled hair disappearing in a lighted mist above her head; three women sit at an angled table, further angling their chairs as they smile and finger the table in unison; a man peers over a low-slung corrugated wall against the white screen; a young runner stops in mid-flight, balancing himself suddenly on one leg—and so on, with different actions for the remaining eight actors. Accompanying these movements is a one-finger piano rendition of the song made popular by Peggy Lee, "Is that all there is?"

When the dumb show ends, the actors pull a black curtain over the white screen, moving the furniture into the same configuration, but against the back wall this time, with its curtain pulled to reveal another white screen. And with this new perspective on precisely the same repeated actions, the text actually begins, spoken by several actors as Hamlet and Ophelia. Müller's part two is then played at another angle in still a third perspective, the right wall a white screen now, while the others are in black. The third part—the scherzo—is played as a relieving interlude in which the actors congregate behind a screen that bisects the space while a film of their ritual is played with Müller's words as subtitles; all this is accompanied by Jessye Norman's voluptuous recording of Schubert's narrative song *Der Zwerg (The Dwarf)*, the story of a dwarf who kills the queen he has loved because she left him for the king, the dwarf condemning himself to perpetual exile on the sea.

Oddly, the musical elements are the only real interpolations. While completing the play with the last two parts in new perspectives—the fourth played against us as if we were the white screen, the fifth returning the entire work full circle to its original position in the dumb show—Wilson is nonetheless absolutely faithful to Müller's words and stage directions (the latter heard if not seen); all of them are offered in this oblique nonliteral manner so that they must be heard or read even more intensively than they would be in a blind attempt to illustrate directly. When different parts of the text appear over actions already seen either silently or with other words, the resonating effects are startling: we never see the three television sets on the stage, but we do see the three women, staring once again into black space. Müller was once horrified by Disney's *Fantasia* because it uses images "to prevent experiences," Beethoven's *Pastoral* Symphony permanently violated by cuddly, leaping lambs. Wilson's images are affinities rather than equivalencies of Müller's politically charged landscape. We are free to make our own associations. Müller wants the public to make up its own mind; Wilson lets the public think.

New York University's student actors under his confident, measured direction perform with a quiet and beautiful grace, unable to disguise their innocence, yet all the more touching in the way their straightforward intensity cuts like the tearing of the photograph into the work's innate complexities. Müller suggests that English-speaking productions can use an entire quote from Marx that he shortens in his text, and Wilson does so: "The main point is to overthrow all existing conditions where humans are suppressed, abandoned, humiliated, contemptuous." Wilson and the students are emblems of that overthrow, triumphant liberators of a text that shows a mind in action, moving in and around dimensions that can't be caught by a photograph. Nakedly, honestly, Müller and Wilson are presenting the torments and pleasures of true argument.   *GR(May 1986)*

The Elusive Object, The Fading Craft

Ezra Pound rambles but usually lands on target: "Criticism," he says, "is the fruit of maturity, *flair* is a faculty of the rarest." It was 1917, and his subject was *Irony, Laforgue, and Some Satire.* In Pound's world, there was only art; the rest was something else. Which is to say he was scarcely ever writing criticism of the dramatic event. In his *Literary Essays,* Shakespeare is in the index, but only as "the greatest English technician bar none." Not Shakespeare the dramatist, however. If Pound thought of plays, he left very little evidence. Shakespeare's fabulous technique was not, for him, about theatrical arrangements, scenes, characters in balance and opposition to one another, or even the *flair*—rare indeed—of stagecraft intoxicated by the actor's art. Instead, technique was about "the arrangement of his sounds . . . on the quality and duration of syllables and on the varying weights of his accent." Pound goes further than he had to in assigning the word "technique" to poetry alone. "Shakespeare," he adds, "had the wit to concentrate his technique where the most enlightened intellect would naturally concentrate"—that is, on sounds.

The enlightened intellect, then, doesn't concentrate on theatre. Criticism is about reading, words, alliteration, assonance, rhythms, structures, and shapes. Pound alludes to painting and music, but drama is either "fustian" (Corneille) or, in effect, it is nothing at all. Pound is only one of thousands who rarely applies enlightened intellect to theatre. I am exaggerating only a little when I say that it just isn't done. Everybody goes to plays, and some of the most Poundian enlightened intellects—Eliot, James—have even written them not very effectively, but theatre has not often inspired demanding ruminations. Flirting with popularity much of the time—a charge not often leveled at poetry—and certainly impure, respected only when the words seem right and when the words are heard, the theatrical act itself has suffered a prolonged history of loathing and denial.

While scorn heaped on theatre has not been a sport limited to America alone (Jonas Barish's formidable study, *The Anti-Theatrical Prejudice,* has uncovered a consistent Western tradition), American refinements have been operating, like the country itself, in a different time zone. Theatrical energies everywhere in the nineteenth century were populist where they existed at all. The century was not curious about serious drama until the last quarter. Even then, news from the Ibsen, Strindberg, and Chekhov fronts took decades to reach the world; English poets, for one example, proved to be cloistered dramatists, stylistically retrograde in ways having nothing to do with the adventures they took when writing poetry alone. True, the British were virtual inventors of evocative, descriptive criticism directed mainly at performance (Leigh Hunt, William Hazlitt, and George Henry Lewes), the first, perhaps, to reflect a public that was beginning to take acting seriously. Yet it would be stretching a point to see those journalistic experiments as a movement that actually released theatre from prejudicial bondage.

Given that bondage, an aspiring theatre critic must first confront several threats to his or her ambition. If theatre itself is either scorned or ignored by even an intelligent public, the act of criticism is disarmed almost before it begins. Without an inquiring public, there is not likely to be a hospitable editorial policy. Furthermore, the young critic will soon discover that, despite Hazlitt, Shaw, Beerbohm, James Agate, and Tynan in England, and Stark Young, Clurman, Bentley, Brustein, Gilman, and Kauffmann in America, there is no acknowledged tradition. The passionate act itself, the presence of such critical force from time to time has done nothing to insure its survival or renewal. Theatre critics, more than others, often possess hidden agendas. Shaw wrote cunningly on behalf of plays he was about to write, sometimes disguising that self-interest by presenting Ibsen and Wagner as models or by publishing extended tributes to modern, yet glamorous, actors. Theatre criticism for him was a job—well done, yes, but not a job for a lifetime.

Has anybody noticed that the best theatre critics are almost always doing something else? Economic necessity is surely one plausible explanation (those disinterested editors, again). Even so, it is a mysterious truth that theatre critics move regularly in or out of the act itself or away from it altogether. The loss to criticism may be a gain for playwriting, painting, teaching, novels, directing, or adventures in other nonfictional realms. Still, it is difficult to think of another craft or profession so consistently abandoned by its most gifted practitioners; if not always abandoned, at the least, shoved to one side while pursuing other occupations, some of them theatrical.

A clue to why this has happened may lie in the behavior of an earlier generation that stuck to its last: George Jean Nathan, John Mason Brown, and Brooks Atkinson are remembered (*if* they are remembered) only as theatre reviewers. They didn't teach, produce, write novels or translations (as Stark Young did), or venture into other territories in their writing, such as political journalism, aesthetics, religion, biography, or history. They did not even review another performing art, as John Simon and Stanley Kauffmann continue to do today with films. Clearly, their various missions and forms of survival could be subsumed in the work of viewing plays and productions almost daily. Newspapers, magazines, and book publishers were everlastingly hospitable to them, suggesting that theatre was for a time a subject of some importance.

Their public success, however, also suggests that what was important about theatre was its sheen and glamour. Writing about stars from the Barrymores to the Lunts was almost like producing a royal (and written) version of *People* magazine. True, Nathan and Atkinson together made the world safe for Eugene O'Neill: America needed a heavyweight playwriting contender and they were only too willing to nominate and elect him as he pursued the longest apprenticeship in playwriting history. Facile, humorous, acerbic, adolescently in love with theatre as an occasion, a reliable bright spot in a clouded landscape, they were enthusiastic reflections of an affirmative period. Covering an immensely inventive and energetic Broadway, their pieces read now as much like fan mail as criticism, albeit more selective and vigorously phrased. Among the brightest, but certainly not the best—Stark Young and, later, Eric Bentley were far more eloquent about acting and plays respectively—Nathan, Brown, and Atkinson flourished at the presumed level of New York's sophisticated audience.

That level, however, was populist, shockingly ignorant and parochial. *Theatre Arts Monthly* almost alone, with Stark Young as its most elegant writer, kept America in touch not only with itself, but also with events and innovations abroad. Broadway was as isolationist as FDR's Republican enemies. Even the enforced exiles of gifted anti-Nazi Germans did not touch American theatre in any way similar to the exiles' effect on music, painting, architecture, and physics. (Consider the difference between Schoenberg and Hindemith, operating here within dimensions and systems refined in Europe, and Kurt Weill, a theatre composer who adapted swiftly, brilliantly—and eagerly—to Broadway, reducing his musical vocabulary, simplifying harmonies and orchestrations, too often exchanging the tart ironies of his Brecht collaborations and symphonic music for the sweet, drooping sentiments of the new, perky, but narrow world.) As usual, theatre cultivated standards that sustained themselves outside the stream of aesthetic discussion and philosophy. The great innovations were often technical: American stage designers kept realizing dreams described earlier by Appia and Craig, while Craig himself remained isolated and uninvited.

Which was quite an irony: Craig made everything possible—from the technologically fluid American musical (now apparently dying its ninth life) to Robert Wilson—but he remained only a textbook legend, never permitted, as he had been in Moscow and Stockholm, to make trouble on his own. He may stand as the model pointing to American theatre's strange and pragmatic inventiveness, always maneuvering with disarming innocence a few light years from history. When Americans touched idioms removed from graphic realism, such as poetic drama or expressionism, the result was highfalutin' blather (Maxwell Anderson) or humdrum banalities in modern drag (Elmer Rice). Energy, good will, talent, inspired low-down comedy in writing and performance were never in doubt or question; all that was missing were the density and reflectiveness of the modern novel, the merciless complexities found in painting and music, the reach into imaginative realms and vocabularies that might have challenged an audience enchanted and numbed by movies and radio.

The critics weren't there; rather, they were in the same mental space, sharing the same intoxicated values, as the audience. With the exception of Bentley, eventually inheriting Stark Young's position in the *New Republic,* and Harold Clurman in the *Nation,* the situation wasn't much better after the Second World War. It would be naive to expect anything else. In broad terms, we get the criticism we deserve. By now it is clear that the movement of all the arts in America is more firmly linked to the market than in any other country; so too, inevitably, is criticism.

Every practicing critic has a story to tell. (Mine is about the new young publisher of the *Saturday Review* informing me in 1978 that I "know too much about the theatre.") Newspapers and magazines sell advertising, part of a chain of "special interests" that make it desirable to have hits on Broadway and even Off-Broadway. These hits, in turn, can provide further commercial nourishment to innumerable dependencies—restaurants, taxis, tourism, and banks—by being recycled for movies and television. Part of Hollywood's oblique charm and shameless honesty is that it so proudly and casually labels as "property" or "product" any play, book, or actor that might be famous for a minute next season. Criticism struggles in America to be about art, but no one can review what little there is without soon feeling the pressure to respond mainly to personalities and trends.

It may be too easy, even too automatic, to charge the *New York Times* with setting corruptive standards that send powerful signals to critics, audiences, and other journals, but the *Times* continues to be positioned as the central arbiter, an imperial power telling the natives how to live. Standards in theatre criticism were probably set and built into an airtight, continuing scheme when Adolph Ochs fired Stark Young as theatre critic in 1925, telling him (as reported by Young in a letter to the Julian Huxleys) that Young's "writing was too abstract; that he [Ochs] wanted the theatre page to be popularized; that he wanted no point of view set forth upon it." In the late sixties, history repeated itself ridiculously when the *Times* did much the same to Stanley Kauffmann. Conspiracy theorists like to imagine angry telephone calls from producers and the Shuberts pressuring the *Times* to get somebody in there without a point of view, but surely Ochs made it clear long ago that the *Times* could always be trusted to act primarily as a consumer guide. From time to time, there may be a critic with a gift for a mocking phrase or even a nicely tailored description of a performance or design; there may even be a moment or two when a *Times* reviewer wrestles with an idea, or struggles with the possibility that a flawed play passionately felt and true unto itself might actually be worth more hyperbole than a mechanically smooth, coldly manipulated play about nothing but the latest comforting apology for middle-class mendacity. Chances are, however, that *Times*'s reviewers will never stir

Ochs in his grave. The trouble with Stark Young's "abstract" writing was that it was dangerously specific.

Indeed, it wasn't about hyperbole at all. Young didn't need it. Even his most minutely described enthusiasms were tempered by an insistent attention to qualifying detail. If, for him, Barrymore's Hamlet was "the most satisfying that I have ever seen," that did not restrain him from suggesting that Barrymore "must give us—and already promises—the sense of a larger inner tumult . . ." Is it abstract to notice that the actor "allows the phrases to fall apart in such a way that the essential musical pattern of the verse—which is a portion of the idea itself—is lost"? To say that a performer "already promises," but isn't yet there, is not a thought or a phrase that submits comfortably to the apostrophized extractions from reviews used by press agents in giant ads published—where?—in the New York Times. Even Barrymore's virtues—"shy and humorous mystery, the proud irony, the terrible storms of pain"—would never be quoted: "terrible storms" might sound like a Bad Thing. Young was all for seasons, but surely not for these Times.

One excuse heard often from those explaining why the Times does not use "fine" writers, such as Young, is that the overnight deadline demands a quickly engineered response, a punching-bag style, swift and unequivocal judgments matched by easy-come adjectives that just as easily avoid ambiguity and resonance. The excuse means less now that critics can see previews, taking a day or more to file their reviews. And it never applied to Walter Kerr, a muscular, stylish writer of Sunday Times pieces reflective of his rigid, restrictive, rulebook notions of a good play.

Kerr's criticism doesn't require an Ochs to gore it into acceptable position. Informed about the ways plays are developed and rehearsed, he is at his best when describing what he actually sees. When assessing what he hasn't known before or what isn't immediately visible, he scolds and threatens like the White Queen: he could see Bert Lahr's Gogo was funny, but he couldn't forgive Beckett's radical redefinition of playwriting or his apparent obscurities. Similarly, he is the worst audience (and critic) for Chekhov, Pirandello, Strindberg, and the Absurd, which means that he was compelled to be hostile or silent when faced with every experiment, good and not so good, since the Living Theatre opened the floodgates.

(One should not be sidetracked here by issues of agreement or disagreement. My quarrel with Kerr is not that every Pirandello play is, by definition, better than every Lanford Wilson or Jean Kerr play; rather, it is the way he uses his authority as a fancier of Wilson-Kerr apples to denounce Pirandello oranges. In book reviews for the Times, nobody builds a critical career by assuming that Harold Robbins is operating in the same medium or genre as Saul Bellow or Donald Barthelme. The same distinctions are usually honored in the other arts: one can adore George Gershwin without expecting the same kind of lift from Stravinsky; nor is it "elitist," finally, to prefer Stravinsky. Theatre, however, attracts a special kind of closed mind. What may be worse is an editorial policy, such as the *New Yorker's*, which publishes George Steiner, John Updike, and V. S. Pritchett on literature, Andrew Porter on music, Pauline Kael on movies, Arlene Croce on dance, and once, the late Harold Rosenberg on art. But for theatre—with only Tynan's brief interlude in the late fifties—the *New Yorker* offers such chatty flyweights as Brendan Gill, Edith Oliver, and [before Tynan] Wolcott Gibbs, each writing flippantly and hyperbolically in a manner that clearly wouldn't be acceptable editorially for the other arts. If Porter denounced Handel as often as Gibbs denounced Shakespeare, he would have been shipped back to London years ago. It's ironic, too, that a more popular medium such as film should be given more discursive space for a more demanding critic. The *New Yorker* seems to be telling us not merely that apples and oranges are the same, but that theatrical apples have less crunch and bite than musical or literary apples: *New Yorker* policy unmasks that anti-theatrical prejudice once again.)

Popular criticism doesn't have to shift any gears to slip into what Tynan once called, in a different context, "the bland leading the bland." Apt and amusing as that is, the blind leading the blind will do well enough to describe current criticism's craven relationship to the audience. Can there be any point in a criticism that merely reports a perception of public taste? And why is theatre the art most often subjected to so much proud ignorance? Or, to put it another way, why does the intelligent, yet populist, critic exchange direct response for an audience response? That same critic hears canned laughter in his living room, knowing why it has been programmed. Why, then, does he surrender to laughter or boredom in the theatre that are no less automated, protective, and unfelt?

One accidental answer to these questions was furnished by the *New York Times* on February 2, 1985, when it published Frank Rich's review of Simon Gray's *The Common Pursuit* side-by-side with Mel Gussow's interview with Jan Kott on the occasion of the publication of Kott's collected essays, *The Theater of Essence*. Where Kott's method is described by Gussow as "a search for esthetic and historical perspective," Rich's method emerges as a search for mental somersaults in which the critic is always striving for balance rather than judgment. Rich had seen the play earlier in London, where he found it to be "a formulaic effort." Clearly, such a phrase is the beginning of an assessment that is not merely negative: one has reason to believe at this point that Rich will account for the formulas and the ways in which they sabotage what might have been a more provocative occasion. Instead, he rushes headlong into sabotaging himself. "The play is still superficial," he tells us, "but highly entertaining in its superficiality." Gray "has polished the script—not to the extent of deepening it" (which we must suppose would be asking too much), "but certainly to the point of sharpening its cleverness." Leaving aside the unanswerable question of why sharper cleverness hasn't led to deeper experience, one has a right to know why Rich seems satisfied with less. (Vocabulary is an early casualty in this exercise, with Gray made to sound more like a shoemaker than a playwright.) Who has actually attended the event—Rich or a surrogate figure, a happy-go-lucky, undemanding understudy? Later, he refers to "upscale soap-opera plot twists." Does this mean that he has uncovered secrets about soap operas, namely that some are truly downscale, others upscale?

Not that he relinquishes values: he knows about "authorial determinism," the way in which a playwright allows plot to decree "its characters' behavior rather than the other way around." Yet, in still another double-twist, he blames the playwright for the leading actor's "strained" performance, announcing what would have been news to Alfred Lunt, Laurence Olivier, or any abundantly imaginative, suggestive actor, that the role is "beyond any actor's power to fill in the blanks." Rich kills his own review with strained kindness, tumbling all over himself to avoid his own opinion. In the end, bouncing into position, he makes a fifty-yard dash into one of those phrases that is meant to be all things to all people: where before he found that Gray had failed to polish the play "to the extent of deepening it," he concludes finally that David Jenkins's set "adds just the right gloss of sweep and depth to an evening of shallow but captivating fun." Suddenly it seems possible to guess that, for Rich, upscale soap operas are passable because they've managed to dislodge right gloss from wrong gloss. Speaking of two characters in Gray's play, one of which he calls "the most generous-spirited of nerds," Rich says that they "make moral weakness seem an appealing spiritual calling." Is this criticism or just a job description for the popular press?

Kott, on the other hand, not only covers more territory more deeply, he locates also the source of such critical acrobatics. "To my mind," he tells Gussow (who neglects to report the burning of his own ears), "a deep limitation of the American critic is that he does not write as a man who has a political, sexual, emotional and national life." Kott himself writes *around* theatrical events, floating in and out of experience with all his lives in full sail—an indefatigable searcher (like Bentley earlier), gallantly finding links, mirror images, and pressure points where others find only isolated, unconnected episodes. Again, I might not always agree with him, but here that becomes precisely the point: criticism works well when casual sentiments recede into the background, making way for ideas, argument, persuasive evidence that the critic is always looking for something better. Many of us—including me—too easily become cranky about the load of rubbish dumped upon us from one week to the next. At our worst, we complain that the subject has disappeared. With Kott, the subject is always there, operating with the presence and passion of the critic himself.

Kott's criticism does not stand alone. The systems of publication these days do not, unfortunately, welcome such criticism on its own terms. Hence, Kott—like so many similarly inclined critics—has never borne witness to his visions and ideas on a regular basis. The big "trade" publishers, shamelessly delivering monstrous picture books to coffee tables, have consigned collected critical essays to the limbo earlier reserved for short stories. University presses and small publishers such as PAJ Publications take up some of the slack, but for the most part the idea of theatre criticism as historical record—indeed as witness—no longer has reliable status.

Reliability is also a problem for the best critics themselves. In Martin Esslin's admiring introduction to Kott's collection, he cites "some of the shortcomings that flow" from "Kott's ability to be enthralled and exhilarated by new ideas, new insights, and new discoveries . . . a premature readiness perhaps to be seduced by the new and seemingly original, a tendency to accept it before it has been tested by time." A network of automatic oppositions persists whenever criticism perceives itself as lonely defender of the new. At one time or another, otherwise reliable critics become suddenly uncritical, ceasing to analyze while adopting a tone of enthralled adoration which simply can't be accurate all the time. If nothing else, going to a Peter Brook, Andrei Serban, or Robert Wilson event is not yet the aesthetic equivalent of a pilgrimage to Lourdes.

Criticism has too often abdicated its responsibility to all aspects of theatrical art. Are directors, after all, the only source of the new? Are they even the major source? If theatrical newness has lately depended more on directorial scenarios than dramatists' plays, isn't that cause for alarm? Is cleverly used technology as satisfying as a great actor's inventions, or is it simply easier to applaud and describe? Are directors' program notes visible on stage? If theatre seems like an endangered species, could it be that its only unique component—the collision of textual complexity with the live actor—plays very little part in most contemporary criticism? These may be self-conscious questions for critics who are, in fact, uncommonly enlightened, but they are questions that call now for urgent attention.

It's a battlefield out there, one good reason why critics often lose sight of their own vision. Before the dust settles, however, critics might pause to reflect on one power they possess that isn't shared by producers, press agents, or publishers: the gift of language. In her acceptance speech on receiving the George Jean Nathan Award for Dramatic Criticism (1983–84), Bonnie Marranca said that she would like to see the "borders abolished . . . between what is called criticism and what is called writing." I take this to mean, in part, that she sees theatre as a natural metaphor for the way we live. It follows, then, that the responsible critic will be performing as writers must perform, discovering subject, language, and meaning in an act of the imagination. "To live life fully," said Marranca, "is to live it as an act of criticism." If this is scarcely self-evident in our own history, surely it is reason for insisting on a tradition despite the odds.

Pound again: his famous definition that "literature is language charged with meaning" must also stand for the literature of criticism. That Pound himself was defeated by theatre, that he couldn't begin to find a language for its meaning ("the medium of drama is people moving about on a stage and using words") is no reason for critical surrender. Pound notwithstanding, the theatrical event can always be rescued by and for intelligence. When he declared that Aeschylus and Sophocles are not "up to Homer," he was a step away from dismissing their special craft altogether. Odd for a literary critic to deny the critical act, but theatre critics need not be bullied or humbled. Pound's refusal or incapacity to charge the literature of theatre with critical meaning is just the challenge needed for recharging theatre criticism with a meaning and language longing for release.   *GR(October 1985)*

Index